GRIMM FAIRY TALES
DAY OF THE DEAD

zenescope

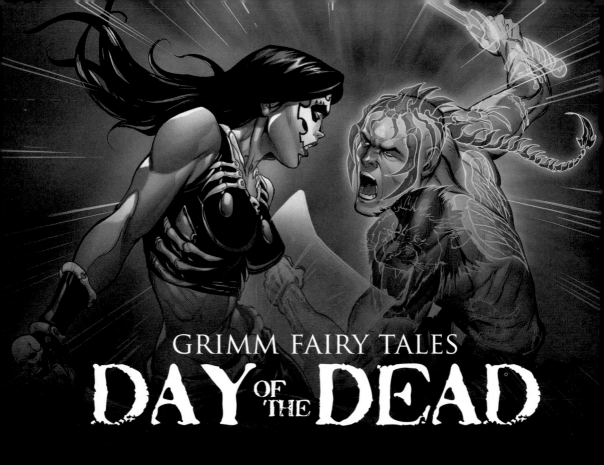

GRIMM FAIRY TALES
DAY OF THE DEAD

Story **JOE BRUSHA** Writer **DAWN P. MARQUEZ**

Artwork **ALLAN OTERO** CH. 1-5 **SEDAT OEZGEN** CH. 4

MARCELO SALAZA CH. 4 & 6

Colors **ERICK ARCINIEGA** CH. 1-5 **ROBBY BEVARD** CH. 4

MARCO LESKO CH. 5-6 **JORGE CORTES** CH. 5

Letters **KURT HATHAWAY** Editor **JESSICA ROSSANA**

Production & Design **CHRISTOPHER COTE & ASHLEY VANACORE**

Cover Artwork **ALLAN OTERO & IVAN NUNES**

Grimm Universe created by **JOE BRUSHA & RALPH TEDESCO**

This volume reprints Grimm Fairy Tales: Day of the Dead issues 1-6 published by Zenescope Entertainment. First Edition, February 2019 • ISBN: 978-1942275589

Joe Brusha • President & Chief Creative Officer
Ralph Tedesco • VP Film & Television
Christopher Cote • Art Director
Dave Franchini • Editor
Christina Barbieri • Assistant Editor
Kellie Supplee • Assistant Editor
Ashley Vanacore • Graphic Designer

Lauren Klasik • Director of Sales & Marketing
Jennifer Bermel • Business Development & Licensing Manager
Jason Condeelis • Direct Sales Representative
Rebecca Pons • Marketing & VIP Coordinator
Kisha Pio • Social Media Manager
Stu Kropnick • Operations Manager

WWW.ZENESCOPE.COM

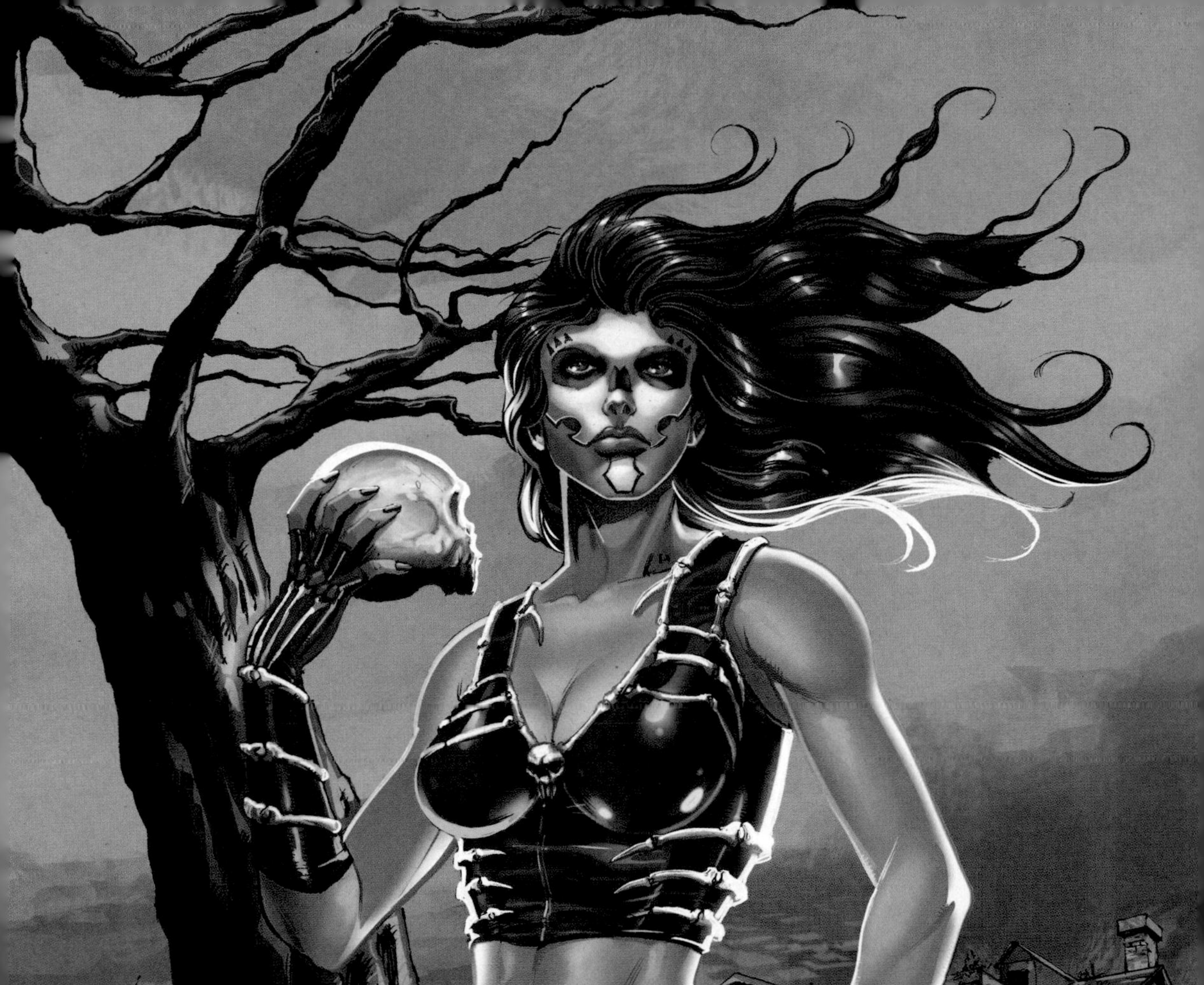

THE STORY SO FAR...

Mary Medina was born different than most. Both gifted and cursed with the powers to raise and control the dead, it's safe to say she has struggled to fit in among the living. On her own since childhood, she was finally taken in by those who understood her at Arcane Acre, a school for beings with special abilities. After learning to hone her skills, Mary is ready to venture back into the world to live her life and learn who she really is.

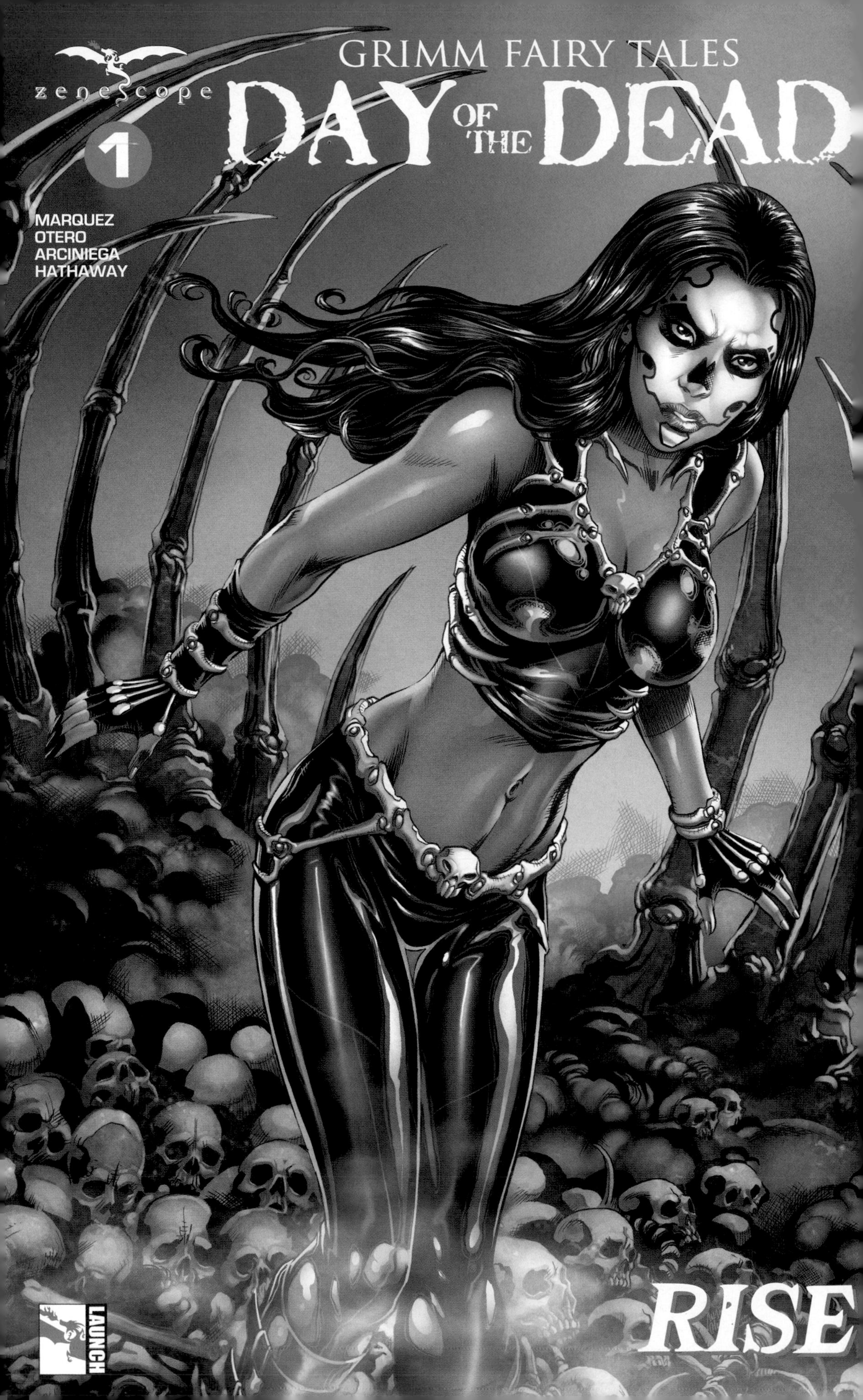
zenescope
GRIMM FAIRY TALES
DAY OF THE DEAD
1
MARQUEZ
OTERO
ARCINIEGA
HATHAWAY
LAUNCH
RISE

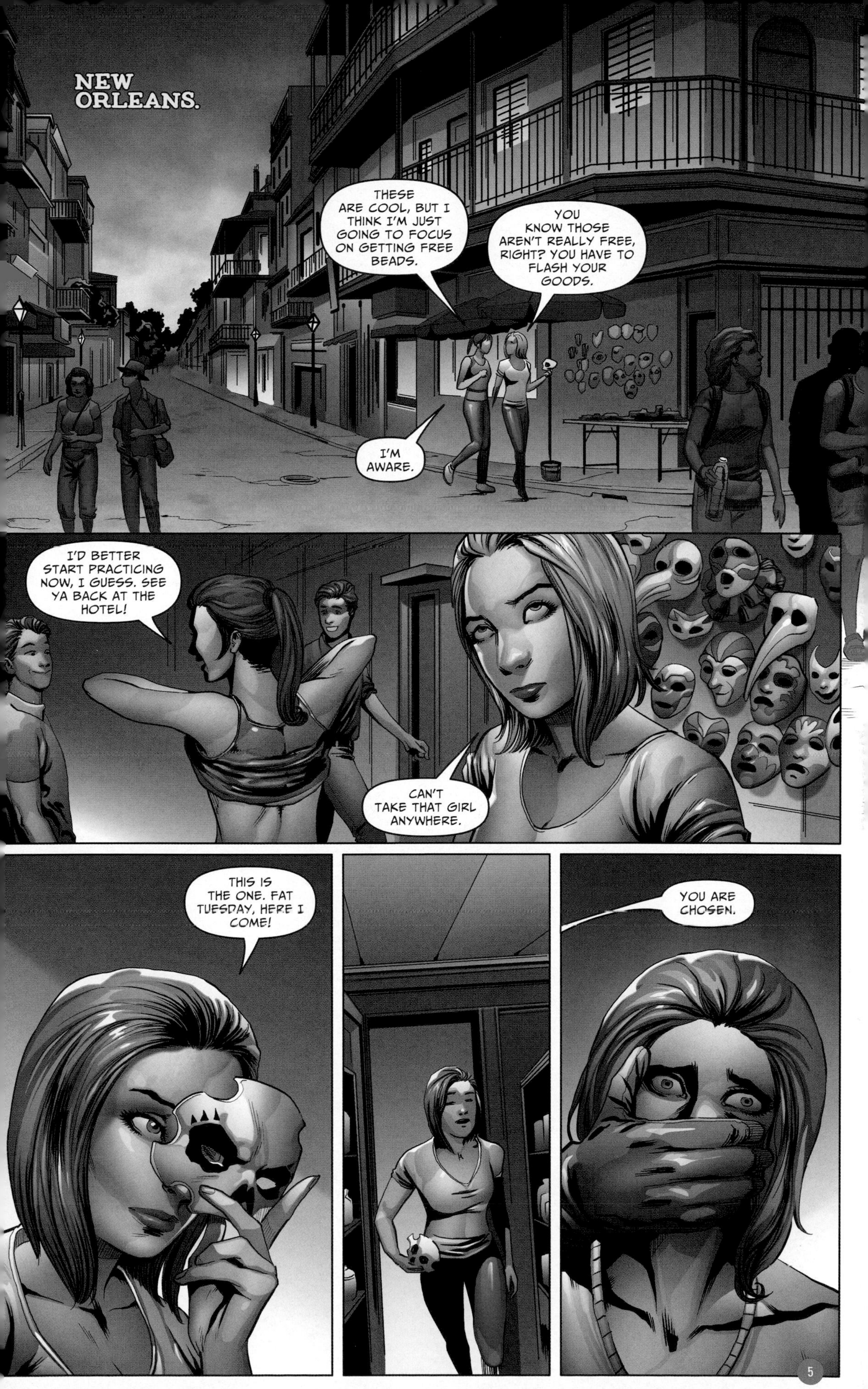
NEW ORLEANS.
THESE ARE COOL, BUT I THINK I'M JUST GOING TO FOCUS ON GETTING FREE BEADS.
YOU KNOW THOSE AREN'T REALLY FREE, RIGHT? YOU HAVE TO FLASH YOUR GOODS.
I'M AWARE.
I'D BETTER START PRACTICING NOW, I GUESS. SEE YA BACK AT THE HOTEL!
CAN'T TAKE THAT GIRL ANYWHERE.
THIS IS THE ONE. FAT TUESDAY, HERE I COME!
YOU ARE CHOSEN.

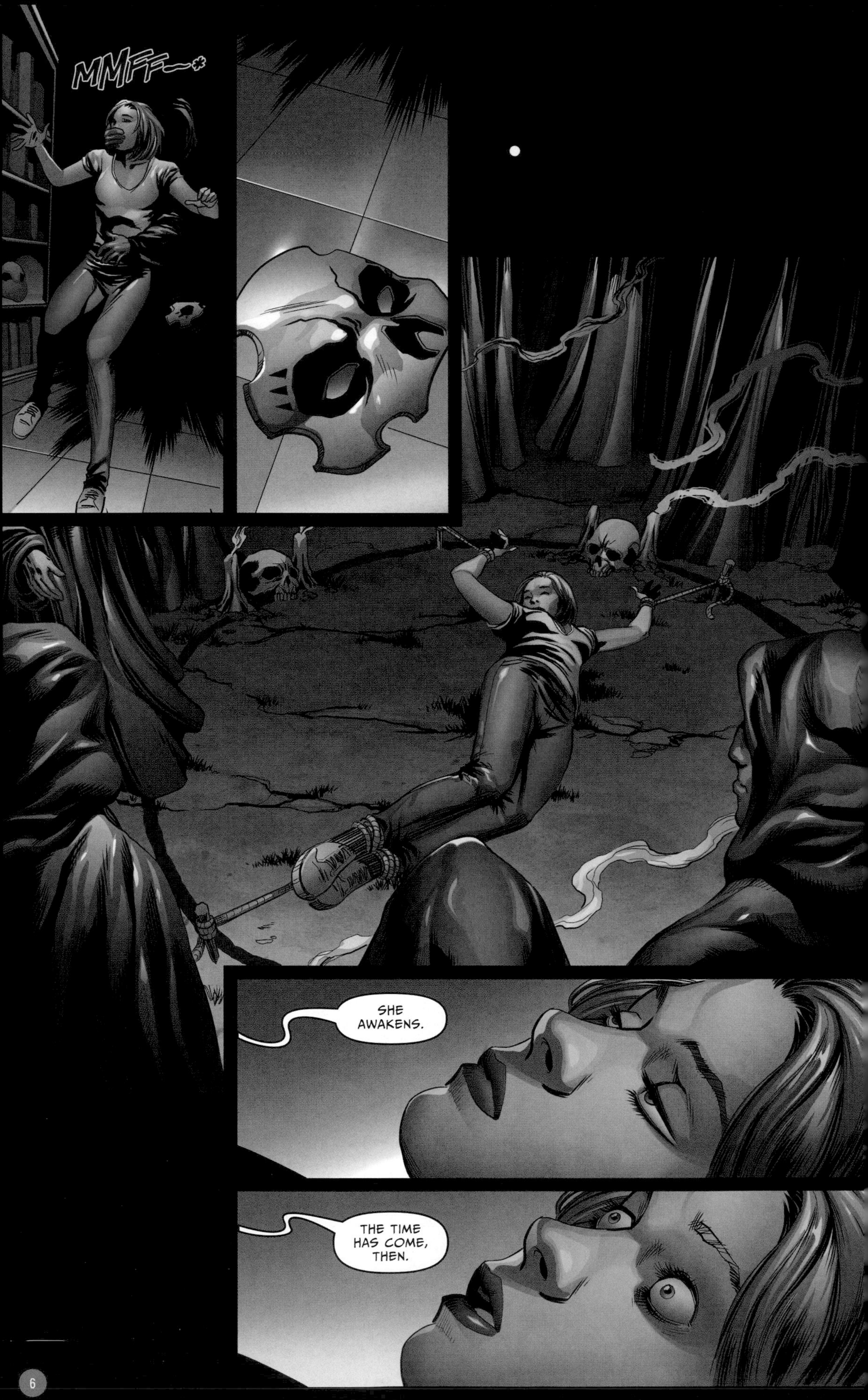
MMFF—*
SHE AWAKENS.
THE TIME HAS COME, THEN.

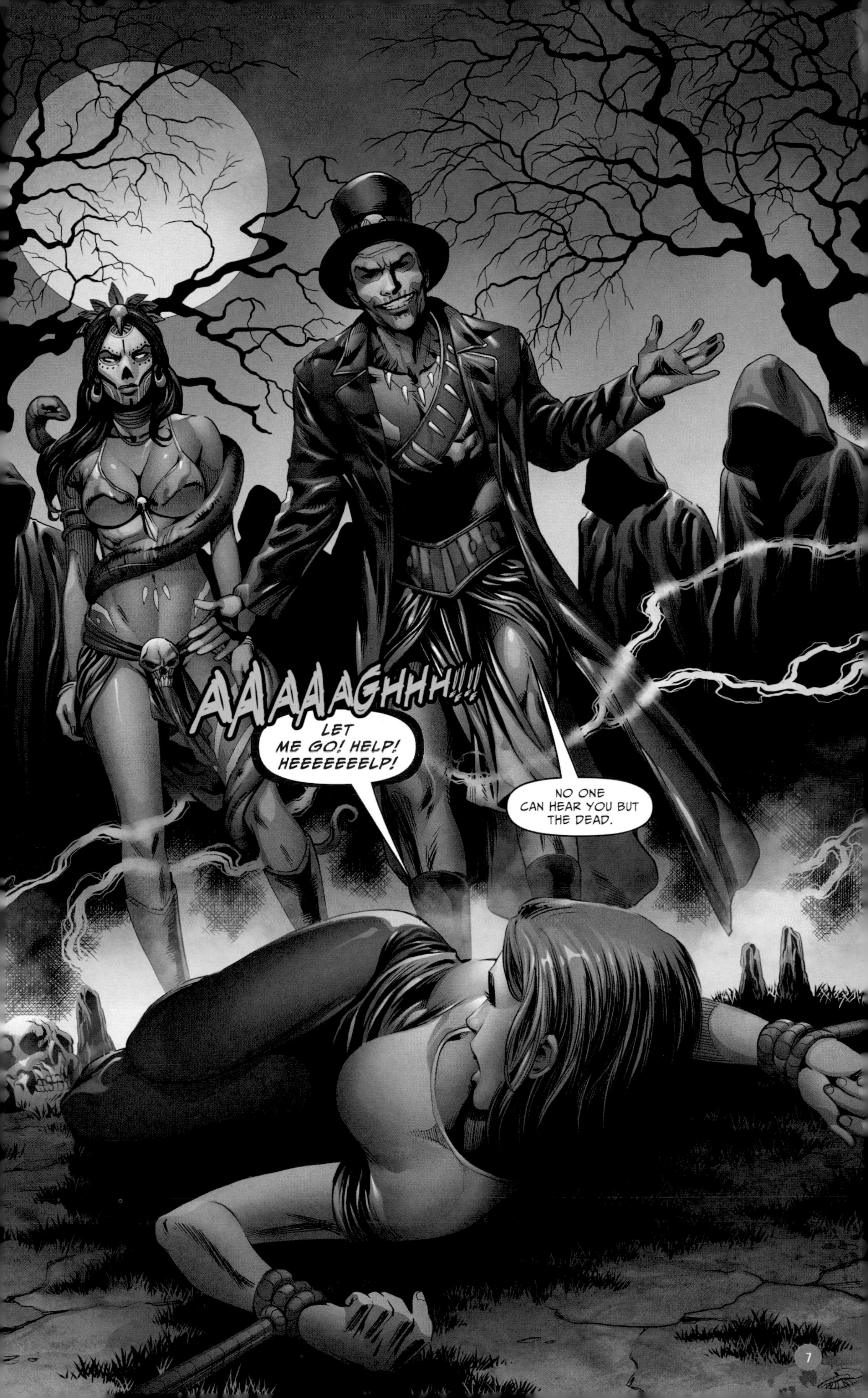
AAAAAGHHH!!!
LET ME GO! HELP! HEEEEEEELP!
NO ONE CAN HEAR YOU BUT THE DEAD.

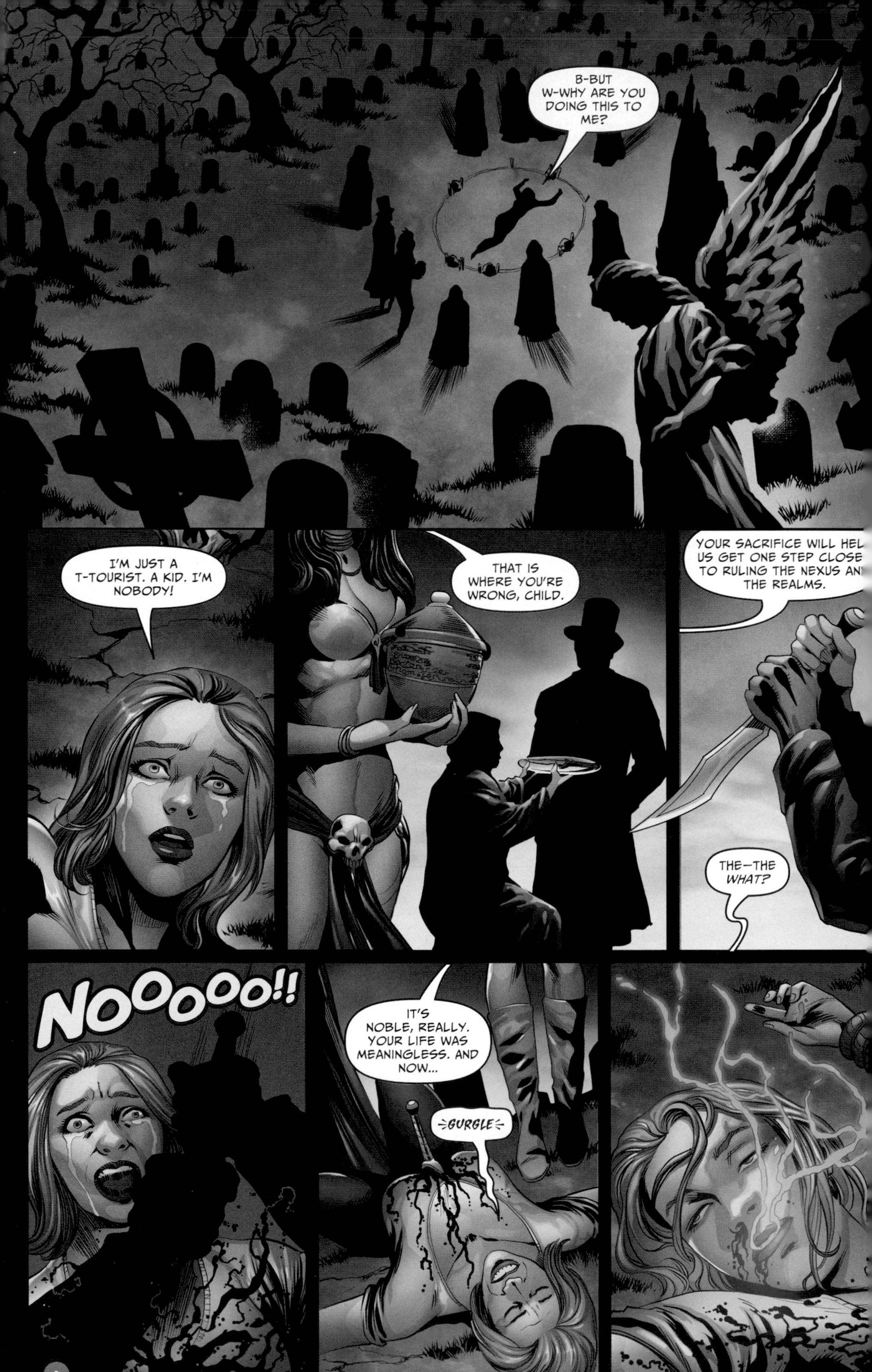

B-BUT W-WHY ARE YOU DOING THIS TO ME?
I'M JUST A T-TOURIST. A KID. I'M NOBODY!
THAT IS WHERE YOU'RE WRONG, CHILD.
YOUR SACRIFICE WILL HEL US GET ONE STEP CLOSE TO RULING THE NEXUS AN THE REALMS.
THE—THE *WHAT?*
NOOOOOO!!
IT'S NOBLE, REALLY. YOUR LIFE WAS MEANINGLESS. AND NOW...
GURGLE

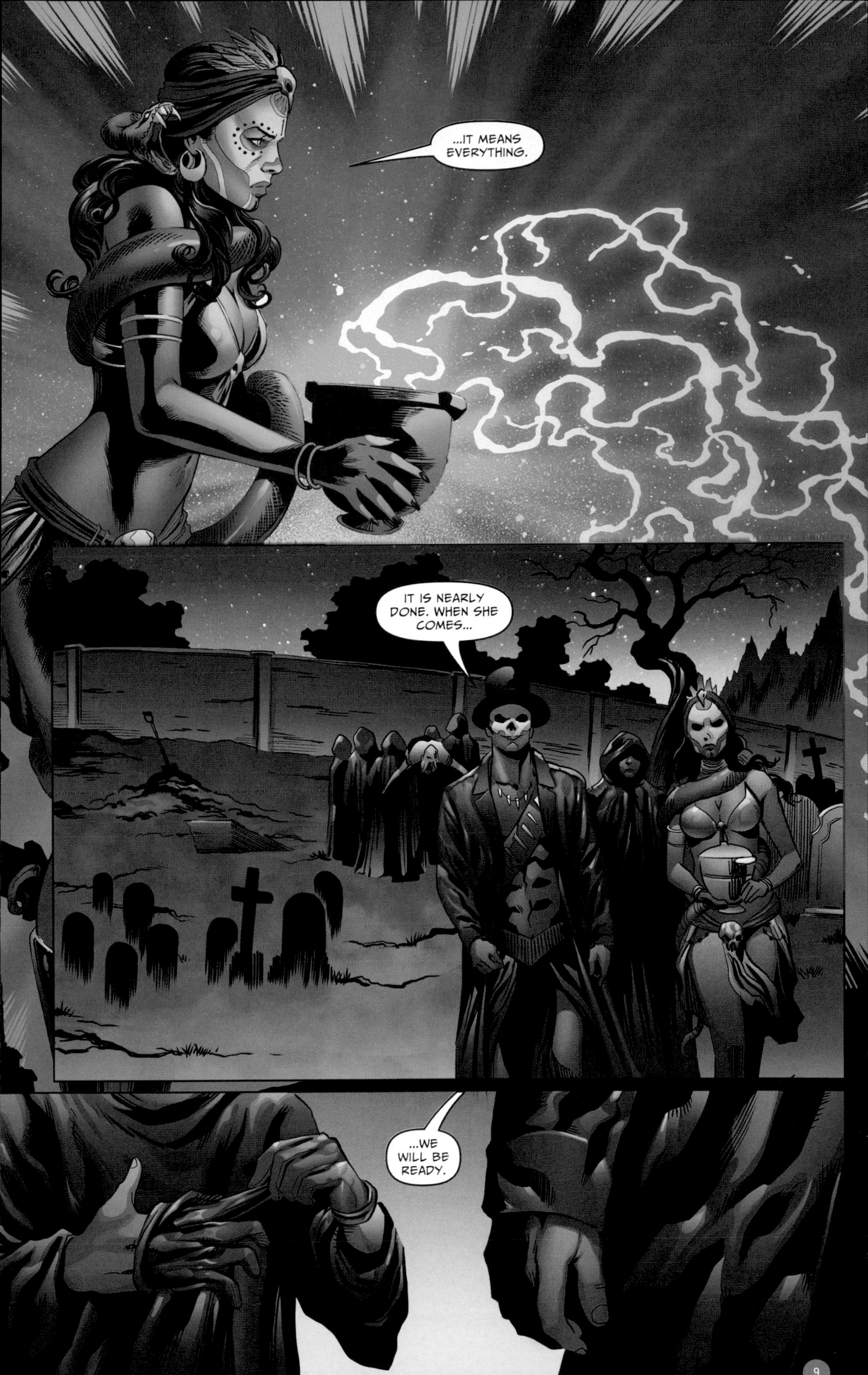
...IT MEANS EVERYTHING.
IT IS NEARLY DONE. WHEN SHE COMES...
...WE WILL BE READY.

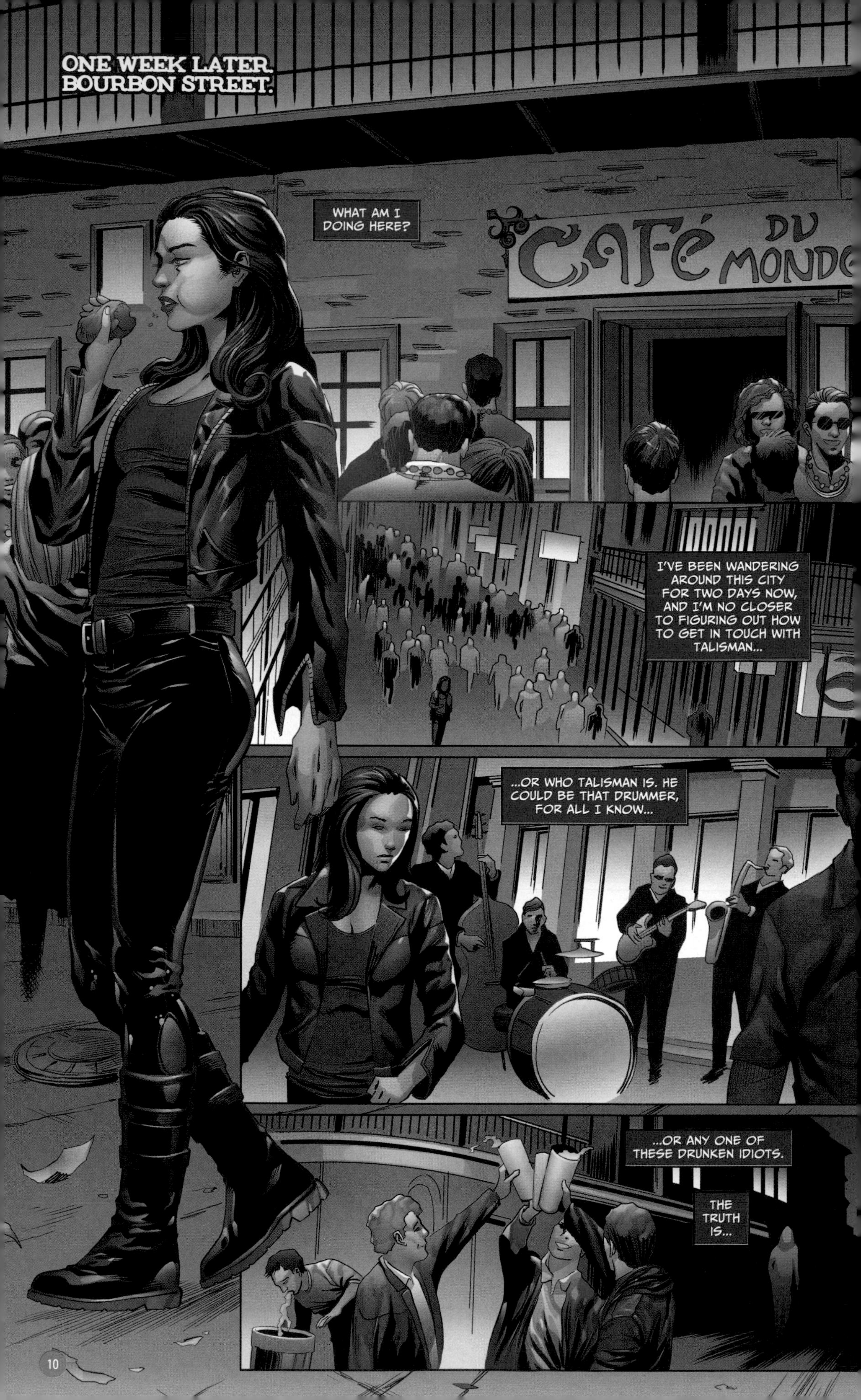
ONE WEEK LATER. BOURBON STREET.
WHAT AM I DOING HERE?
CAFÉ DU MONDE
I'VE BEEN WANDERING AROUND THIS CITY FOR TWO DAYS NOW, AND I'M NO CLOSER TO FIGURING OUT HOW TO GET IN TOUCH WITH TALISMAN...
...OR WHO TALISMAN IS. HE COULD BE THAT DRUMMER, FOR ALL I KNOW...
...OR ANY ONE OF THESE DRUNKEN IDIOTS.
THE TRUTH IS...

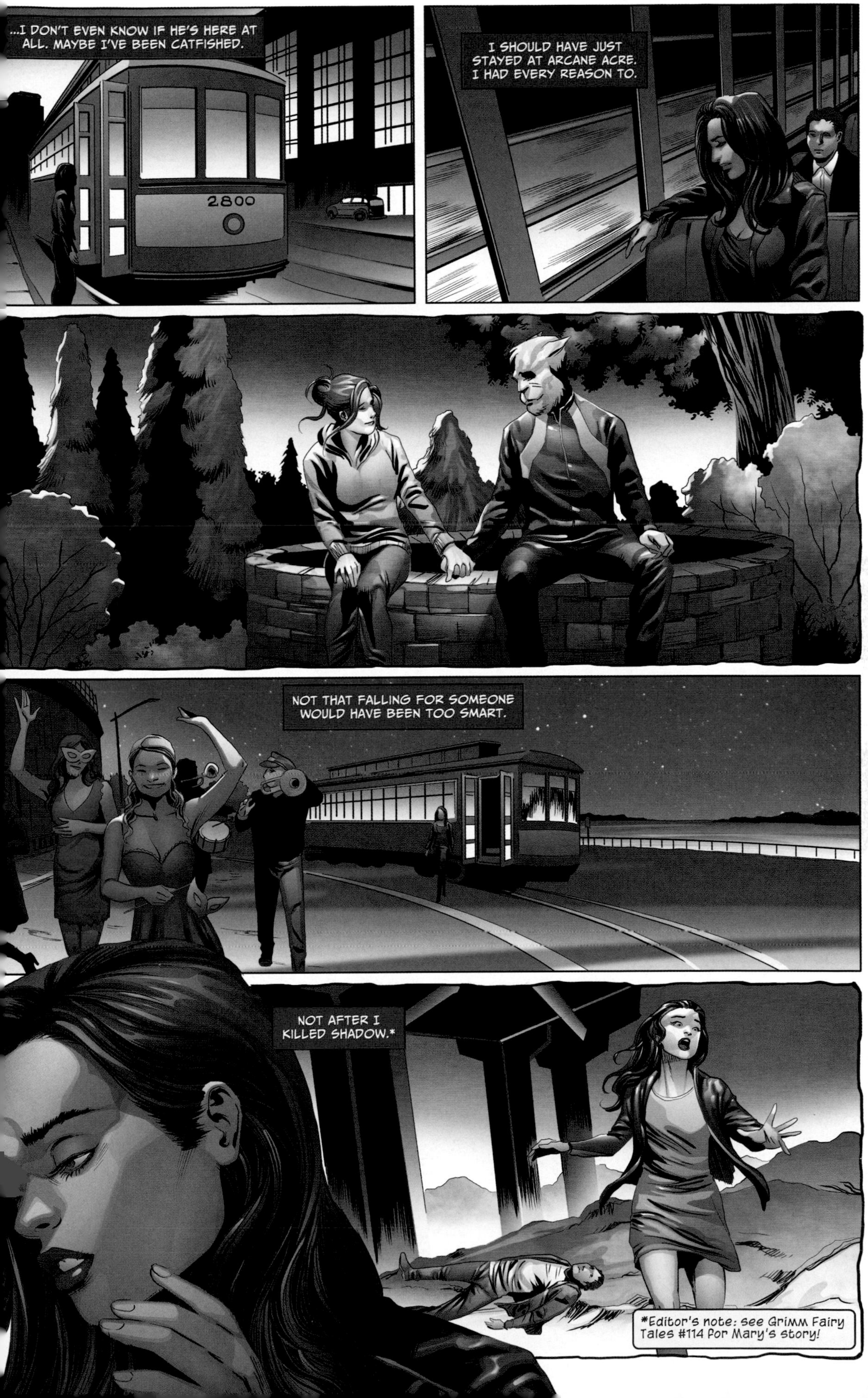
...I DON'T EVEN KNOW IF HE'S HERE AT ALL. MAYBE I'VE BEEN CATFISHED.
2800
I SHOULD HAVE JUST STAYED AT ARCANE ACRE. I HAD EVERY REASON TO.
NOT THAT FALLING FOR SOMEONE WOULD HAVE BEEN TOO SMART.
NOT AFTER I KILLED SHADOW.*
*Editor's note: see Grimm Fairy Tales #114 for Mary's story!

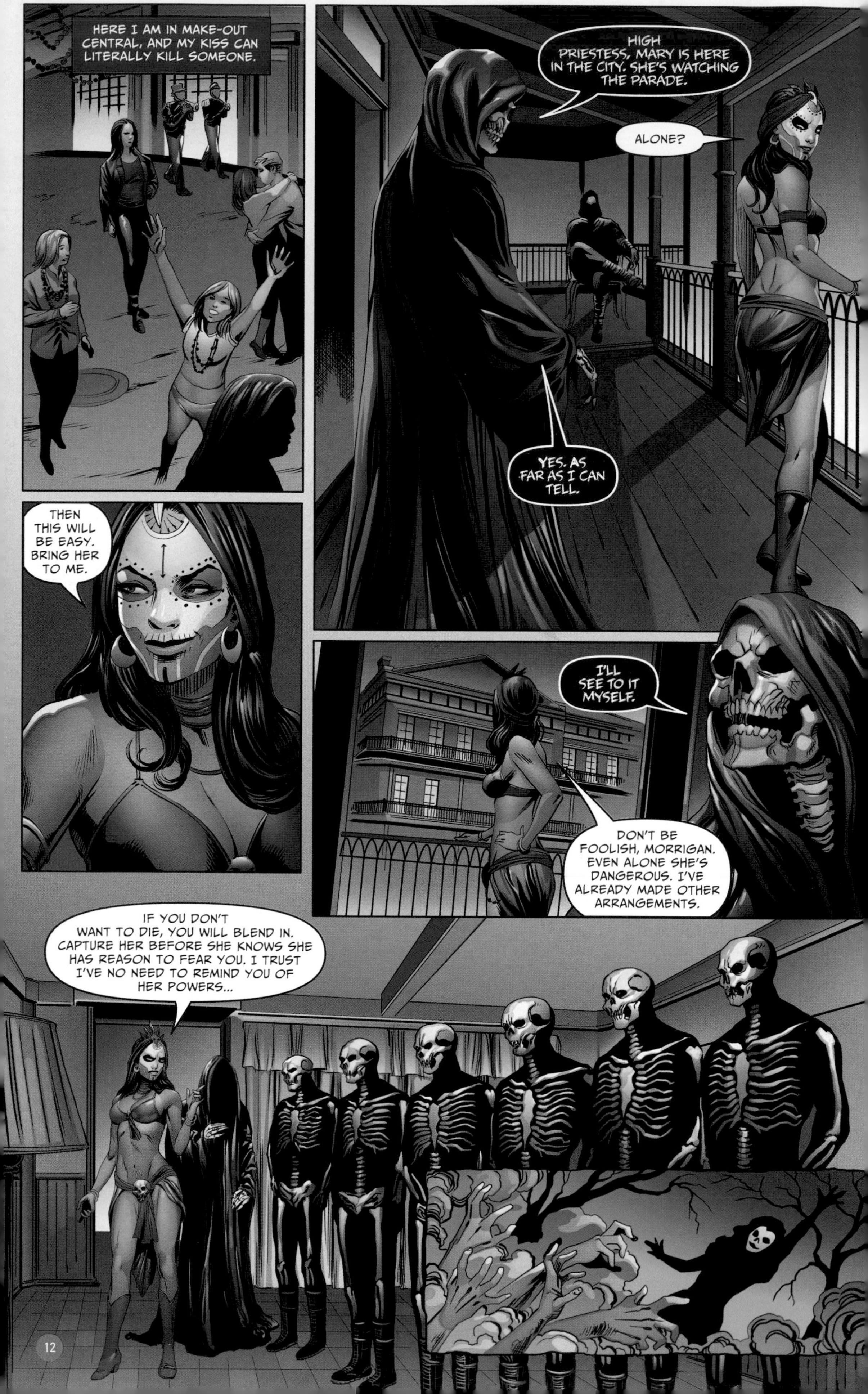

HERE I AM IN MAKE-OUT CENTRAL, AND MY KISS CAN LITERALLY KILL SOMEONE.
HIGH PRIESTESS, MARY IS HERE IN THE CITY. SHE'S WATCHING THE PARADE.
ALONE?
YES. AS FAR AS I CAN TELL.
THEN THIS WILL BE EASY. BRING HER TO ME.
I'LL SEE TO IT MYSELF.
DON'T BE FOOLISH, MORRIGAN. EVEN ALONE SHE'S DANGEROUS. I'VE ALREADY MADE OTHER ARRANGEMENTS.
IF YOU DON'T WANT TO DIE, YOU WILL BLEND IN. CAPTURE HER BEFORE SHE KNOWS SHE HAS REASON TO FEAR YOU. I TRUST I'VE NO NEED TO REMIND YOU OF HER POWERS...

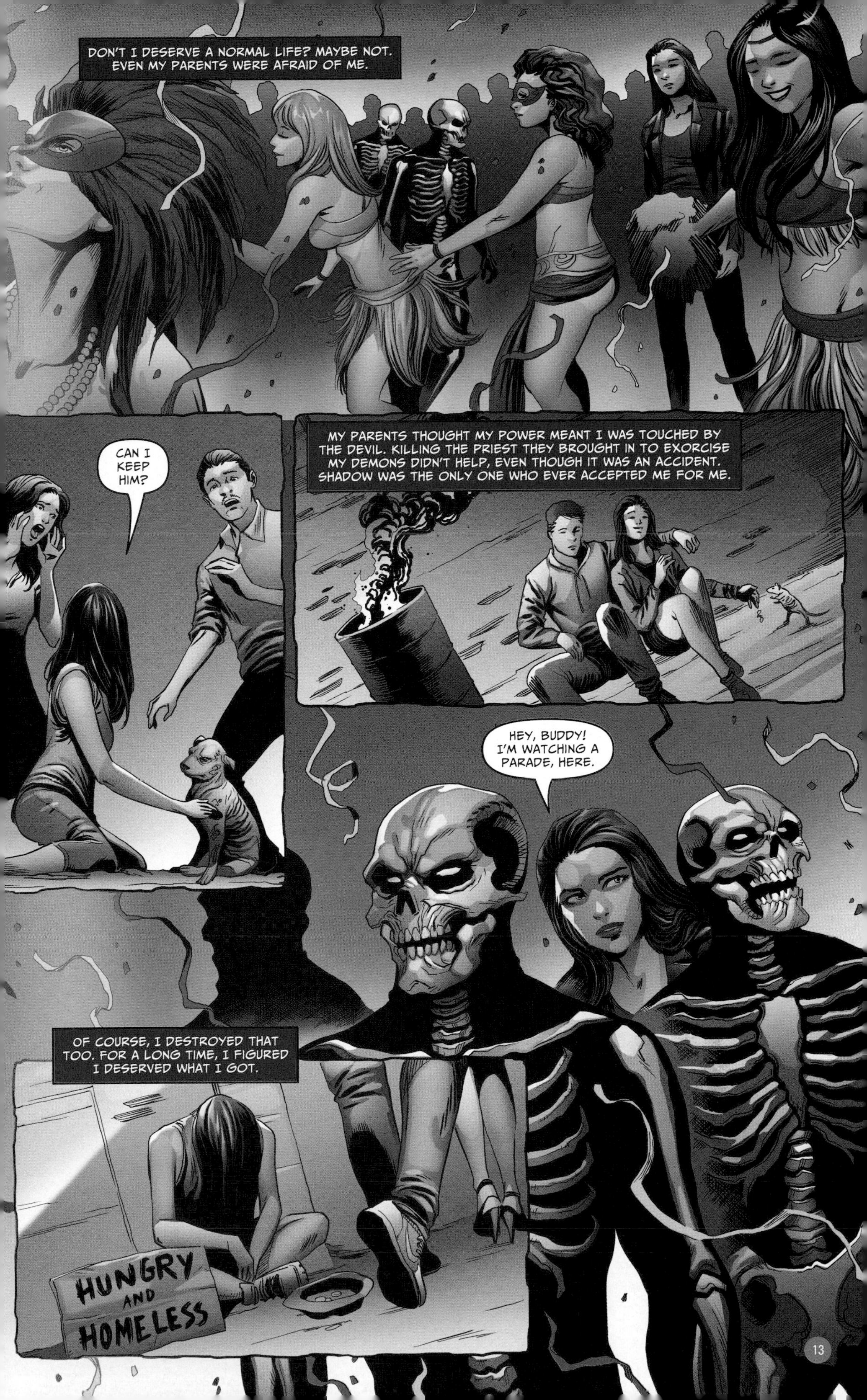
DON'T I DESERVE A NORMAL LIFE? MAYBE NOT. EVEN MY PARENTS WERE AFRAID OF ME.
CAN I KEEP HIM?
MY PARENTS THOUGHT MY POWER MEANT I WAS TOUCHED BY THE DEVIL. KILLING THE PRIEST THEY BROUGHT IN TO EXORCISE MY DEMONS DIDN'T HELP, EVEN THOUGH IT WAS AN ACCIDENT. SHADOW WAS THE ONLY ONE WHO EVER ACCEPTED ME FOR ME.
HEY, BUDDY! I'M WATCHING A PARADE, HERE.
OF COURSE, I DESTROYED THAT TOO. FOR A LONG TIME, I FIGURED I DESERVED WHAT I GOT.
HUNGRY AND HOMELESS

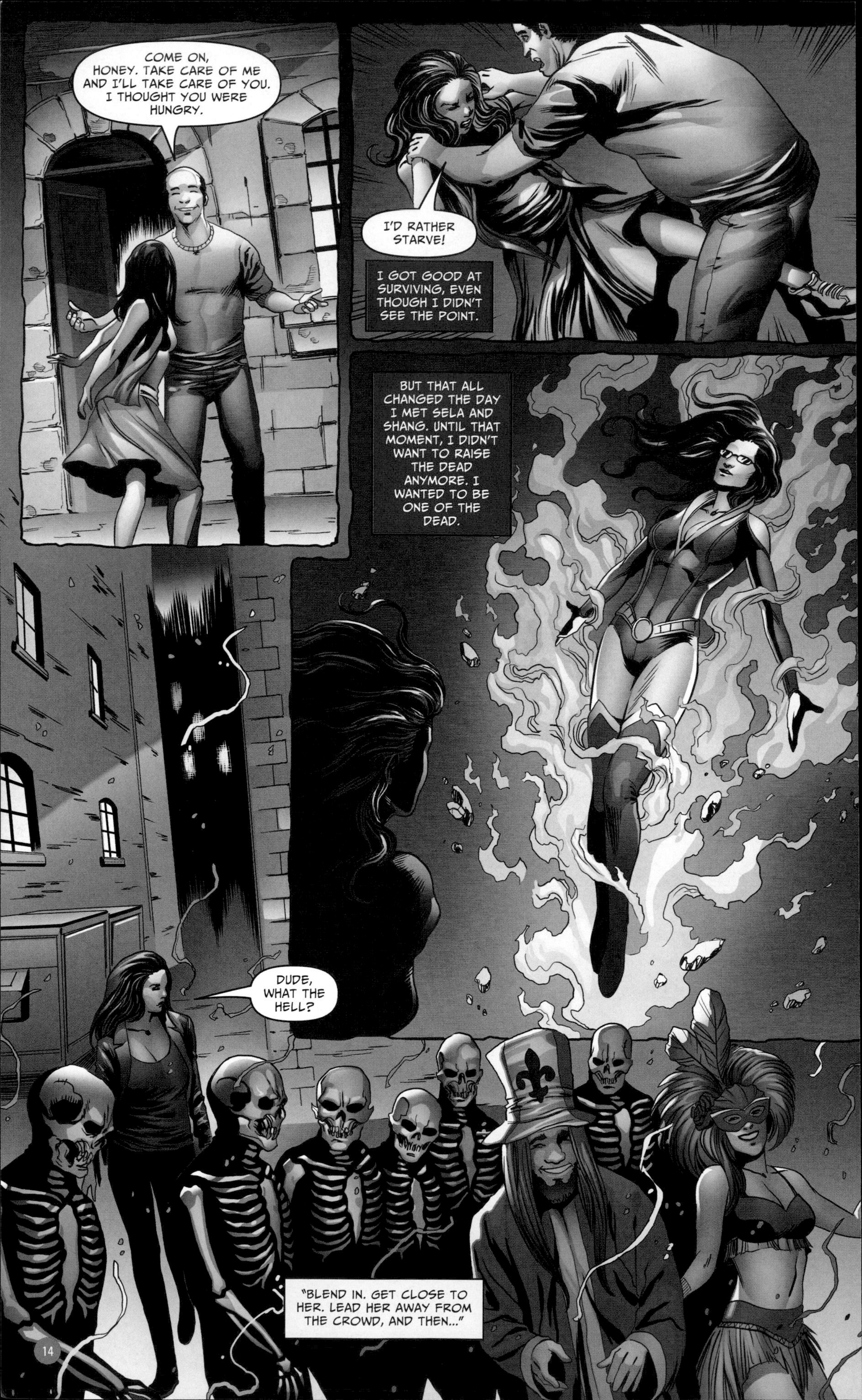

COME ON, HONEY. TAKE CARE OF ME AND I'LL TAKE CARE OF YOU. I THOUGHT YOU WERE HUNGRY.
I'D RATHER STARVE!
I GOT GOOD AT SURVIVING, EVEN THOUGH I DIDN'T SEE THE POINT.
BUT THAT ALL CHANGED THE DAY I MET SELA AND SHANG. UNTIL THAT MOMENT, I DIDN'T WANT TO RAISE THE DEAD ANYMORE. I WANTED TO BE ONE OF THE DEAD.
DUDE, WHAT THE HELL?
"BLEND IN. GET CLOSE TO HER. LEAD HER AWAY FROM THE CROWD, AND THEN..."

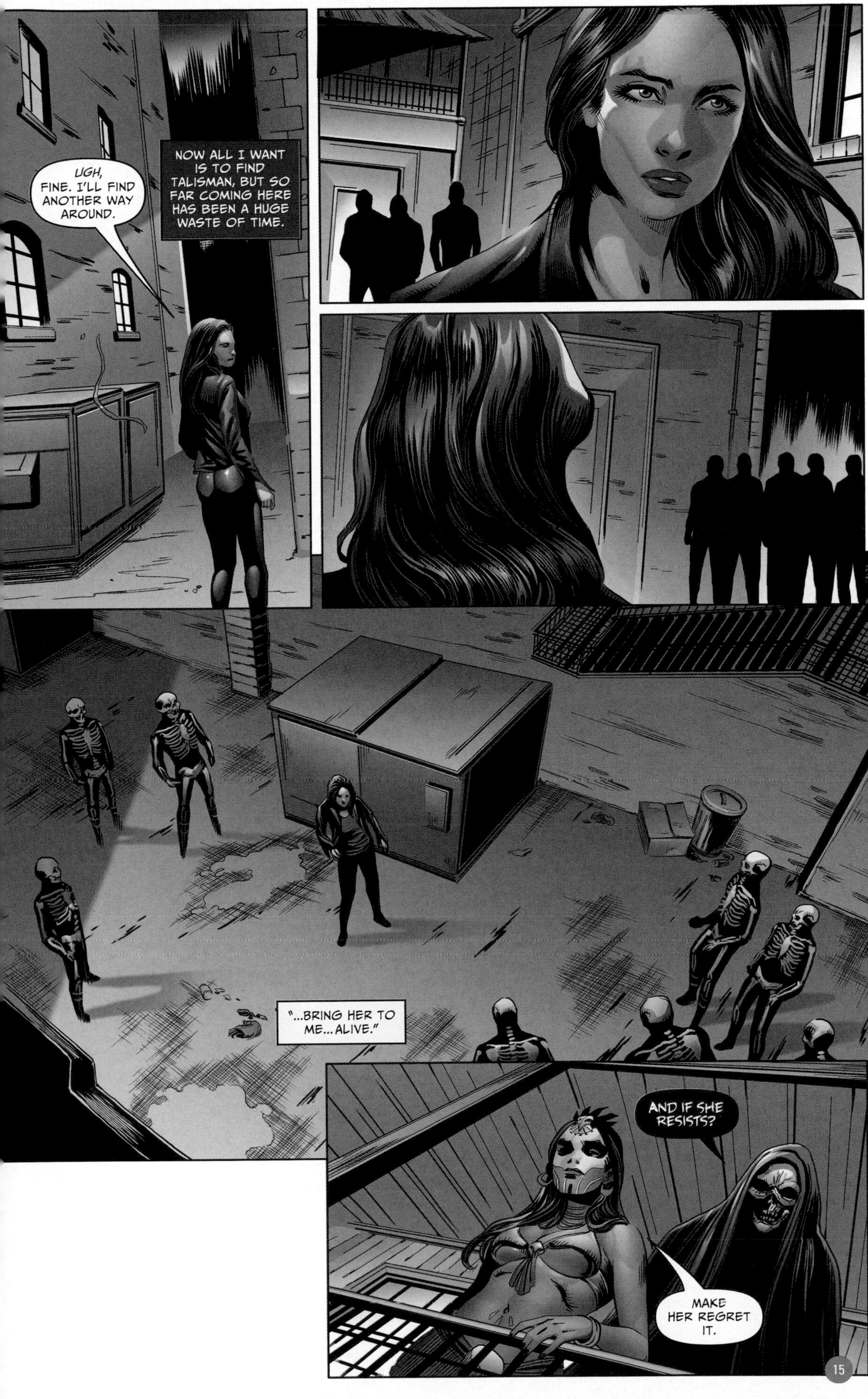
UGH, FINE. I'LL FIND ANOTHER WAY AROUND.
NOW ALL I WANT IS TO FIND TALISMAN, BUT SO FAR COMING HERE HAS BEEN A HUGE WASTE OF TIME.
"...BRING HER TO ME...ALIVE."
AND IF SHE RESISTS?
MAKE HER REGRET IT.

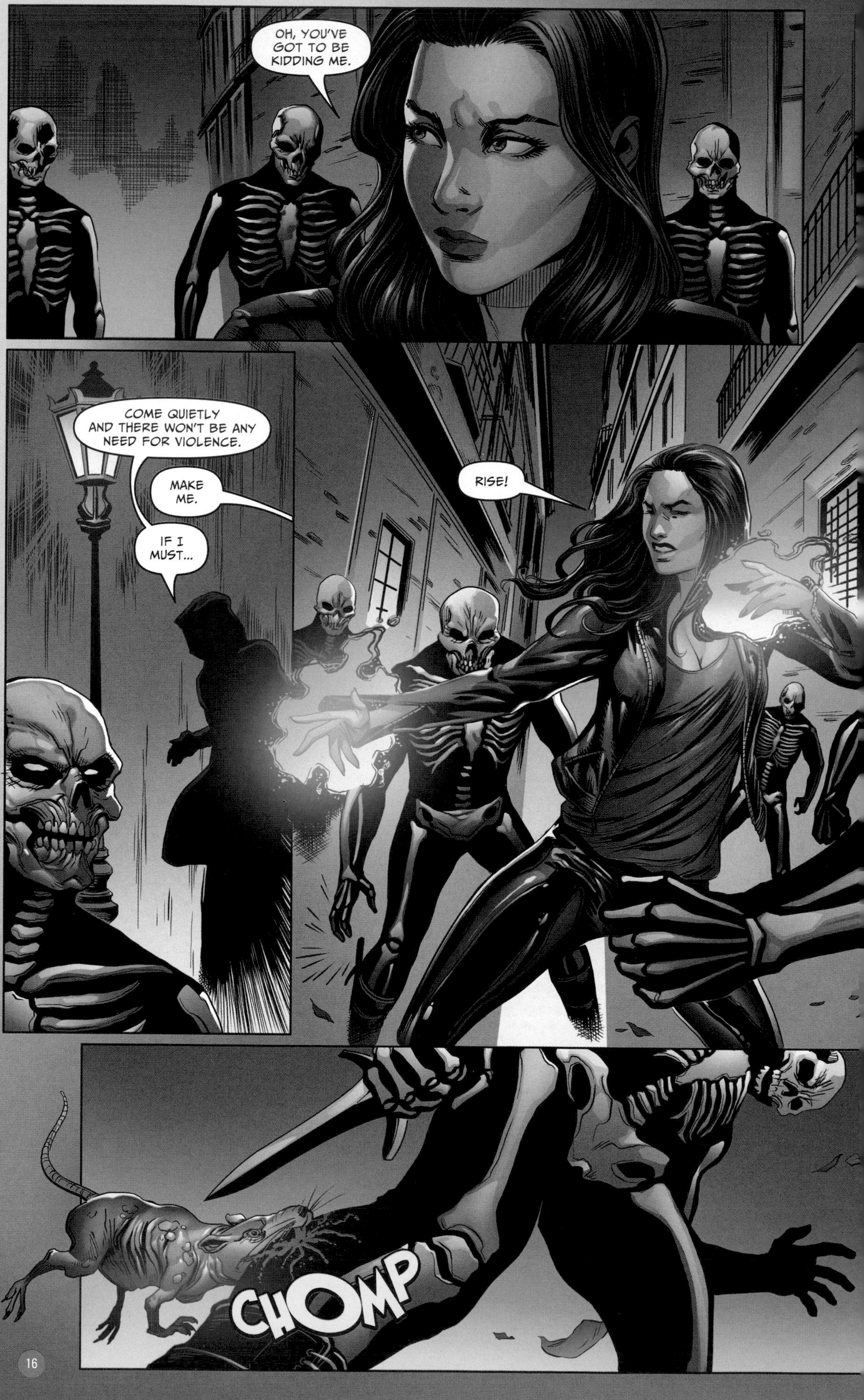
OH, YOU'VE GOT TO BE KIDDING ME.
COME QUIETLY AND THERE WON'T BE ANY NEED FOR VIOLENCE.
MAKE ME.
IF I MUST...
RISE!
CHOMP

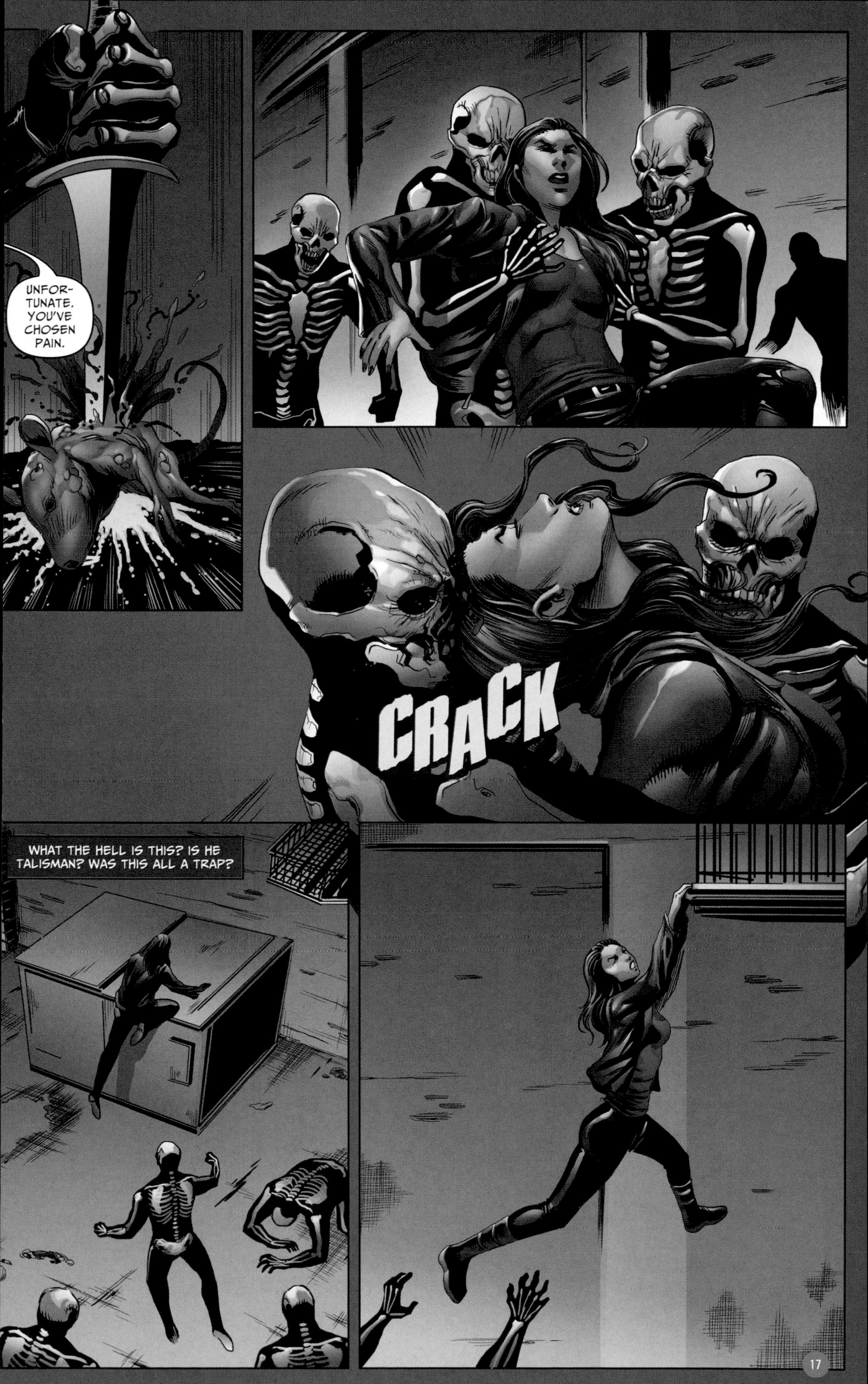
UNFORTUNATE. YOU'VE CHOSEN PAIN.
CRACK
WHAT THE HELL IS THIS? IS HE TALISMAN? WAS THIS ALL A TRAP?

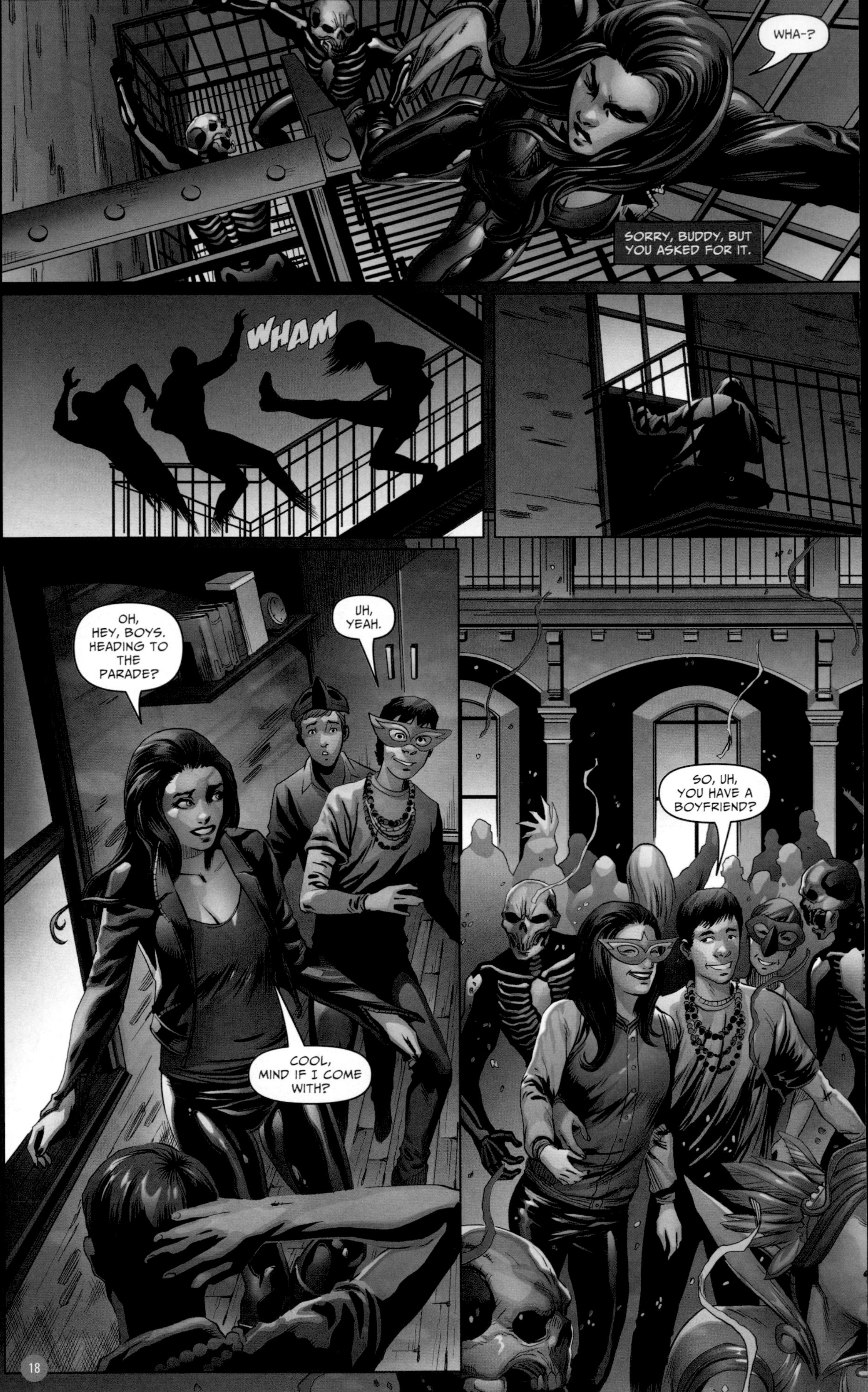
WHA-?
SORRY, BUDDY, BUT YOU ASKED FOR IT.
WHAM
OH, HEY, BOYS. HEADING TO THE PARADE?
UH, YEAH.
COOL, MIND IF I COME WITH?
SO, UH, YOU HAVE A BOYFRIEND?

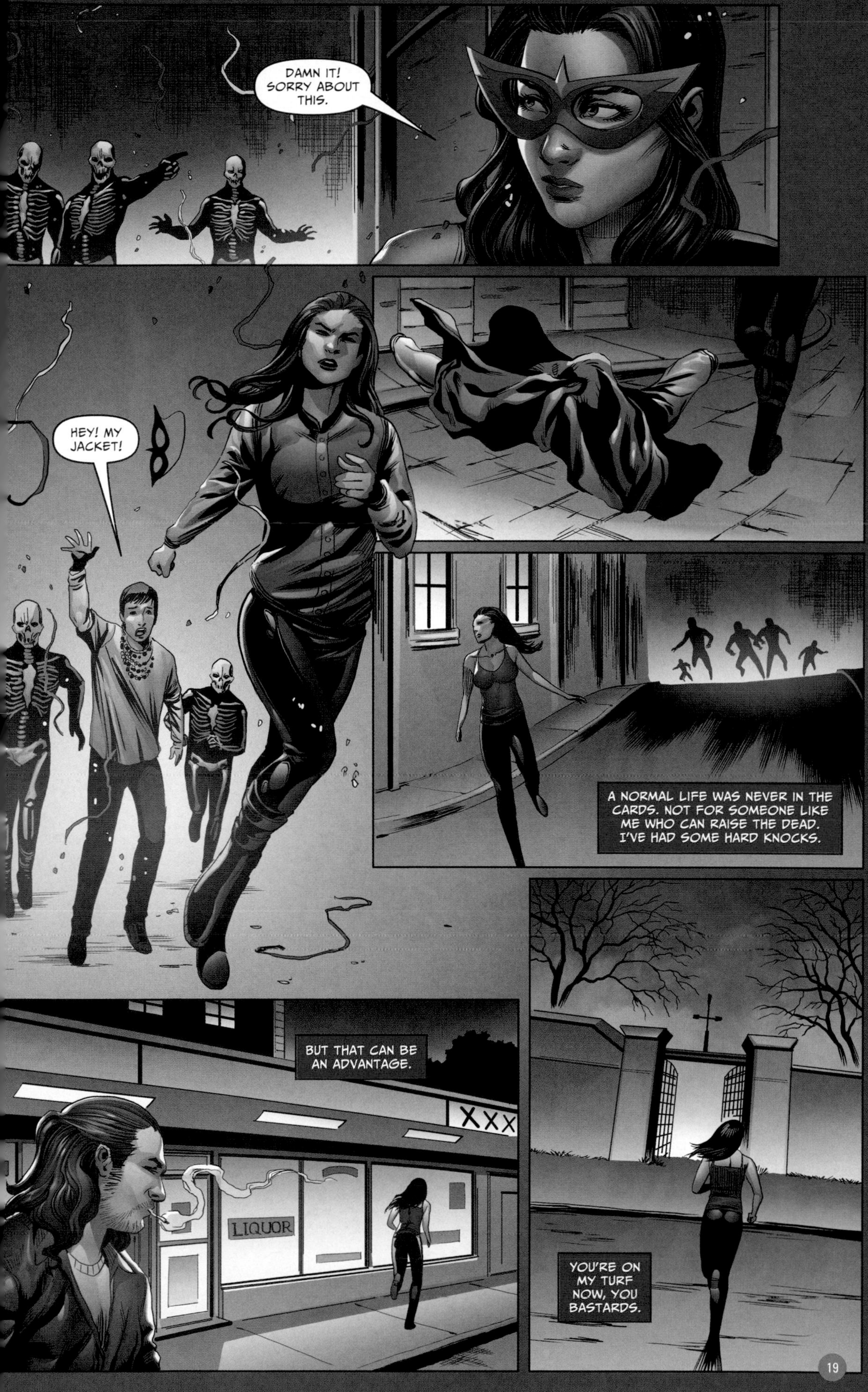
DAMN IT! SORRY ABOUT THIS.
HEY! MY JACKET!
A NORMAL LIFE WAS NEVER IN THE CARDS. NOT FOR SOMEONE LIKE ME WHO CAN RAISE THE DEAD. I'VE HAD SOME HARD KNOCKS.
BUT THAT CAN BE AN ADVANTAGE.
XXX
LIQUOR
YOU'RE ON MY TURF NOW, YOU BASTARDS.

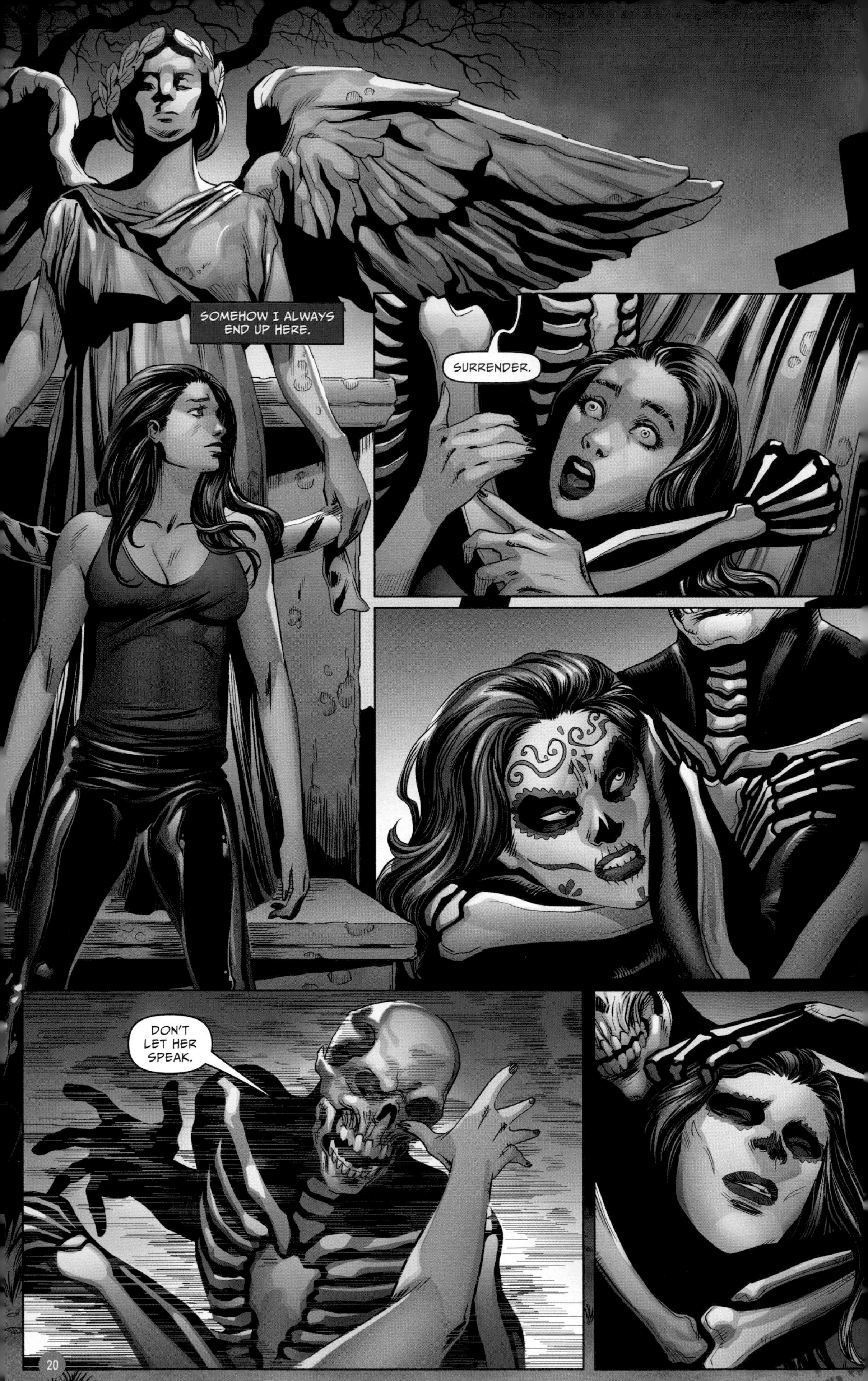
SOMEHOW I ALWAYS END UP HERE.
SURRENDER.
DON'T LET HER SPEAK.

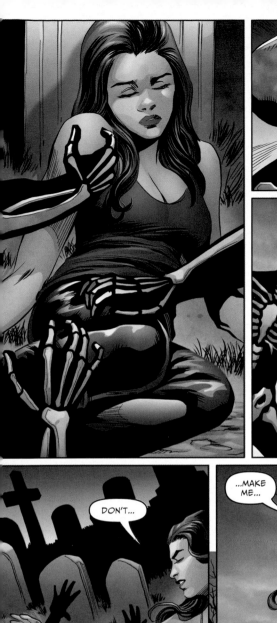

BACK OFF!

DON'T...

...MAKE ME...

...DO THIS!

OOOF!

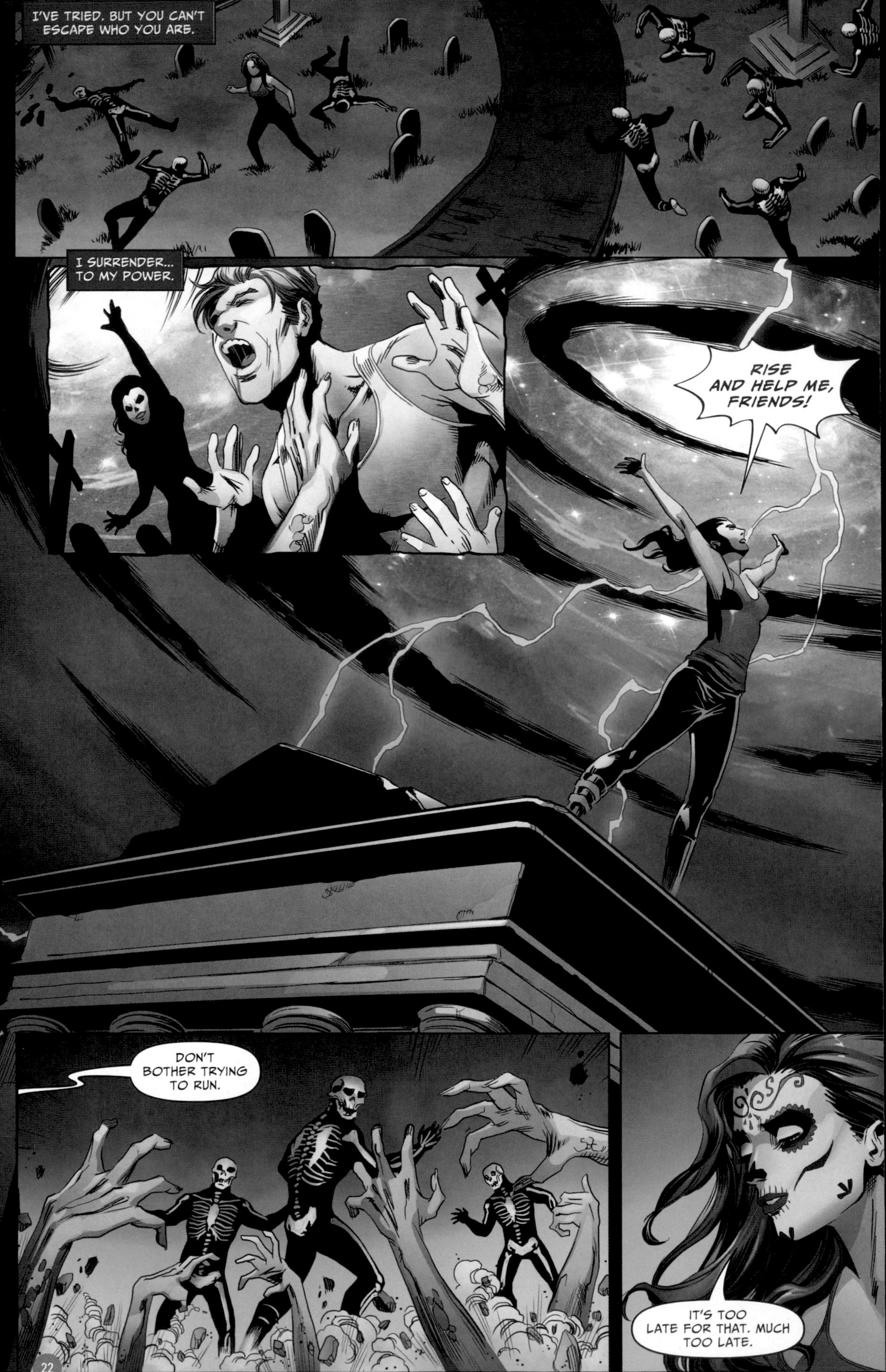

I'VE TRIED. BUT YOU CAN'T ESCAPE WHO YOU ARE.
I SURRENDER... TO MY POWER.
RISE AND HELP ME, FRIENDS!
DON'T BOTHER TRYING TO RUN.
IT'S TOO LATE FOR THAT. MUCH TOO LATE.

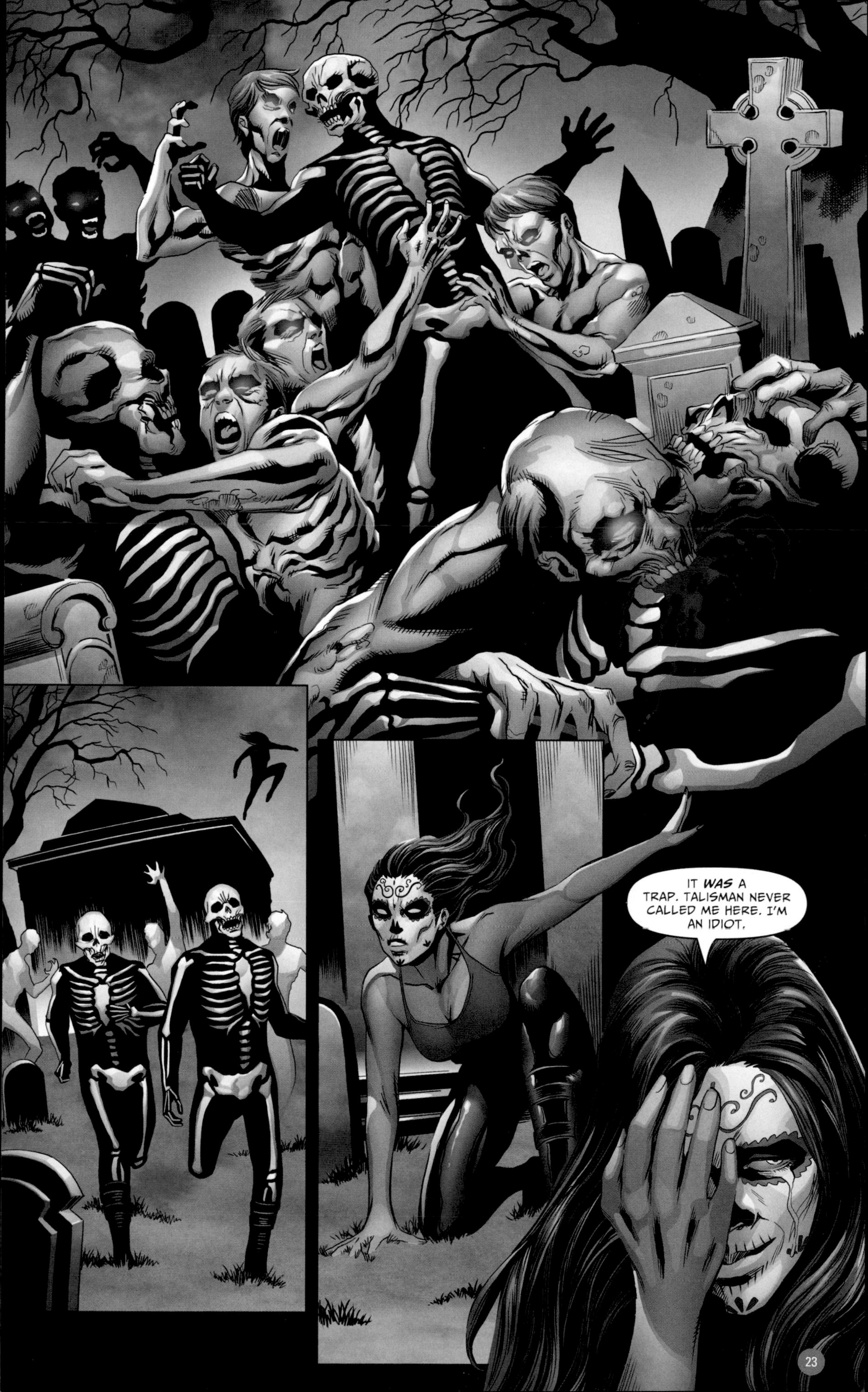
IT WAS A TRAP. TALISMAN NEVER CALLED ME HERE. I'M AN IDIOT.

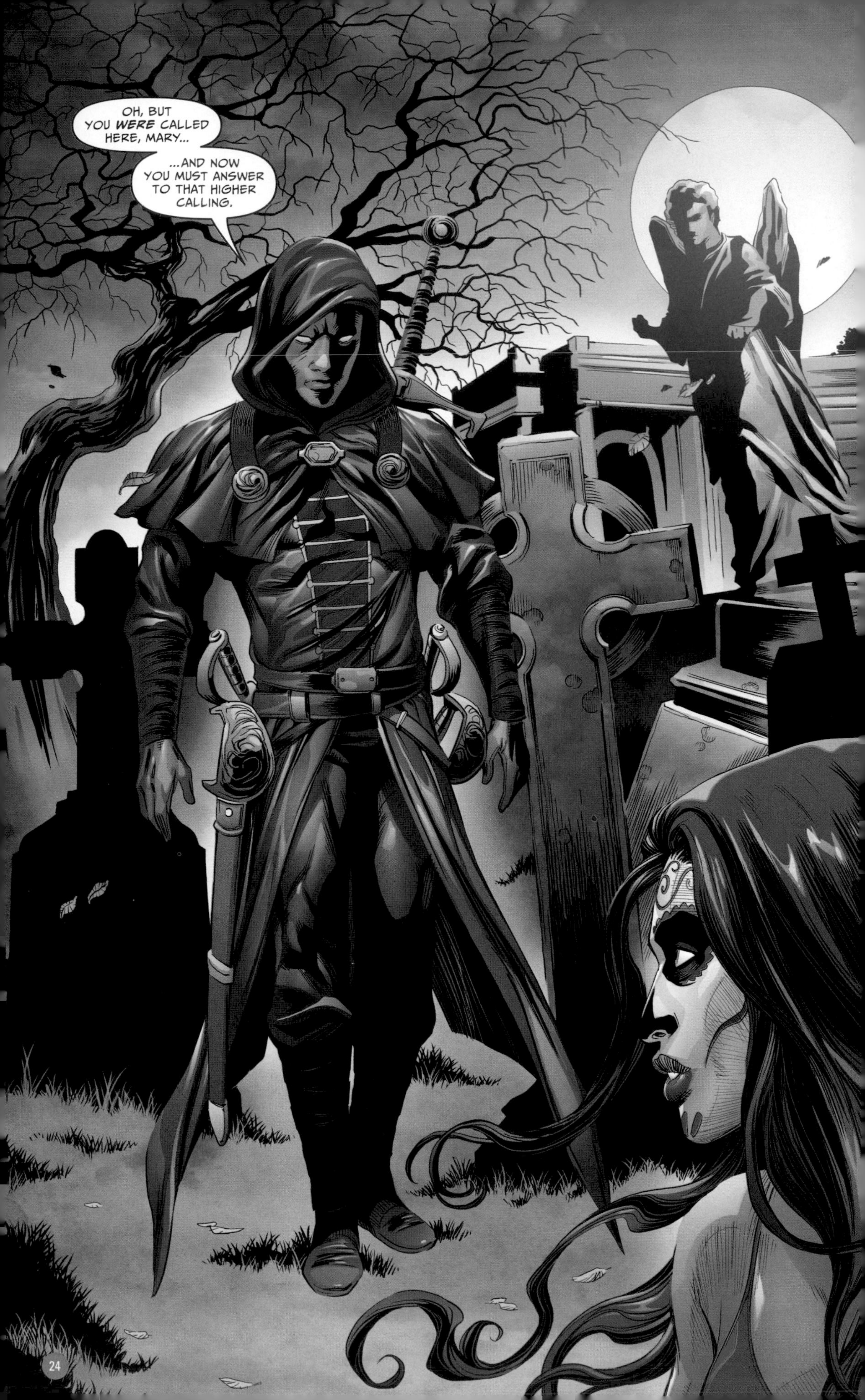
OH, BUT YOU WERE CALLED HERE, MARY...
...AND NOW YOU MUST ANSWER TO THAT HIGHER CALLING.

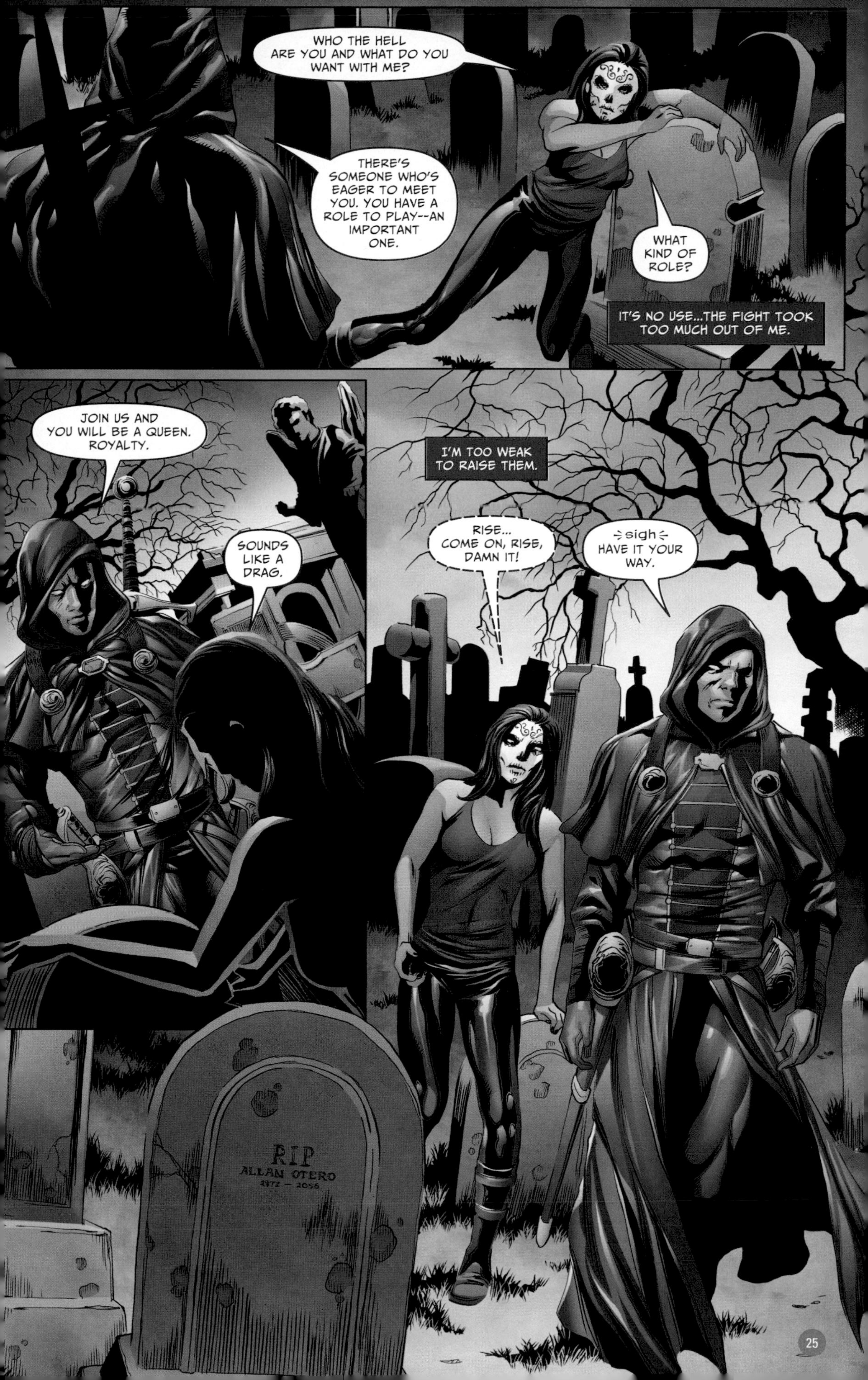
WHO THE HELL ARE YOU AND WHAT DO YOU WANT WITH ME?
THERE'S SOMEONE WHO'S EAGER TO MEET YOU. YOU HAVE A ROLE TO PLAY--AN IMPORTANT ONE.
WHAT KIND OF ROLE?
IT'S NO USE...THE FIGHT TOOK TOO MUCH OUT OF ME.
JOIN US AND YOU WILL BE A QUEEN. ROYALTY.
SOUNDS LIKE A DRAG.
I'M TOO WEAK TO RAISE THEM.
RISE... COME ON, RISE, DAMN IT!
sigh HAVE IT YOUR WAY.
RIP
ALLAN OTERO
1972 — 2056

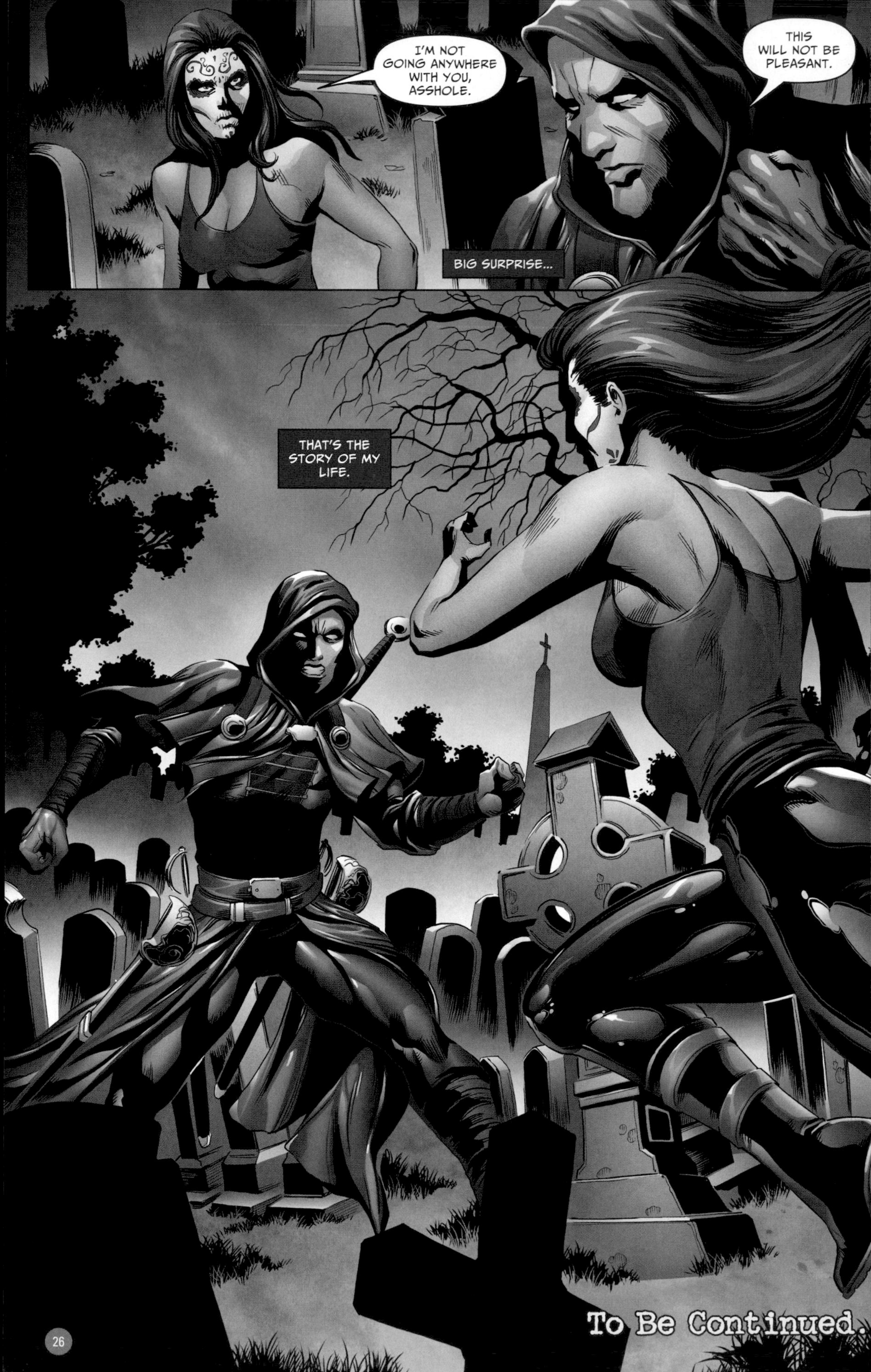

I'M NOT GOING ANYWHERE WITH YOU, ASSHOLE.
THIS WILL NOT BE PLEASANT.
BIG SURPRISE...
THAT'S THE STORY OF MY LIFE.
To Be Continued.

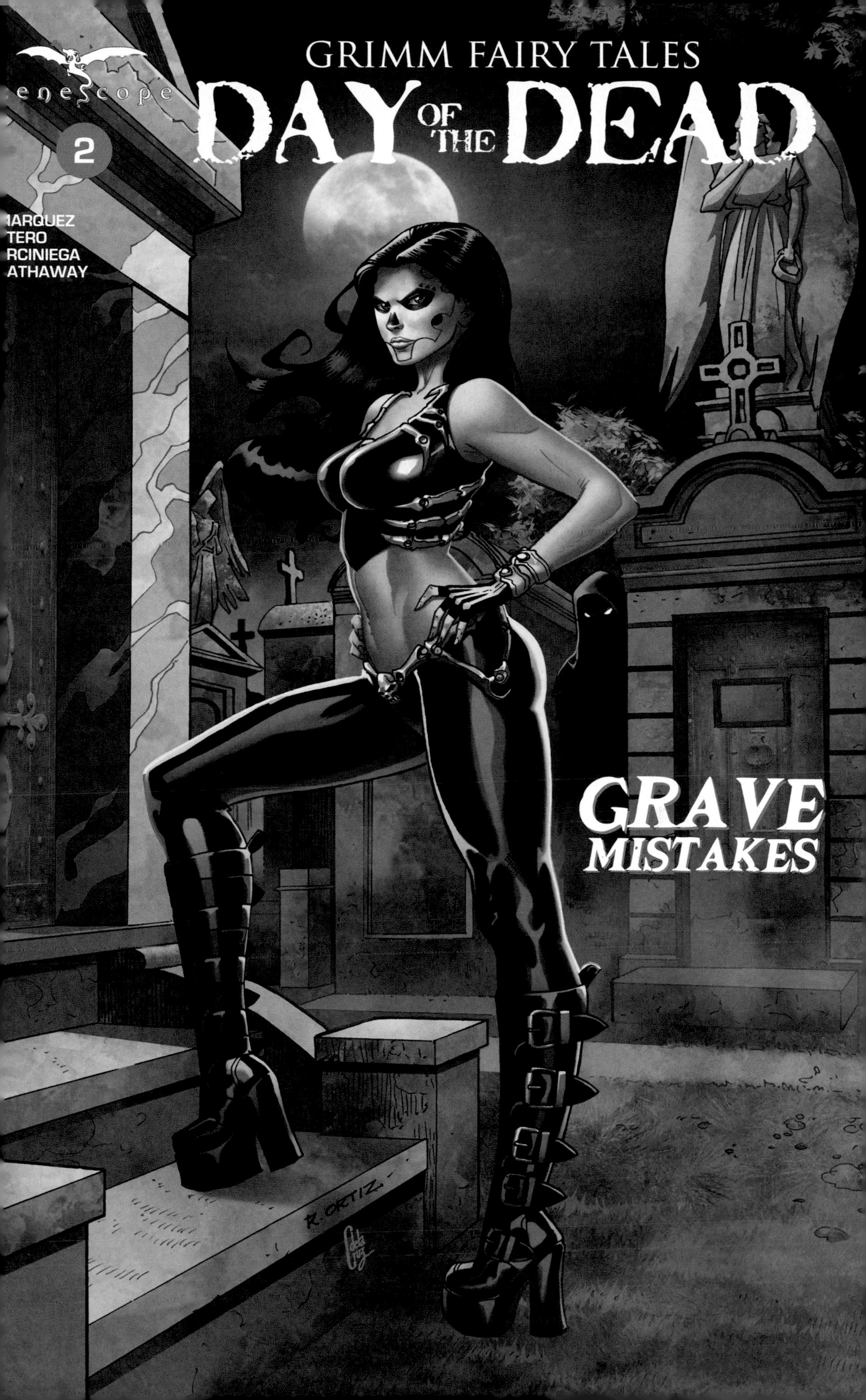

zenescope
2
GRIMM FAIRY TALES
DAY OF THE DEAD
IARQUEZ
TERO
RCINIEGA
ATHAWAY
GRAVE
MISTAKES
R. ORTIZ

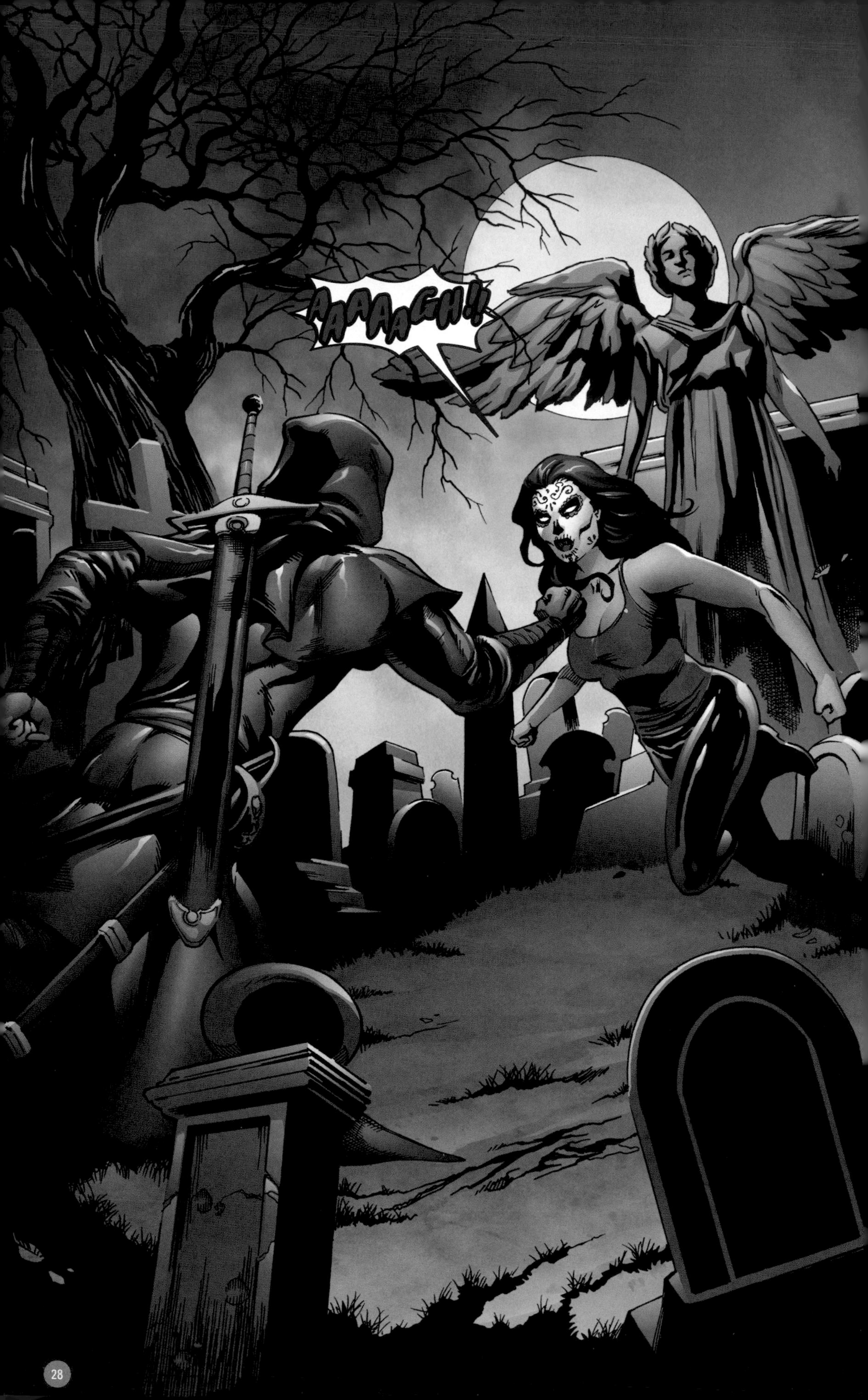
AAAAAAGH!!

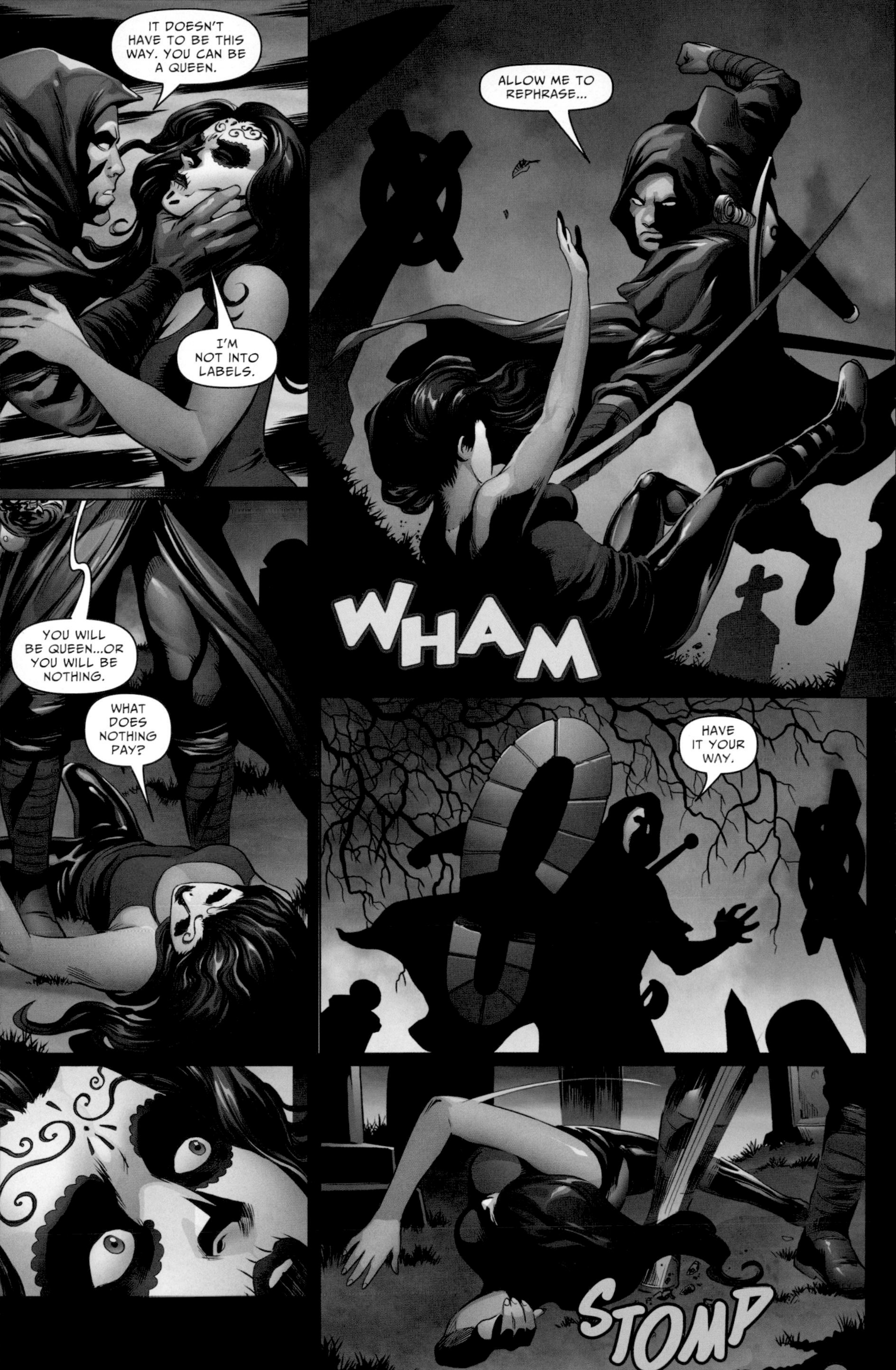
IT DOESN'T HAVE TO BE THIS WAY. YOU CAN BE A QUEEN.
I'M NOT INTO LABELS.
ALLOW ME TO REPHRASE...
WHAM
YOU WILL BE QUEEN...OR YOU WILL BE NOTHING.
WHAT DOES NOTHING PAY?
HAVE IT YOUR WAY.
STOMP

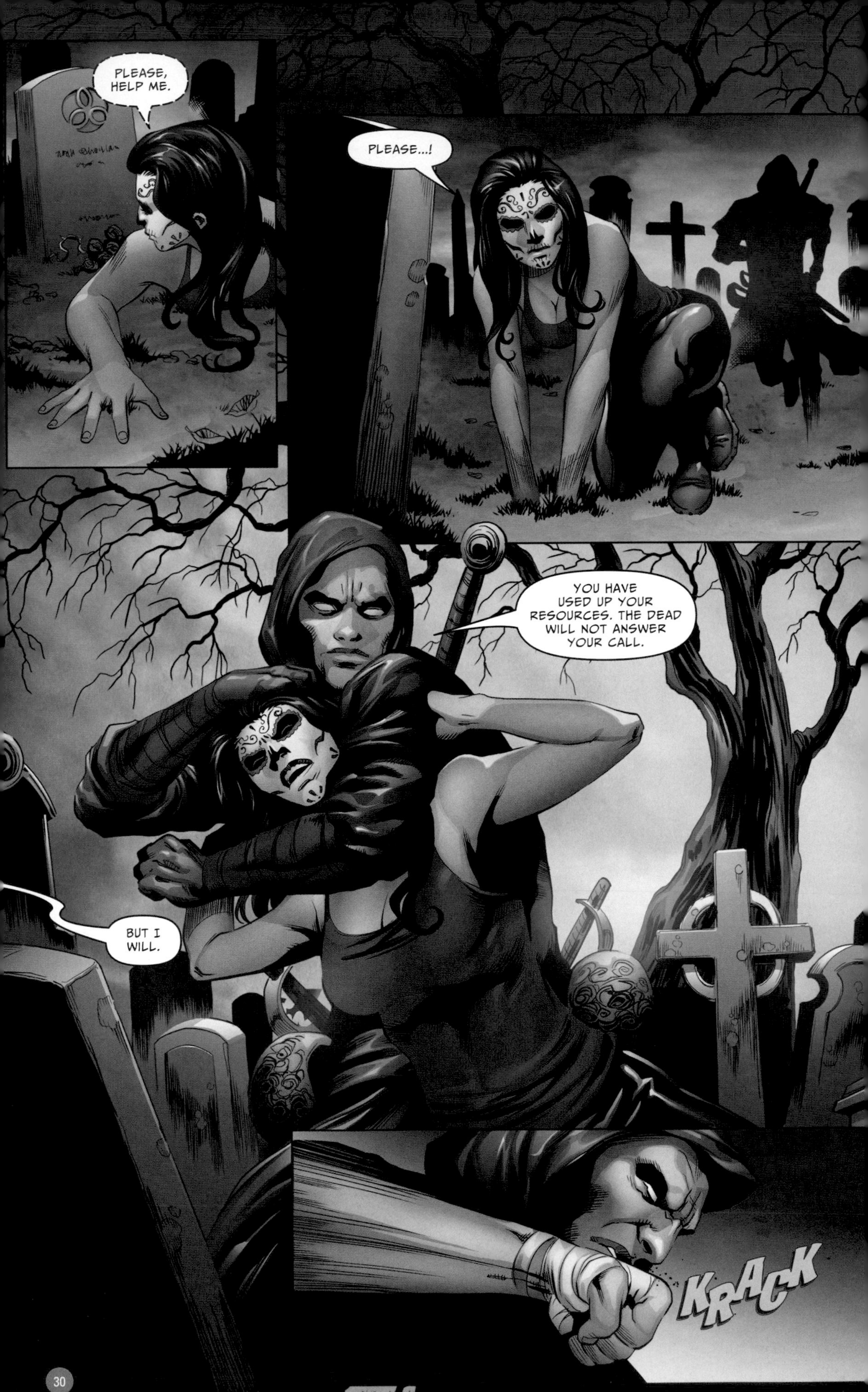
PLEASE, HELP ME.
PLEASE...!
YOU HAVE USED UP YOUR RESOURCES. THE DEAD WILL NOT ANSWER YOUR CALL.
BUT I WILL.
KRACK

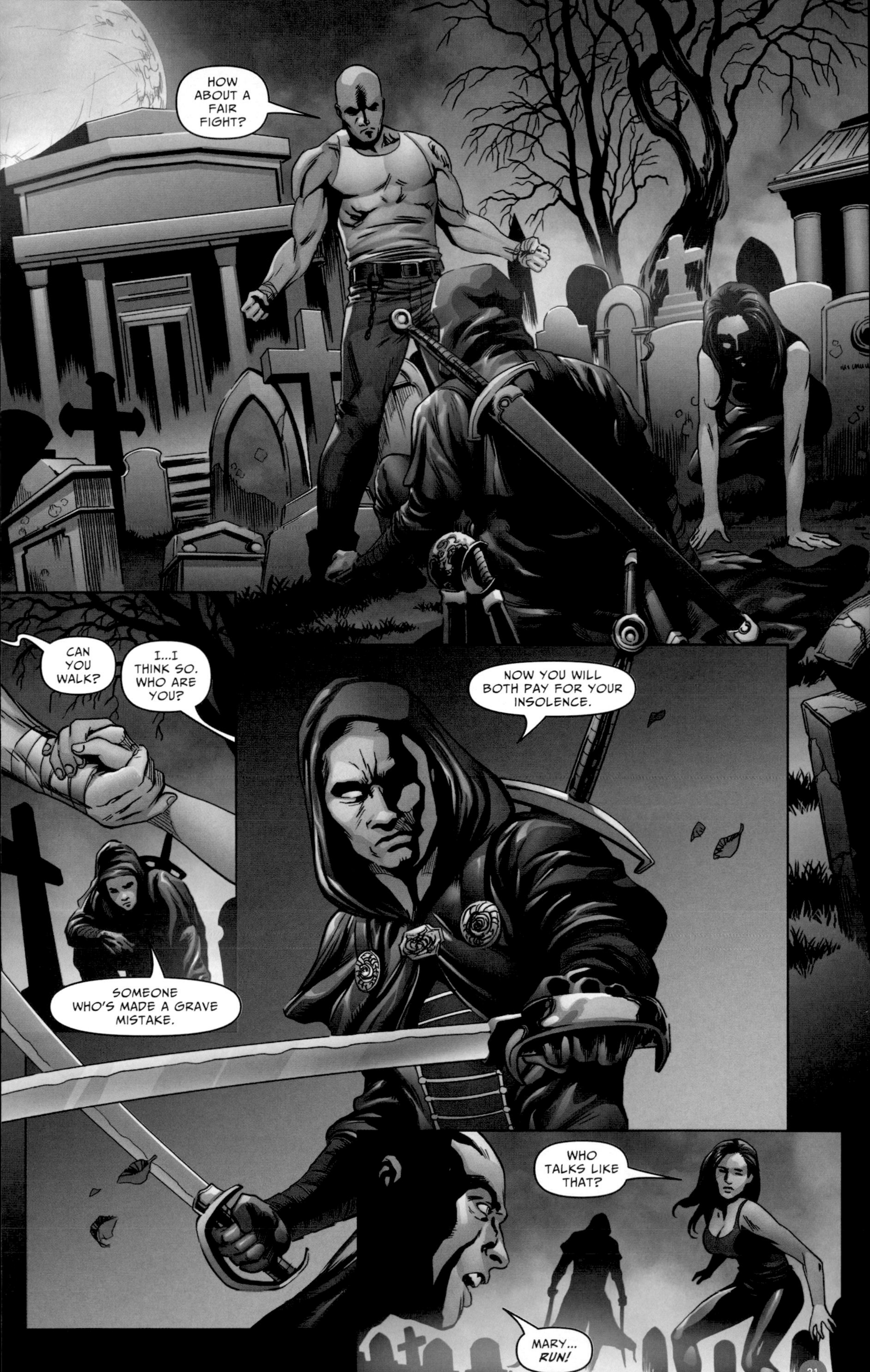

HOW ABOUT A FAIR FIGHT?
CAN YOU WALK?
I...I THINK SO. WHO ARE YOU?
SOMEONE WHO'S MADE A GRAVE MISTAKE.
NOW YOU WILL BOTH PAY FOR YOUR INSOLENCE.
WHO TALKS LIKE THAT?
MARY... *RUN!*

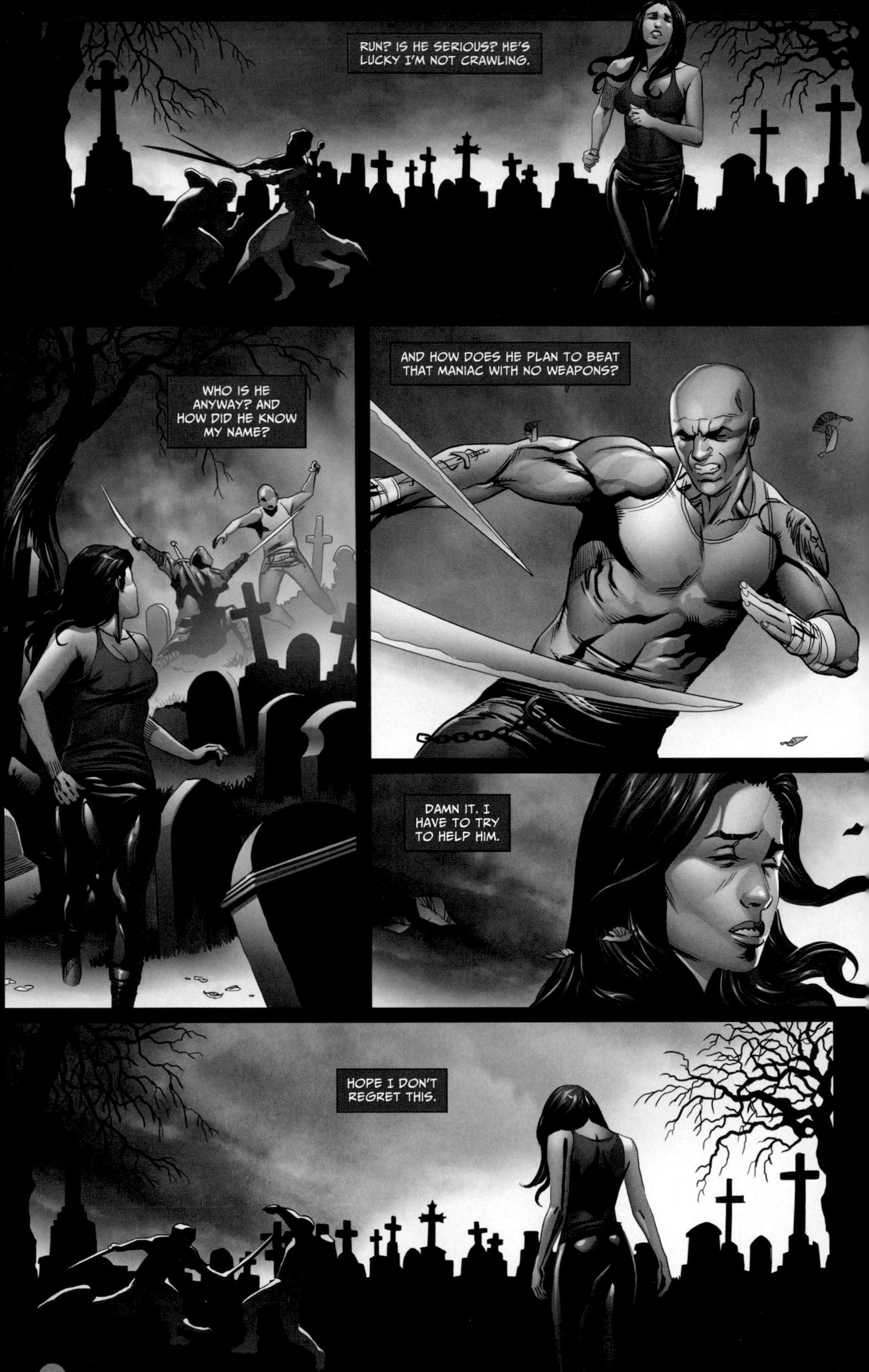
RUN? IS HE SERIOUS? HE'S LUCKY I'M NOT CRAWLING.
WHO IS HE ANYWAY? AND HOW DID HE KNOW MY NAME?
AND HOW DOES HE PLAN TO BEAT THAT MANIAC WITH NO WEAPONS?
DAMN IT. I HAVE TO TRY TO HELP HIM.
HOPE I DON'T REGRET THIS.

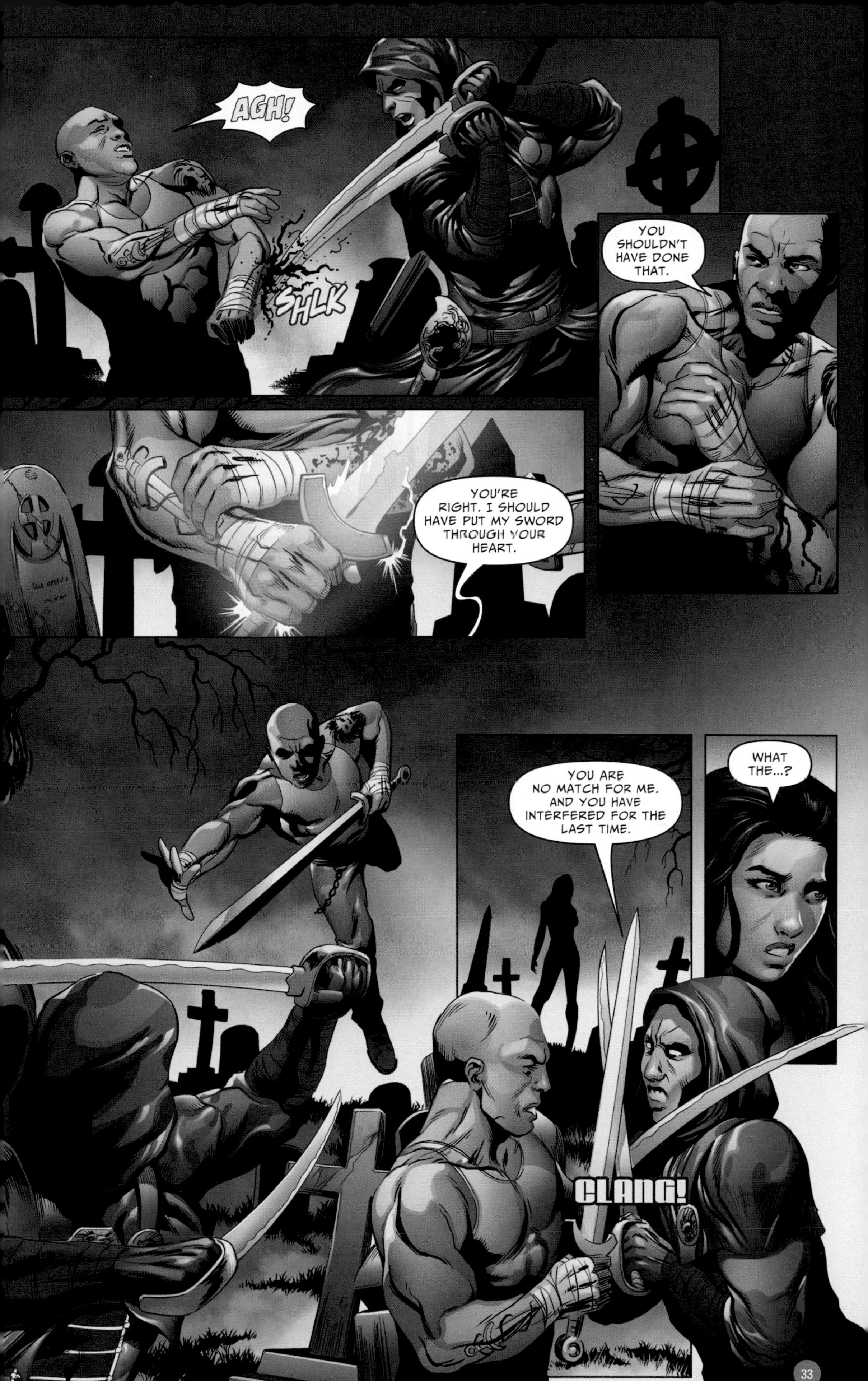
AGH!
SHLK
YOU SHOULDN'T HAVE DONE THAT.
YOU'RE RIGHT. I SHOULD HAVE PUT MY SWORD THROUGH YOUR HEART.
YOU ARE NO MATCH FOR ME. AND YOU HAVE INTERFERED FOR THE LAST TIME.
WHAT THE...?
CLANG!

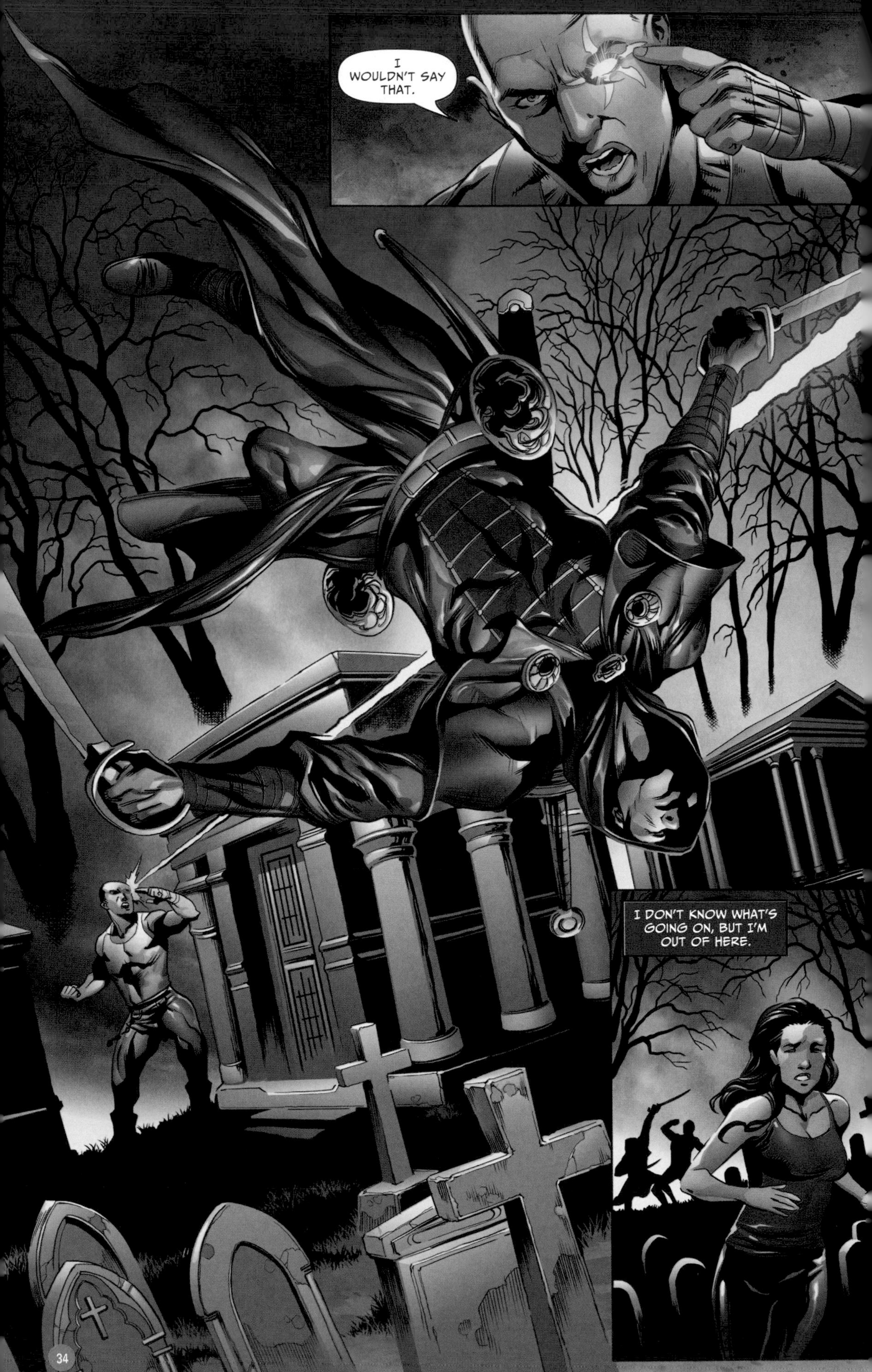
I WOULDN'T SAY THAT.
I DON'T KNOW WHAT'S GOING ON, BUT I'M OUT OF HERE.

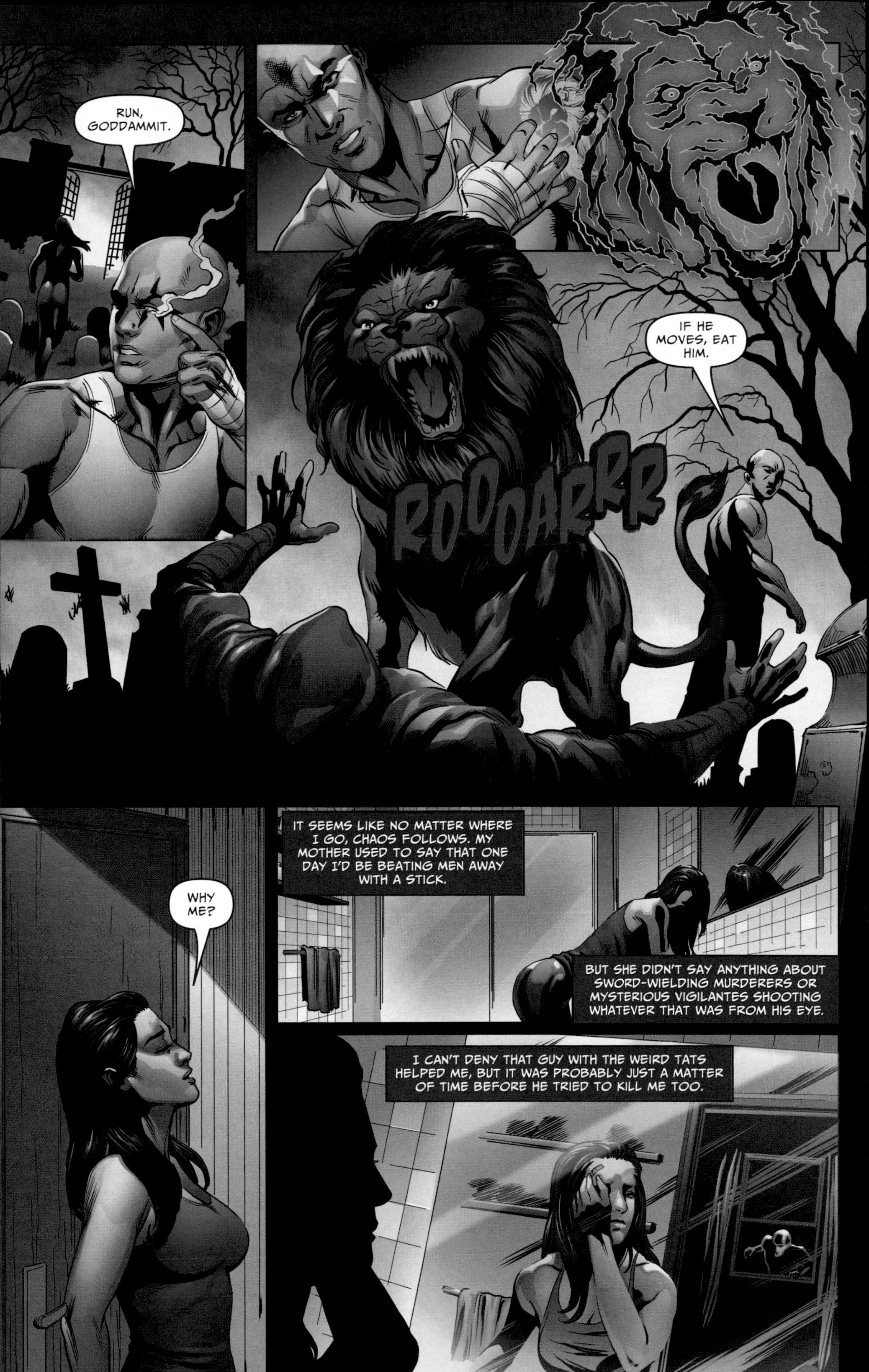
RUN, GODDAMMIT.
IF HE MOVES, EAT HIM.
ROOOARRR
WHY ME?
IT SEEMS LIKE NO MATTER WHERE I GO, CHAOS FOLLOWS. MY MOTHER USED TO SAY THAT ONE DAY I'D BE BEATING MEN AWAY WITH A STICK.
BUT SHE DIDN'T SAY ANYTHING ABOUT SWORD-WIELDING MURDERERS OR MYSTERIOUS VIGILANTES SHOOTING WHATEVER THAT WAS FROM HIS EYE.
I CAN'T DENY THAT GUY WITH THE WEIRD TATS HELPED ME, BUT IT WAS PROBABLY JUST A MATTER OF TIME BEFORE HE TRIED TO KILL ME TOO.

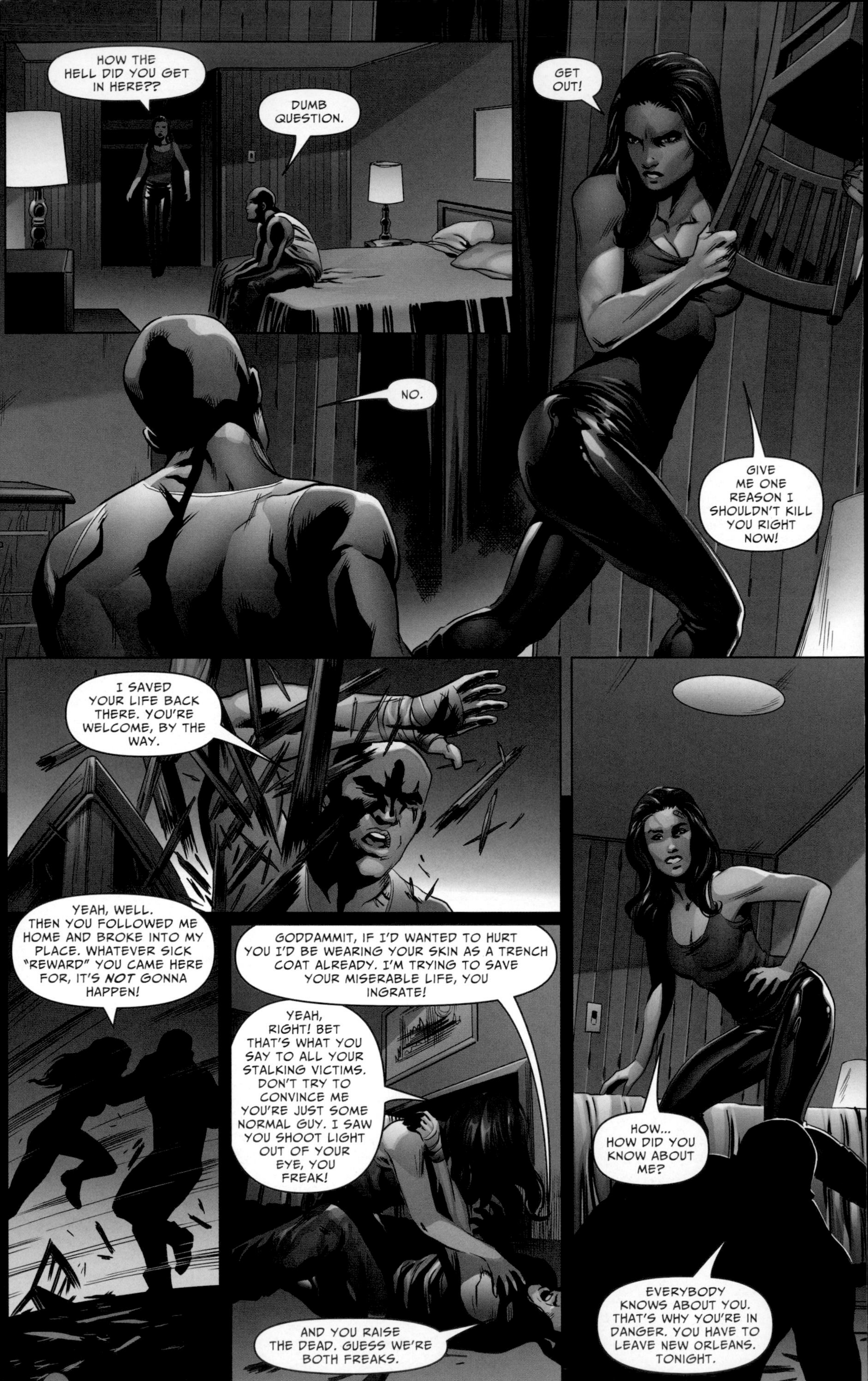
HOW THE HELL DID YOU GET IN HERE??
DUMB QUESTION.
GET OUT!
NO.
GIVE ME ONE REASON I SHOULDN'T KILL YOU RIGHT NOW!
I SAVED YOUR LIFE BACK THERE. YOU'RE WELCOME, BY THE WAY.
YEAH, WELL. THEN YOU FOLLOWED ME HOME AND BROKE INTO MY PLACE. WHATEVER SICK "REWARD" YOU CAME HERE FOR, IT'S *NOT* GONNA HAPPEN!
GODDAMMIT, IF I'D WANTED TO HURT YOU I'D BE WEARING YOUR SKIN AS A TRENCH COAT ALREADY. I'M TRYING TO SAVE YOUR MISERABLE LIFE, YOU INGRATE!
YEAH, RIGHT! BET THAT'S WHAT YOU SAY TO ALL YOUR STALKING VICTIMS. DON'T TRY TO CONVINCE ME YOU'RE JUST SOME NORMAL GUY. I SAW YOU SHOOT LIGHT OUT OF YOUR EYE, YOU FREAK!
AND YOU RAISE THE DEAD. GUESS WE'RE BOTH FREAKS.
HOW... HOW DID YOU KNOW ABOUT ME?
EVERYBODY KNOWS ABOUT YOU. THAT'S WHY YOU'RE IN DANGER. YOU HAVE TO LEAVE NEW ORLEANS. TONIGHT.

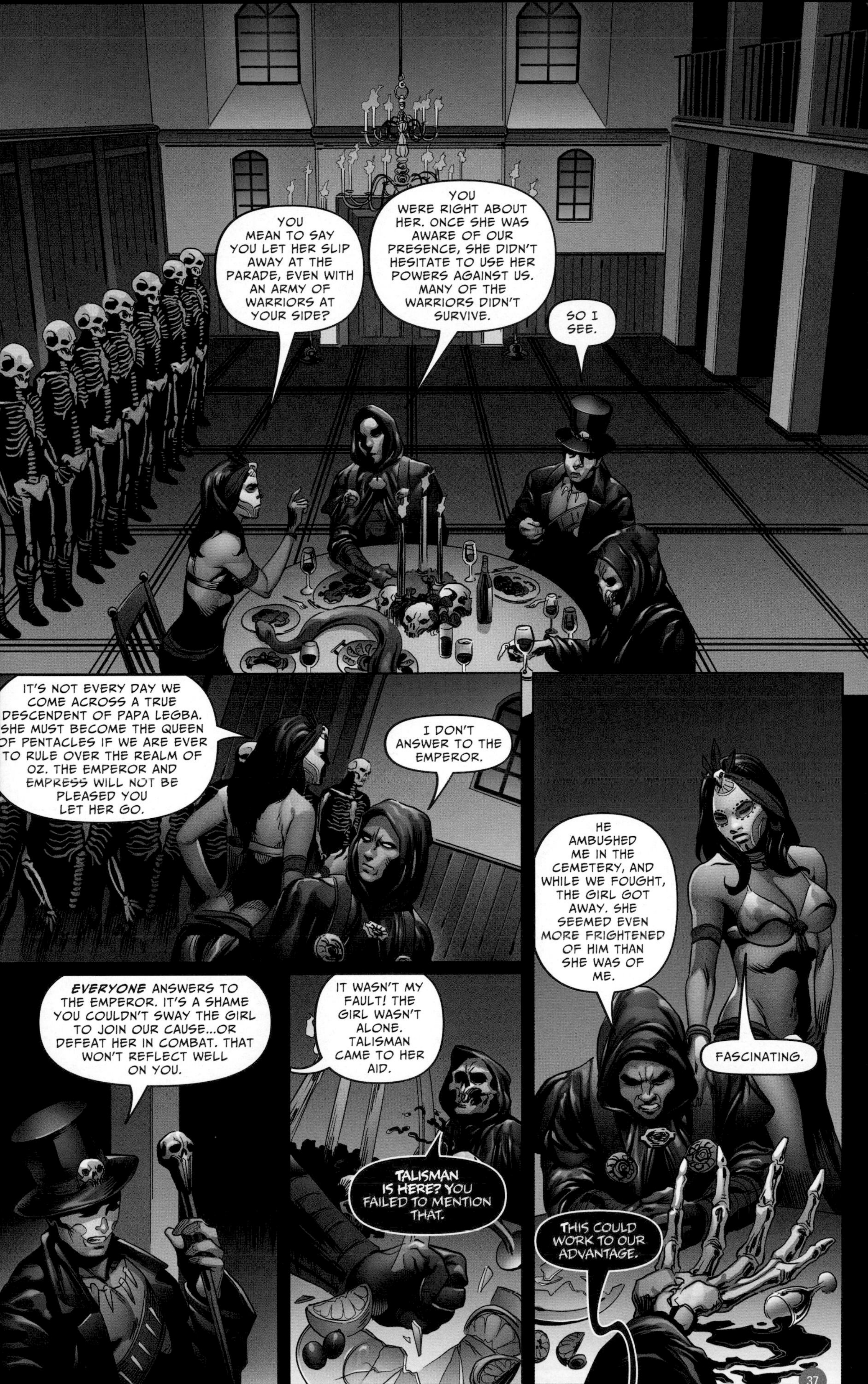
YOU MEAN TO SAY YOU LET HER SLIP AWAY AT THE PARADE, EVEN WITH AN ARMY OF WARRIORS AT YOUR SIDE?
YOU WERE RIGHT ABOUT HER. ONCE SHE WAS AWARE OF OUR PRESENCE, SHE DIDN'T HESITATE TO USE HER POWERS AGAINST US. MANY OF THE WARRIORS DIDN'T SURVIVE.
SO I SEE.
IT'S NOT EVERY DAY WE COME ACROSS A TRUE DESCENDENT OF PAPA LEGBA. SHE MUST BECOME THE QUEEN OF PENTACLES IF WE ARE EVER TO RULE OVER THE REALM OF OZ. THE EMPEROR AND EMPRESS WILL NOT BE PLEASED YOU LET HER GO.
I DON'T ANSWER TO THE EMPEROR.
HE AMBUSHED ME IN THE CEMETERY, AND WHILE WE FOUGHT, THE GIRL GOT AWAY. SHE SEEMED EVEN MORE FRIGHTENED OF HIM THAN SHE WAS OF ME.
FASCINATING.
EVERYONE ANSWERS TO THE EMPEROR. IT'S A SHAME YOU COULDN'T SWAY THE GIRL TO JOIN OUR CAUSE...OR DEFEAT HER IN COMBAT. THAT WON'T REFLECT WELL ON YOU.
IT WASN'T MY FAULT! THE GIRL WASN'T ALONE. TALISMAN CAME TO HER AID.
TALISMAN IS HERE? YOU FAILED TO MENTION THAT.
THIS COULD WORK TO OUR ADVANTAGE.

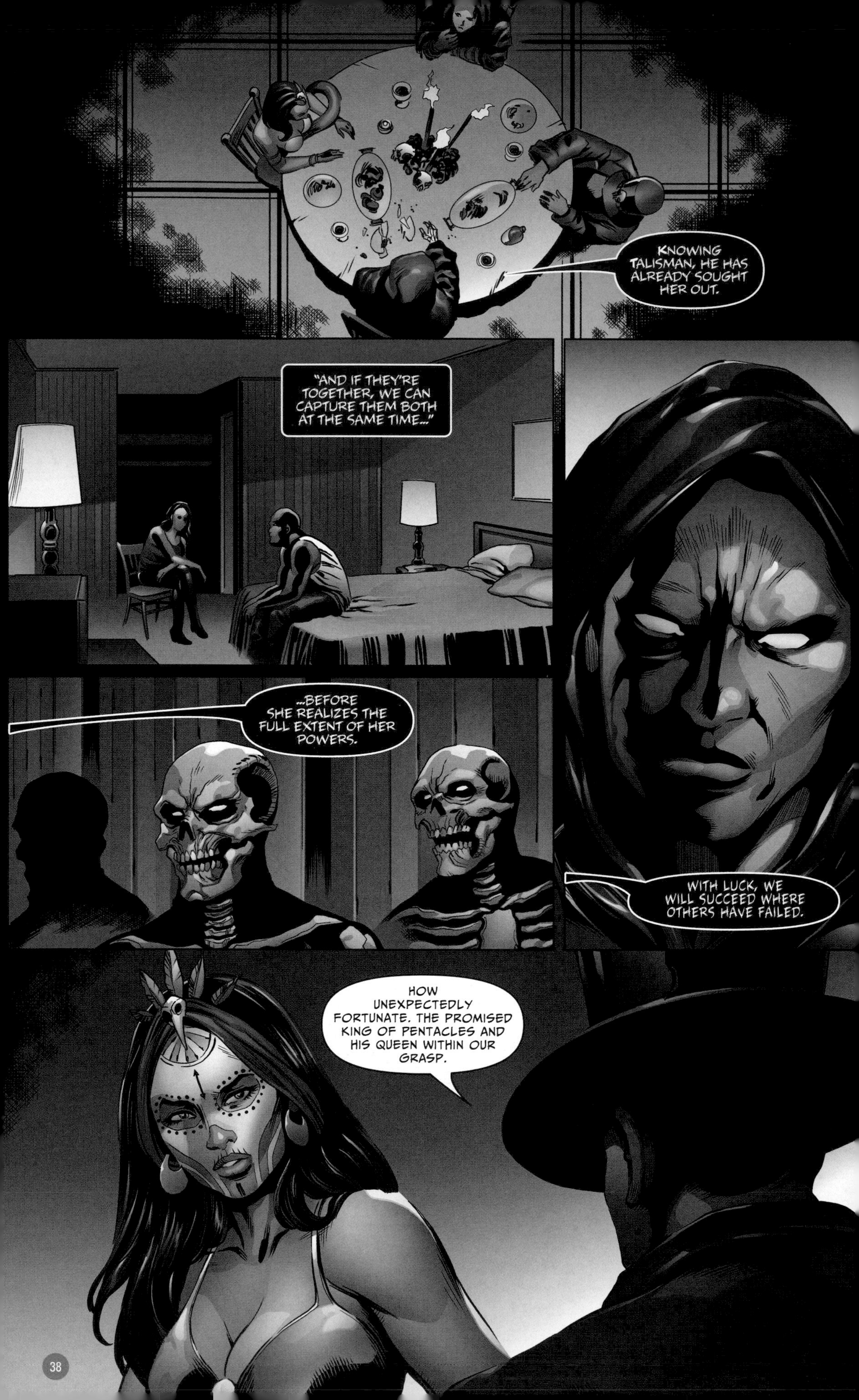
KNOWING TALISMAN, HE HAS ALREADY SOUGHT HER OUT.
"AND IF THEY'RE TOGETHER, WE CAN CAPTURE THEM BOTH AT THE SAME TIME..."
...BEFORE SHE REALIZES THE FULL EXTENT OF HER POWERS.
WITH LUCK, WE WILL SUCCEED WHERE OTHERS HAVE FAILED.
HOW UNEXPECTEDLY FORTUNATE. THE PROMISED KING OF PENTACLES AND HIS QUEEN WITHIN OUR GRASP.

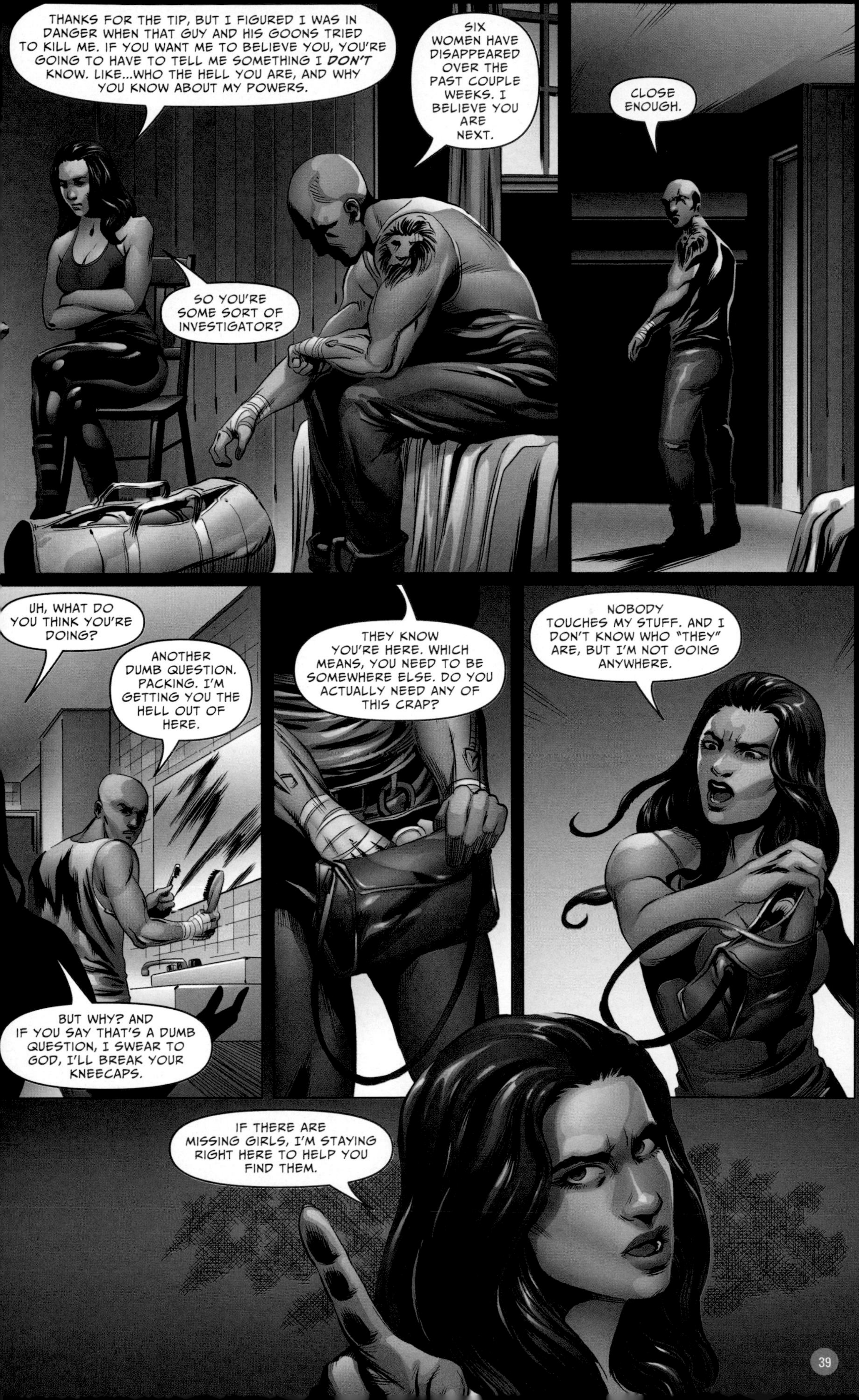

THANKS FOR THE TIP, BUT I FIGURED I WAS IN DANGER WHEN THAT GUY AND HIS GOONS TRIED TO KILL ME. IF YOU WANT ME TO BELIEVE YOU, YOU'RE GOING TO HAVE TO TELL ME SOMETHING I *DON'T* KNOW. LIKE...WHO THE HELL YOU ARE, AND WHY YOU KNOW ABOUT MY POWERS.
SIX WOMEN HAVE DISAPPEARED OVER THE PAST COUPLE WEEKS. I BELIEVE YOU ARE NEXT.
SO YOU'RE SOME SORT OF INVESTIGATOR?
CLOSE ENOUGH.
UH, WHAT DO YOU THINK YOU'RE DOING?
ANOTHER DUMB QUESTION. PACKING. I'M GETTING YOU THE HELL OUT OF HERE.
BUT WHY? AND IF YOU SAY THAT'S A DUMB QUESTION, I SWEAR TO GOD, I'LL BREAK YOUR KNEECAPS.
THEY KNOW YOU'RE HERE. WHICH MEANS, YOU NEED TO BE SOMEWHERE ELSE. DO YOU ACTUALLY NEED ANY OF THIS CRAP?
NOBODY TOUCHES MY STUFF. AND I DON'T KNOW WHO "THEY" ARE, BUT I'M NOT GOING ANYWHERE.
IF THERE ARE MISSING GIRLS, I'M STAYING RIGHT HERE TO HELP YOU FIND THEM.

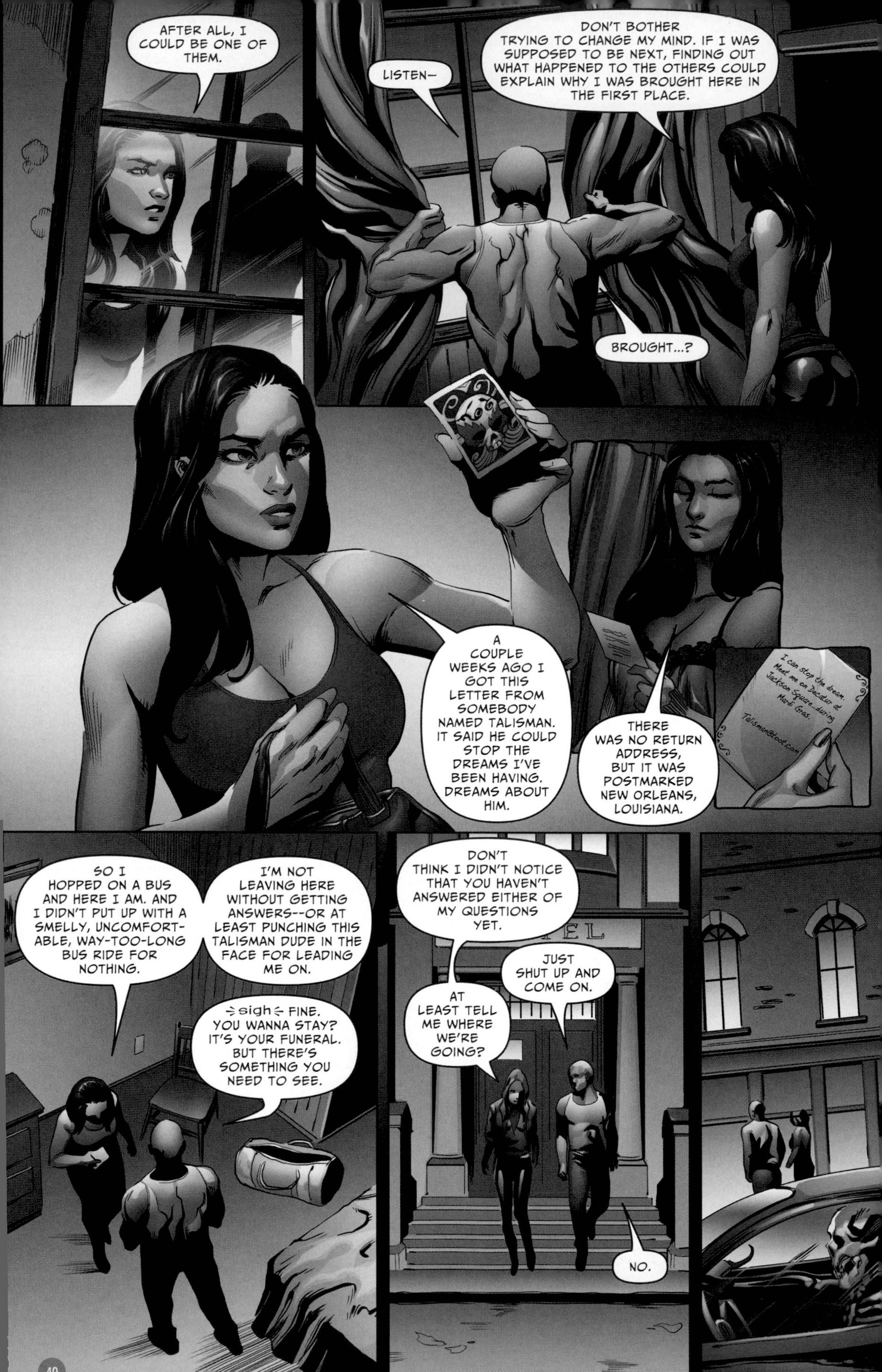
AFTER ALL, I COULD BE ONE OF THEM.
LISTEN—
DON'T BOTHER TRYING TO CHANGE MY MIND. IF I WAS SUPPOSED TO BE NEXT, FINDING OUT WHAT HAPPENED TO THE OTHERS COULD EXPLAIN WHY I WAS BROUGHT HERE IN THE FIRST PLACE.
BROUGHT...?
A COUPLE WEEKS AGO I GOT THIS LETTER FROM SOMEBODY NAMED TALISMAN. IT SAID HE COULD STOP THE DREAMS I'VE BEEN HAVING. DREAMS ABOUT HIM.
THERE WAS NO RETURN ADDRESS, BUT IT WAS POSTMARKED NEW ORLEANS, LOUISIANA.
I can stop the dream. Meet me on Decatur at Jackson Square...during Mardi Gras.
Talisman@toot.com
SO I HOPPED ON A BUS AND HERE I AM. AND I DIDN'T PUT UP WITH A SMELLY, UNCOMFORT-ABLE, WAY-TOO-LONG BUS RIDE FOR NOTHING.
I'M NOT LEAVING HERE WITHOUT GETTING ANSWERS--OR AT LEAST PUNCHING THIS TALISMAN DUDE IN THE FACE FOR LEADING ME ON.
⇒sigh⇐ FINE. YOU WANNA STAY? IT'S YOUR FUNERAL. BUT THERE'S SOMETHING YOU NEED TO SEE.
DON'T THINK I DIDN'T NOTICE THAT YOU HAVEN'T ANSWERED EITHER OF MY QUESTIONS YET.
JUST SHUT UP AND COME ON.
AT LEAST TELL ME WHERE WE'RE GOING?
NO.

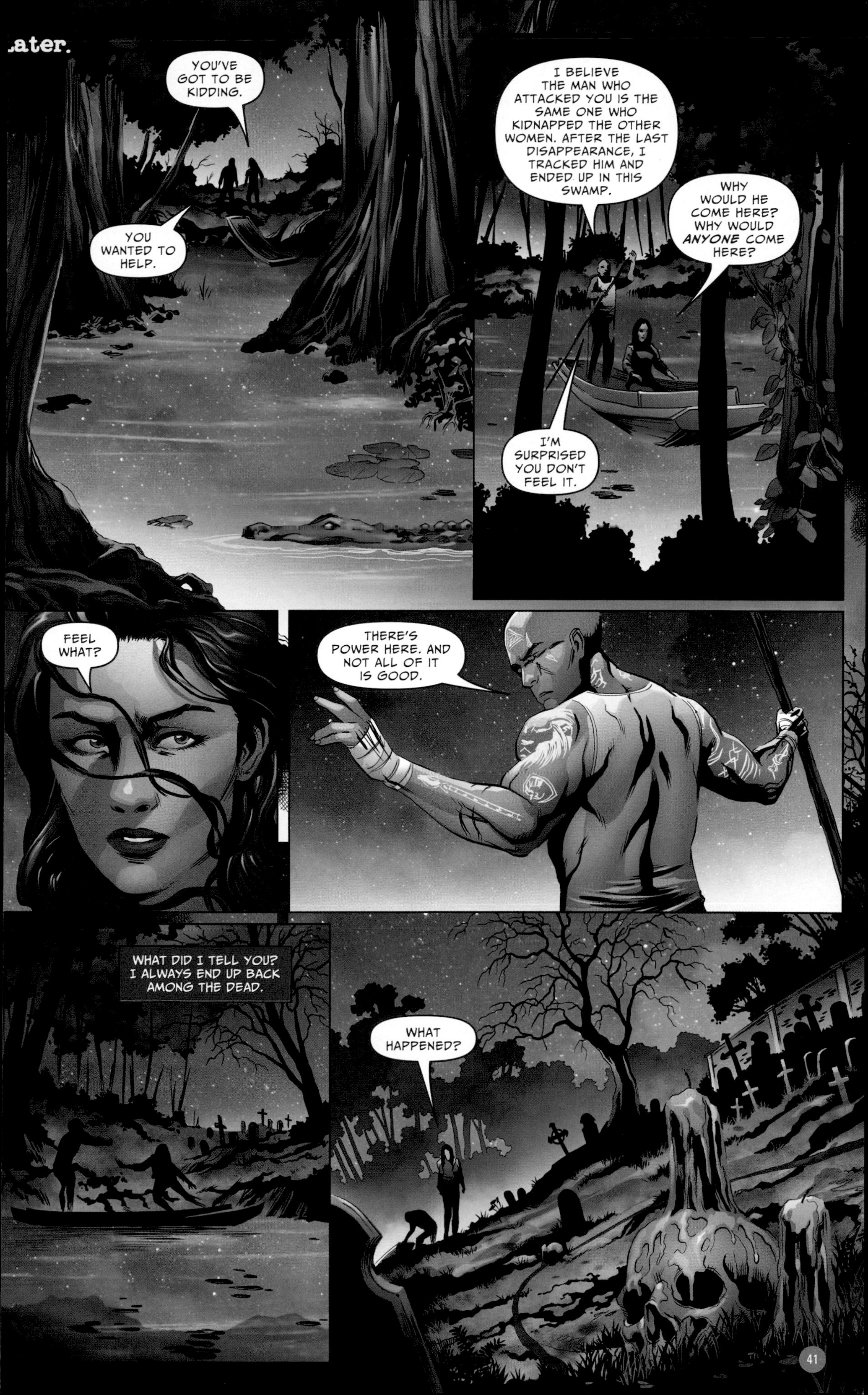
ater.
YOU'VE GOT TO BE KIDDING.
YOU WANTED TO HELP.
I BELIEVE THE MAN WHO ATTACKED YOU IS THE SAME ONE WHO KIDNAPPED THE OTHER WOMEN. AFTER THE LAST DISAPPEARANCE, I TRACKED HIM AND ENDED UP IN THIS SWAMP.
WHY WOULD HE COME HERE? WHY WOULD *ANYONE* COME HERE?
I'M SURPRISED YOU DON'T FEEL IT.
FEEL WHAT?
THERE'S POWER HERE. AND NOT ALL OF IT IS GOOD.
WHAT DID I TELL YOU? I ALWAYS END UP BACK AMONG THE DEAD.
WHAT HAPPENED?

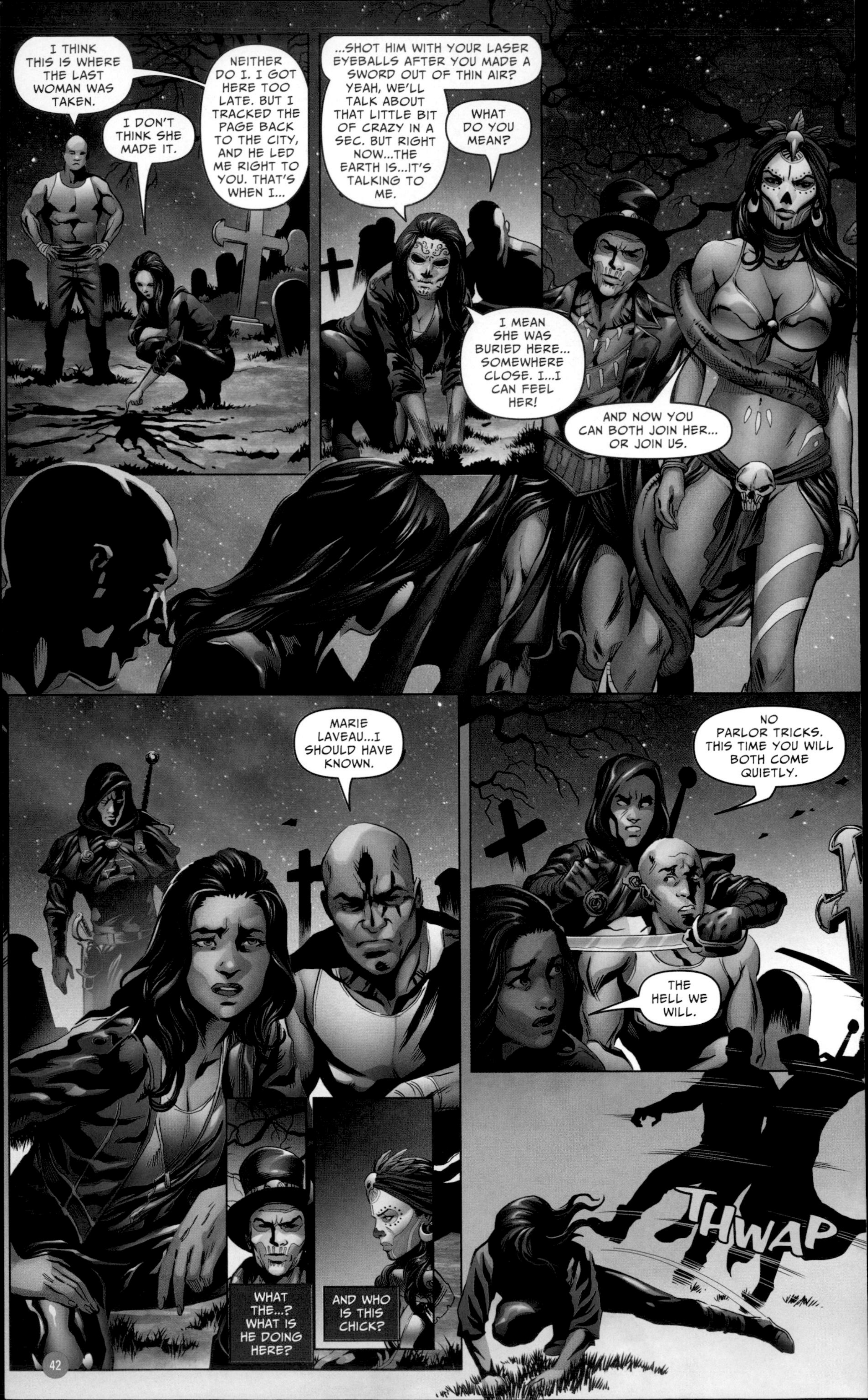
I THINK THIS IS WHERE THE LAST WOMAN WAS TAKEN.
I DON'T THINK SHE MADE IT.
NEITHER DO I. I GOT HERE TOO LATE. BUT I TRACKED THE PAGE BACK TO THE CITY, AND HE LED ME RIGHT TO YOU. THAT'S WHEN I...
...SHOT HIM WITH YOUR LASER EYEBALLS AFTER YOU MADE A SWORD OUT OF THIN AIR? YEAH, WE'LL TALK ABOUT THAT LITTLE BIT OF CRAZY IN A SEC. BUT RIGHT NOW...THE EARTH IS...IT'S TALKING TO ME.
WHAT DO YOU MEAN?
I MEAN SHE WAS BURIED HERE... SOMEWHERE CLOSE. I...I CAN FEEL HER!
AND NOW YOU CAN BOTH JOIN HER... OR JOIN US.
MARIE LAVEAU...I SHOULD HAVE KNOWN.
WHAT THE...? WHAT IS HE DOING HERE?
AND WHO IS THIS CHICK?
NO PARLOR TRICKS. THIS TIME YOU WILL BOTH COME QUIETLY.
THE HELL WE WILL.
THWAP

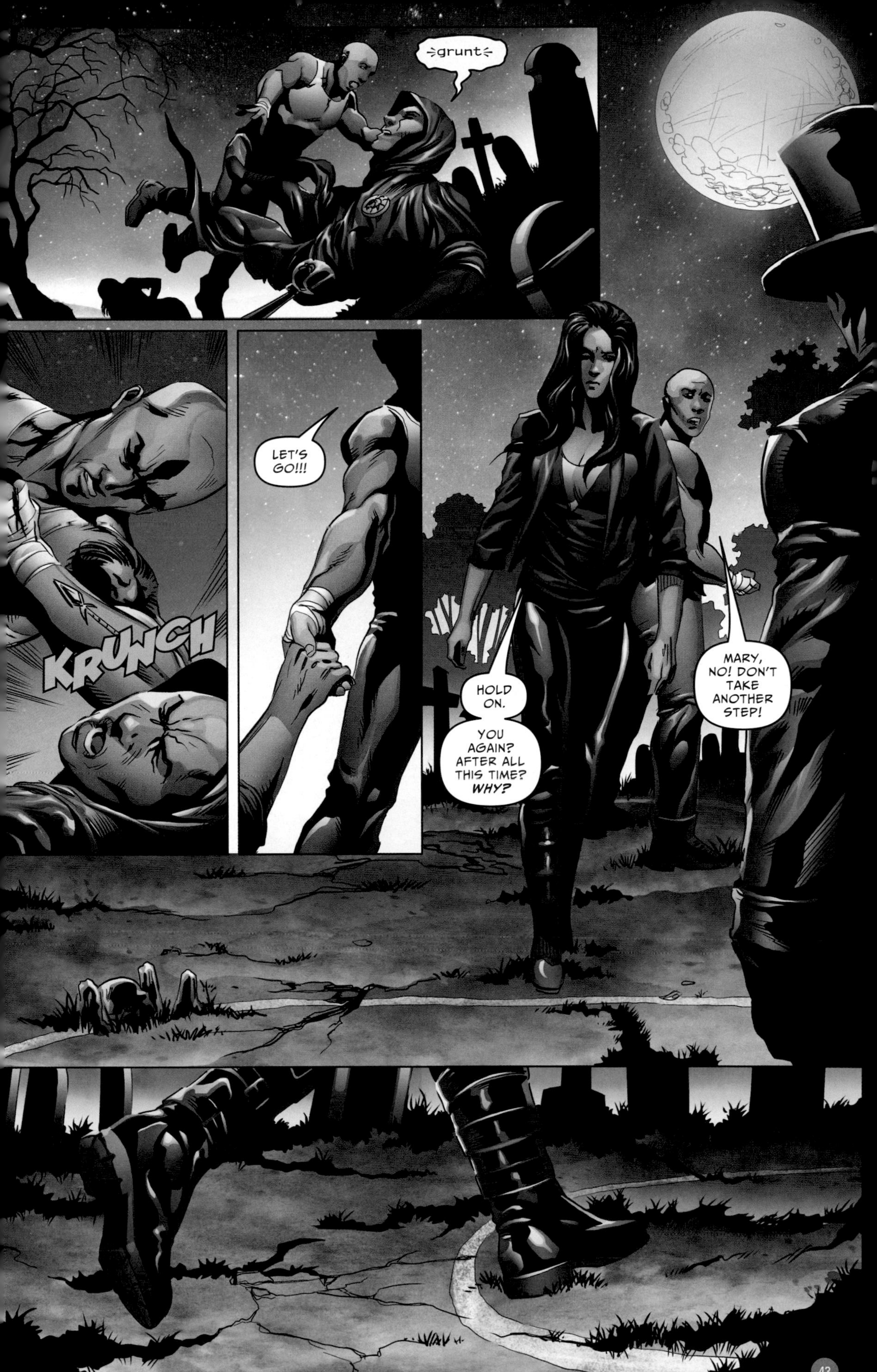
grunt
KRUNCH
LET'S GO!!!
HOLD ON.
YOU AGAIN? AFTER ALL THIS TIME? *WHY?*
MARY, NO! DON'T TAKE ANOTHER STEP!

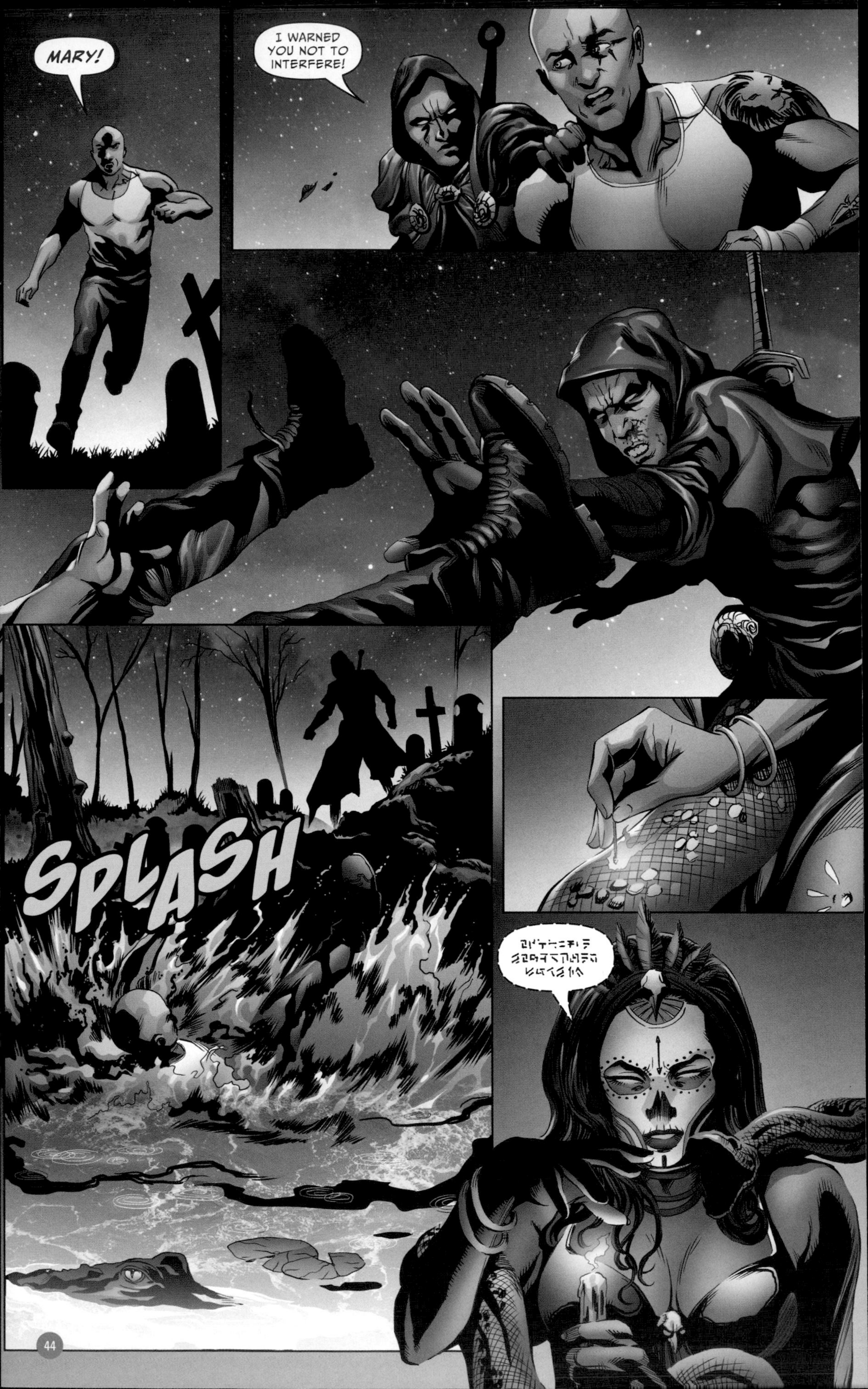
MARY!
I WARNED YOU NOT TO INTERFERE!
SPLASH

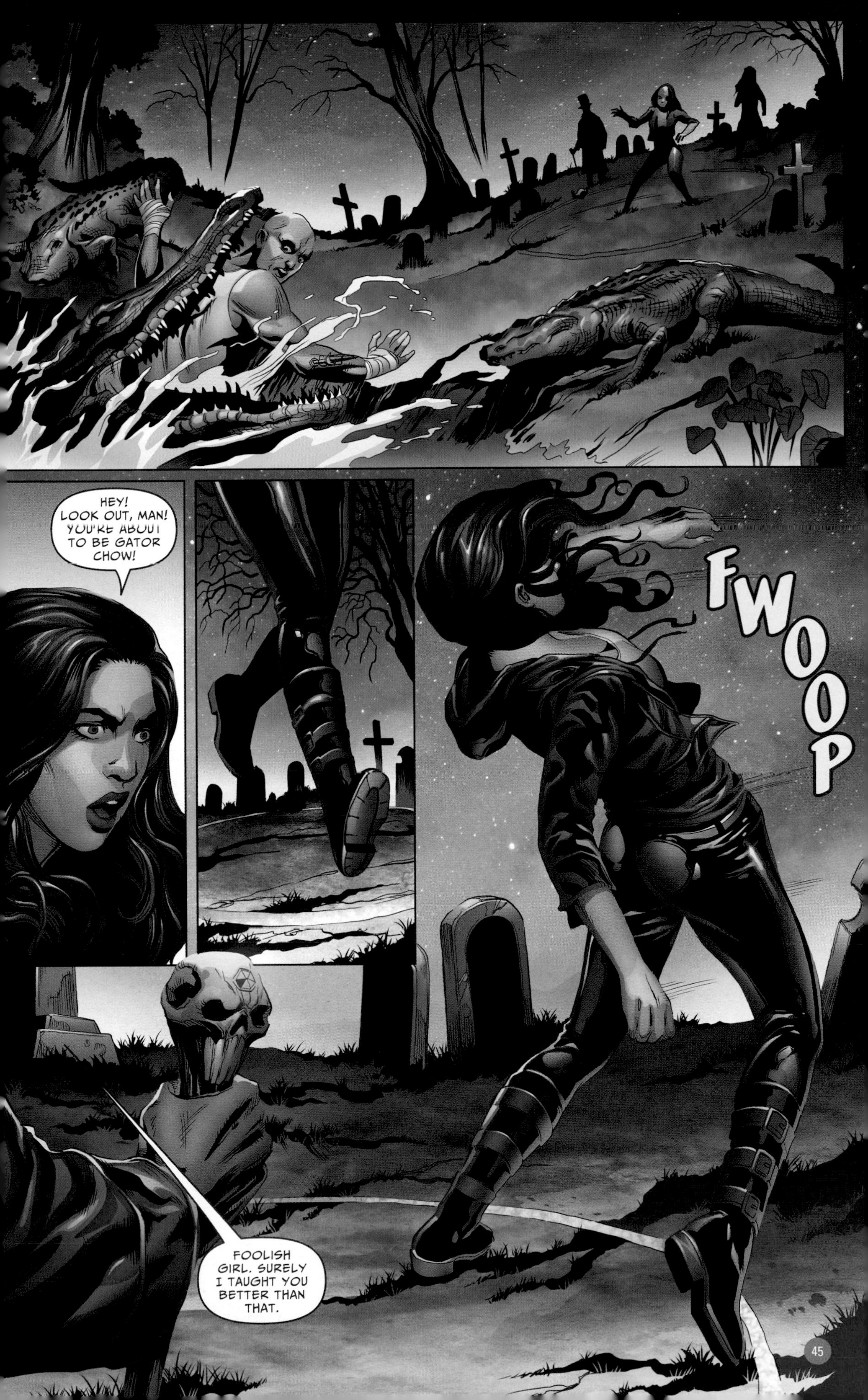
HEY! LOOK OUT, MAN! YOU'RE ABOUT TO BE GATOR CHOW!
FWOOP
FOOLISH GIRL. SURELY I TAUGHT YOU BETTER THAN THAT.

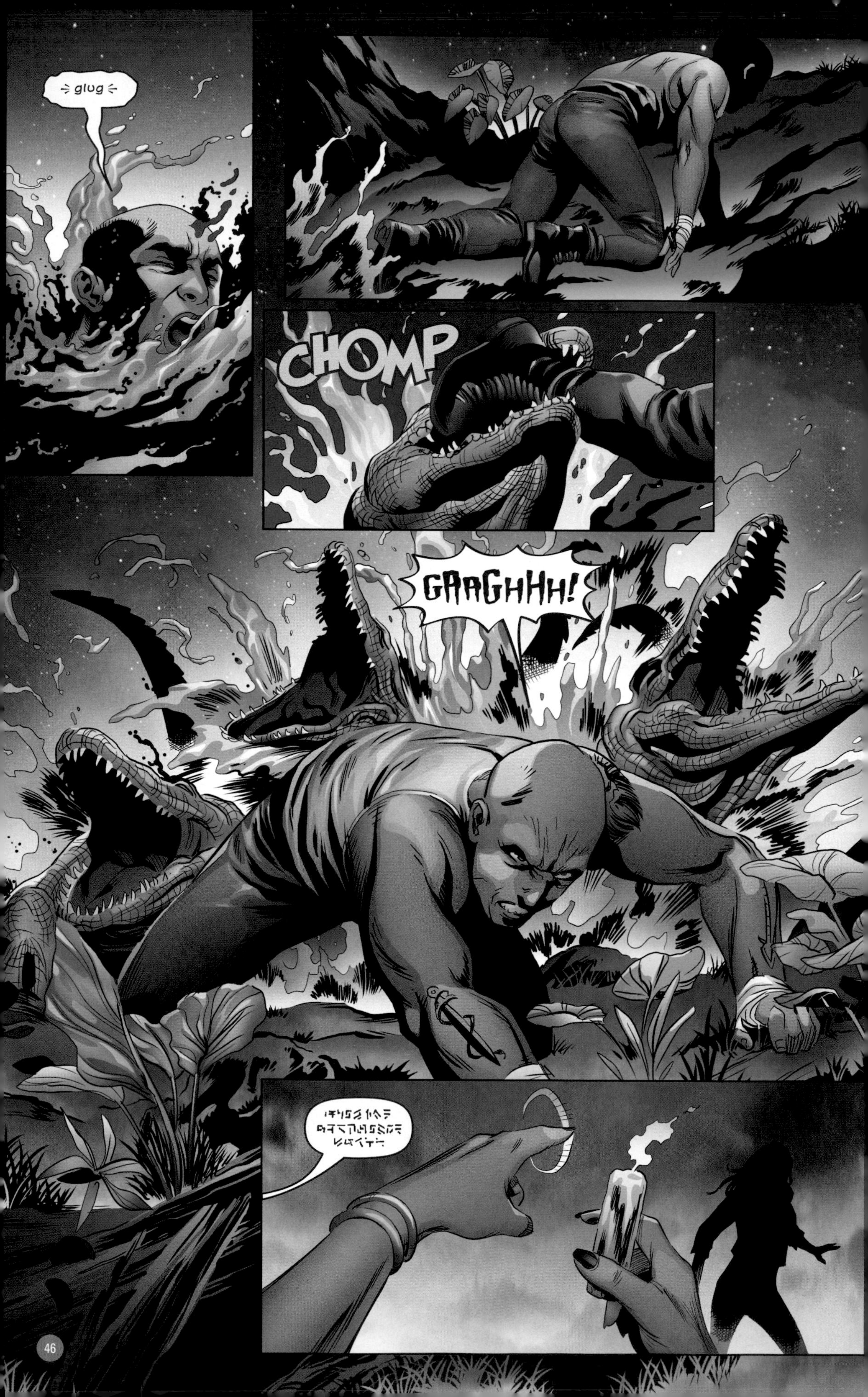
glug
CHOMP
GAAGHHH!

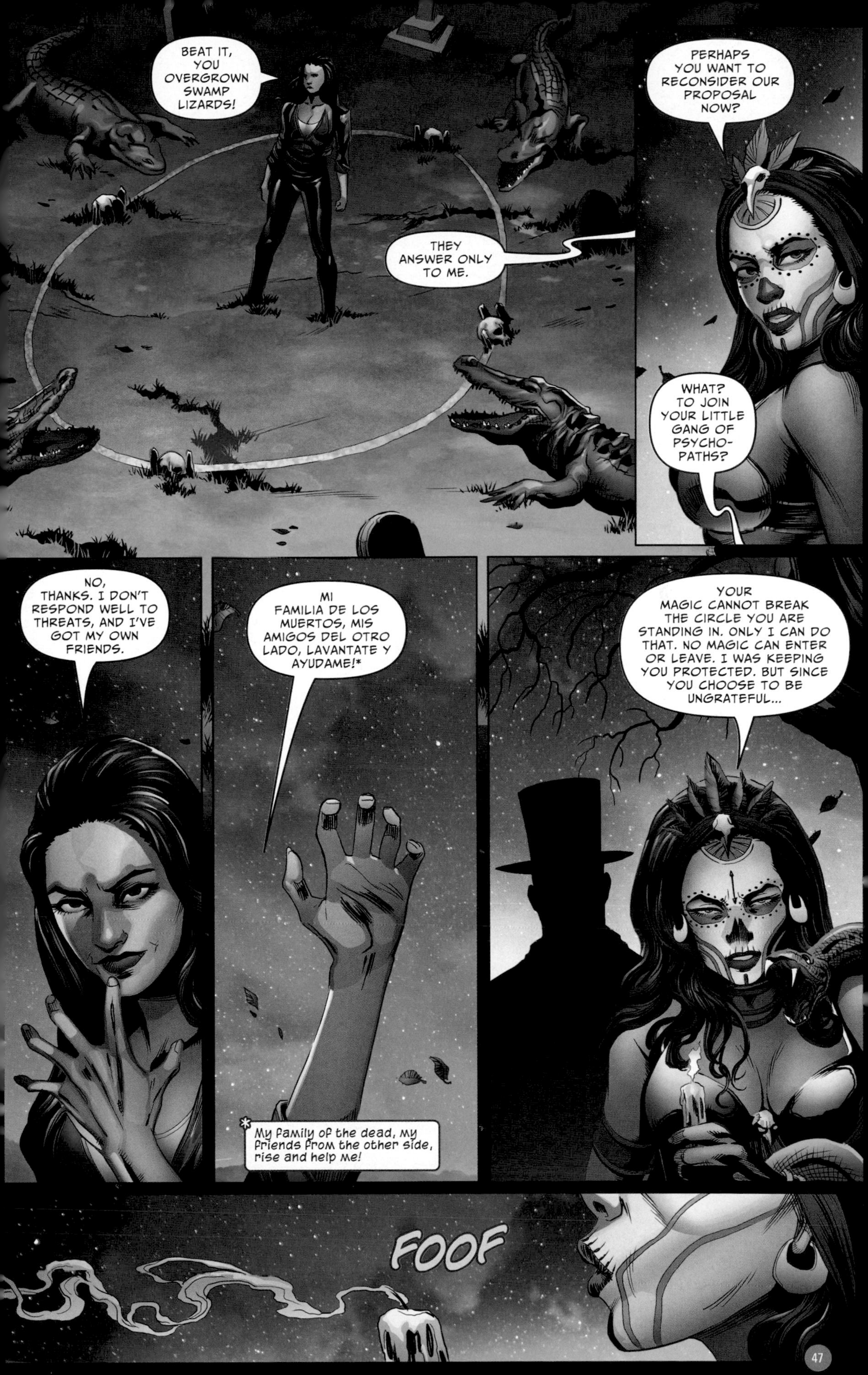
BEAT IT, YOU OVERGROWN SWAMP LIZARDS!
PERHAPS YOU WANT TO RECONSIDER OUR PROPOSAL NOW?
THEY ANSWER ONLY TO ME.
WHAT? TO JOIN YOUR LITTLE GANG OF PSYCHO-PATHS?
NO, THANKS. I DON'T RESPOND WELL TO THREATS, AND I'VE GOT MY OWN FRIENDS.
MI FAMILIA DE LOS MUERTOS, MIS AMIGOS DEL OTRO LADO, LAVANTATE Y AYUDAME!*
*My family of the dead, my friends from the other side, rise and help me!
YOUR MAGIC CANNOT BREAK THE CIRCLE YOU ARE STANDING IN. ONLY I CAN DO THAT. NO MAGIC CAN ENTER OR LEAVE. I WAS KEEPING YOU PROTECTED. BUT SINCE YOU CHOOSE TO BE UNGRATEFUL...
FOOF

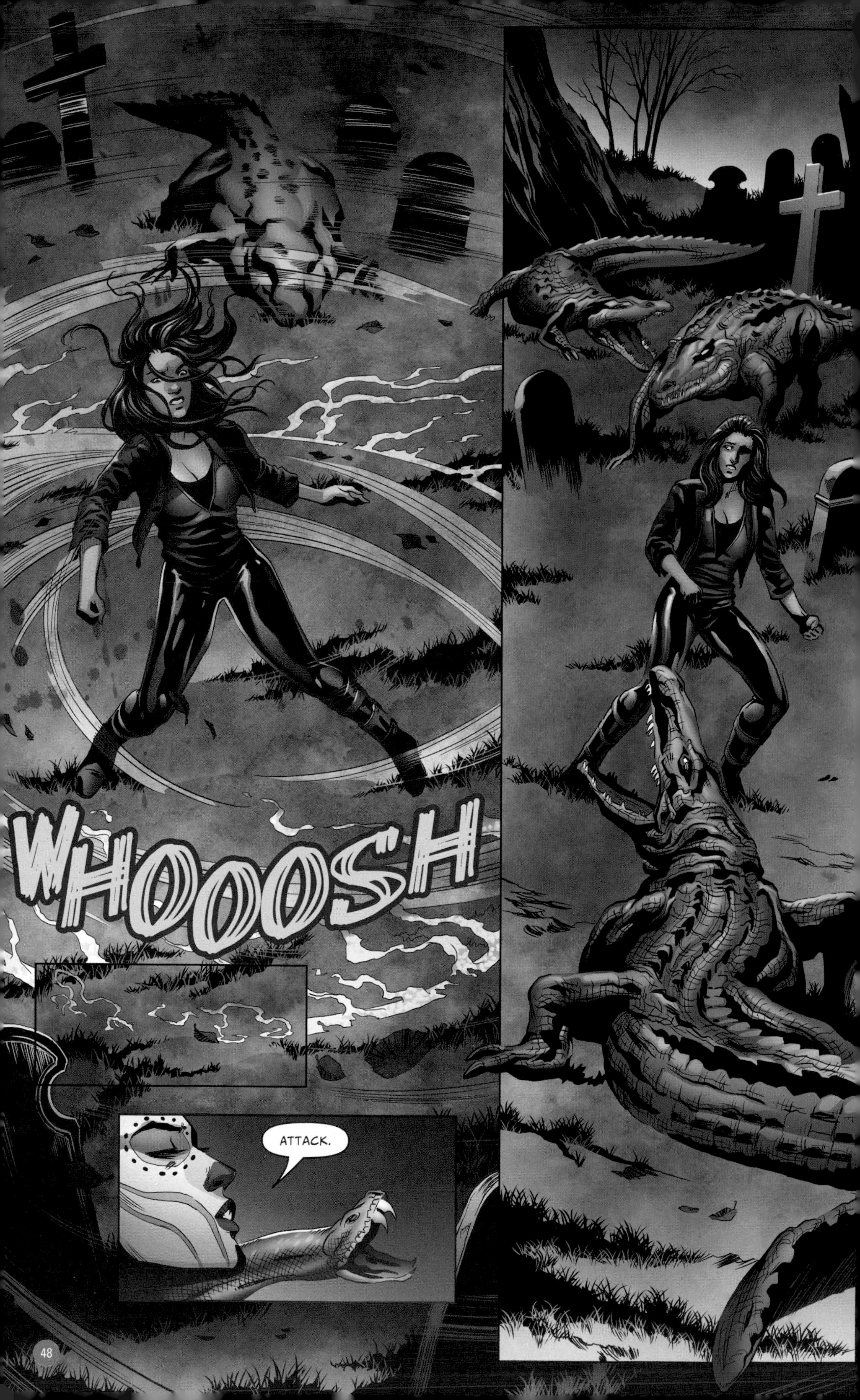
WHOOOSH
ATTACK.

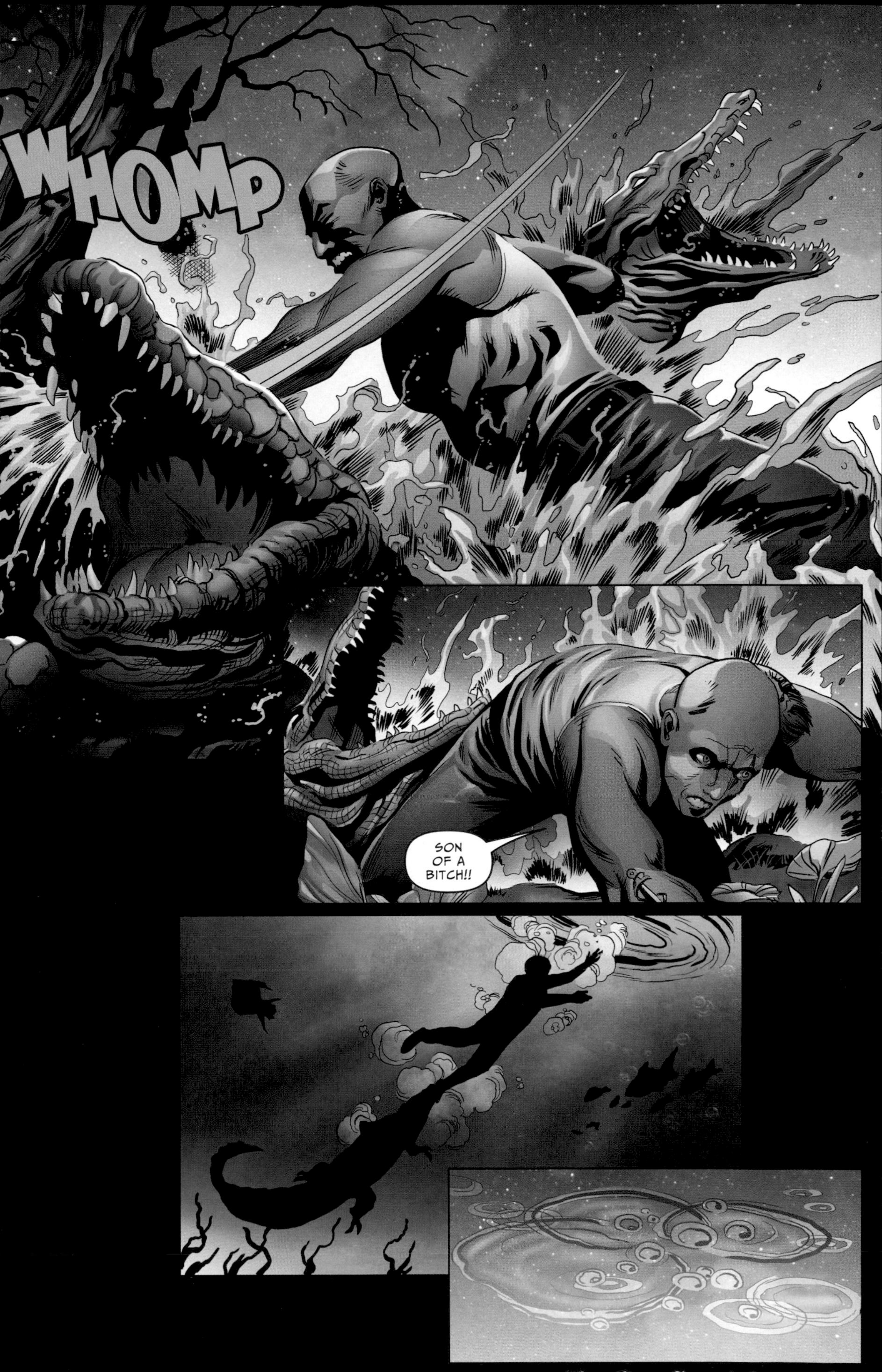
WHOMP
SON OF A BITCH!!

To Be Continued...

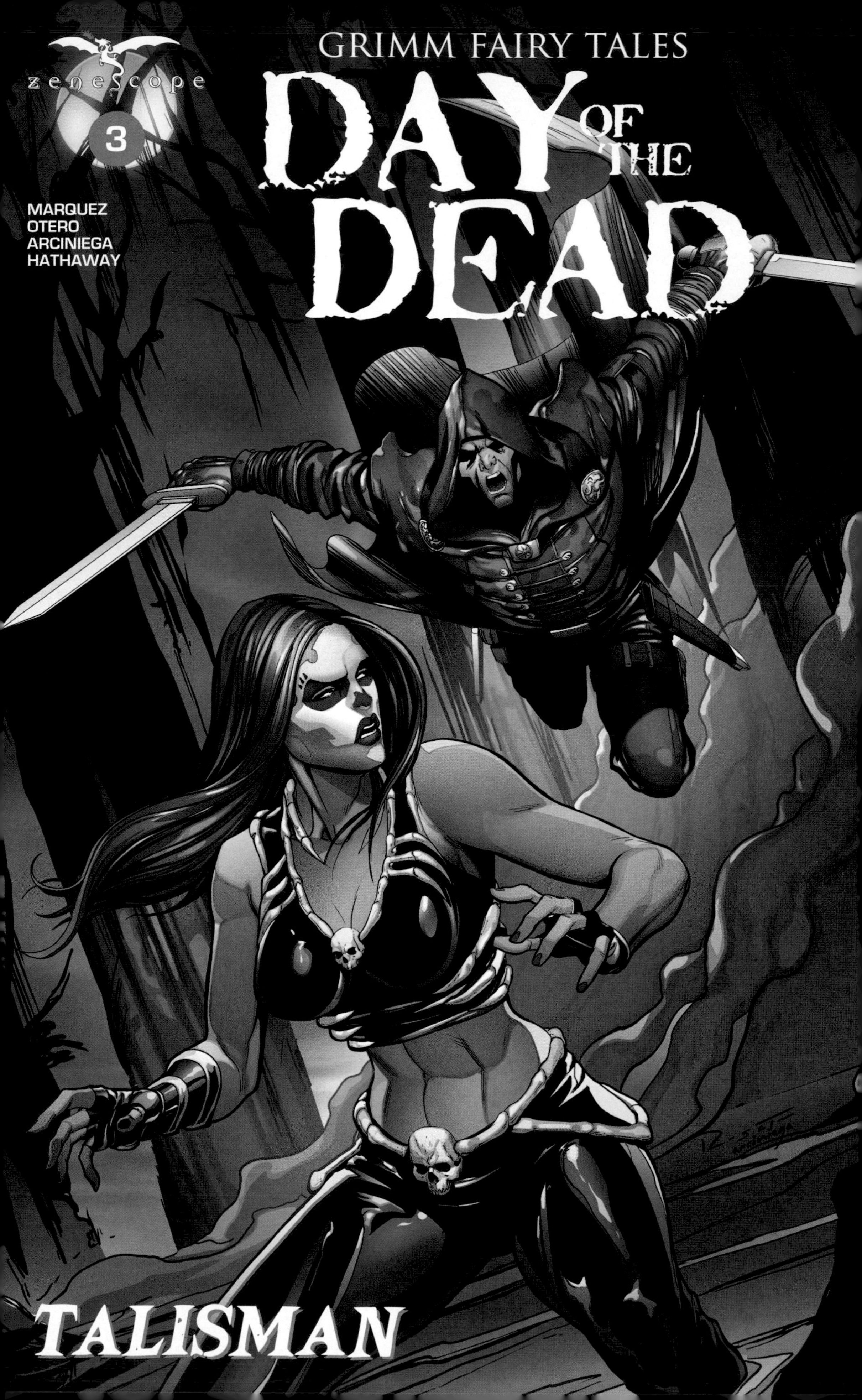
zenescope
3
GRIMM FAIRY TALES
DAY OF THE DEAD
MARQUEZ
OTERO
ARCINIEGA
HATHAWAY
TALISMAN

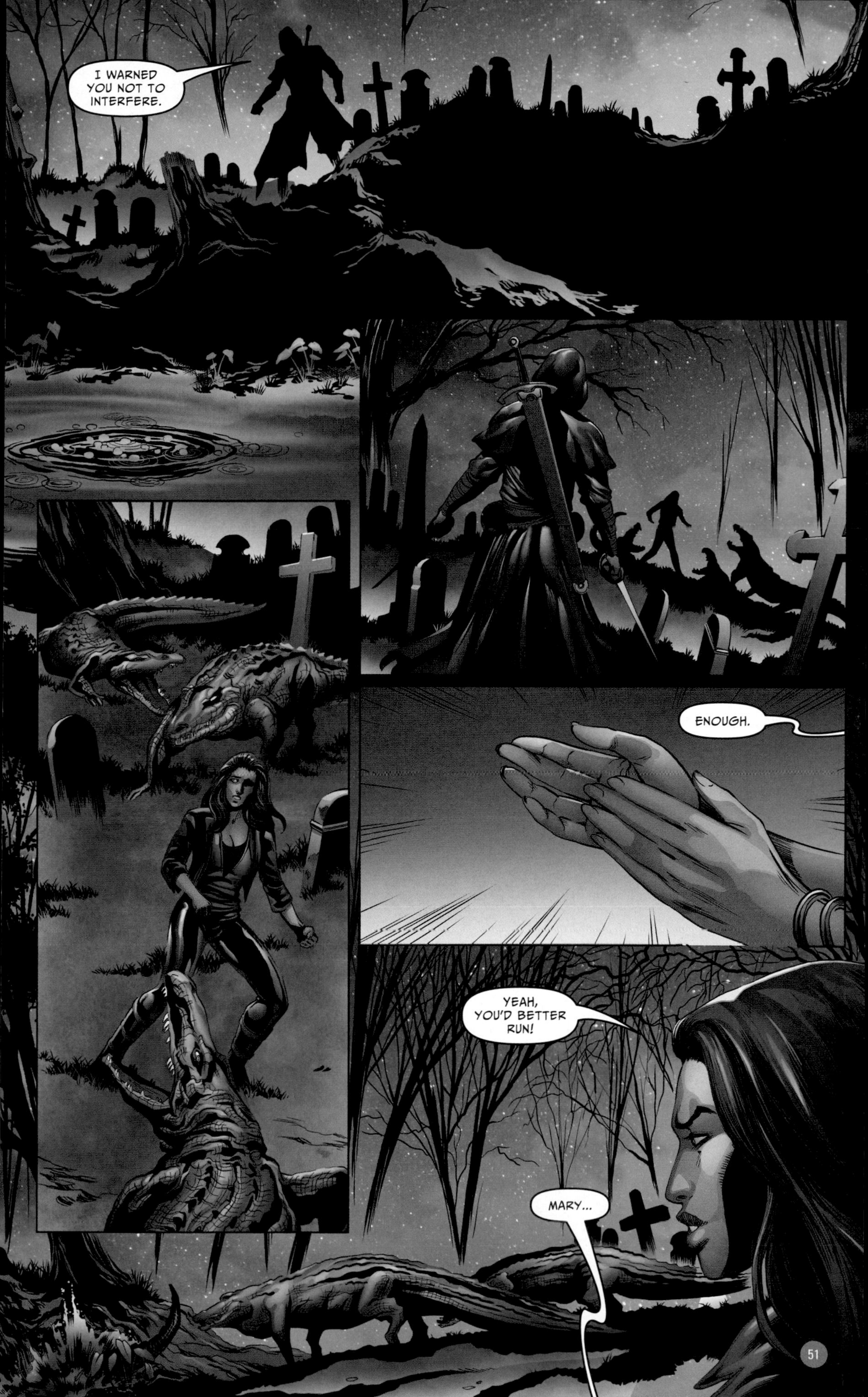
I WARNED YOU NOT TO INTERFERE.
ENOUGH.
YEAH, YOU'D BETTER RUN!
MARY...

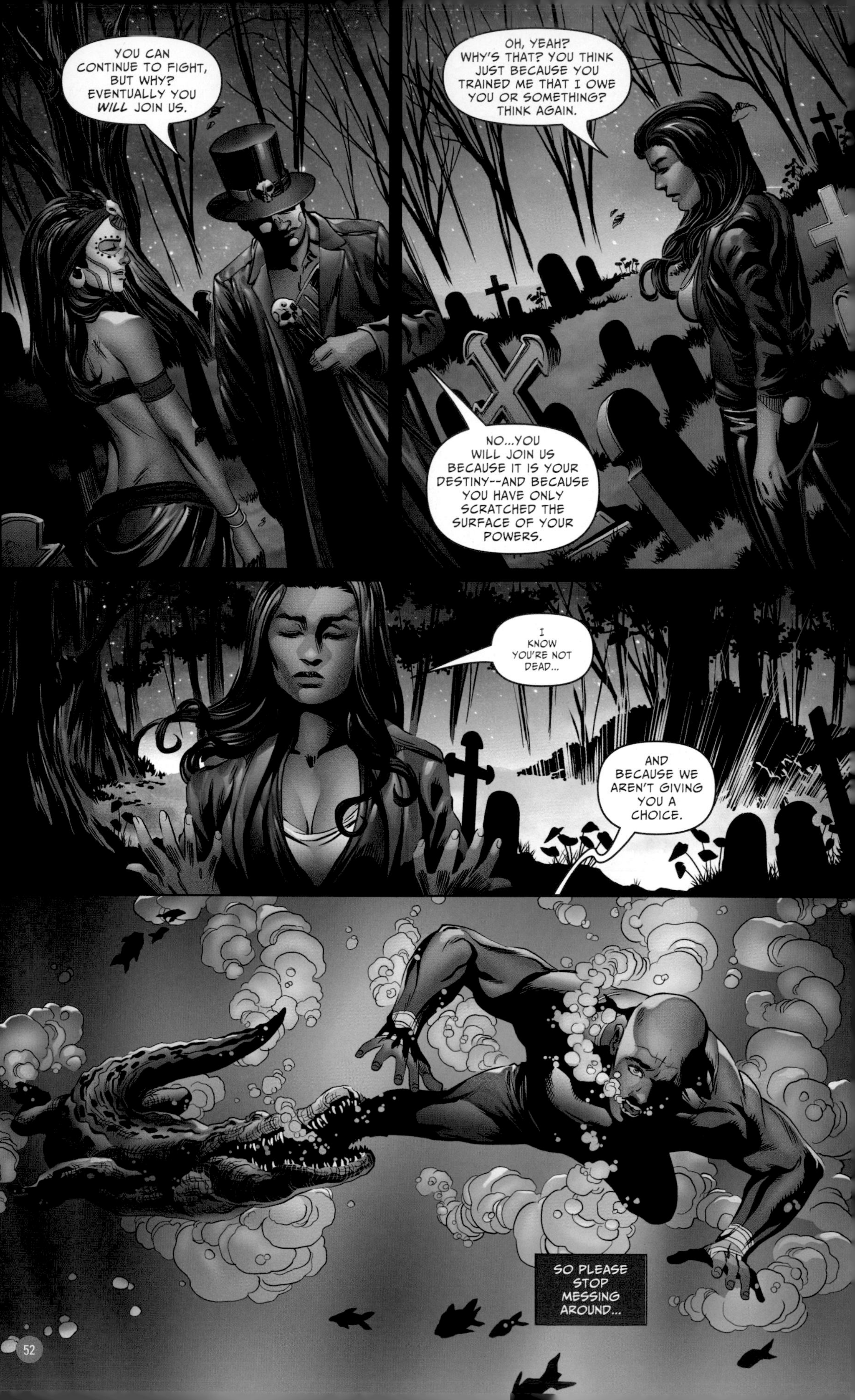
YOU CAN CONTINUE TO FIGHT, BUT WHY? EVENTUALLY YOU *WILL* JOIN US.
OH, YEAH? WHY'S THAT? YOU THINK JUST BECAUSE YOU TRAINED ME THAT I OWE YOU OR SOMETHING? THINK AGAIN.
NO...YOU WILL JOIN US BECAUSE IT IS YOUR DESTINY--AND BECAUSE YOU HAVE ONLY SCRATCHED THE SURFACE OF YOUR POWERS.
I KNOW YOU'RE NOT DEAD...
AND BECAUSE WE AREN'T GIVING YOU A CHOICE.
SO PLEASE STOP MESSING AROUND...

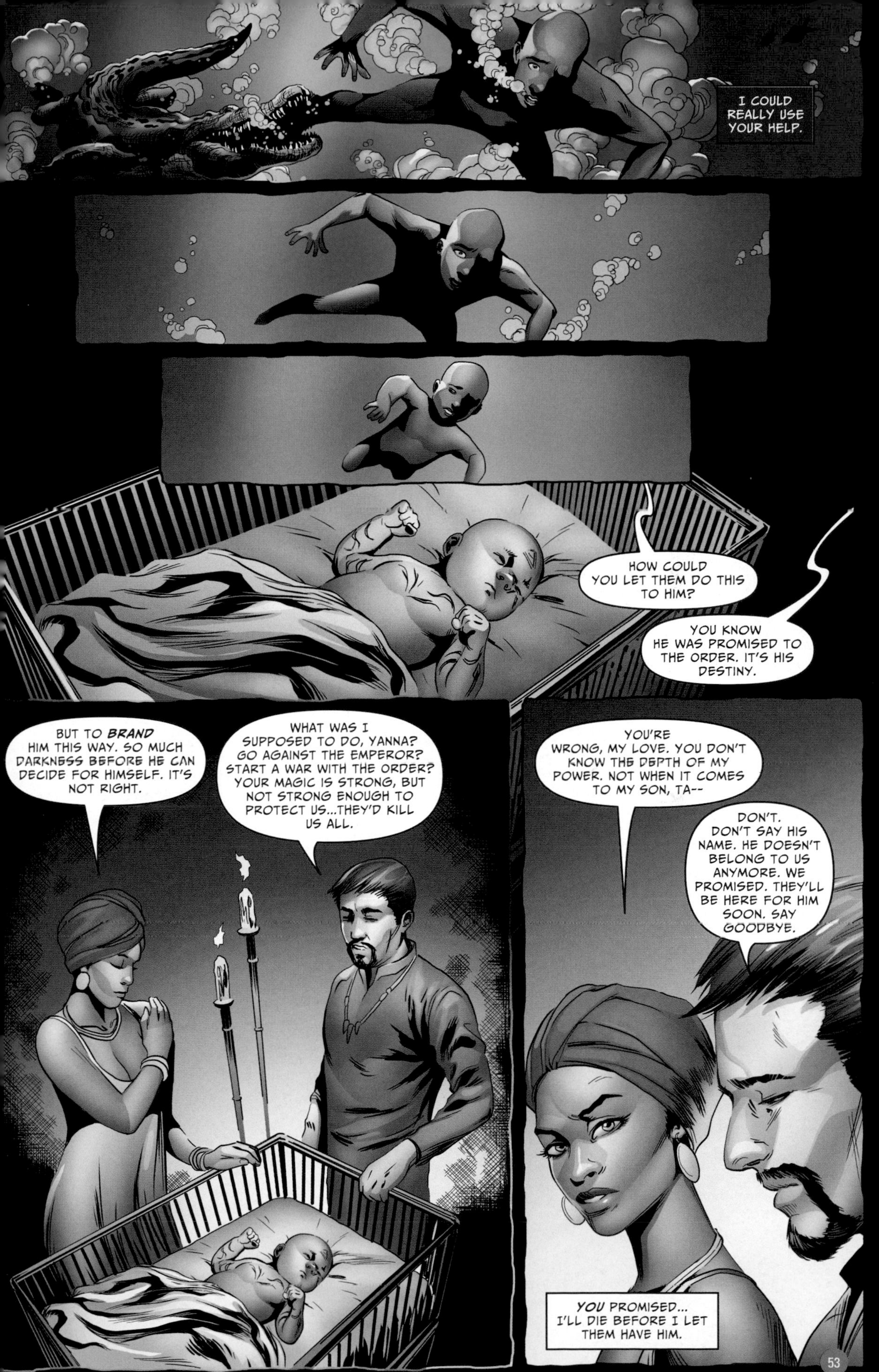

I COULD REALLY USE YOUR HELP.
HOW COULD YOU LET THEM DO THIS TO HIM?
YOU KNOW HE WAS PROMISED TO THE ORDER. IT'S HIS DESTINY.
BUT TO *BRAND* HIM THIS WAY. SO MUCH DARKNESS BEFORE HE CAN DECIDE FOR HIMSELF. IT'S NOT RIGHT.
WHAT WAS I SUPPOSED TO DO, YANNA? GO AGAINST THE EMPEROR? START A WAR WITH THE ORDER? YOUR MAGIC IS STRONG, BUT NOT STRONG ENOUGH TO PROTECT US...THEY'D KILL US ALL.
YOU'RE WRONG, MY LOVE. YOU DON'T KNOW THE DEPTH OF MY POWER. NOT WHEN IT COMES TO MY SON, TA--
DON'T. DON'T SAY HIS NAME. HE DOESN'T BELONG TO US ANYMORE. WE PROMISED. THEY'LL BE HERE FOR HIM SOON. SAY GOODBYE.
YOU PROMISED... I'LL DIE BEFORE I LET THEM HAVE HIM.

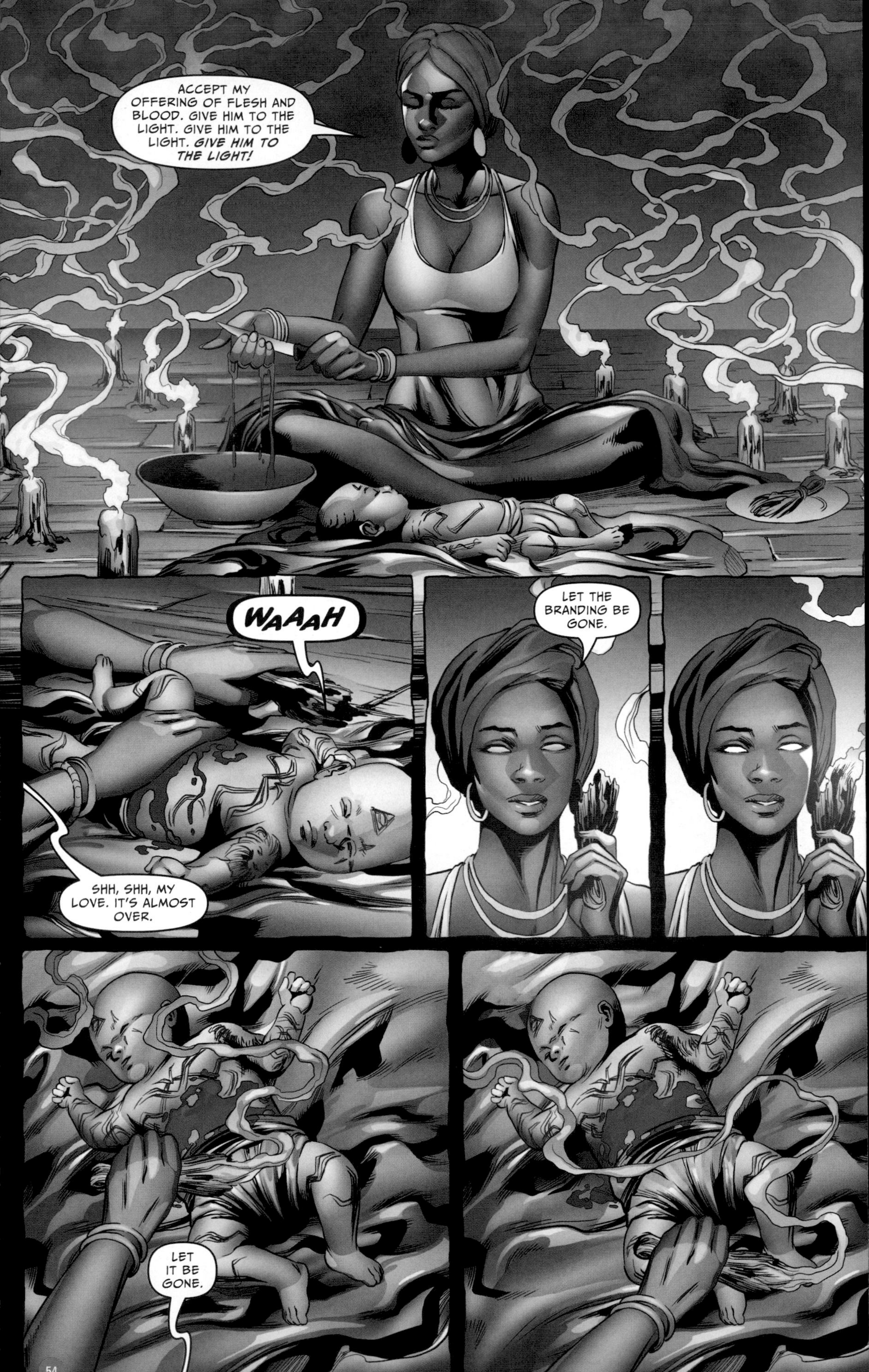
ACCEPT MY OFFERING OF FLESH AND BLOOD. GIVE HIM TO THE LIGHT. GIVE HIM TO THE LIGHT. *GIVE HIM TO THE LIGHT!*
WAAAH
SHH, SHH, MY LOVE. IT'S ALMOST OVER.
LET THE BRANDING BE GONE.
LET IT BE GONE.

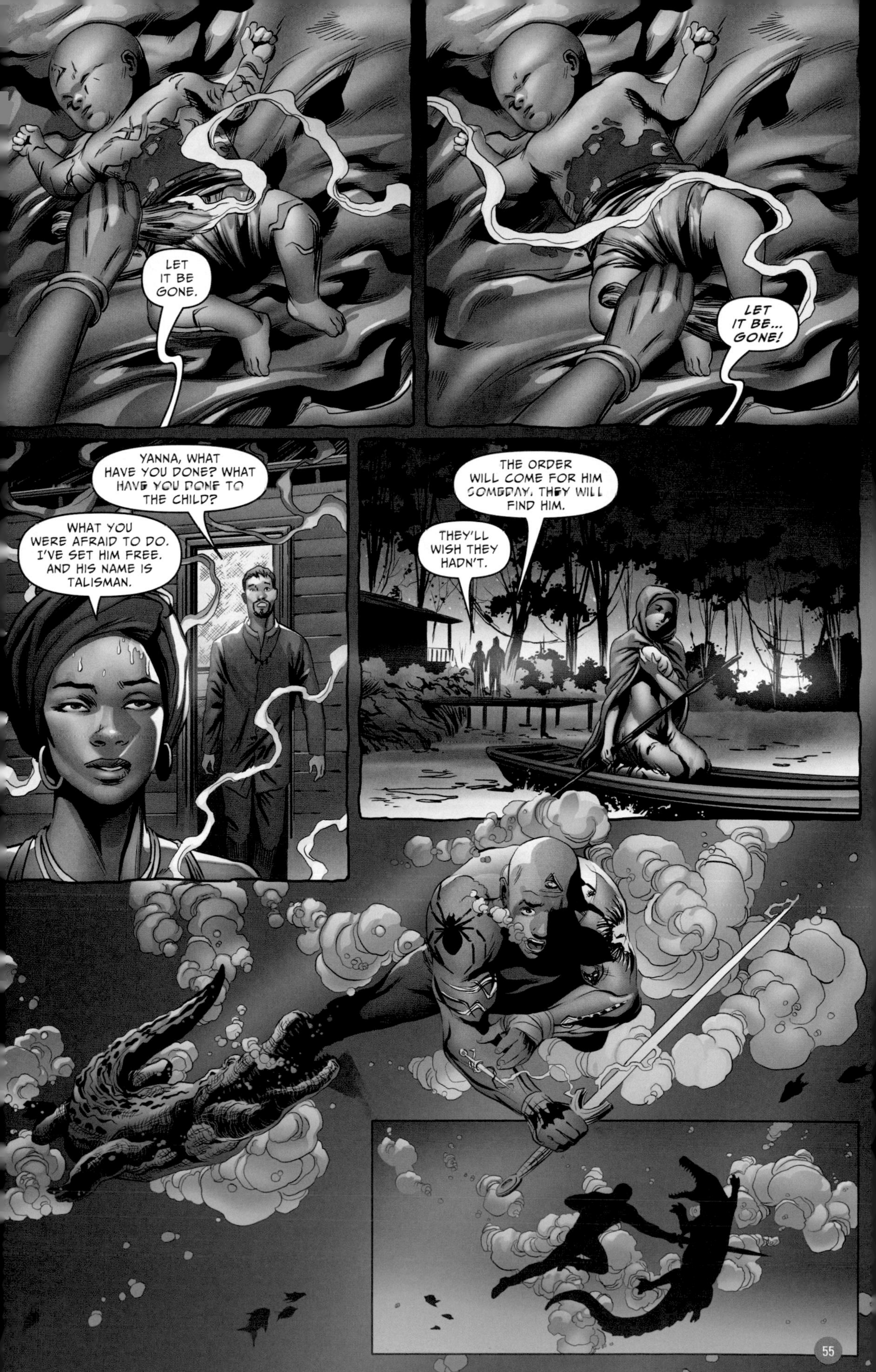
LET IT BE GONE.
LET IT BE... GONE!
YANNA, WHAT HAVE YOU DONE? WHAT HAVE YOU DONE TO THE CHILD?
WHAT YOU WERE AFRAID TO DO. I'VE SET HIM FREE. AND HIS NAME IS TALISMAN.
THE ORDER WILL COME FOR HIM SOMEDAY. THEY WILL FIND HIM.
THEY'LL WISH THEY HADN'T.

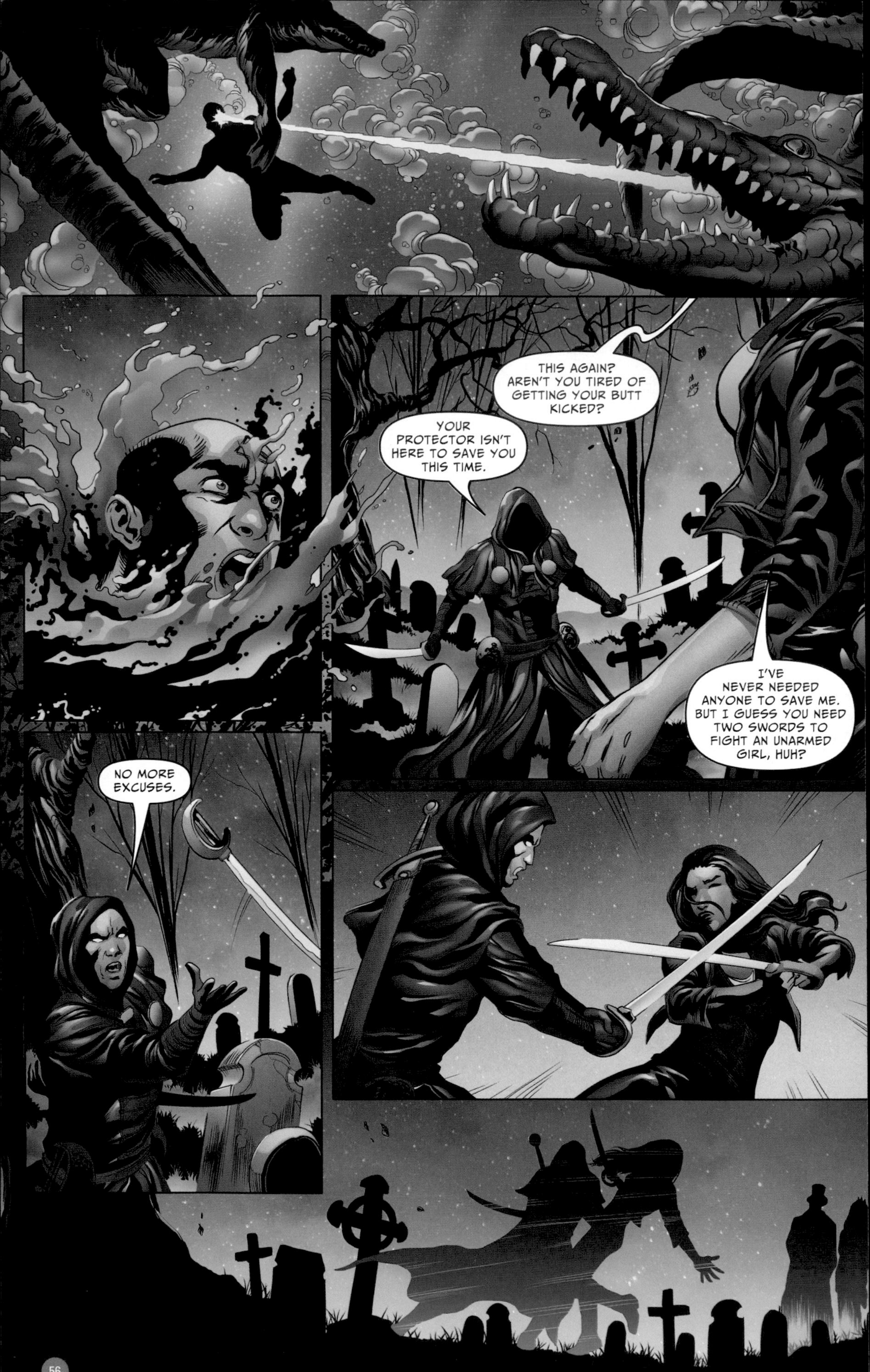
THIS AGAIN? AREN'T YOU TIRED OF GETTING YOUR BUTT KICKED?
YOUR PROTECTOR ISN'T HERE TO SAVE YOU THIS TIME.
I'VE NEVER NEEDED ANYONE TO SAVE ME. BUT I GUESS YOU NEED TWO SWORDS TO FIGHT AN UNARMED GIRL, HUH?
NO MORE EXCUSES.

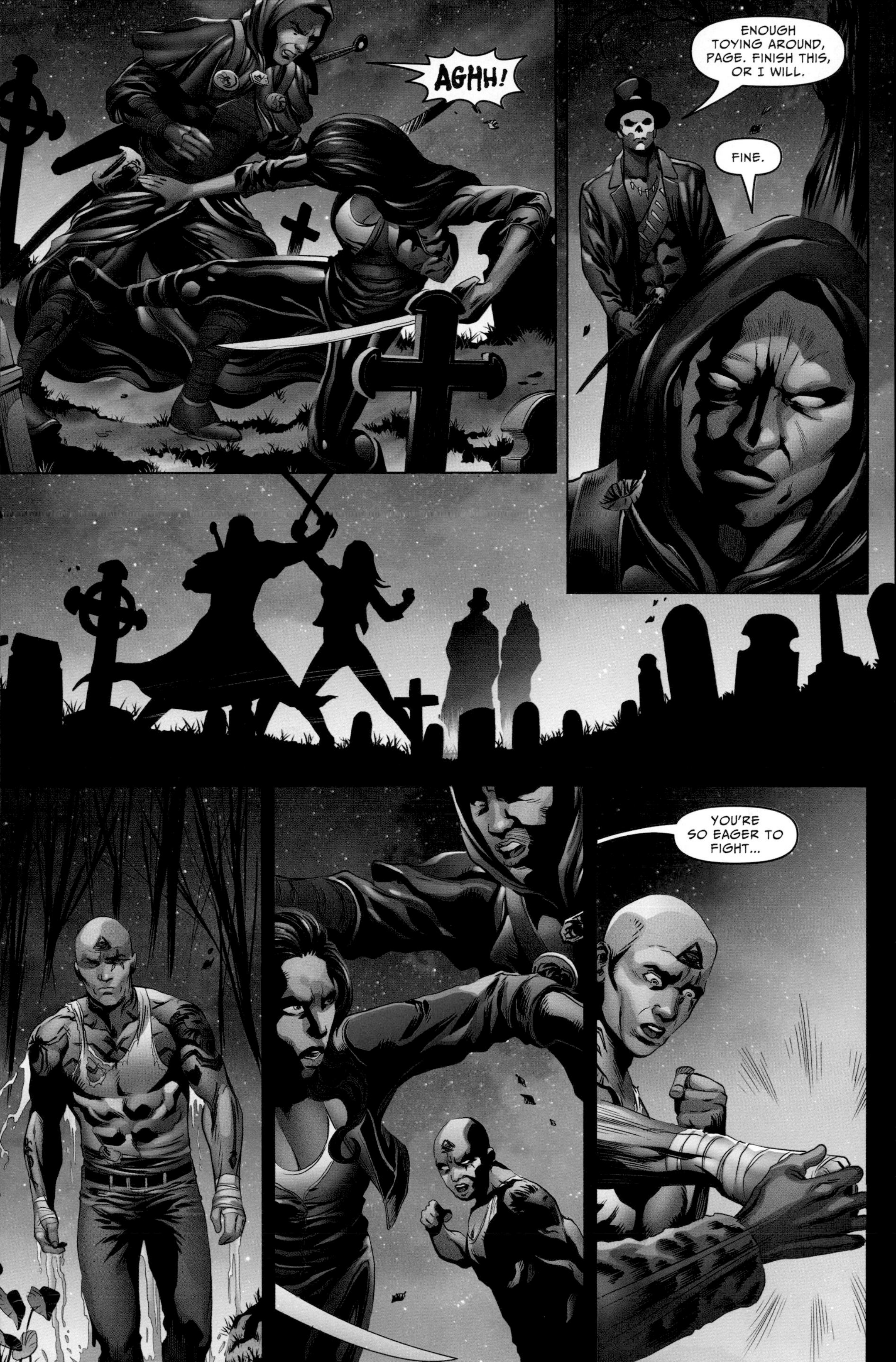
AGHH!
ENOUGH TOYING AROUND, PAGE. FINISH THIS, OR I WILL.
FINE.
YOU'RE SO EAGER TO FIGHT...

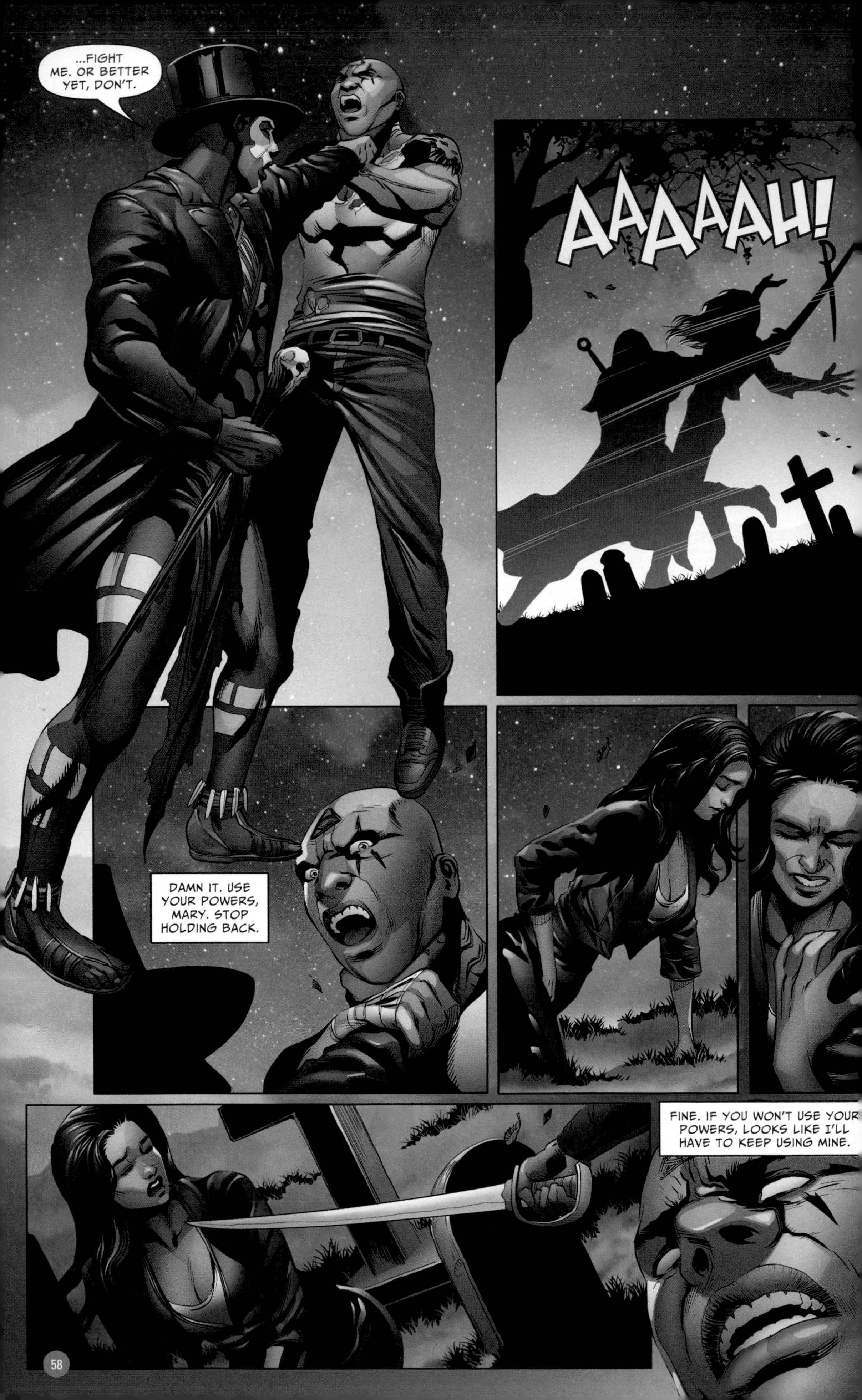
...FIGHT ME. OR BETTER YET, DON'T.
AAAAAH!
DAMN IT. USE YOUR POWERS, MARY. STOP HOLDING BACK.
FINE. IF YOU WON'T USE YOUR POWERS, LOOKS LIKE I'LL HAVE TO KEEP USING MINE.

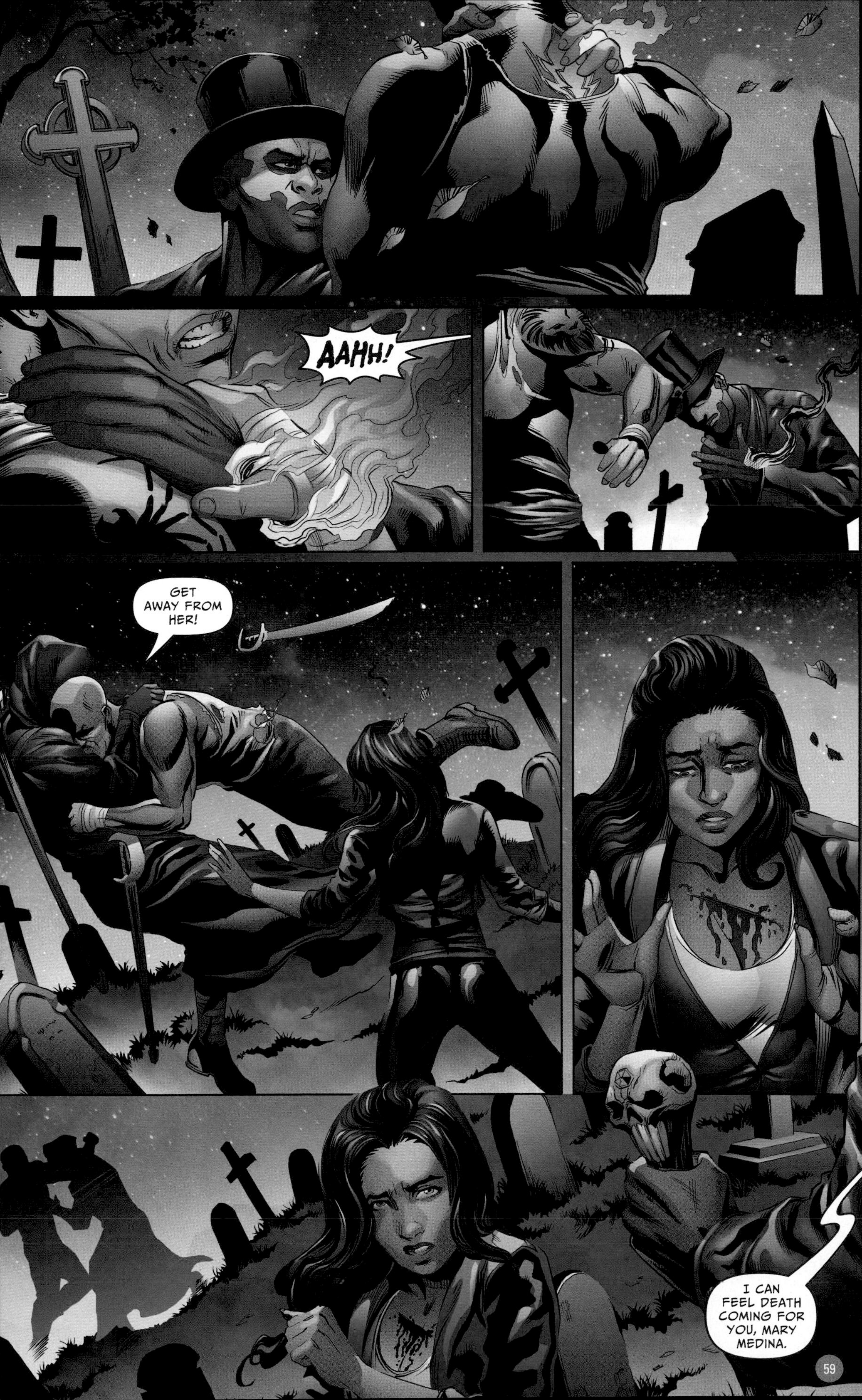
AAHH!
GET AWAY FROM HER!
I CAN FEEL DEATH COMING FOR YOU, MARY MEDINA.

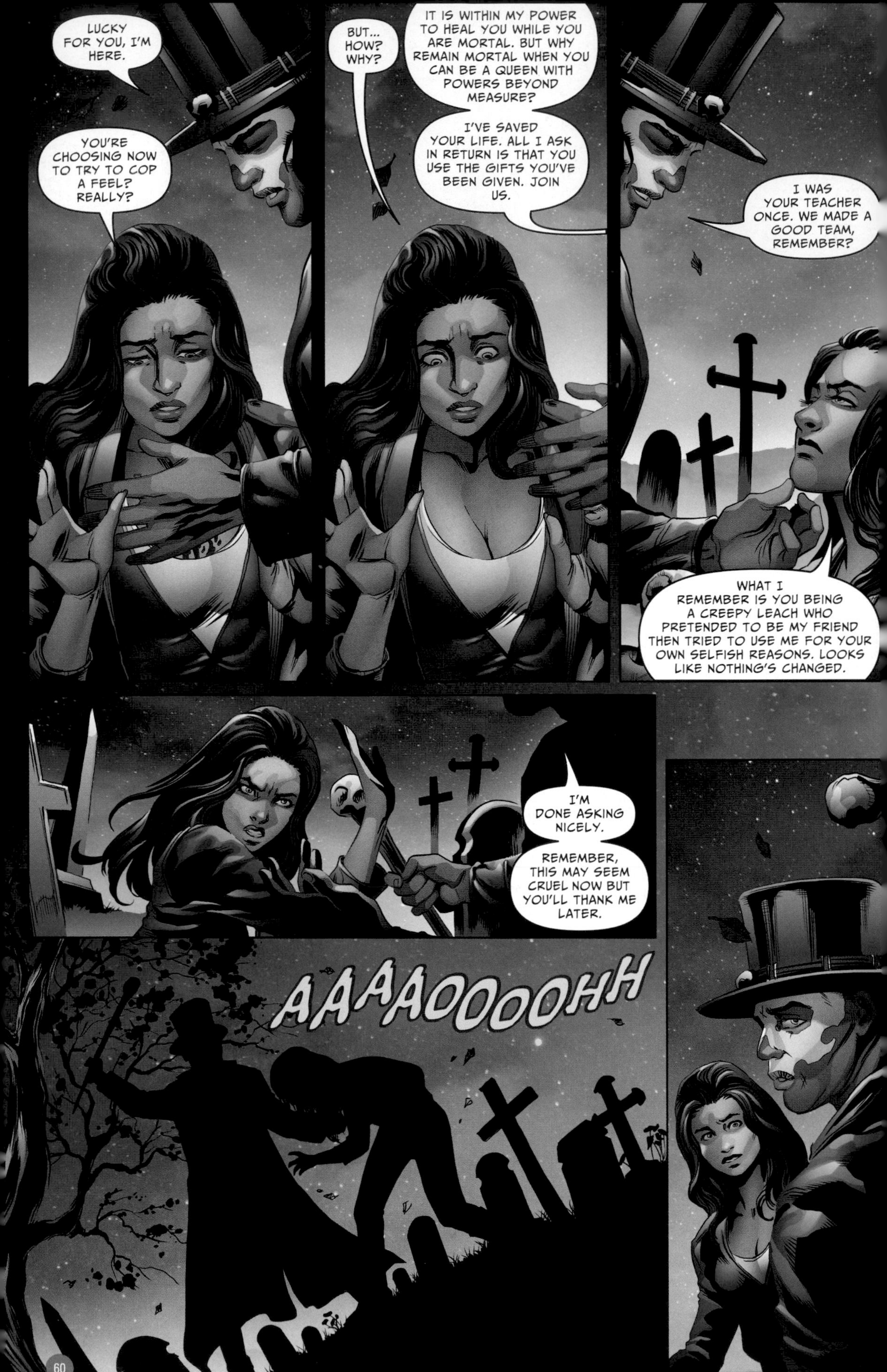
LUCKY FOR YOU, I'M HERE.
YOU'RE CHOOSING NOW TO TRY TO COP A FEEL? REALLY?
BUT... HOW? WHY?
IT IS WITHIN MY POWER TO HEAL YOU WHILE YOU ARE MORTAL. BUT WHY REMAIN MORTAL WHEN YOU CAN BE A QUEEN WITH POWERS BEYOND MEASURE?
I'VE SAVED YOUR LIFE. ALL I ASK IN RETURN IS THAT YOU USE THE GIFTS YOU'VE BEEN GIVEN. JOIN US.
I WAS YOUR TEACHER ONCE. WE MADE A GOOD TEAM, REMEMBER?
WHAT I REMEMBER IS YOU BEING A CREEPY LEACH WHO PRETENDED TO BE MY FRIEND THEN TRIED TO USE ME FOR YOUR OWN SELFISH REASONS. LOOKS LIKE NOTHING'S CHANGED.
I'M DONE ASKING NICELY.
REMEMBER, THIS MAY SEEM CRUEL NOW BUT YOU'LL THANK ME LATER.
AAAAOOOOHH

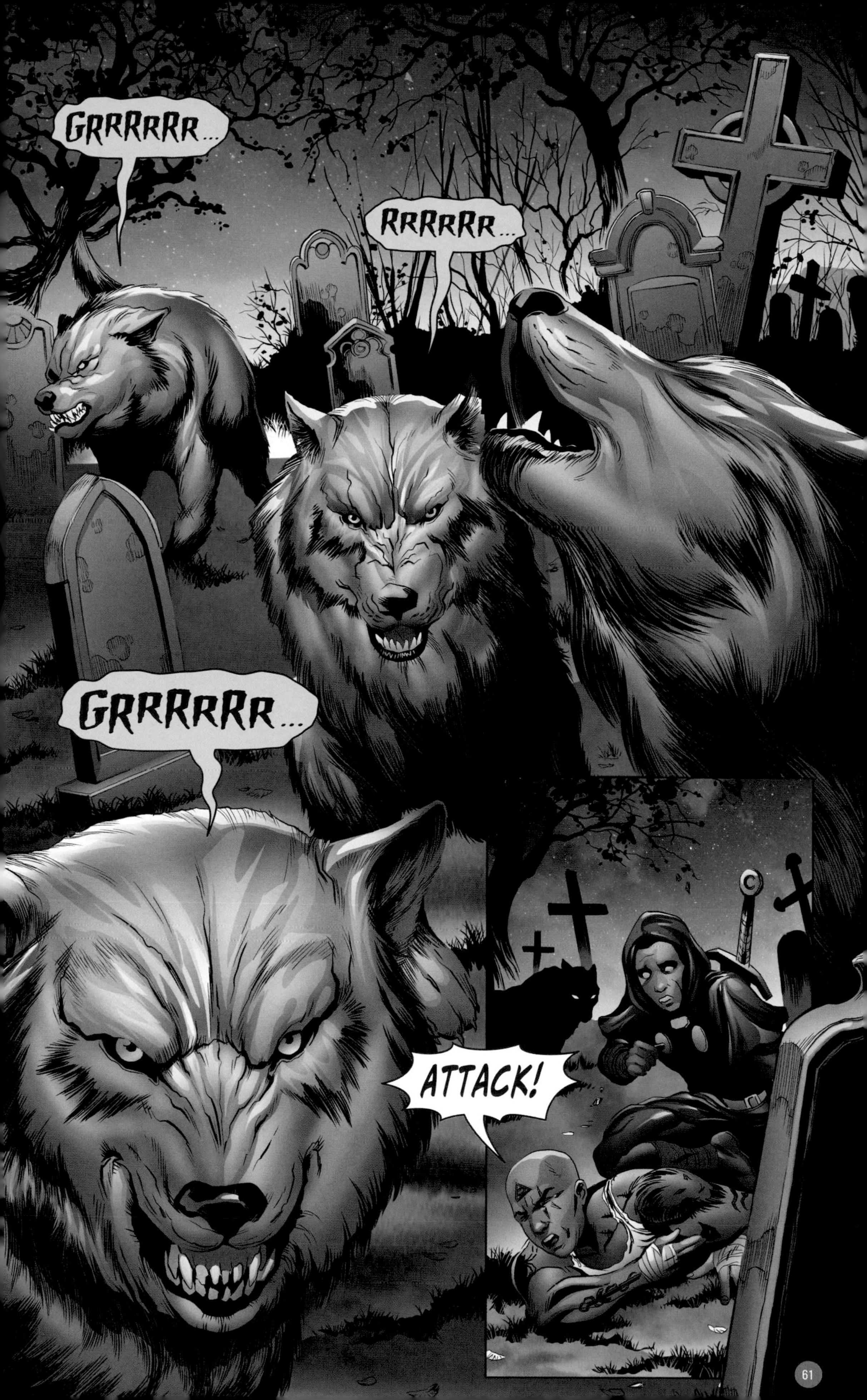
GRRRRRR...
RRRRRR...
GRRRRRR...
ATTACK!

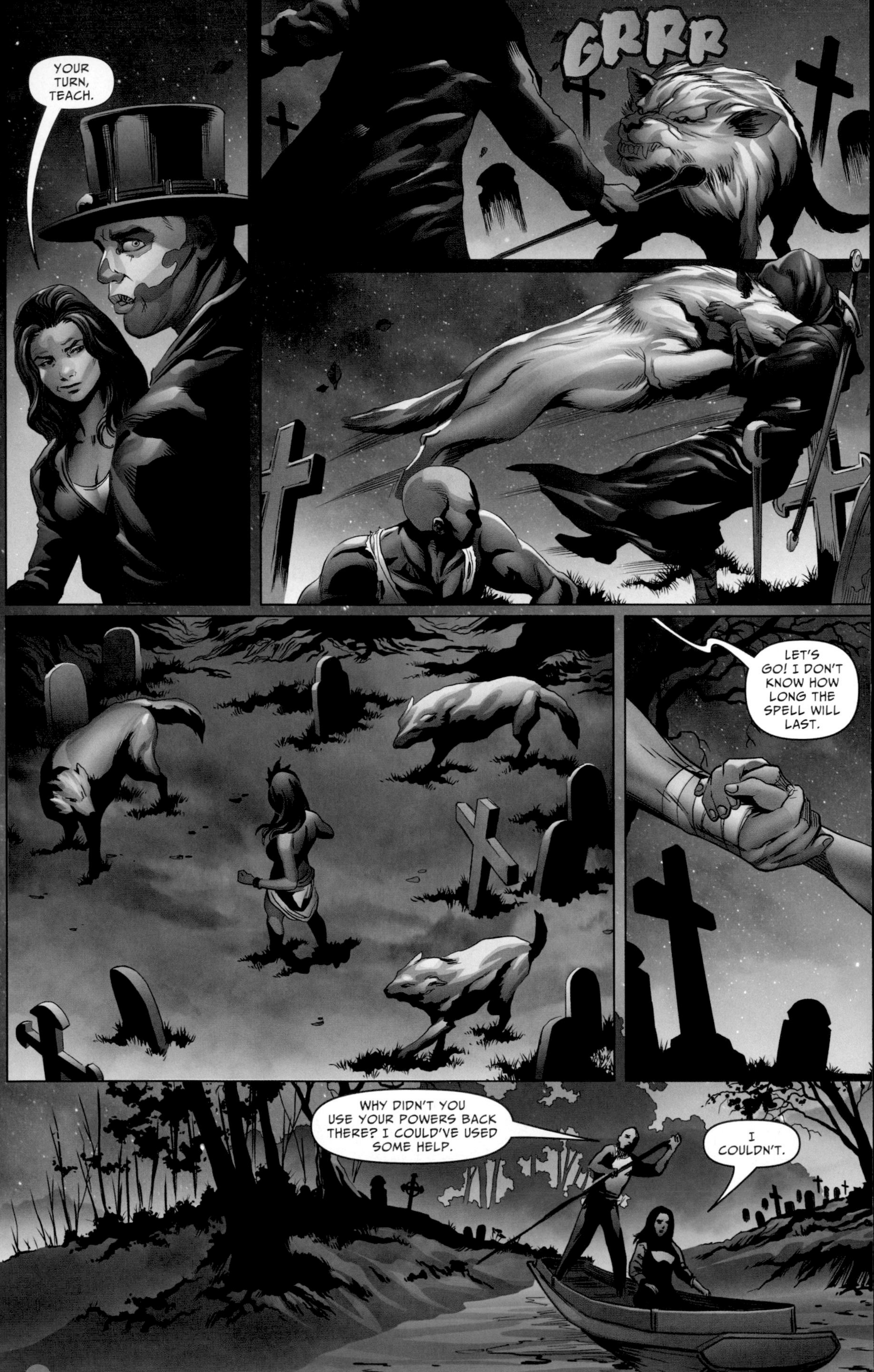
YOUR TURN, TEACH.
GRRR
LET'S GO! I DON'T KNOW HOW LONG THE SPELL WILL LAST.
WHY DIDN'T YOU USE YOUR POWERS BACK THERE? I COULD'VE USED SOME HELP.
I COULDN'T.

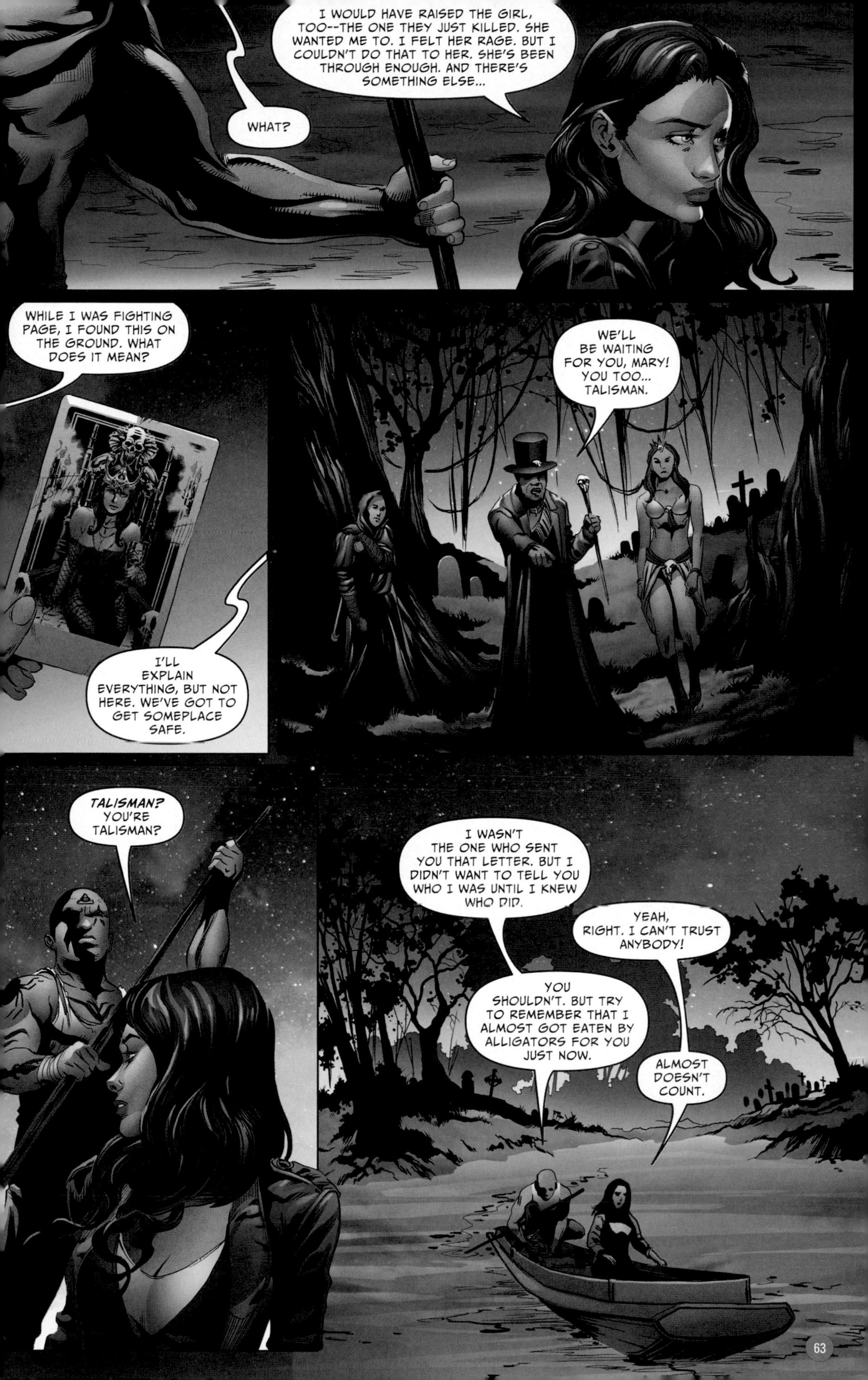
I WOULD HAVE RAISED THE GIRL, TOO--THE ONE THEY JUST KILLED. SHE WANTED ME TO. I FELT HER RAGE. BUT I COULDN'T DO THAT TO HER. SHE'S BEEN THROUGH ENOUGH. AND THERE'S SOMETHING ELSE...
WHAT?
WHILE I WAS FIGHTING PAGE, I FOUND THIS ON THE GROUND. WHAT DOES IT MEAN?
WE'LL BE WAITING FOR YOU, MARY! YOU TOO... TALISMAN.
I'LL EXPLAIN EVERYTHING, BUT NOT HERE. WE'VE GOT TO GET SOMEPLACE SAFE.
TALISMAN? YOU'RE TALISMAN?
I WASN'T THE ONE WHO SENT YOU THAT LETTER. BUT I DIDN'T WANT TO TELL YOU WHO I WAS UNTIL I KNEW WHO DID.
YEAH, RIGHT. I CAN'T TRUST ANYBODY!
YOU SHOULDN'T. BUT TRY TO REMEMBER THAT I ALMOST GOT EATEN BY ALLIGATORS FOR YOU JUST NOW.
ALMOST DOESN'T COUNT.

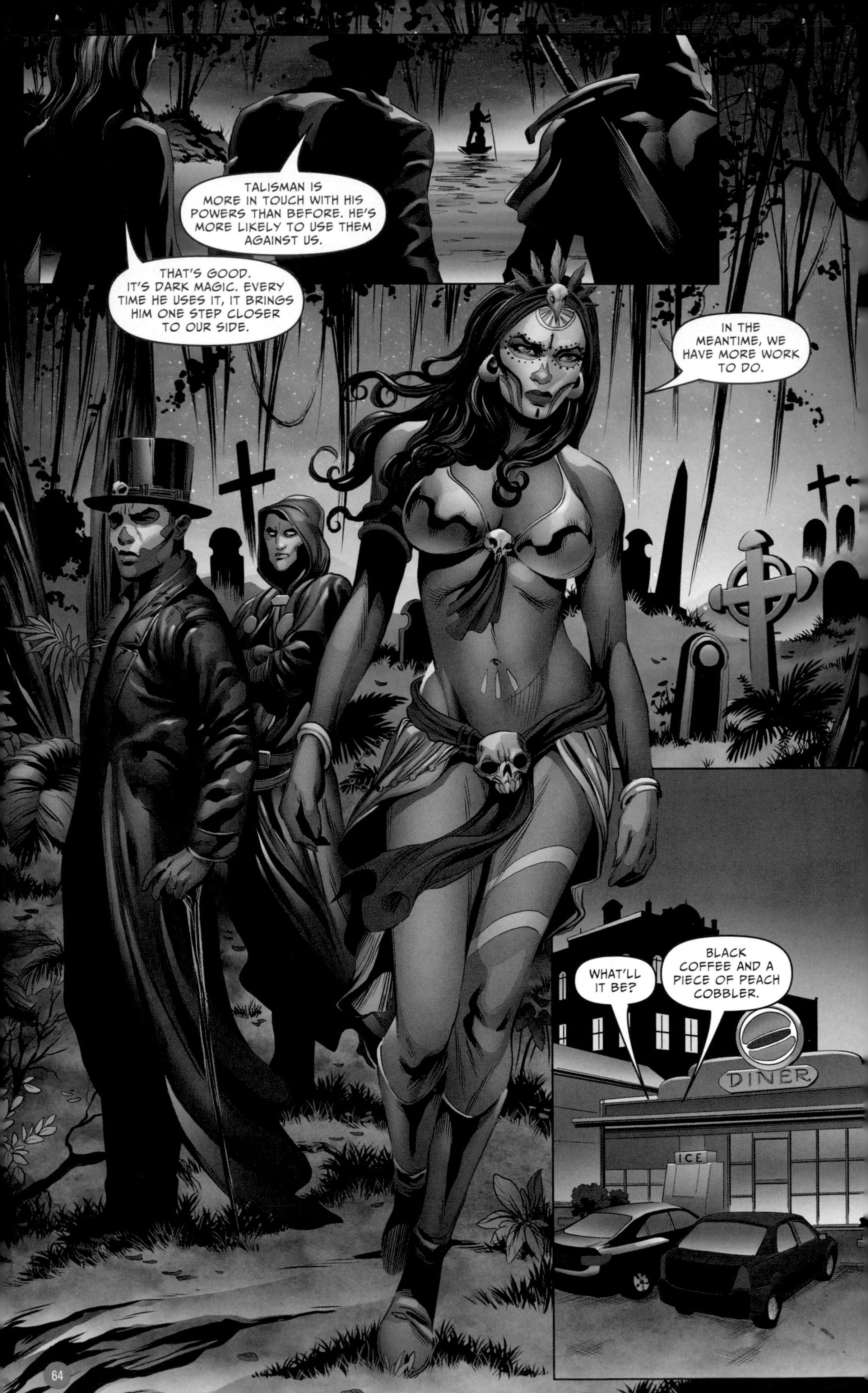
TALISMAN IS MORE IN TOUCH WITH HIS POWERS THAN BEFORE. HE'S MORE LIKELY TO USE THEM AGAINST US.
THAT'S GOOD. IT'S DARK MAGIC. EVERY TIME HE USES IT, IT BRINGS HIM ONE STEP CLOSER TO OUR SIDE.
IN THE MEANTIME, WE HAVE MORE WORK TO DO.
WHAT'LL IT BE?
BLACK COFFEE AND A PIECE OF PEACH COBBLER.
DINER
ICE

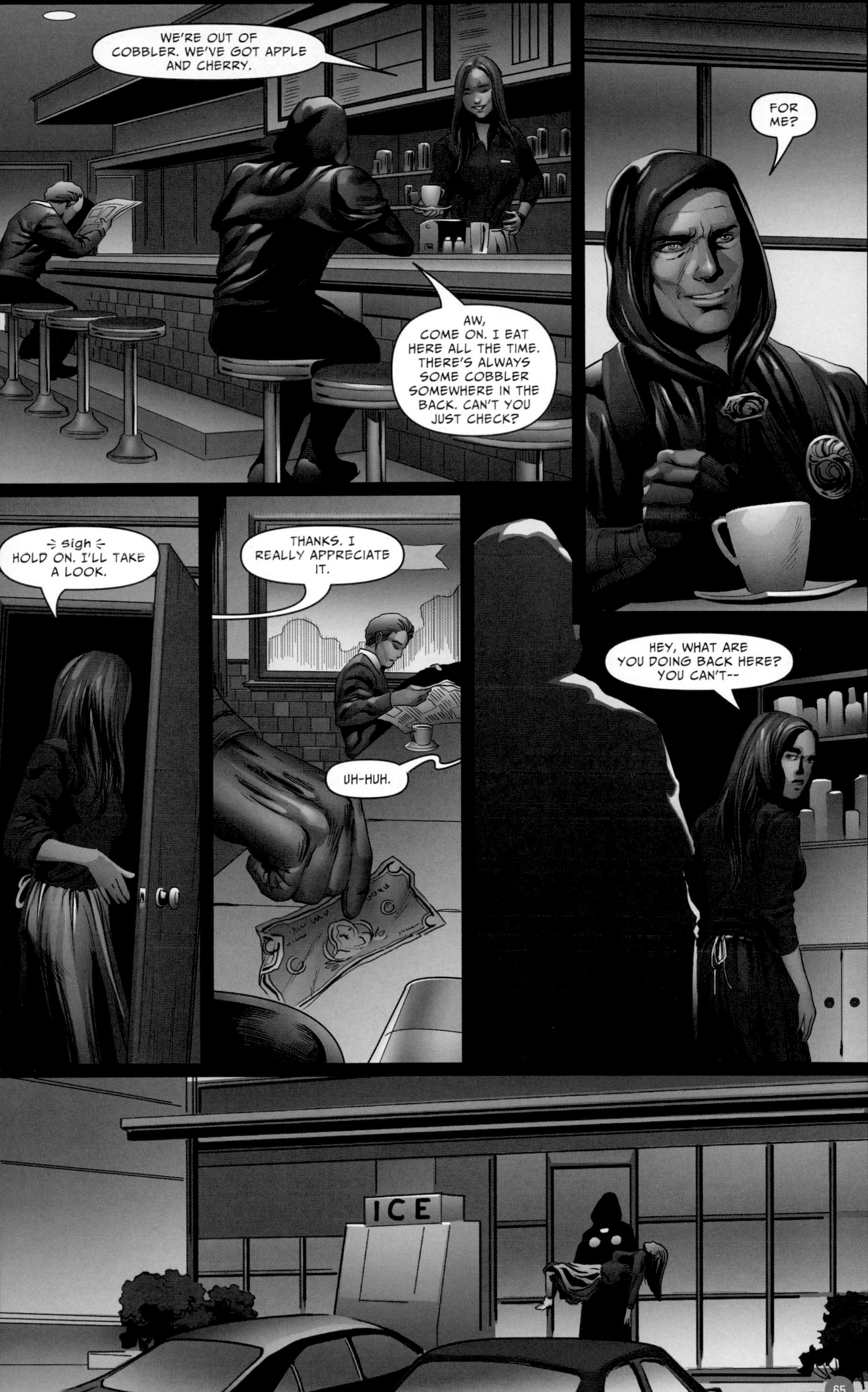
WE'RE OUT OF COBBLER. WE'VE GOT APPLE AND CHERRY.
AW, COME ON. I EAT HERE ALL THE TIME. THERE'S ALWAYS SOME COBBLER SOMEWHERE IN THE BACK. CAN'T YOU JUST CHECK?
FOR ME?
sigh
HOLD ON. I'LL TAKE A LOOK.
THANKS. I REALLY APPRECIATE IT.
UH-HUH.
HEY, WHAT ARE YOU DOING BACK HERE? YOU CAN'T--
ICE

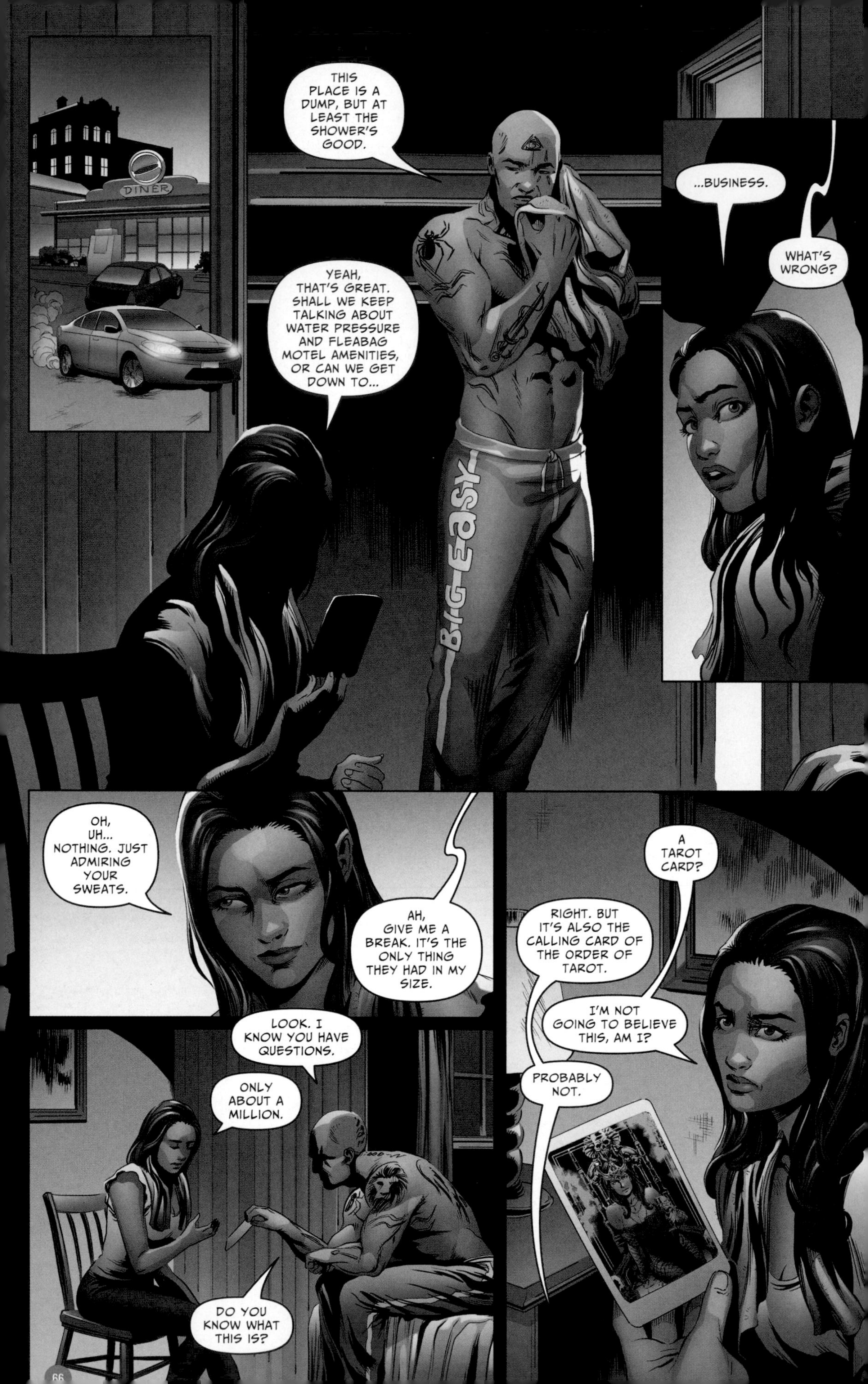
DINER
THIS PLACE IS A DUMP, BUT AT LEAST THE SHOWER'S GOOD.
YEAH, THAT'S GREAT. SHALL WE KEEP TALKING ABOUT WATER PRESSURE AND FLEABAG MOTEL AMENITIES, OR CAN WE GET DOWN TO...
BIG EASY
...BUSINESS.
WHAT'S WRONG?
OH, UH... NOTHING. JUST ADMIRING YOUR SWEATS.
AH, GIVE ME A BREAK. IT'S THE ONLY THING THEY HAD IN MY SIZE.
LOOK. I KNOW YOU HAVE QUESTIONS.
ONLY ABOUT A MILLION.
DO YOU KNOW WHAT THIS IS?
A TAROT CARD?
RIGHT. BUT IT'S ALSO THE CALLING CARD OF THE ORDER OF TAROT.
I'M NOT GOING TO BELIEVE THIS, AM I?
PROBABLY NOT.

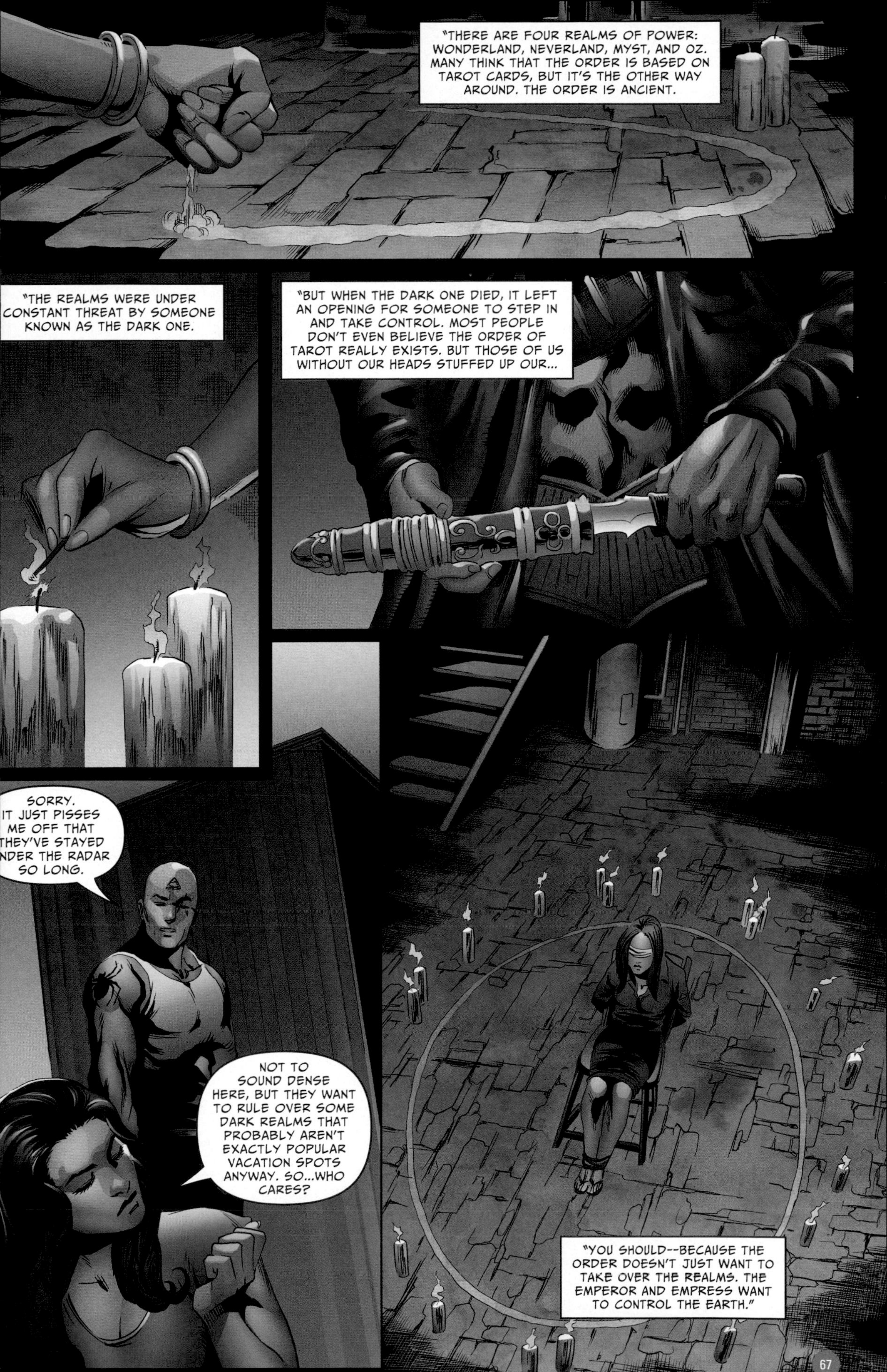
"THERE ARE FOUR REALMS OF POWER: WONDERLAND, NEVERLAND, MYST, AND OZ. MANY THINK THAT THE ORDER IS BASED ON TAROT CARDS, BUT IT'S THE OTHER WAY AROUND. THE ORDER IS ANCIENT.
"THE REALMS WERE UNDER CONSTANT THREAT BY SOMEONE KNOWN AS THE DARK ONE.
"BUT WHEN THE DARK ONE DIED, IT LEFT AN OPENING FOR SOMEONE TO STEP IN AND TAKE CONTROL. MOST PEOPLE DON'T EVEN BELIEVE THE ORDER OF TAROT REALLY EXISTS. BUT THOSE OF US WITHOUT OUR HEADS STUFFED UP OUR...
SORRY. IT JUST PISSES ME OFF THAT THEY'VE STAYED UNDER THE RADAR SO LONG.
NOT TO SOUND DENSE HERE, BUT THEY WANT TO RULE OVER SOME DARK REALMS THAT PROBABLY AREN'T EXACTLY POPULAR VACATION SPOTS ANYWAY. SO...WHO CARES?
"YOU SHOULD--BECAUSE THE ORDER DOESN'T JUST WANT TO TAKE OVER THE REALMS. THE EMPEROR AND EMPRESS WANT TO CONTROL THE EARTH."

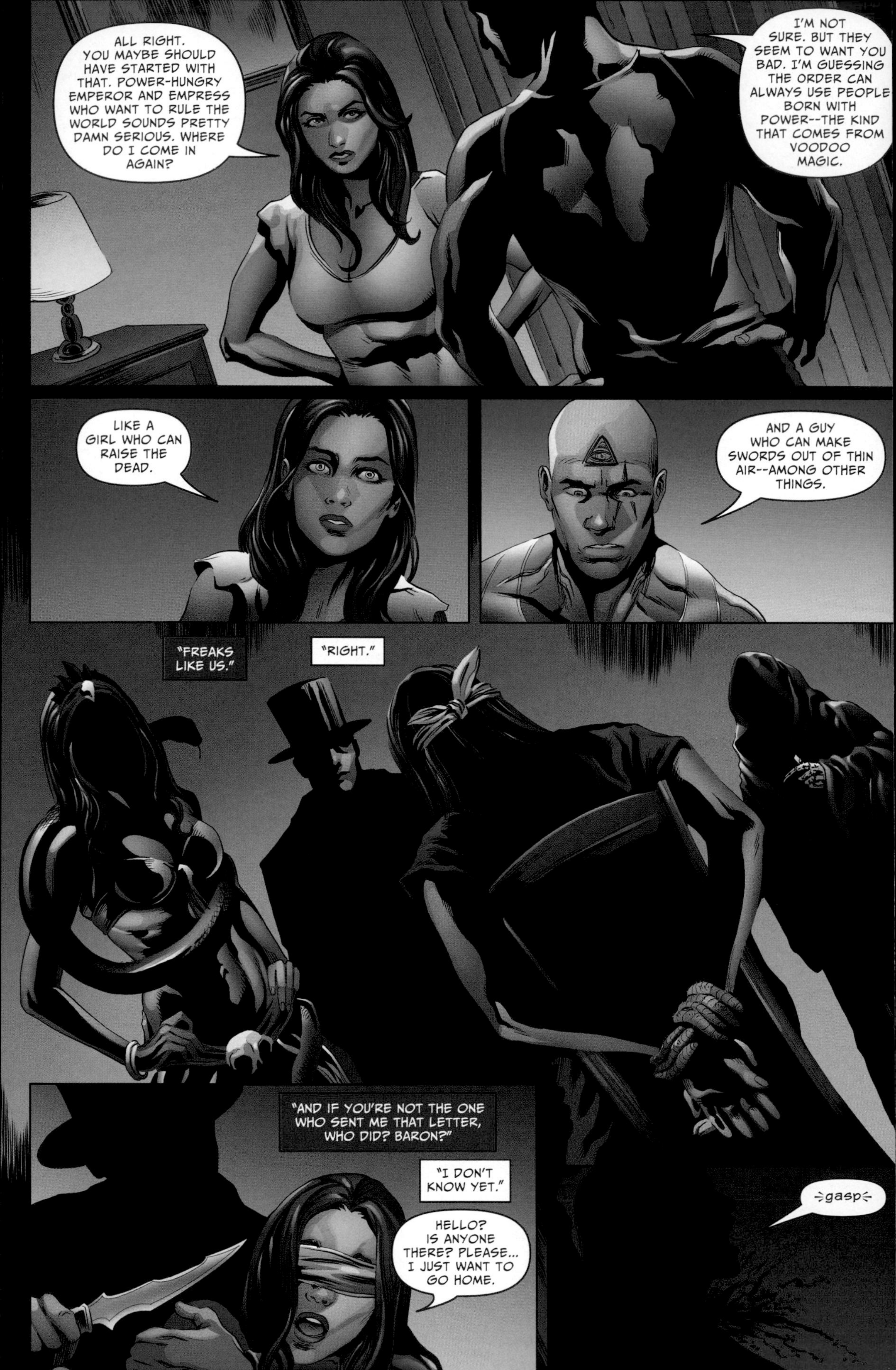
ALL RIGHT. YOU MAYBE SHOULD HAVE STARTED WITH THAT. POWER-HUNGRY EMPEROR AND EMPRESS WHO WANT TO RULE THE WORLD SOUNDS PRETTY DAMN SERIOUS. WHERE DO I COME IN AGAIN?
I'M NOT SURE. BUT THEY SEEM TO WANT YOU BAD. I'M GUESSING THE ORDER CAN ALWAYS USE PEOPLE BORN WITH POWER--THE KIND THAT COMES FROM VOODOO MAGIC.
LIKE A GIRL WHO CAN RAISE THE DEAD.
AND A GUY WHO CAN MAKE SWORDS OUT OF THIN AIR--AMONG OTHER THINGS.
"FREAKS LIKE US."
"RIGHT."
"AND IF YOU'RE NOT THE ONE WHO SENT ME THAT LETTER, WHO DID? BARON?"
"I DON'T KNOW YET."
HELLO? IS ANYONE THERE? PLEASE... I JUST WANT TO GO HOME.
gasp

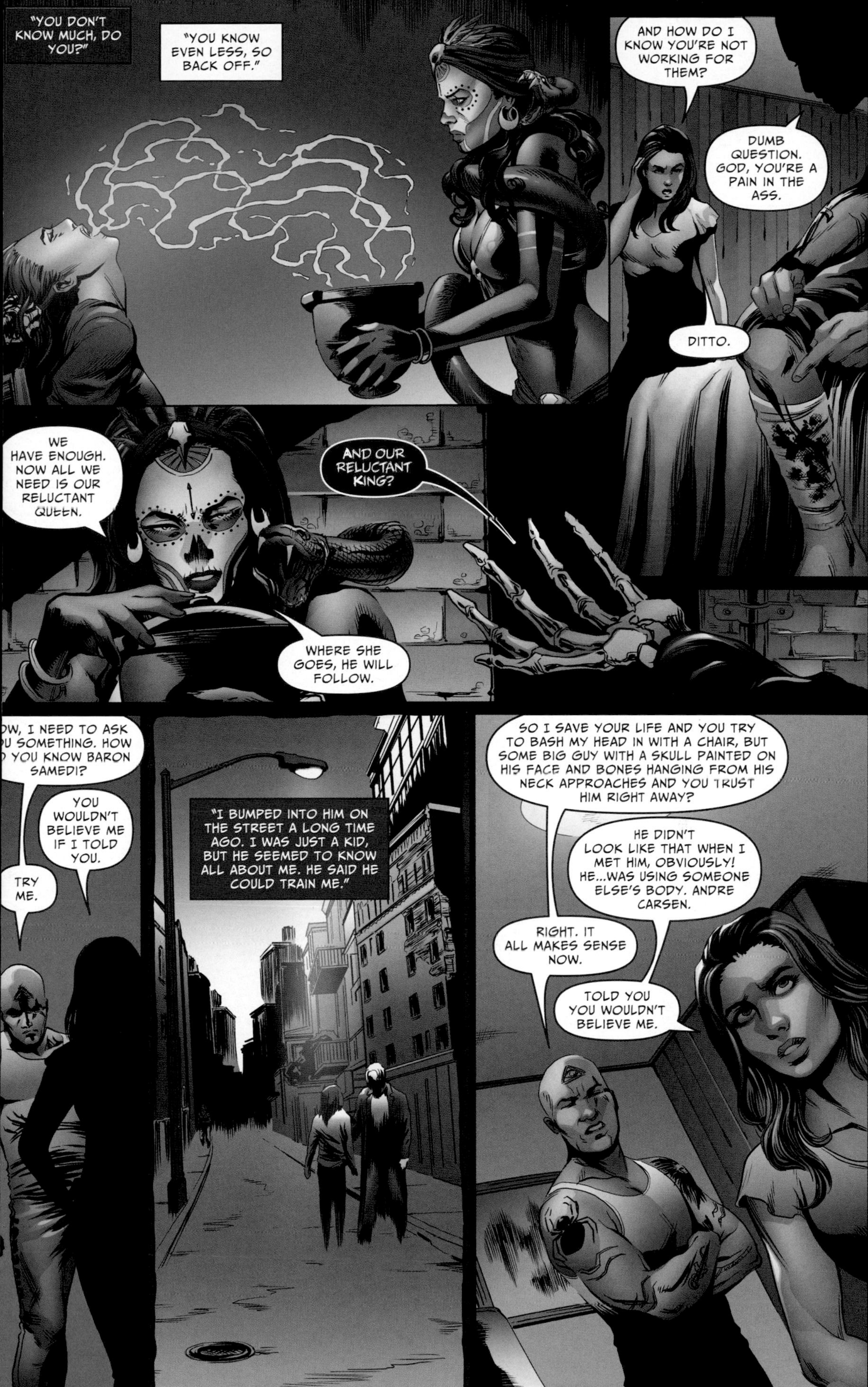
"YOU DON'T KNOW MUCH, DO YOU?"
"YOU KNOW EVEN LESS, SO BACK OFF."
AND HOW DO I KNOW YOU'RE NOT WORKING FOR THEM?
DUMB QUESTION. GOD, YOU'RE A PAIN IN THE ASS.
DITTO.
WE HAVE ENOUGH. NOW ALL WE NEED IS OUR RELUCTANT QUEEN.
AND OUR RELUCTANT KING?
WHERE SHE GOES, HE WILL FOLLOW.
OW, I NEED TO ASK U SOMETHING. HOW YOU KNOW BARON SAMEDI?
YOU WOULDN'T BELIEVE ME IF I TOLD YOU.
TRY ME.
"I BUMPED INTO HIM ON THE STREET A LONG TIME AGO. I WAS JUST A KID, BUT HE SEEMED TO KNOW ALL ABOUT ME. HE SAID HE COULD TRAIN ME."
SO I SAVE YOUR LIFE AND YOU TRY TO BASH MY HEAD IN WITH A CHAIR, BUT SOME BIG GUY WITH A SKULL PAINTED ON HIS FACE AND BONES HANGING FROM HIS NECK APPROACHES AND YOU TRUST HIM RIGHT AWAY?
HE DIDN'T LOOK LIKE THAT WHEN I MET HIM, OBVIOUSLY! HE...WAS USING SOMEONE ELSE'S BODY. ANDRE CARSEN.
RIGHT. IT ALL MAKES SENSE NOW.
TOLD YOU YOU WOULDN'T BELIEVE ME.

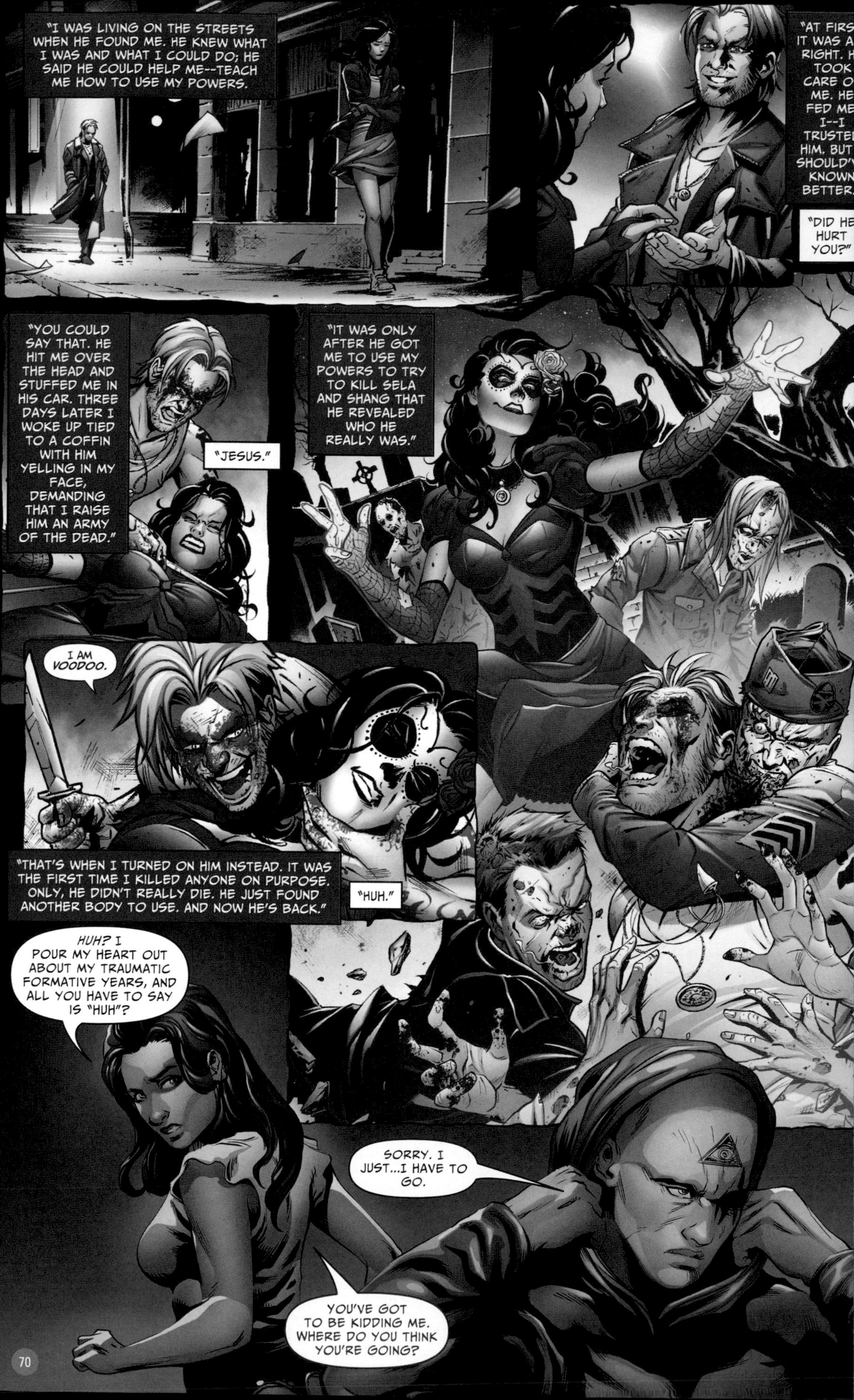
"I WAS LIVING ON THE STREETS WHEN HE FOUND ME. HE KNEW WHAT I WAS AND WHAT I COULD DO; HE SAID HE COULD HELP ME--TEACH ME HOW TO USE MY POWERS.
"AT FIRS IT WAS A RIGHT. H TOOK CARE O ME. HE FED ME I--I TRUSTE HIM. BUT SHOULD'V KNOWN BETTER.
"DID HE HURT YOU?"
"YOU COULD SAY THAT. HE HIT ME OVER THE HEAD AND STUFFED ME IN HIS CAR. THREE DAYS LATER I WOKE UP TIED TO A COFFIN WITH HIM YELLING IN MY FACE, DEMANDING THAT I RAISE HIM AN ARMY OF THE DEAD."
"JESUS."
"IT WAS ONLY AFTER HE GOT ME TO USE MY POWERS TO TRY TO KILL SELA AND SHANG THAT HE REVEALED WHO HE REALLY WAS."
I AM *VOODOO.*
"THAT'S WHEN I TURNED ON HIM INSTEAD. IT WAS THE FIRST TIME I KILLED ANYONE ON PURPOSE. ONLY, HE DIDN'T REALLY DIE. HE JUST FOUND ANOTHER BODY TO USE. AND NOW HE'S BACK."
"HUH."
HUH? I POUR MY HEART OUT ABOUT MY TRAUMATIC FORMATIVE YEARS, AND ALL YOU HAVE TO SAY IS "HUH"?
SORRY. I JUST...I HAVE TO GO.
YOU'VE GOT TO BE KIDDING ME. WHERE DO YOU THINK YOU'RE GOING?

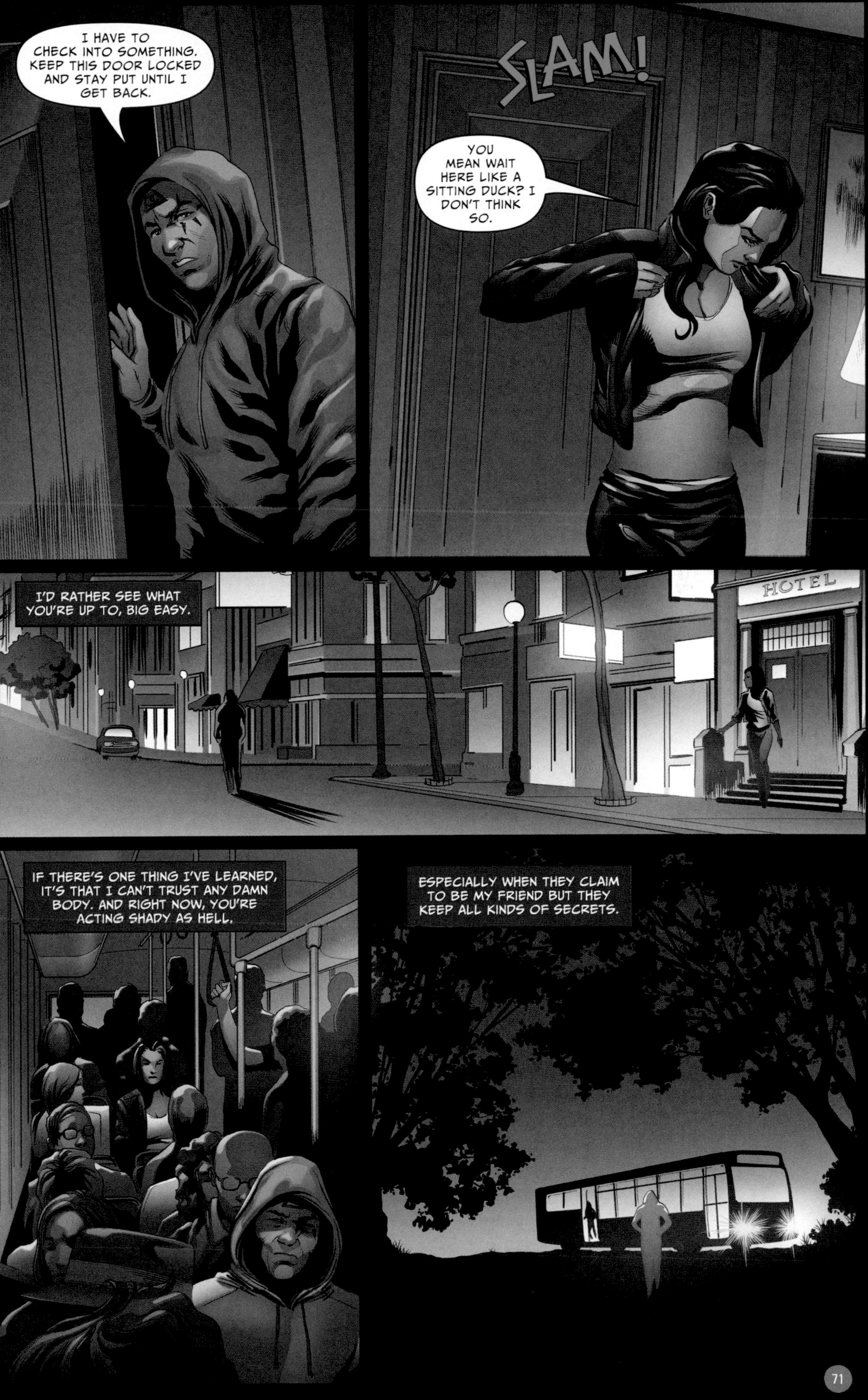
I HAVE TO CHECK INTO SOMETHING. KEEP THIS DOOR LOCKED AND STAY PUT UNTIL I GET BACK.
SLAM!
YOU MEAN WAIT HERE LIKE A SITTING DUCK? I DON'T THINK SO.
I'D RATHER SEE WHAT YOU'RE UP TO, BIG EASY.
HOTEL
IF THERE'S ONE THING I'VE LEARNED, IT'S THAT I CAN'T TRUST ANY DAMN BODY. AND RIGHT NOW, YOU'RE ACTING SHADY AS HELL.
ESPECIALLY WHEN THEY CLAIM TO BE MY FRIEND BUT THEY KEEP ALL KINDS OF SECRETS.

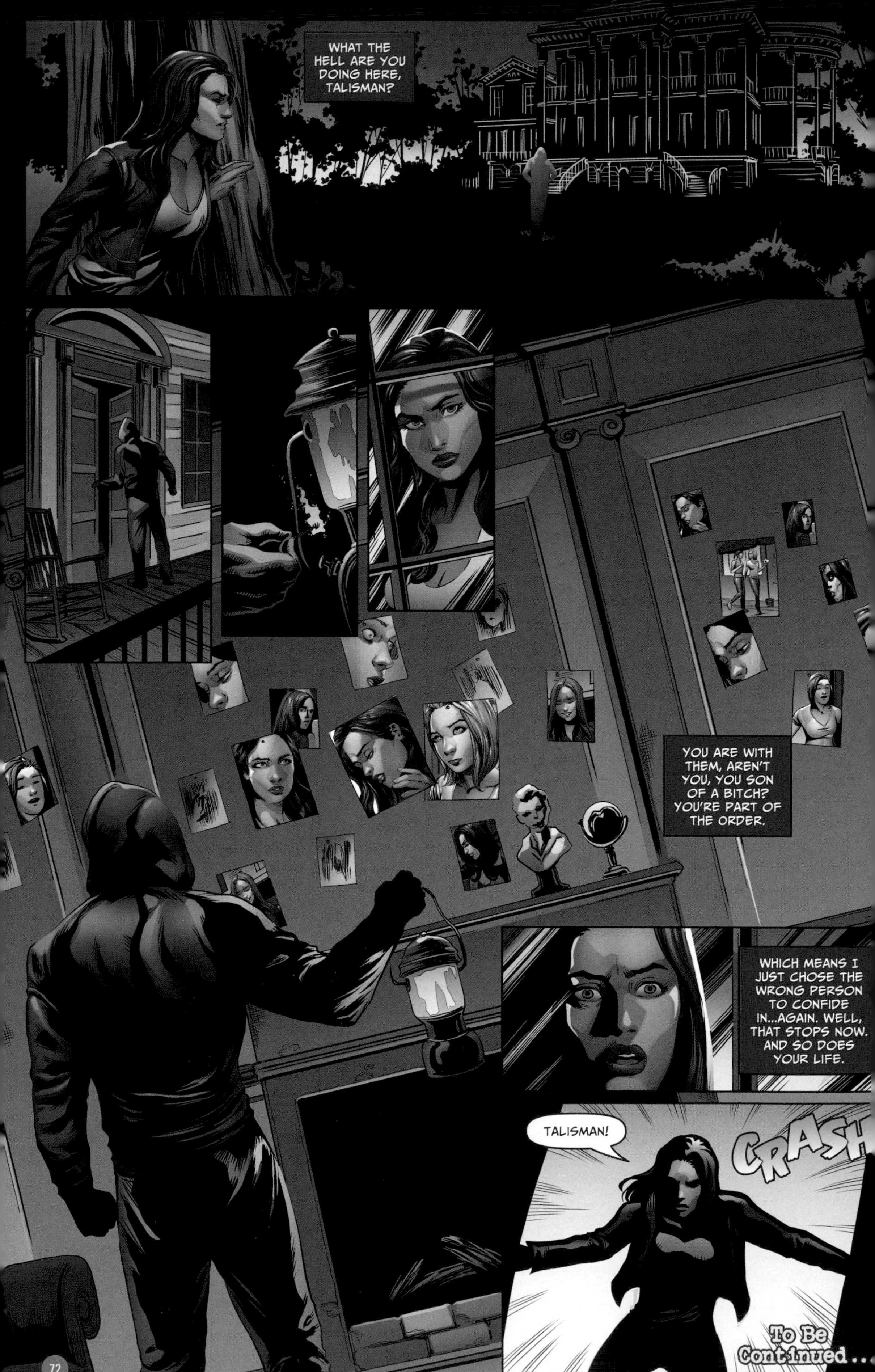

WHAT THE HELL ARE YOU DOING HERE, TALISMAN?
YOU ARE WITH THEM, AREN'T YOU, YOU SON OF A BITCH? YOU'RE PART OF THE ORDER.
WHICH MEANS I JUST CHOSE THE WRONG PERSON TO CONFIDE IN...AGAIN. WELL, THAT STOPS NOW. AND SO DOES YOUR LIFE.
TALISMAN!
CRASH
To Be Continued...

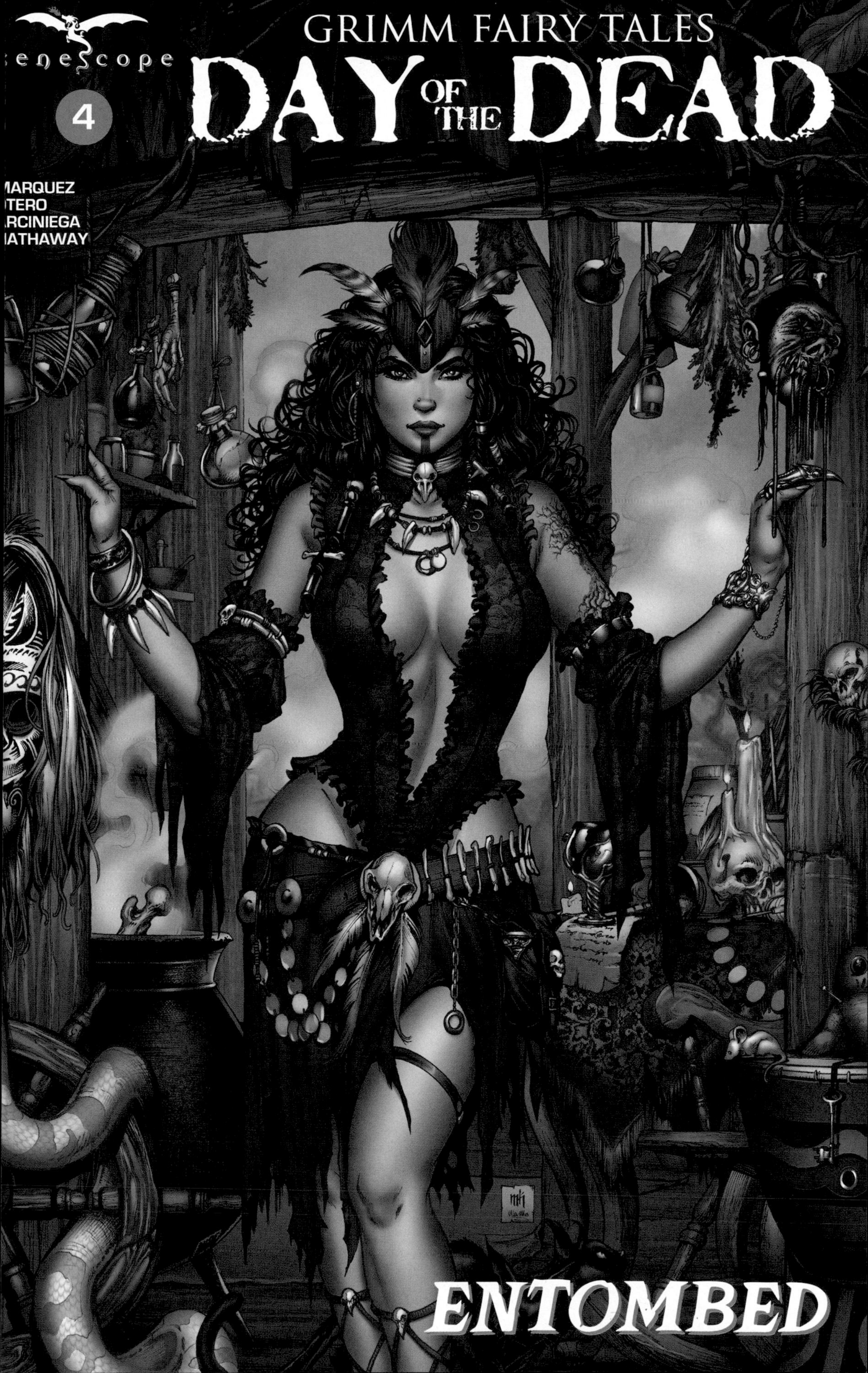

zenescope
4
GRIMM FAIRY TALES
DAY OF THE DEAD
MARQUEZ
OTERO
ARCINIEGA
HATHAWAY
ENTOMBED

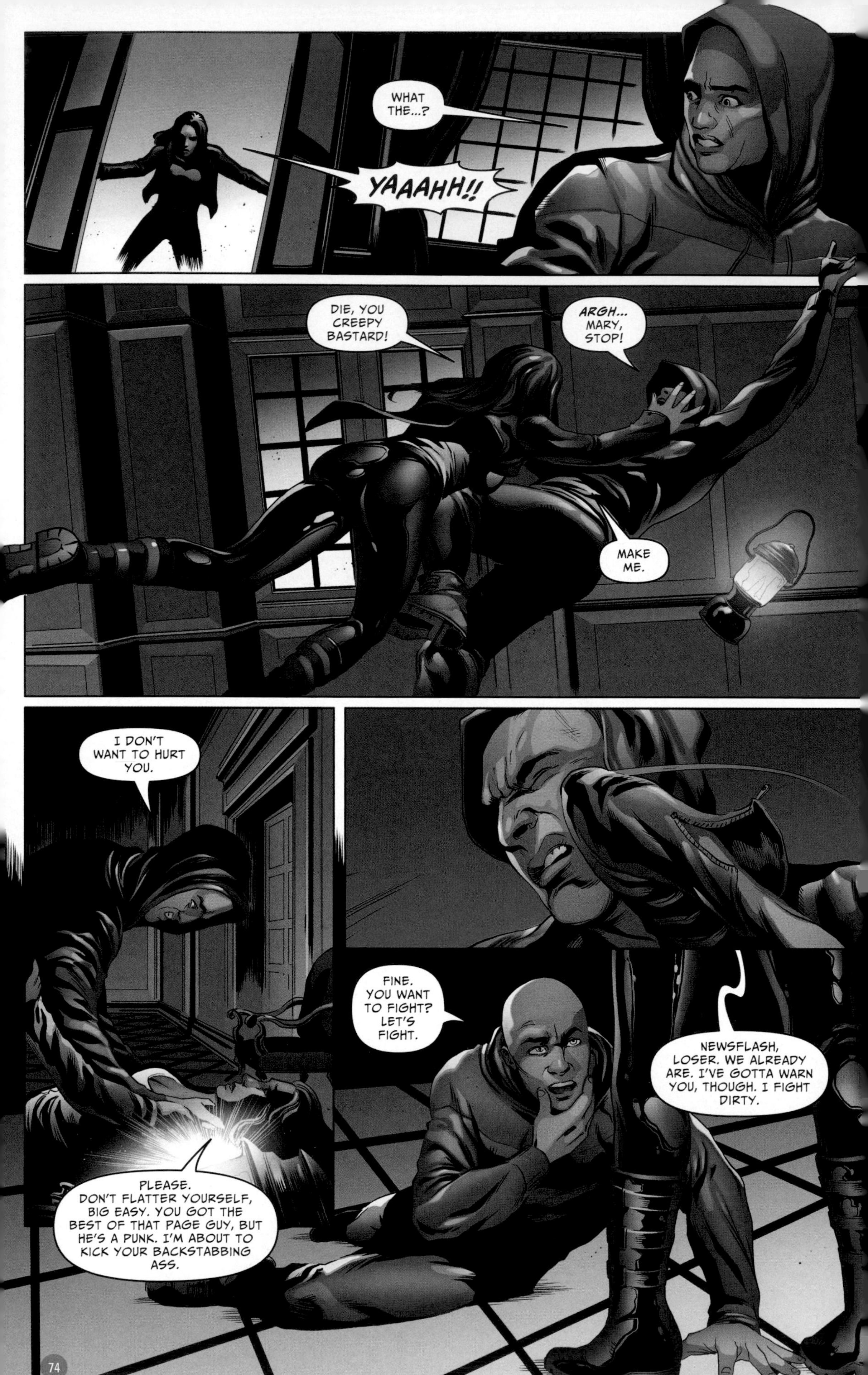
WHAT THE...?
YAAAHH!!
DIE, YOU CREEPY BASTARD!
ARGH... MARY, STOP!
MAKE ME.
I DON'T WANT TO HURT YOU.
PLEASE. DON'T FLATTER YOURSELF, BIG EASY. YOU GOT THE BEST OF THAT PAGE GUY, BUT HE'S A PUNK. I'M ABOUT TO KICK YOUR BACKSTABBING ASS.
FINE. YOU WANT TO FIGHT? LET'S FIGHT.
NEWSFLASH, LOSER. WE ALREADY ARE. I'VE GOTTA WARN YOU, THOUGH. I FIGHT DIRTY.

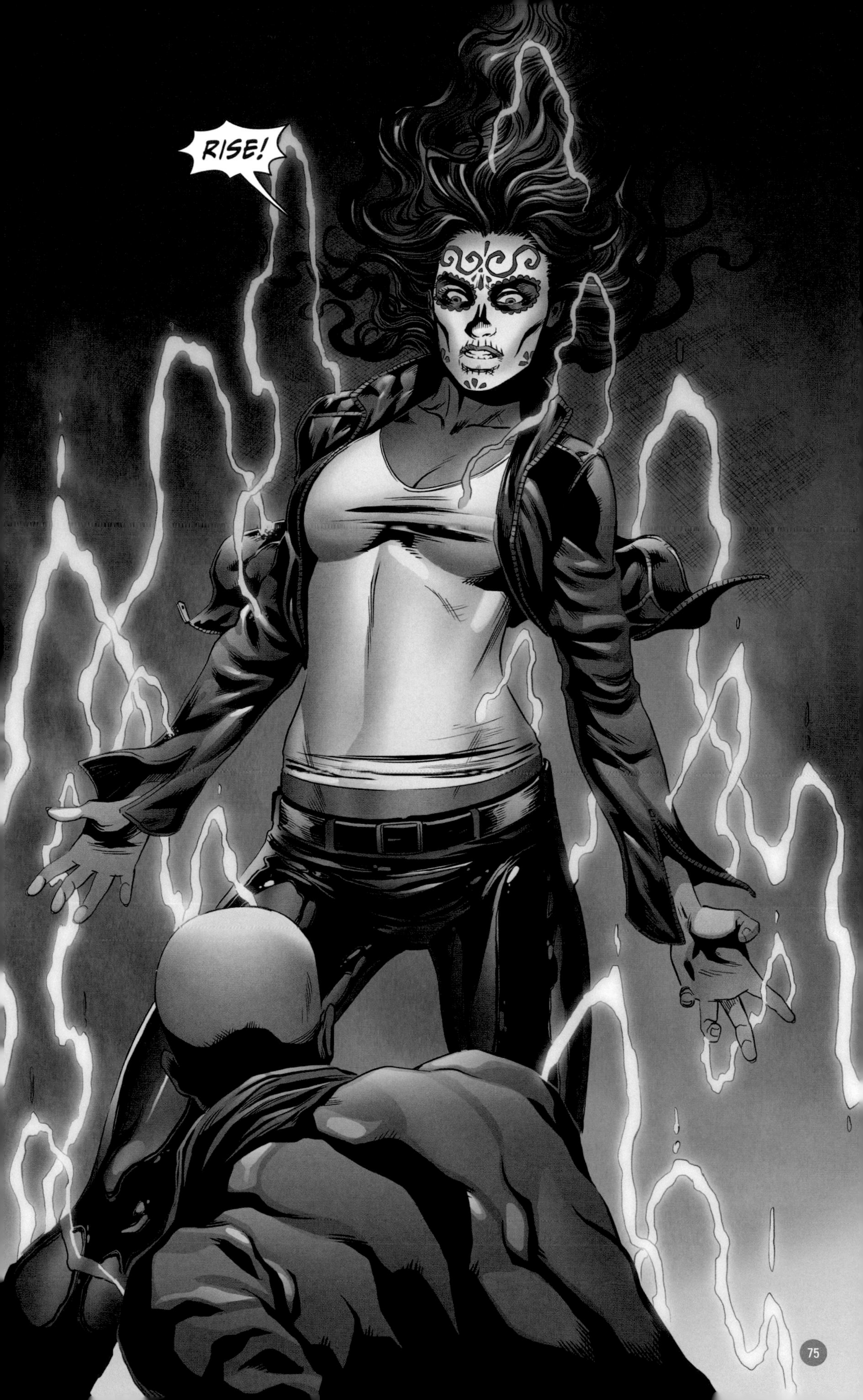
RISE!

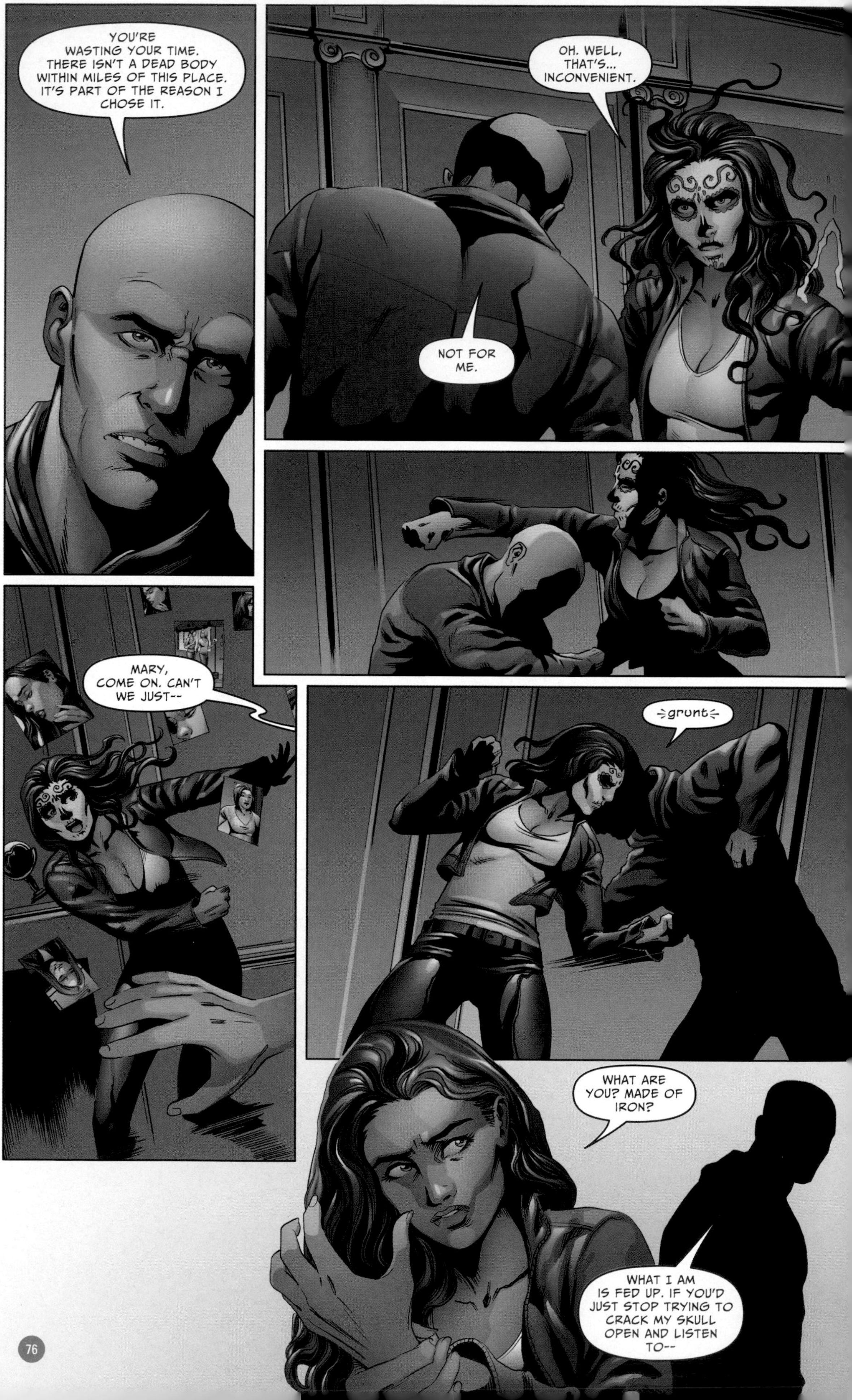
YOU'RE WASTING YOUR TIME. THERE ISN'T A DEAD BODY WITHIN MILES OF THIS PLACE. IT'S PART OF THE REASON I CHOSE IT.
OH. WELL, THAT'S... INCONVENIENT.
NOT FOR ME.
MARY, COME ON. CAN'T WE JUST--
grunt
WHAT ARE YOU? MADE OF IRON?
WHAT I AM IS FED UP. IF YOU'D JUST STOP TRYING TO CRACK MY SKULL OPEN AND LISTEN TO--

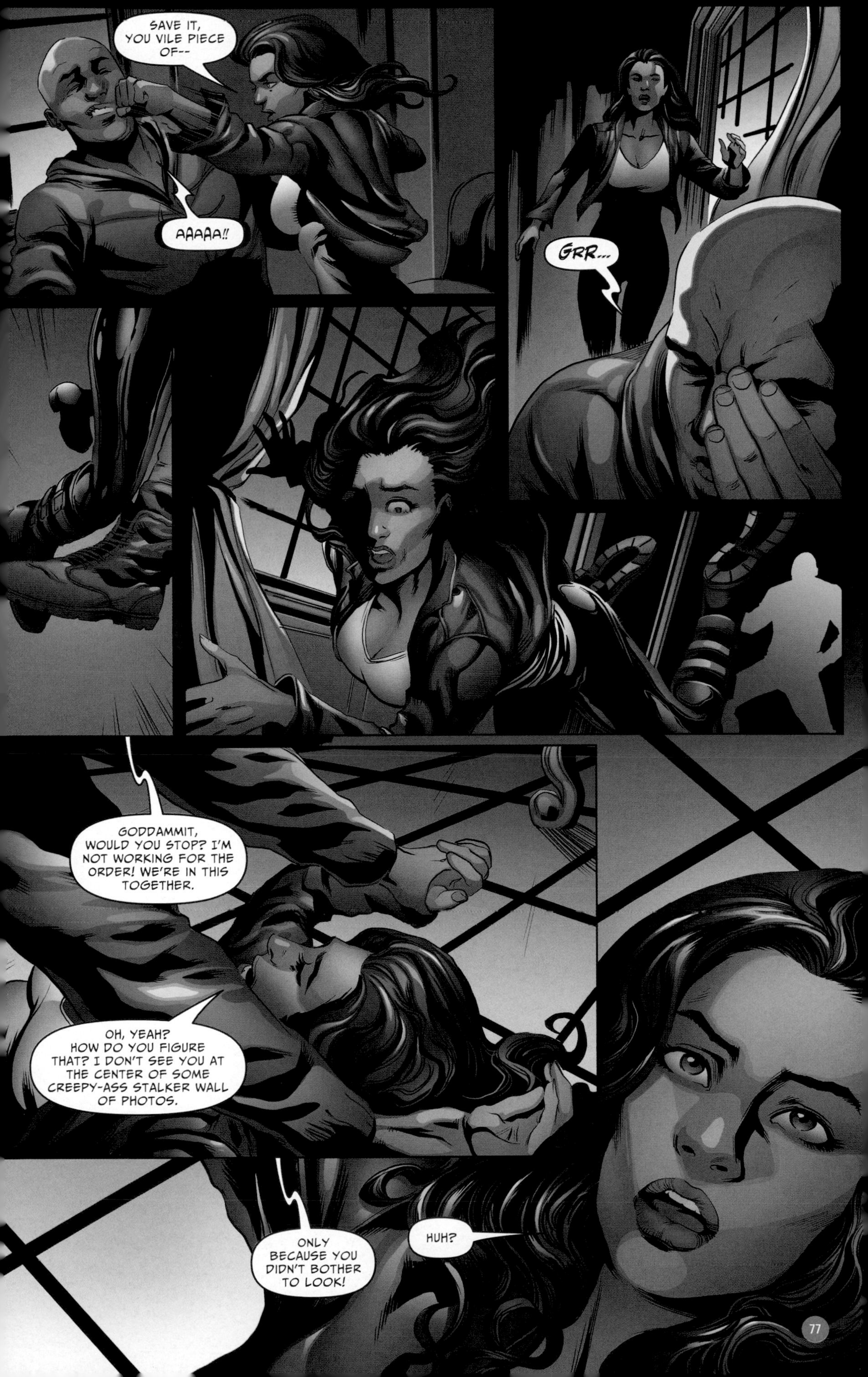
SAVE IT, YOU VILE PIECE OF--
AAAAA!!
GRR...
GODDAMMIT, WOULD YOU STOP? I'M NOT WORKING FOR THE ORDER! WE'RE IN THIS TOGETHER.
OH, YEAH? HOW DO YOU FIGURE THAT? I DON'T SEE YOU AT THE CENTER OF SOME CREEPY-ASS STALKER WALL OF PHOTOS.
ONLY BECAUSE YOU DIDN'T BOTHER TO LOOK!
HUH?

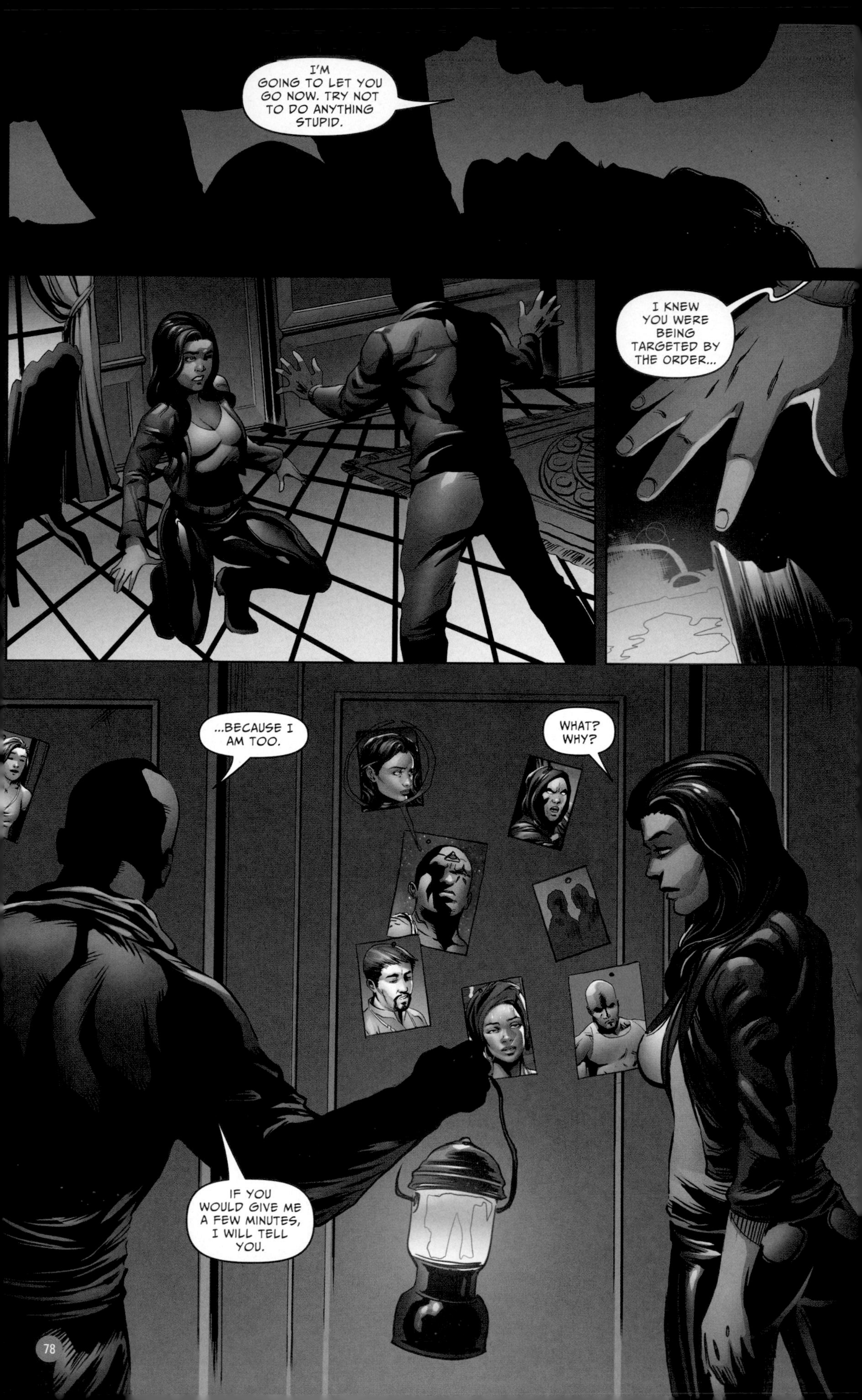
I'M GOING TO LET YOU GO NOW. TRY NOT TO DO ANYTHING STUPID.
I KNEW YOU WERE BEING TARGETED BY THE ORDER...
...BECAUSE I AM TOO.
WHAT? WHY?
IF YOU WOULD GIVE ME A FEW MINUTES, I WILL TELL YOU.

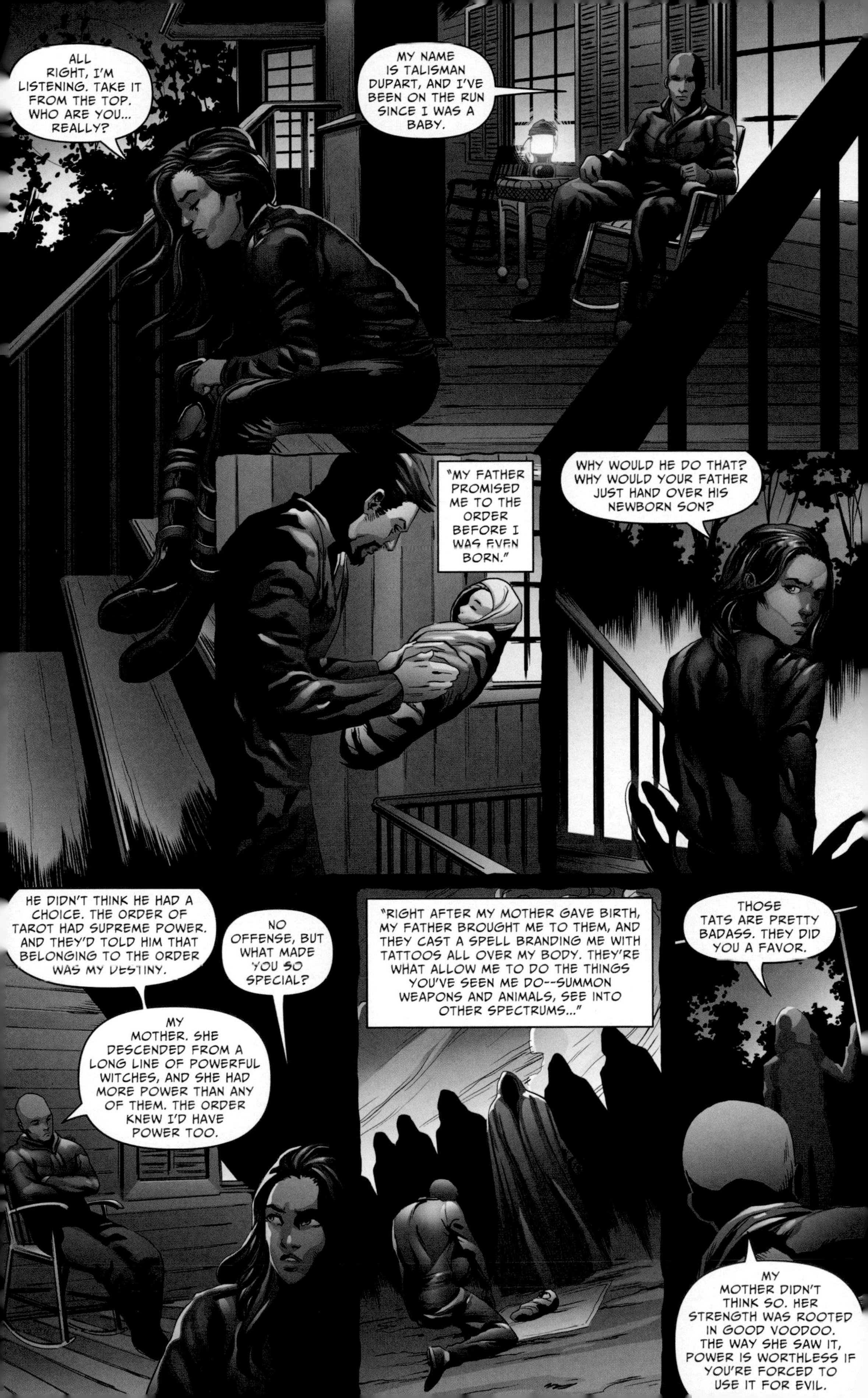
ALL RIGHT, I'M LISTENING. TAKE IT FROM THE TOP. WHO ARE YOU... REALLY?
MY NAME IS TALISMAN DUPART, AND I'VE BEEN ON THE RUN SINCE I WAS A BABY.
"MY FATHER PROMISED ME TO THE ORDER BEFORE I WAS EVEN BORN."
WHY WOULD HE DO THAT? WHY WOULD YOUR FATHER JUST HAND OVER HIS NEWBORN SON?
HE DIDN'T THINK HE HAD A CHOICE. THE ORDER OF TAROT HAD SUPREME POWER. AND THEY'D TOLD HIM THAT BELONGING TO THE ORDER WAS MY DESTINY.
NO OFFENSE, BUT WHAT MADE YOU SO SPECIAL?
MY MOTHER. SHE DESCENDED FROM A LONG LINE OF POWERFUL WITCHES, AND SHE HAD MORE POWER THAN ANY OF THEM. THE ORDER KNEW I'D HAVE POWER TOO.
"RIGHT AFTER MY MOTHER GAVE BIRTH, MY FATHER BROUGHT ME TO THEM, AND THEY CAST A SPELL BRANDING ME WITH TATTOOS ALL OVER MY BODY. THEY'RE WHAT ALLOW ME TO DO THE THINGS YOU'VE SEEN ME DO--SUMMON WEAPONS AND ANIMALS, SEE INTO OTHER SPECTRUMS..."
THOSE TATS ARE PRETTY BADASS. THEY DID YOU A FAVOR.
MY MOTHER DIDN'T THINK SO. HER STRENGTH WAS ROOTED IN GOOD VOODOO. THE WAY SHE SAW IT, POWER IS WORTHLESS IF YOU'RE FORCED TO USE IT FOR EVIL.

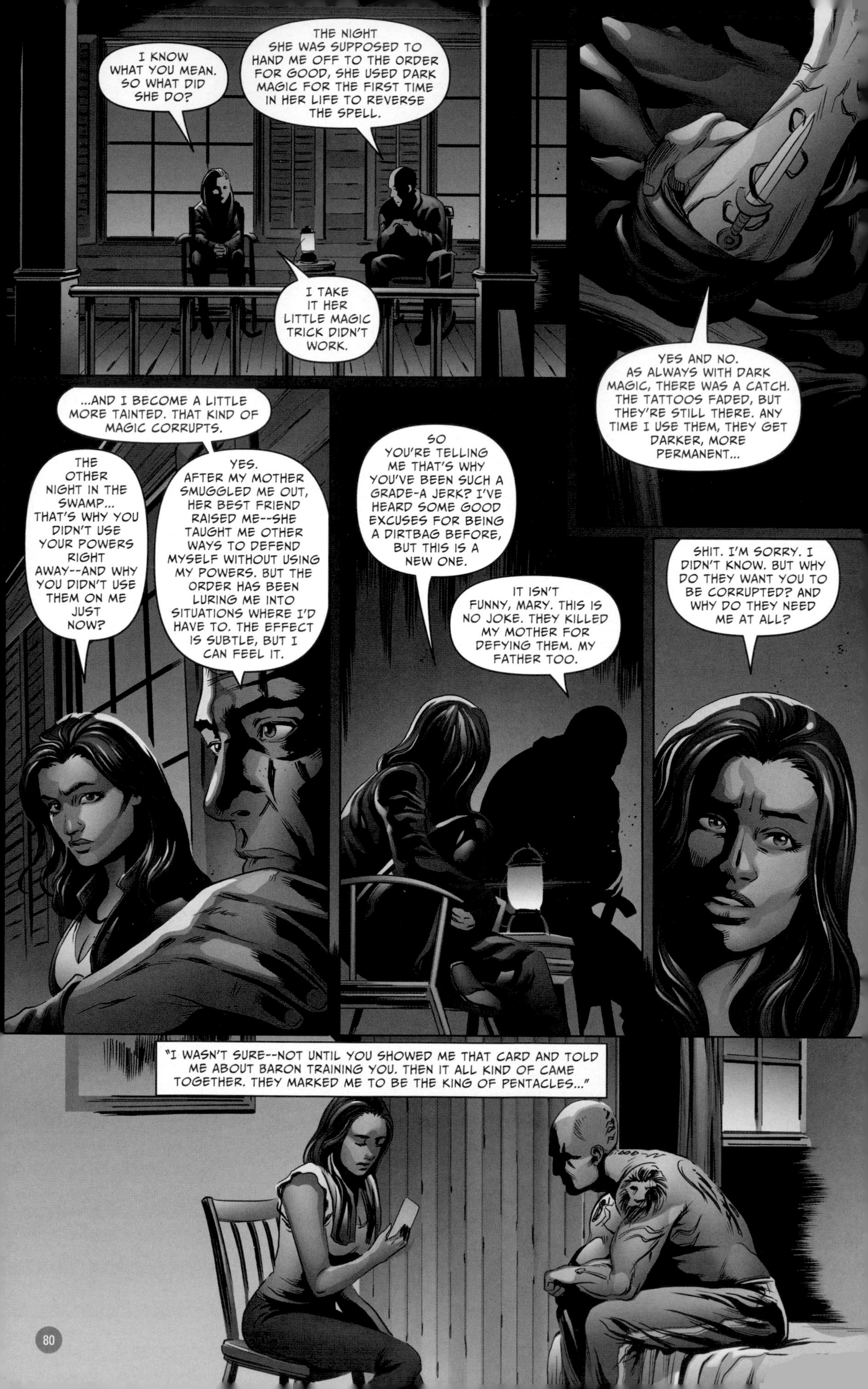
I KNOW WHAT YOU MEAN. SO WHAT DID SHE DO?
THE NIGHT SHE WAS SUPPOSED TO HAND ME OFF TO THE ORDER FOR GOOD, SHE USED DARK MAGIC FOR THE FIRST TIME IN HER LIFE TO REVERSE THE SPELL.
I TAKE IT HER LITTLE MAGIC TRICK DIDN'T WORK.
YES AND NO. AS ALWAYS WITH DARK MAGIC, THERE WAS A CATCH. THE TATTOOS FADED, BUT THEY'RE STILL THERE. ANY TIME I USE THEM, THEY GET DARKER, MORE PERMANENT...
...AND I BECOME A LITTLE MORE TAINTED. THAT KIND OF MAGIC CORRUPTS.
THE OTHER NIGHT IN THE SWAMP... THAT'S WHY YOU DIDN'T USE YOUR POWERS RIGHT AWAY--AND WHY YOU DIDN'T USE THEM ON ME JUST NOW?
YES. AFTER MY MOTHER SMUGGLED ME OUT, HER BEST FRIEND RAISED ME--SHE TAUGHT ME OTHER WAYS TO DEFEND MYSELF WITHOUT USING MY POWERS. BUT THE ORDER HAS BEEN LURING ME INTO SITUATIONS WHERE I'D HAVE TO. THE EFFECT IS SUBTLE, BUT I CAN FEEL IT.
SO YOU'RE TELLING ME THAT'S WHY YOU'VE BEEN SUCH A GRADE-A JERK? I'VE HEARD SOME GOOD EXCUSES FOR BEING A DIRTBAG BEFORE, BUT THIS IS A NEW ONE.
IT ISN'T FUNNY, MARY. THIS IS NO JOKE. THEY KILLED MY MOTHER FOR DEFYING THEM. MY FATHER TOO.
SHIT. I'M SORRY. I DIDN'T KNOW. BUT WHY DO THEY WANT YOU TO BE CORRUPTED? AND WHY DO THEY NEED ME AT ALL?
"I WASN'T SURE--NOT UNTIL YOU SHOWED ME THAT CARD AND TOLD ME ABOUT BARON TRAINING YOU. THEN IT ALL KIND OF CAME TOGETHER. THEY MARKED ME TO BE THE KING OF PENTACLES..."

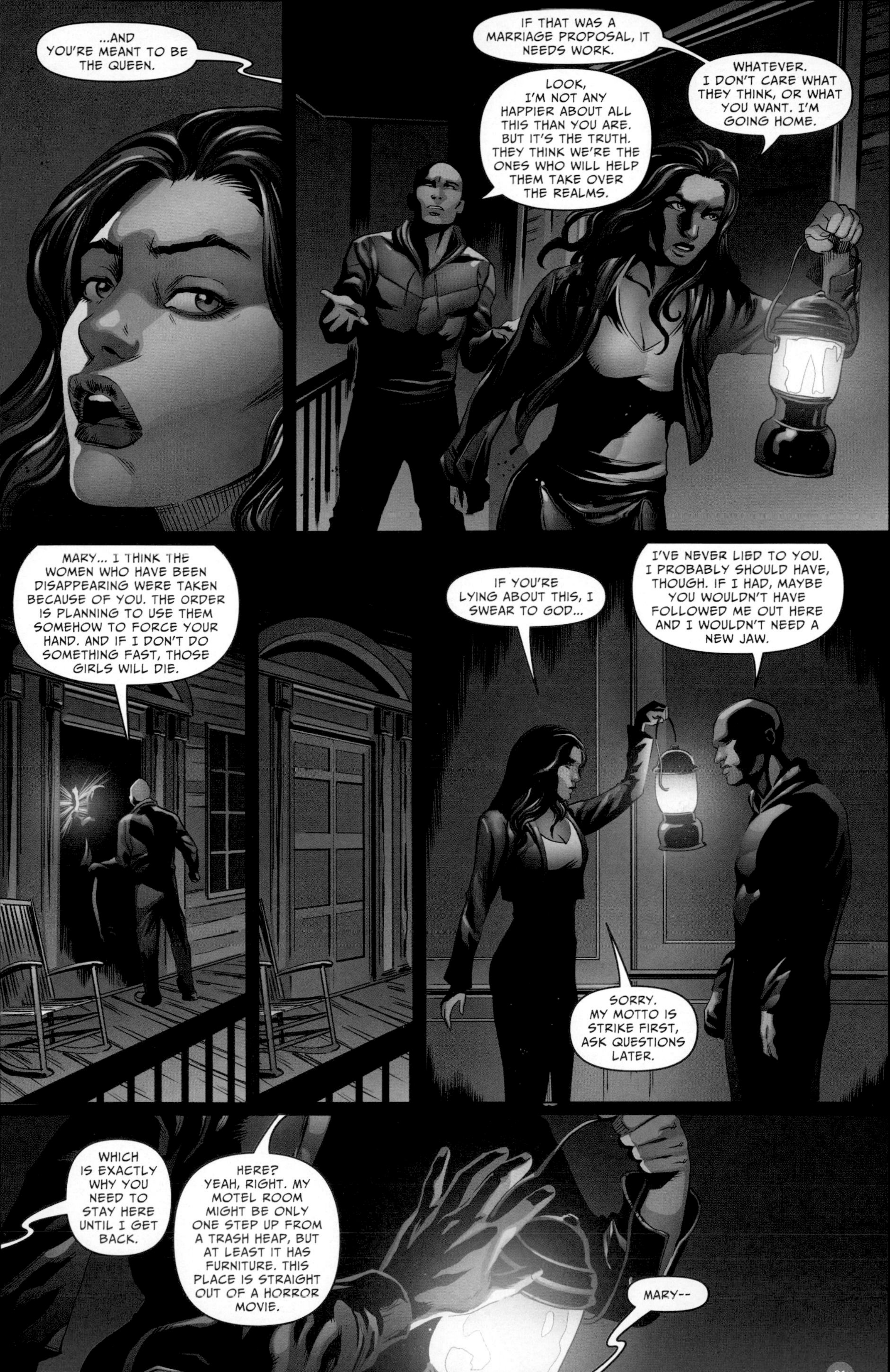
...AND YOU'RE MEANT TO BE THE QUEEN.
IF THAT WAS A MARRIAGE PROPOSAL, IT NEEDS WORK.
LOOK, I'M NOT ANY HAPPIER ABOUT ALL THIS THAN YOU ARE. BUT IT'S THE TRUTH. THEY THINK WE'RE THE ONES WHO WILL HELP THEM TAKE OVER THE REALMS.
WHATEVER. I DON'T CARE WHAT THEY THINK, OR WHAT YOU WANT. I'M GOING HOME.
MARY... I THINK THE WOMEN WHO HAVE BEEN DISAPPEARING WERE TAKEN BECAUSE OF YOU. THE ORDER IS PLANNING TO USE THEM SOMEHOW TO FORCE YOUR HAND. AND IF I DON'T DO SOMETHING FAST, THOSE GIRLS WILL DIE.
IF YOU'RE LYING ABOUT THIS, I SWEAR TO GOD...
I'VE NEVER LIED TO YOU. I PROBABLY SHOULD HAVE, THOUGH. IF I HAD, MAYBE YOU WOULDN'T HAVE FOLLOWED ME OUT HERE AND I WOULDN'T NEED A NEW JAW.
SORRY. MY MOTTO IS STRIKE FIRST, ASK QUESTIONS LATER.
WHICH IS EXACTLY WHY YOU NEED TO STAY HERE UNTIL I GET BACK.
HERE? YEAH, RIGHT. MY MOTEL ROOM MIGHT BE ONLY ONE STEP UP FROM A TRASH HEAP, BUT AT LEAST IT HAS FURNITURE. THIS PLACE IS STRAIGHT OUT OF A HORROR MOVIE.
MARY--

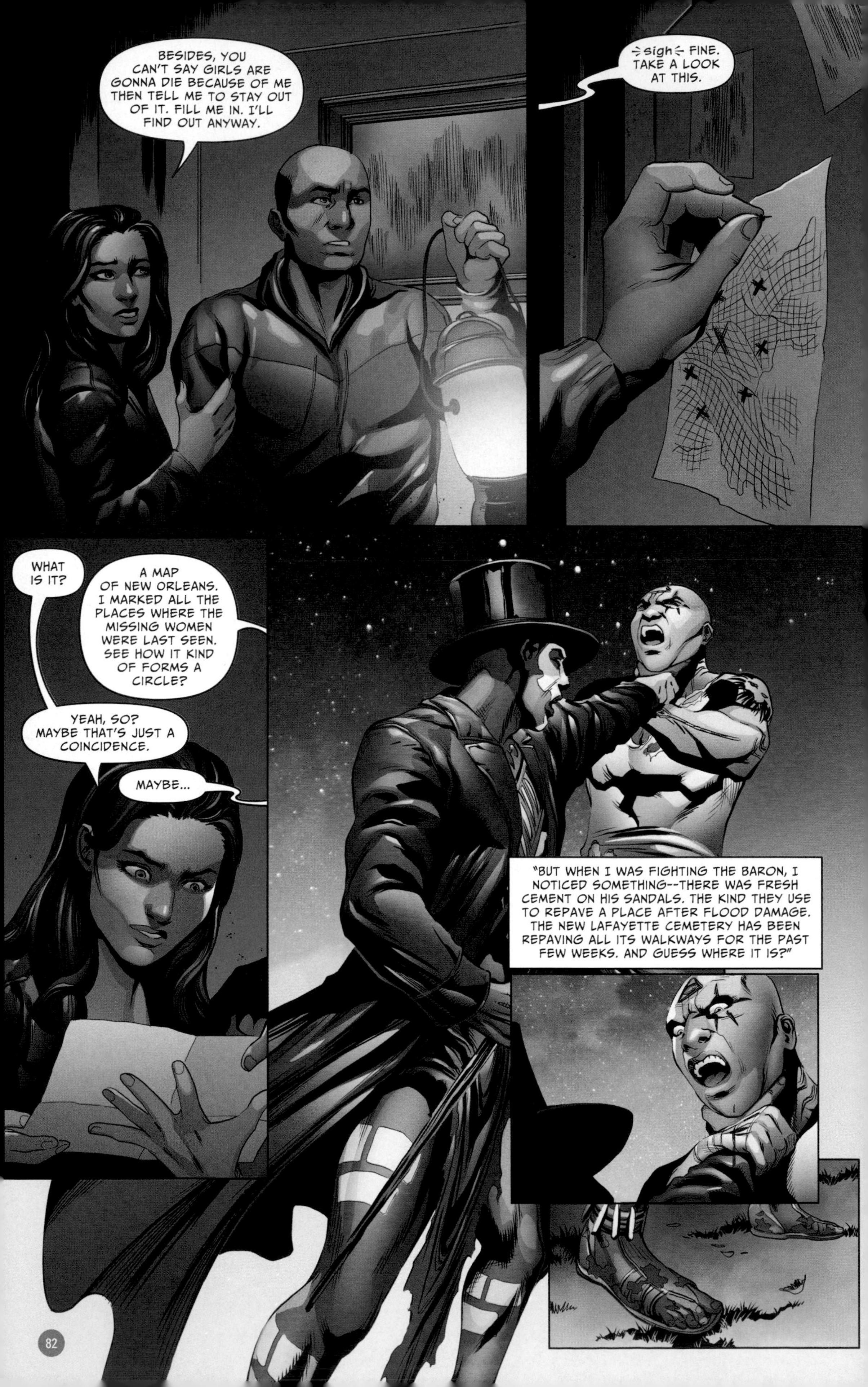
BESIDES, YOU CAN'T SAY GIRLS ARE GONNA DIE BECAUSE OF ME THEN TELL ME TO STAY OUT OF IT. FILL ME IN. I'LL FIND OUT ANYWAY.
≑sigh≑ FINE. TAKE A LOOK AT THIS.
WHAT IS IT?
A MAP OF NEW ORLEANS. I MARKED ALL THE PLACES WHERE THE MISSING WOMEN WERE LAST SEEN. SEE HOW IT KIND OF FORMS A CIRCLE?
YEAH, SO? MAYBE THAT'S JUST A COINCIDENCE.
MAYBE...
"BUT WHEN I WAS FIGHTING THE BARON, I NOTICED SOMETHING--THERE WAS FRESH CEMENT ON HIS SANDALS. THE KIND THEY USE TO REPAVE A PLACE AFTER FLOOD DAMAGE. THE NEW LAFAYETTE CEMETERY HAS BEEN REPAVING ALL ITS WALKWAYS FOR THE PAST FEW WEEKS. AND GUESS WHERE IT IS?"

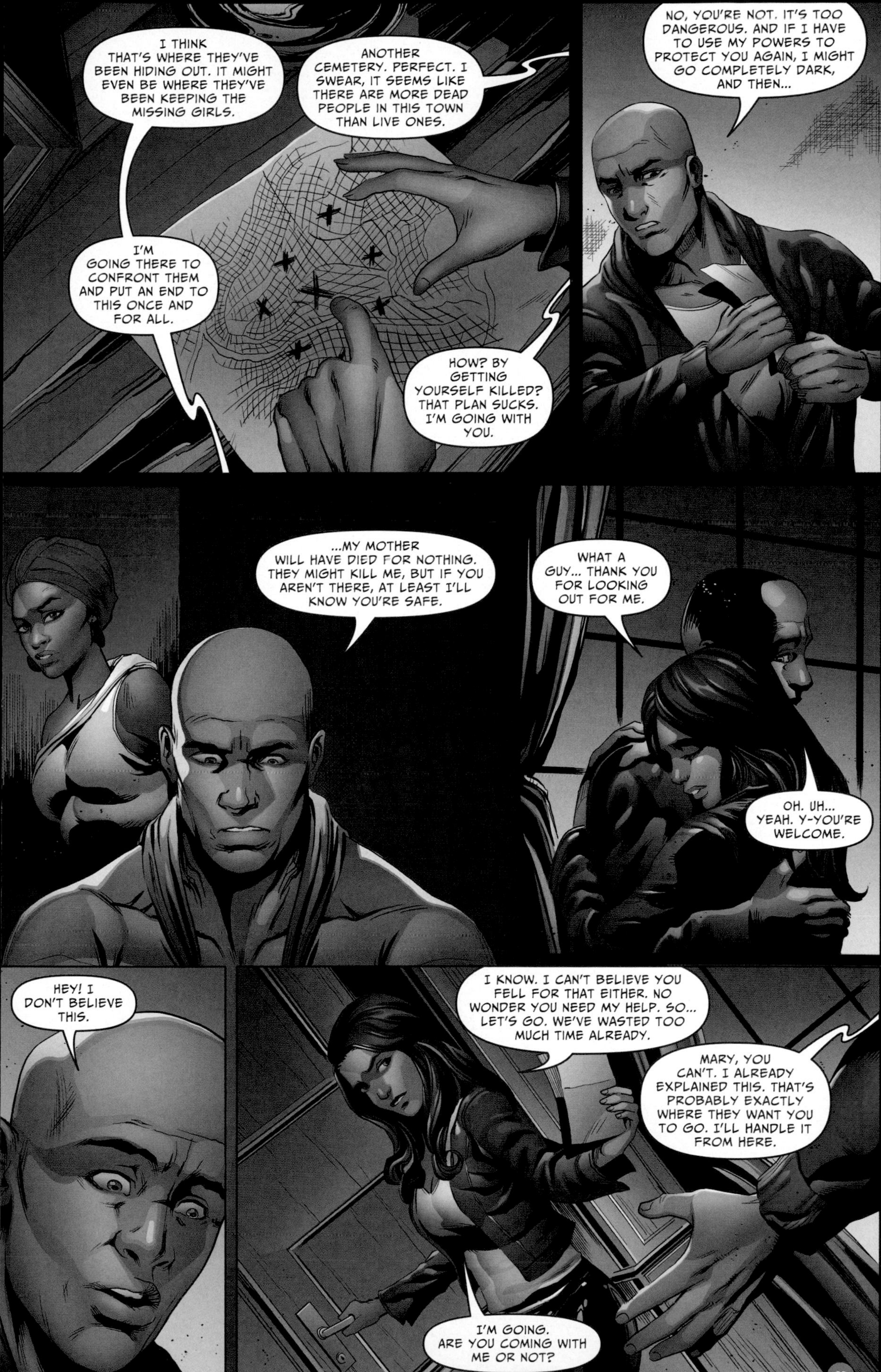
I THINK THAT'S WHERE THEY'VE BEEN HIDING OUT. IT MIGHT EVEN BE WHERE THEY'VE BEEN KEEPING THE MISSING GIRLS.
ANOTHER CEMETERY. PERFECT. I SWEAR, IT SEEMS LIKE THERE ARE MORE DEAD PEOPLE IN THIS TOWN THAN LIVE ONES.
I'M GOING THERE TO CONFRONT THEM AND PUT AN END TO THIS ONCE AND FOR ALL.
HOW? BY GETTING YOURSELF KILLED? THAT PLAN SUCKS. I'M GOING WITH YOU.
NO, YOU'RE NOT. IT'S TOO DANGEROUS. AND IF I HAVE TO USE MY POWERS TO PROTECT YOU AGAIN, I MIGHT GO COMPLETELY DARK, AND THEN...
...MY MOTHER WILL HAVE DIED FOR NOTHING. THEY MIGHT KILL ME, BUT IF YOU AREN'T THERE, AT LEAST I'LL KNOW YOU'RE SAFE.
WHAT A GUY... THANK YOU FOR LOOKING OUT FOR ME.
OH. UH... YEAH. Y-YOU'RE WELCOME.
HEY! I DON'T BELIEVE THIS.
I KNOW. I CAN'T BELIEVE YOU FELL FOR THAT EITHER. NO WONDER YOU NEED MY HELP. SO... LET'S GO. WE'VE WASTED TOO MUCH TIME ALREADY.
MARY, YOU CAN'T. I ALREADY EXPLAINED THIS. THAT'S PROBABLY EXACTLY WHERE THEY WANT YOU TO GO. I'LL HANDLE IT FROM HERE.
I'M GOING. ARE YOU COMING WITH ME OR NOT?

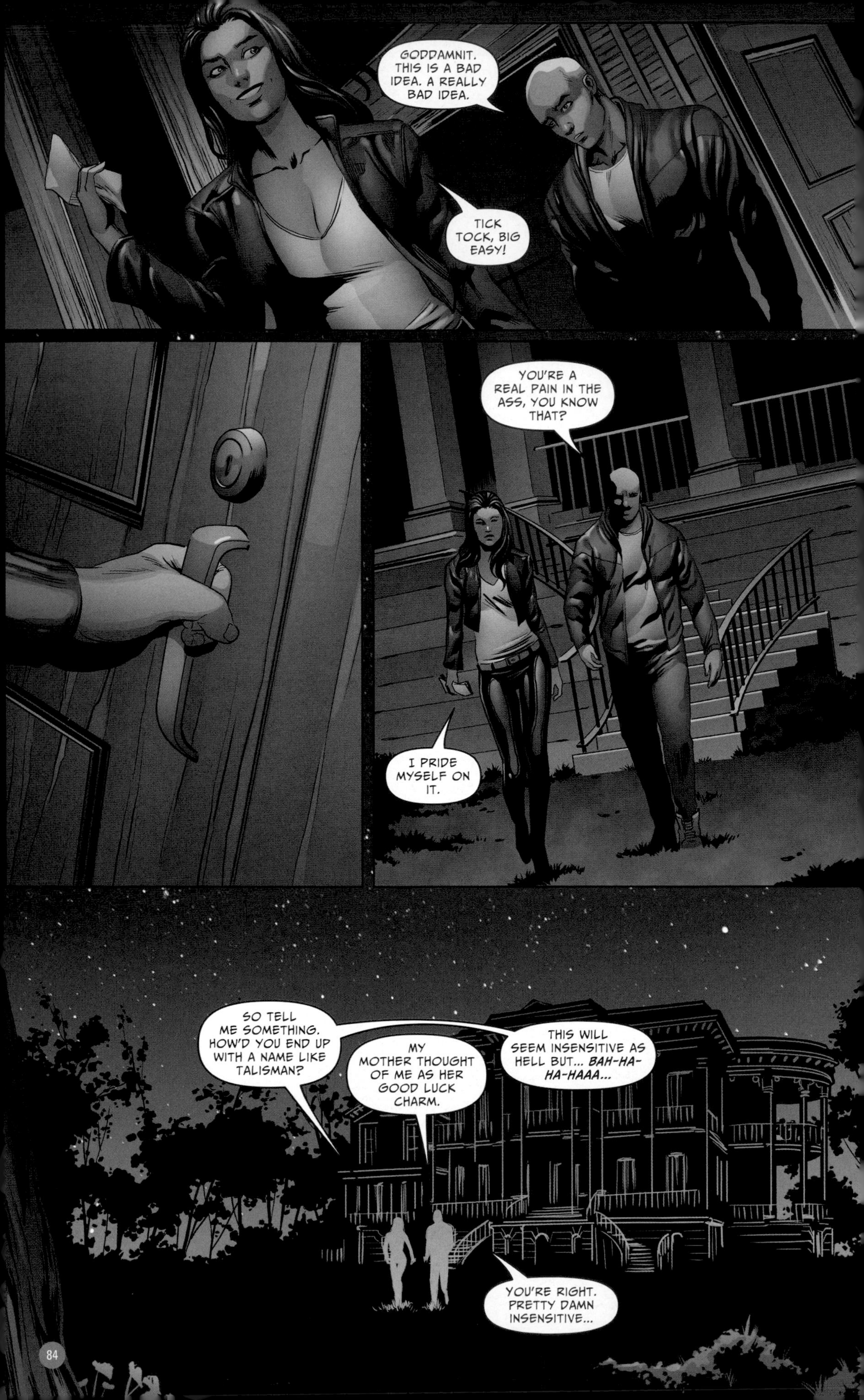
GODDAMNIT. THIS IS A BAD IDEA. A REALLY BAD IDEA.
TICK TOCK, BIG EASY!
YOU'RE A REAL PAIN IN THE ASS, YOU KNOW THAT?
I PRIDE MYSELF ON IT.
SO TELL ME SOMETHING. HOW'D YOU END UP WITH A NAME LIKE TALISMAN?
MY MOTHER THOUGHT OF ME AS HER GOOD LUCK CHARM.
THIS WILL SEEM INSENSITIVE AS HELL BUT... *BAH-HA-HA-HAAA...*
YOU'RE RIGHT. PRETTY DAMN INSENSITIVE...

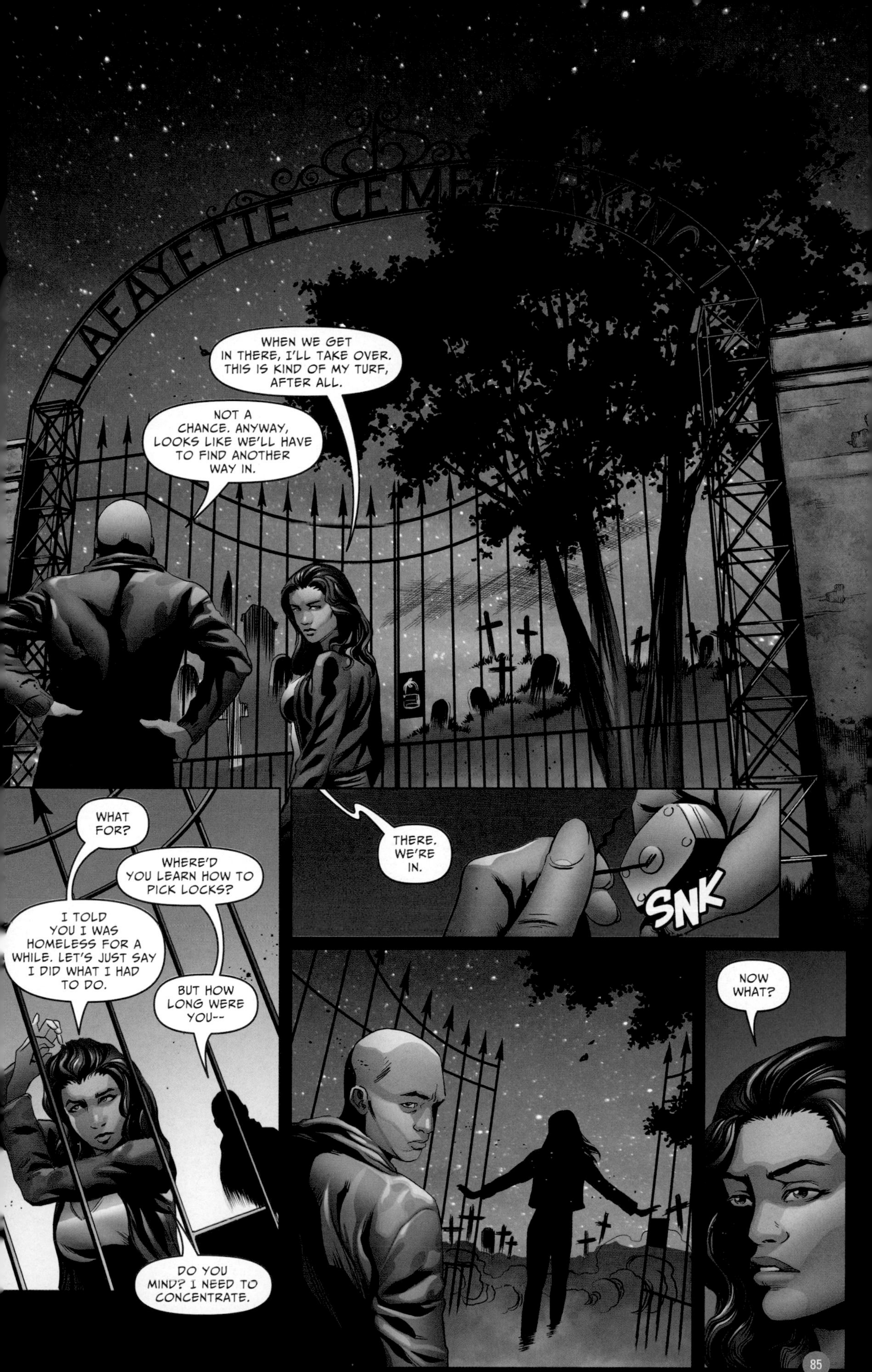
LAFAYETTE CEME
WHEN WE GET IN THERE, I'LL TAKE OVER. THIS IS KIND OF MY TURF, AFTER ALL.
NOT A CHANCE. ANYWAY, LOOKS LIKE WE'LL HAVE TO FIND ANOTHER WAY IN.
WHAT FOR?
WHERE'D YOU LEARN HOW TO PICK LOCKS?
I TOLD YOU I WAS HOMELESS FOR A WHILE. LET'S JUST SAY I DID WHAT I HAD TO DO.
BUT HOW LONG WERE YOU--
DO YOU MIND? I NEED TO CONCENTRATE.
THERE. WE'RE IN.
SNK
NOW WHAT?

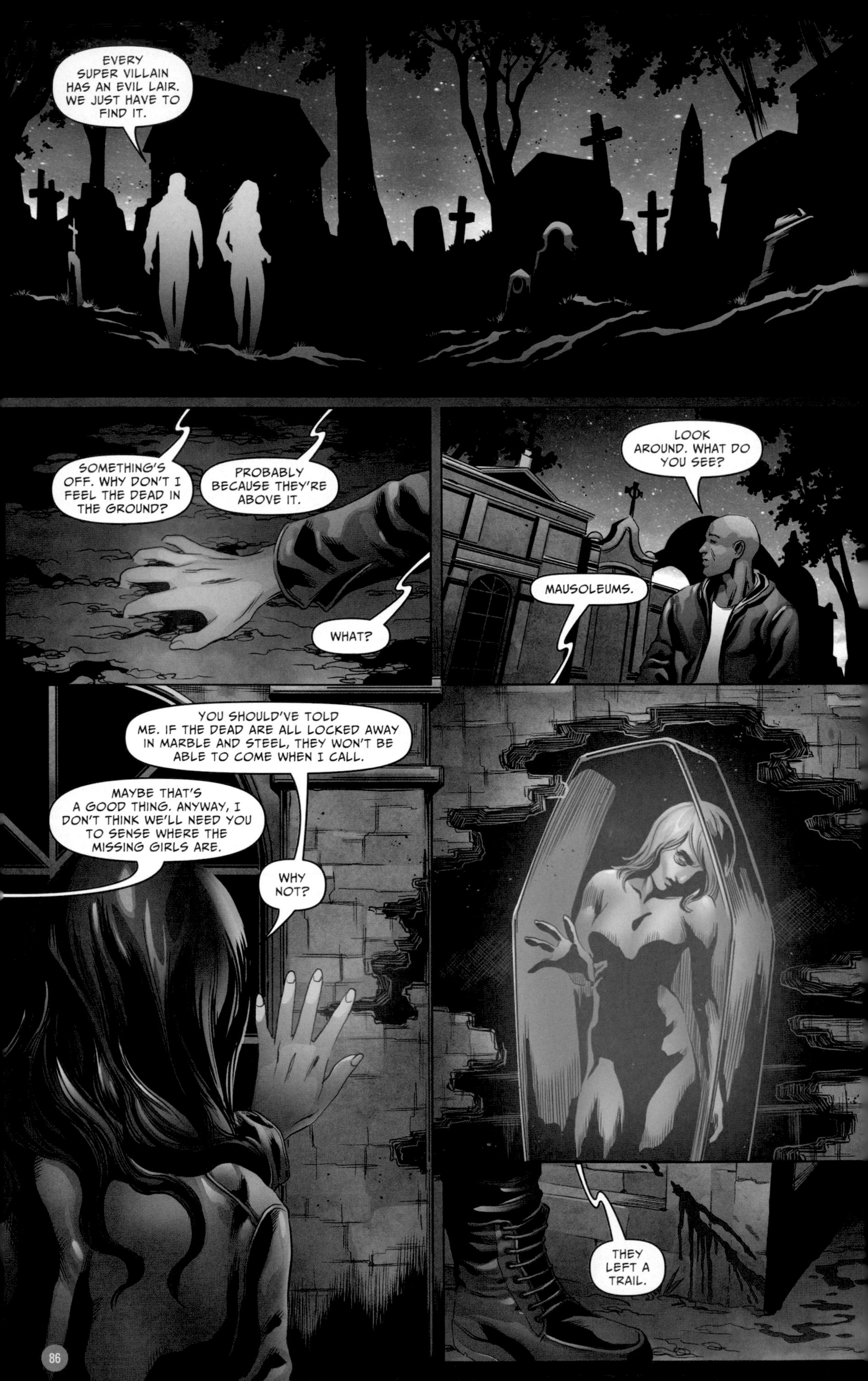
EVERY SUPER VILLAIN HAS AN EVIL LAIR. WE JUST HAVE TO FIND IT.
SOMETHING'S OFF. WHY DON'T I FEEL THE DEAD IN THE GROUND?
PROBABLY BECAUSE THEY'RE ABOVE IT.
WHAT?
LOOK AROUND. WHAT DO YOU SEE?
MAUSOLEUMS.
YOU SHOULD'VE TOLD ME. IF THE DEAD ARE ALL LOCKED AWAY IN MARBLE AND STEEL, THEY WON'T BE ABLE TO COME WHEN I CALL.
MAYBE THAT'S A GOOD THING. ANYWAY, I DON'T THINK WE'LL NEED YOU TO SENSE WHERE THE MISSING GIRLS ARE.
WHY NOT?
THEY LEFT A TRAIL.

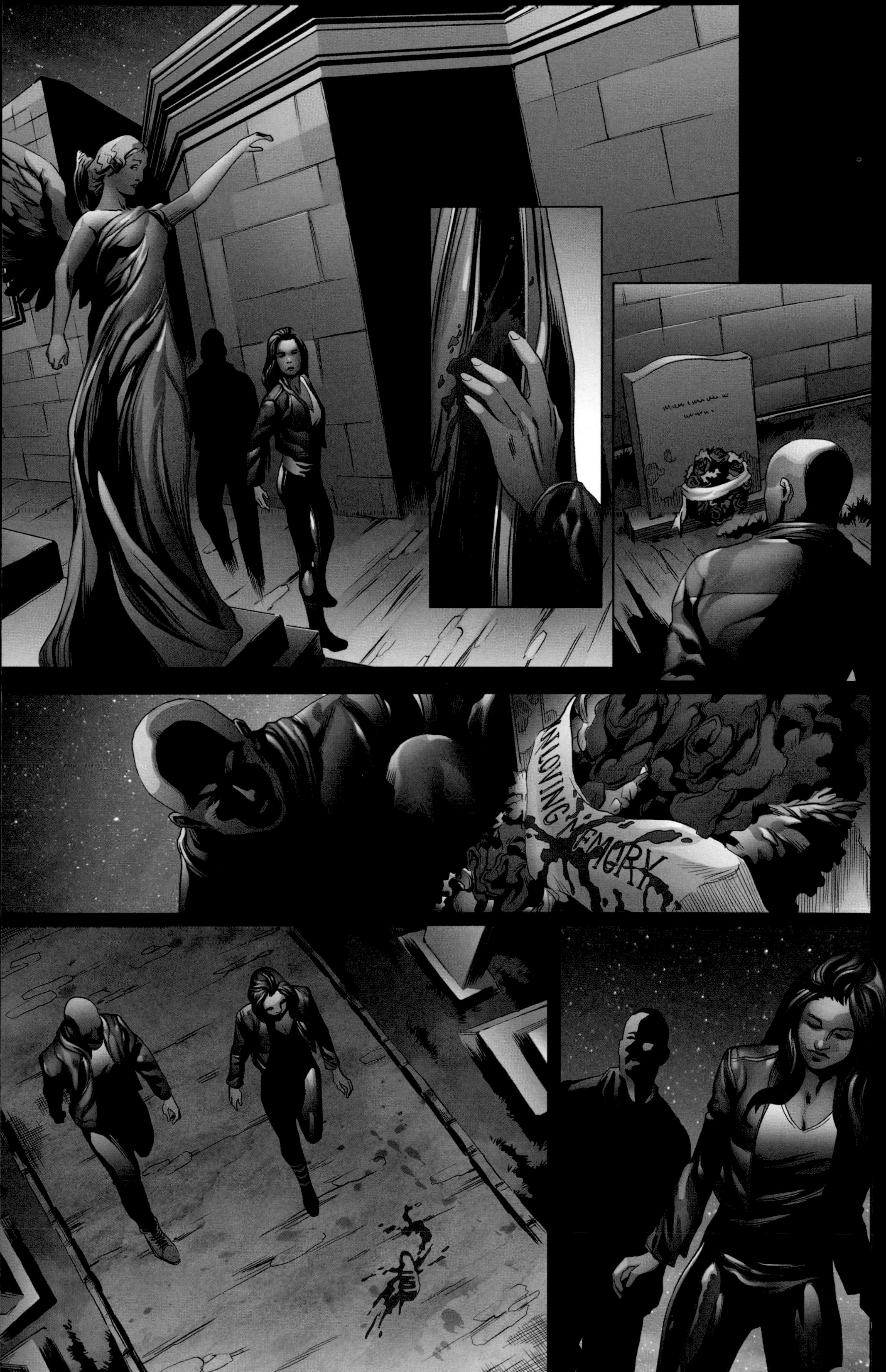
N LOVING MEMORY

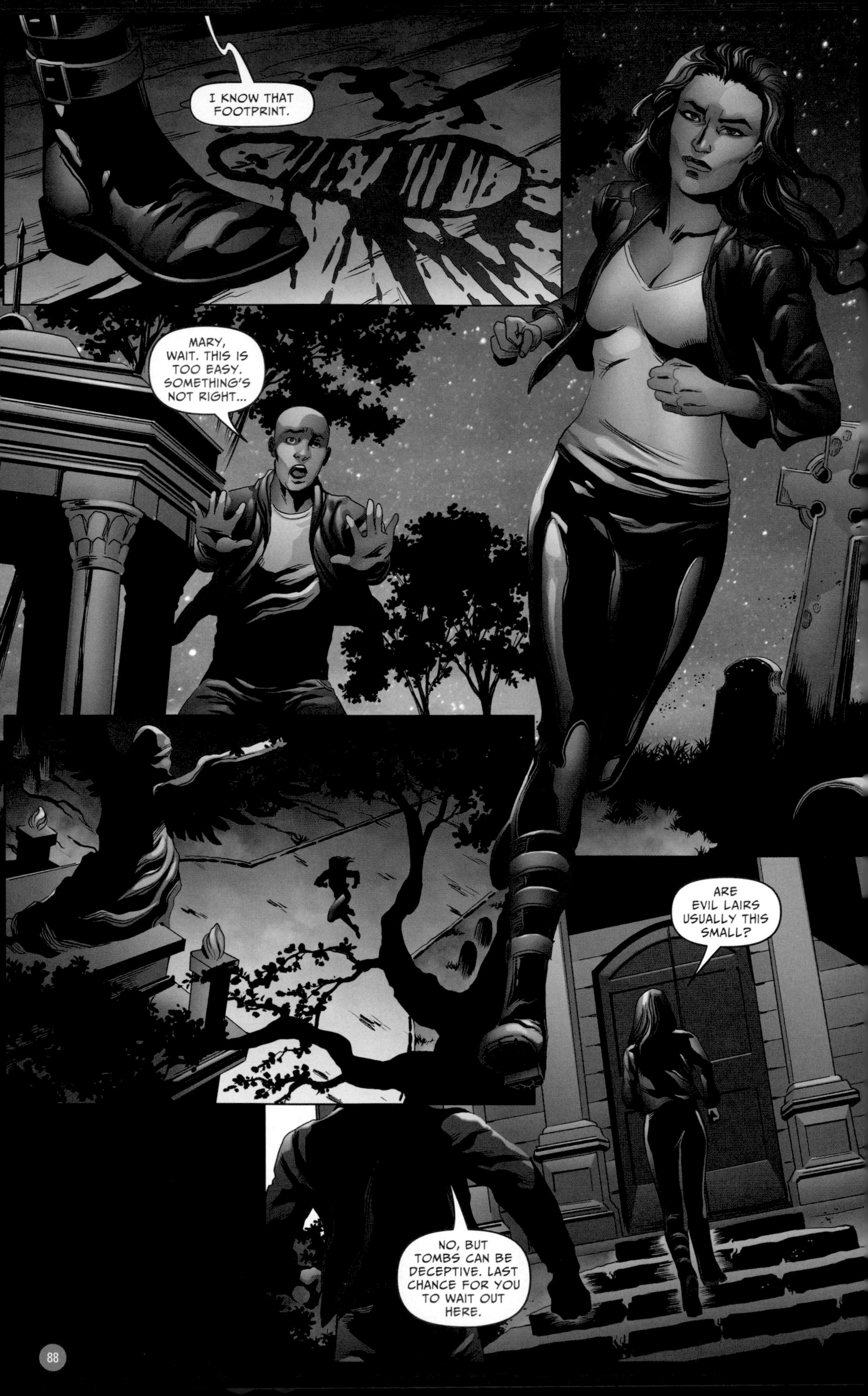
I KNOW THAT FOOTPRINT.
MARY, WAIT. THIS IS TOO EASY. SOMETHING'S NOT RIGHT...
ARE EVIL LAIRS USUALLY THIS SMALL?
NO, BUT TOMBS CAN BE DECEPTIVE. LAST CHANCE FOR YOU TO WAIT OUT HERE.

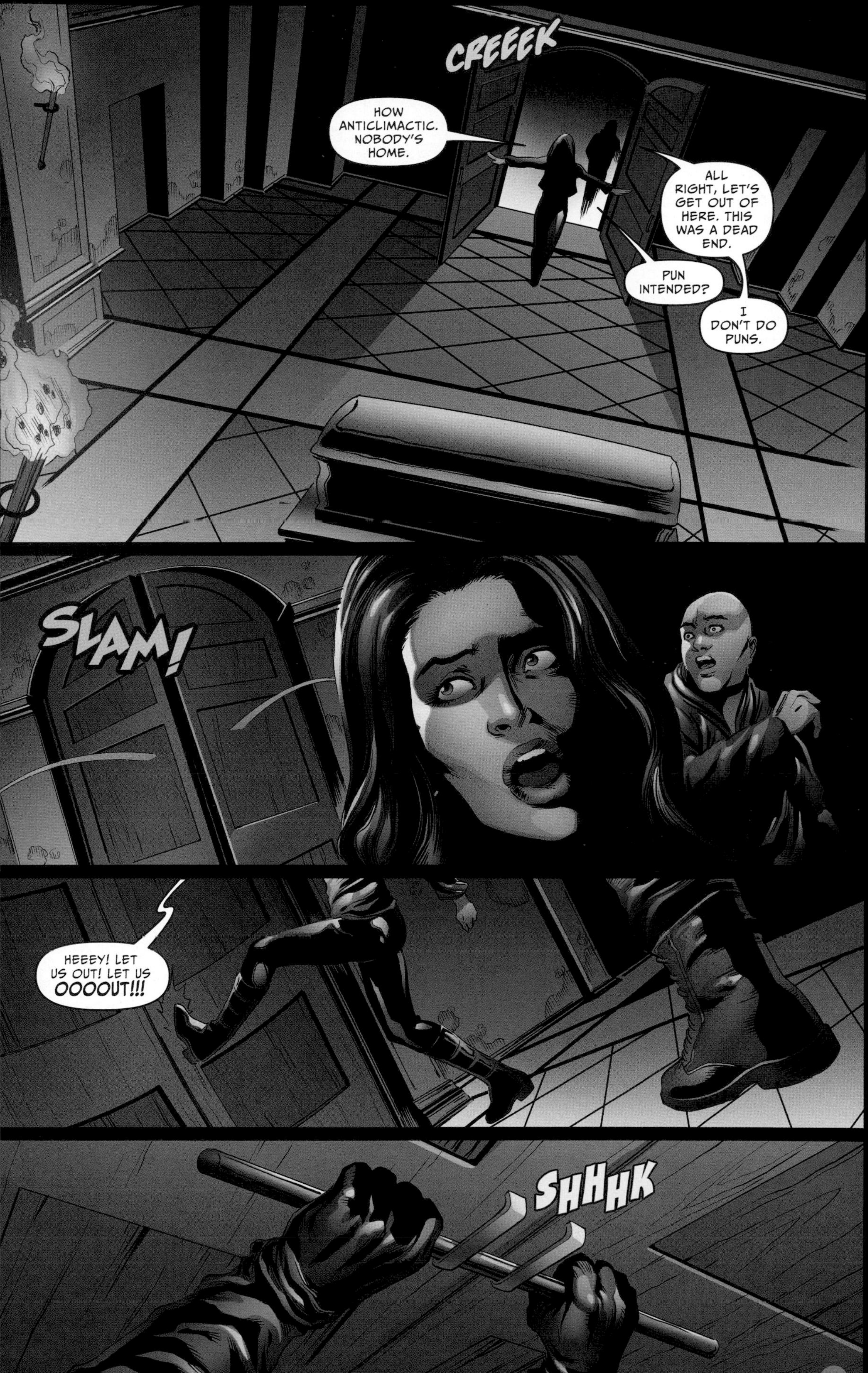
CREEEK
HOW ANTICLIMACTIC. NOBODY'S HOME.
ALL RIGHT, LET'S GET OUT OF HERE. THIS WAS A DEAD END.
PUN INTENDED?
I DON'T DO PUNS.
SLAM!
HEEEY! LET US OUT! LET US OOOOUT!!!
SHHHK

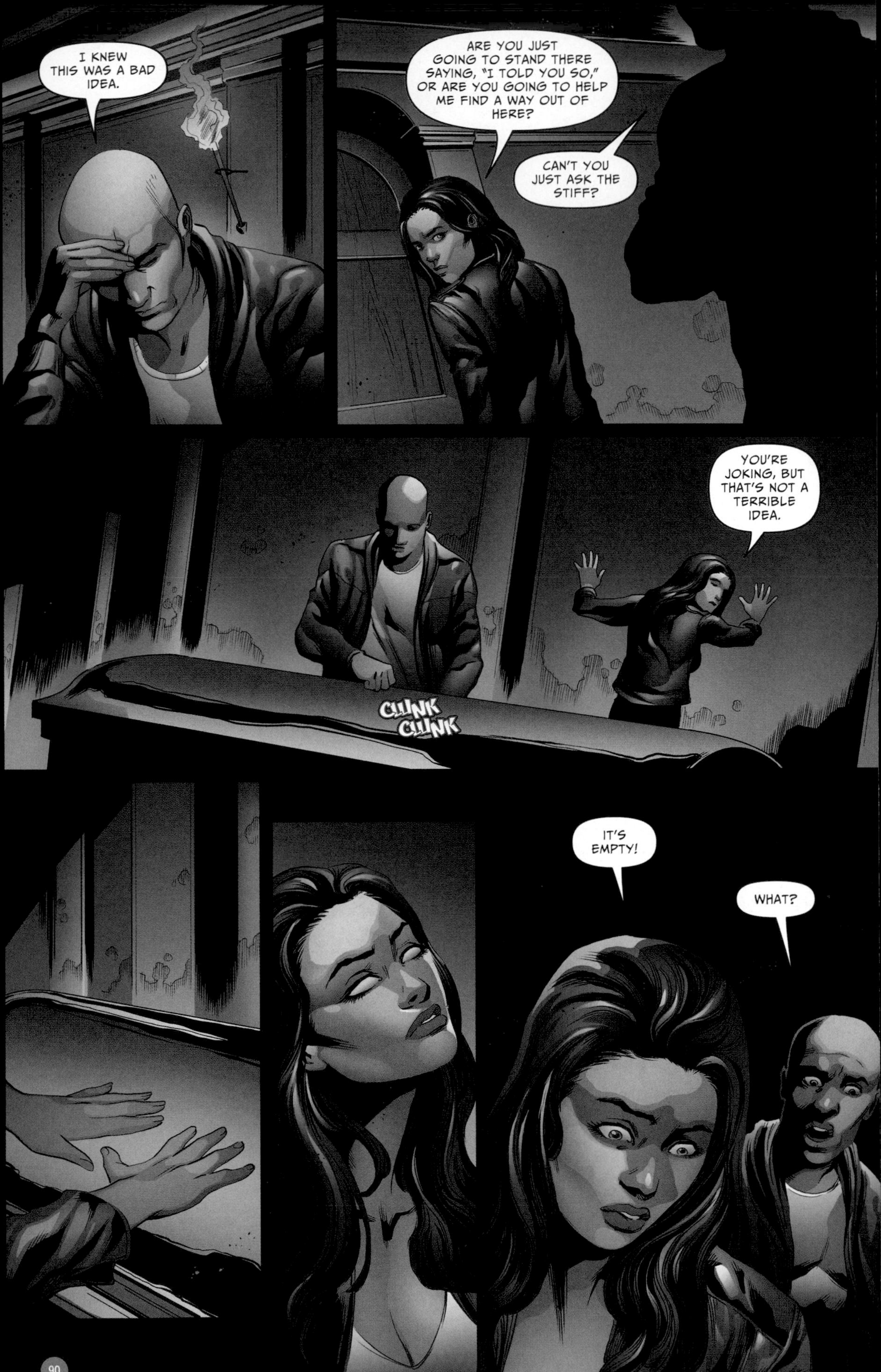
I KNEW THIS WAS A BAD IDEA.
ARE YOU JUST GOING TO STAND THERE SAYING, "I TOLD YOU SO," OR ARE YOU GOING TO HELP ME FIND A WAY OUT OF HERE?
CAN'T YOU JUST ASK THE STIFF?
YOU'RE JOKING, BUT THAT'S NOT A TERRIBLE IDEA.
CLINK CLINK
IT'S EMPTY!
WHAT?

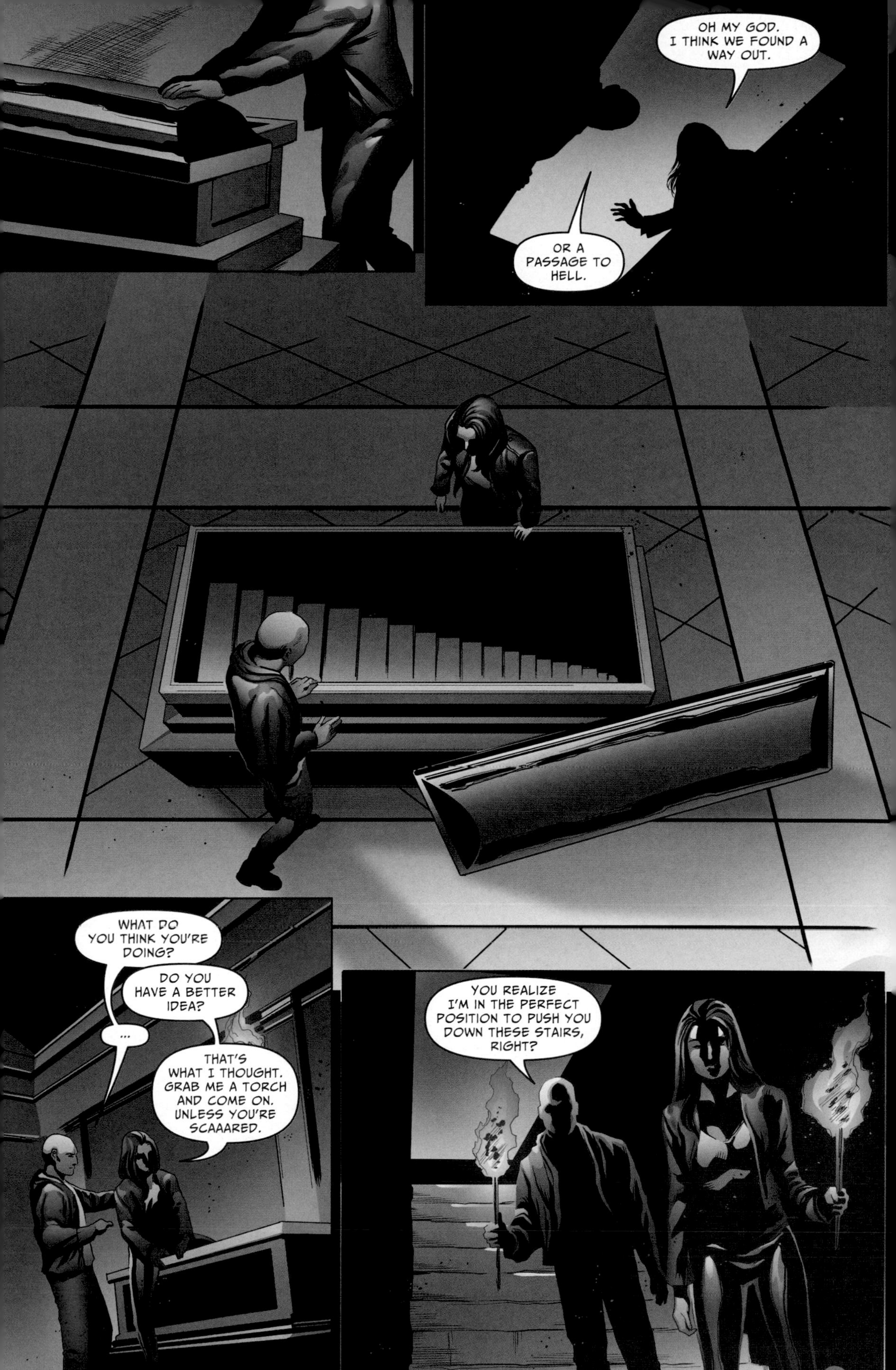
OH MY GOD. I THINK WE FOUND A WAY OUT.
OR A PASSAGE TO HELL.
WHAT DO YOU THINK YOU'RE DOING?
DO YOU HAVE A BETTER IDEA?
...
THAT'S WHAT I THOUGHT. GRAB ME A TORCH AND COME ON. UNLESS YOU'RE SCAAARED.
YOU REALIZE I'M IN THE PERFECT POSITION TO PUSH YOU DOWN THESE STAIRS, RIGHT?

I'VE MADE SOME BAD CALLS IN MY LIFE. TOOK LOTS OF WRONG TURNS.

AND YOU MIGHT BE THINKING THIS SEEMS LIKE ONE MORE...

I THINK IT'S A MAZE.

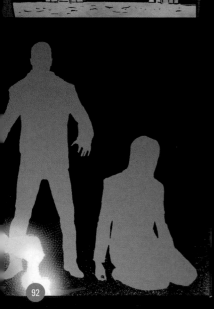

AND YOU WOULD BE RIGHT.

NOOOOO!!

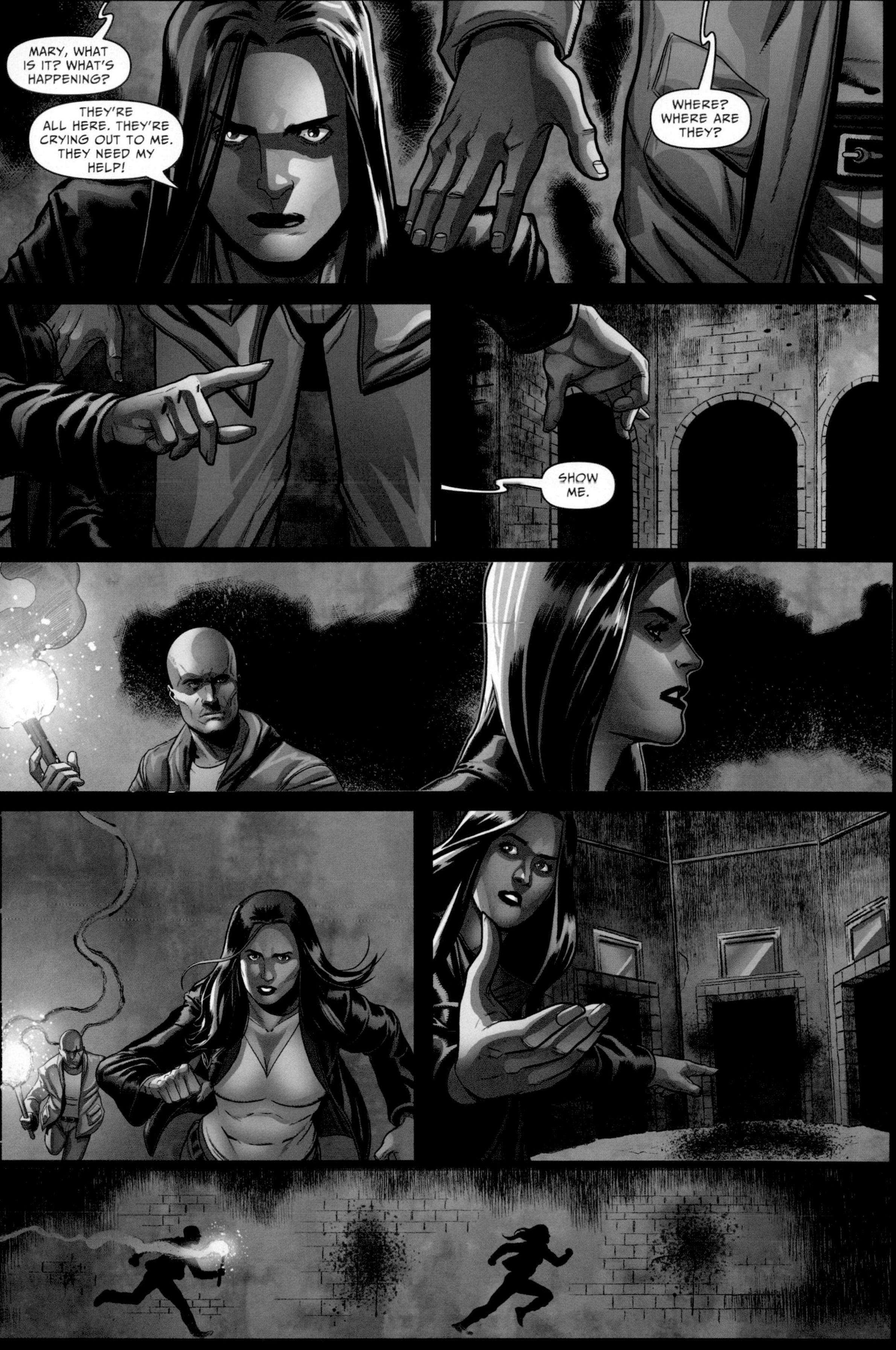
MARY, WHAT IS IT? WHAT'S HAPPENING?
THEY'RE ALL HERE. THEY'RE CRYING OUT TO ME. THEY NEED MY HELP!
WHERE? WHERE ARE THEY?
SHOW ME.

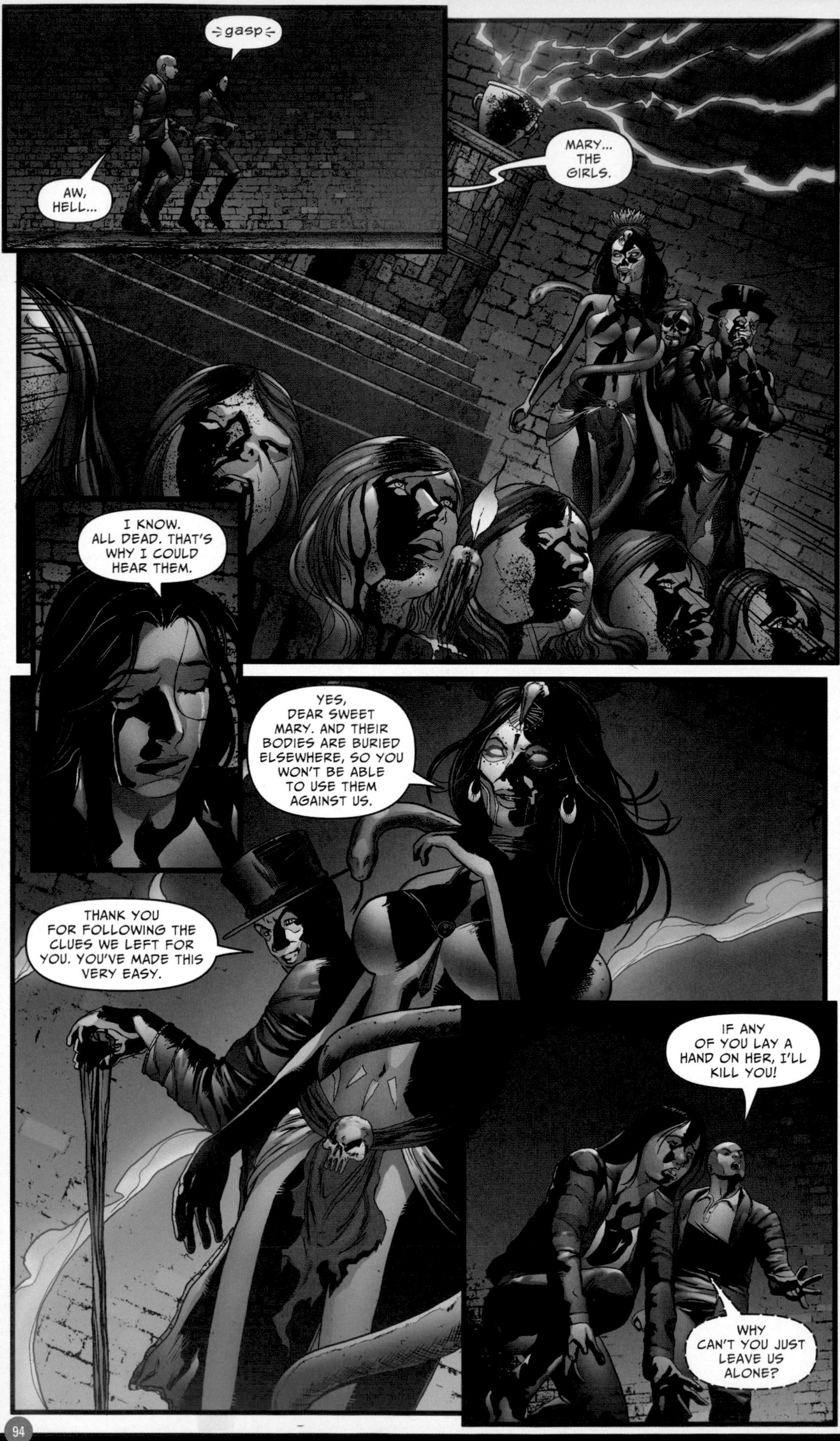
gasp
AW, HELL...
MARY... THE GIRLS.
I KNOW. ALL DEAD. THAT'S WHY I COULD HEAR THEM.
YES, DEAR SWEET MARY. AND THEIR BODIES ARE BURIED ELSEWHERE, SO YOU WON'T BE ABLE TO USE THEM AGAINST US.
THANK YOU FOR FOLLOWING THE CLUES WE LEFT FOR YOU. YOU'VE MADE THIS VERY EASY.
IF ANY OF YOU LAY A HAND ON HER, I'LL KILL YOU!
WHY CAN'T YOU JUST LEAVE US ALONE?

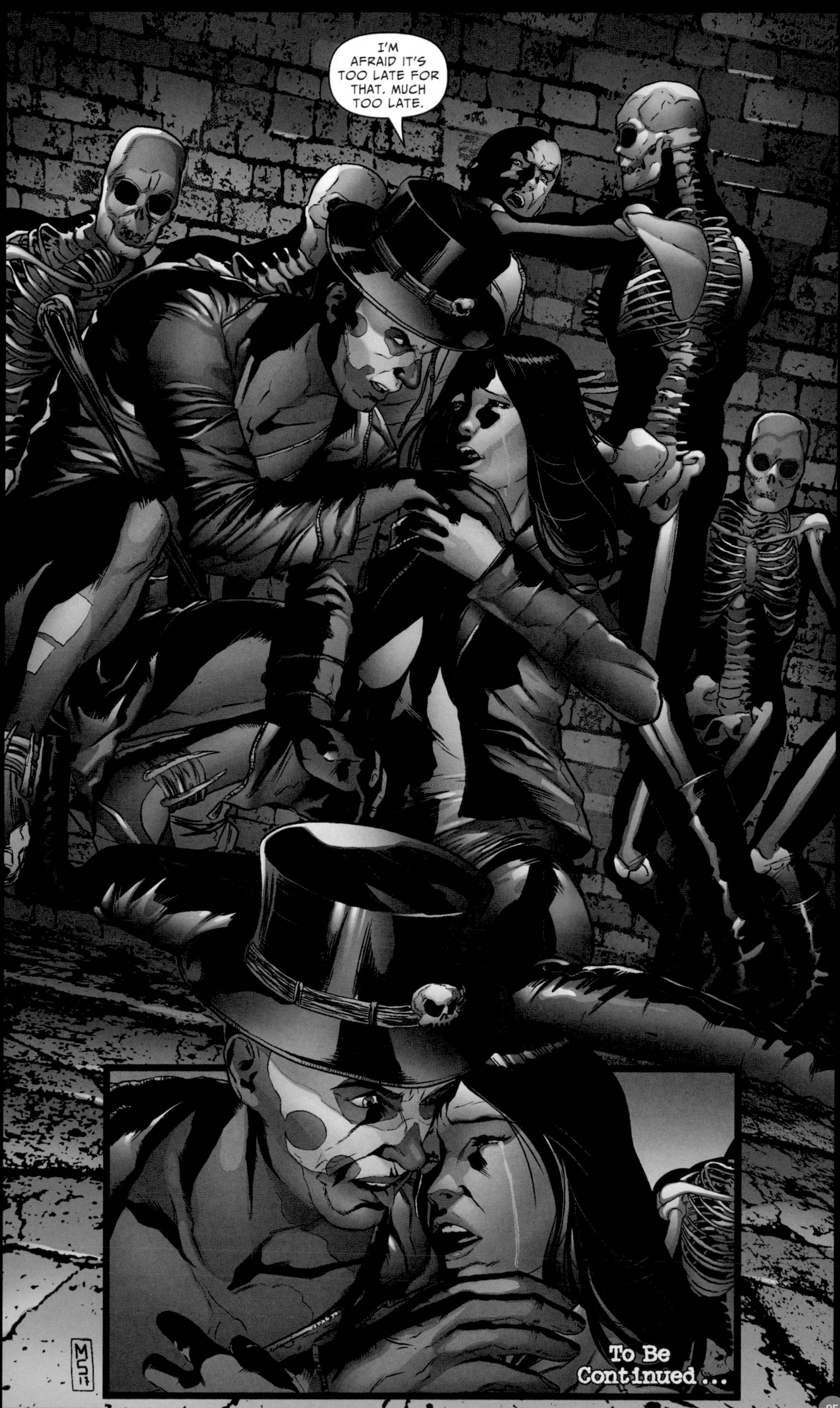
I'M AFRAID IT'S TOO LATE FOR THAT. MUCH TOO LATE.
To Be Continued...

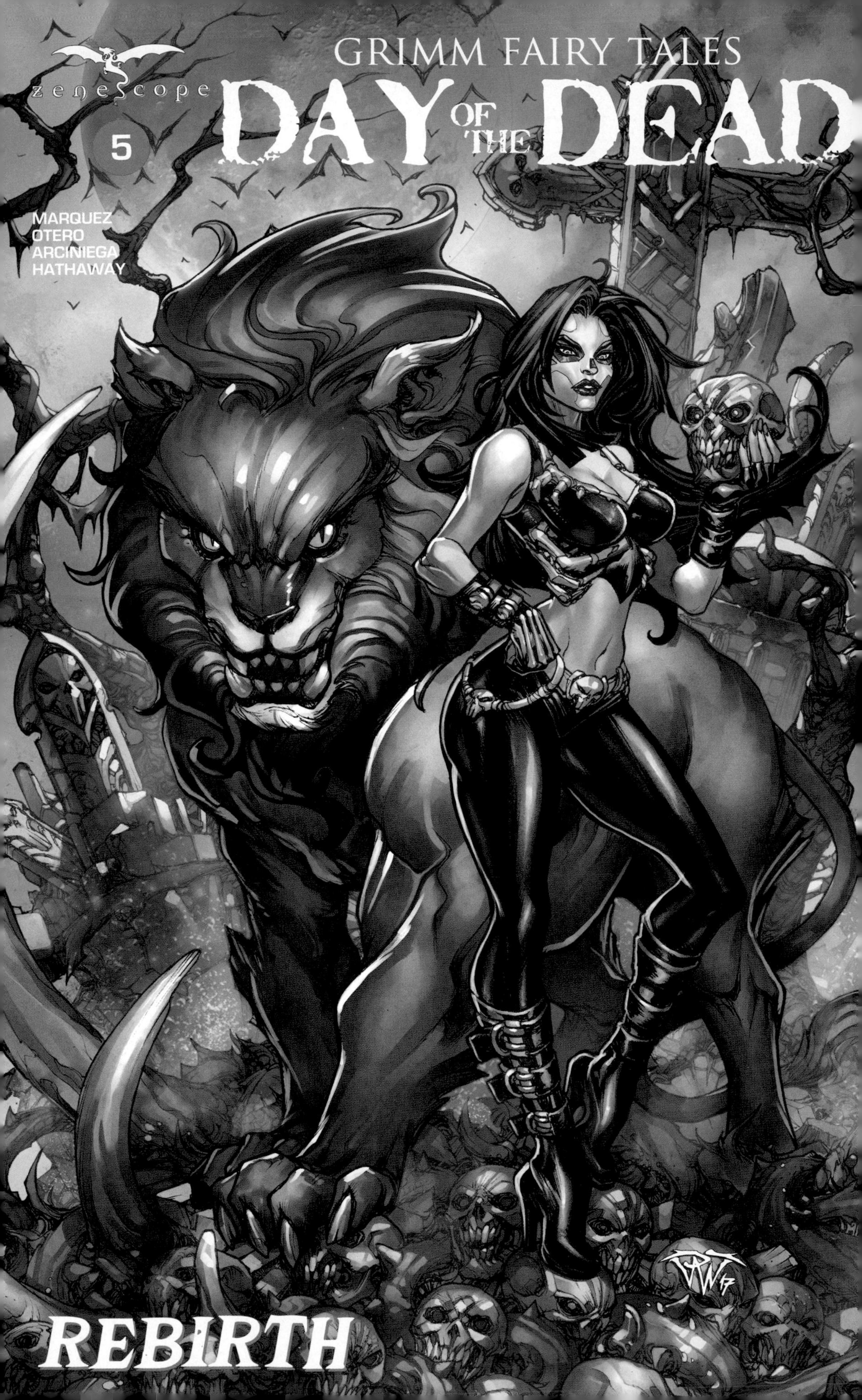

zenescope
GRIMM FAIRY TALES
DAY OF THE DEAD
5
MARQUEZ
OTERO
ARCINIEGA
HATHAWAY
REBIRTH

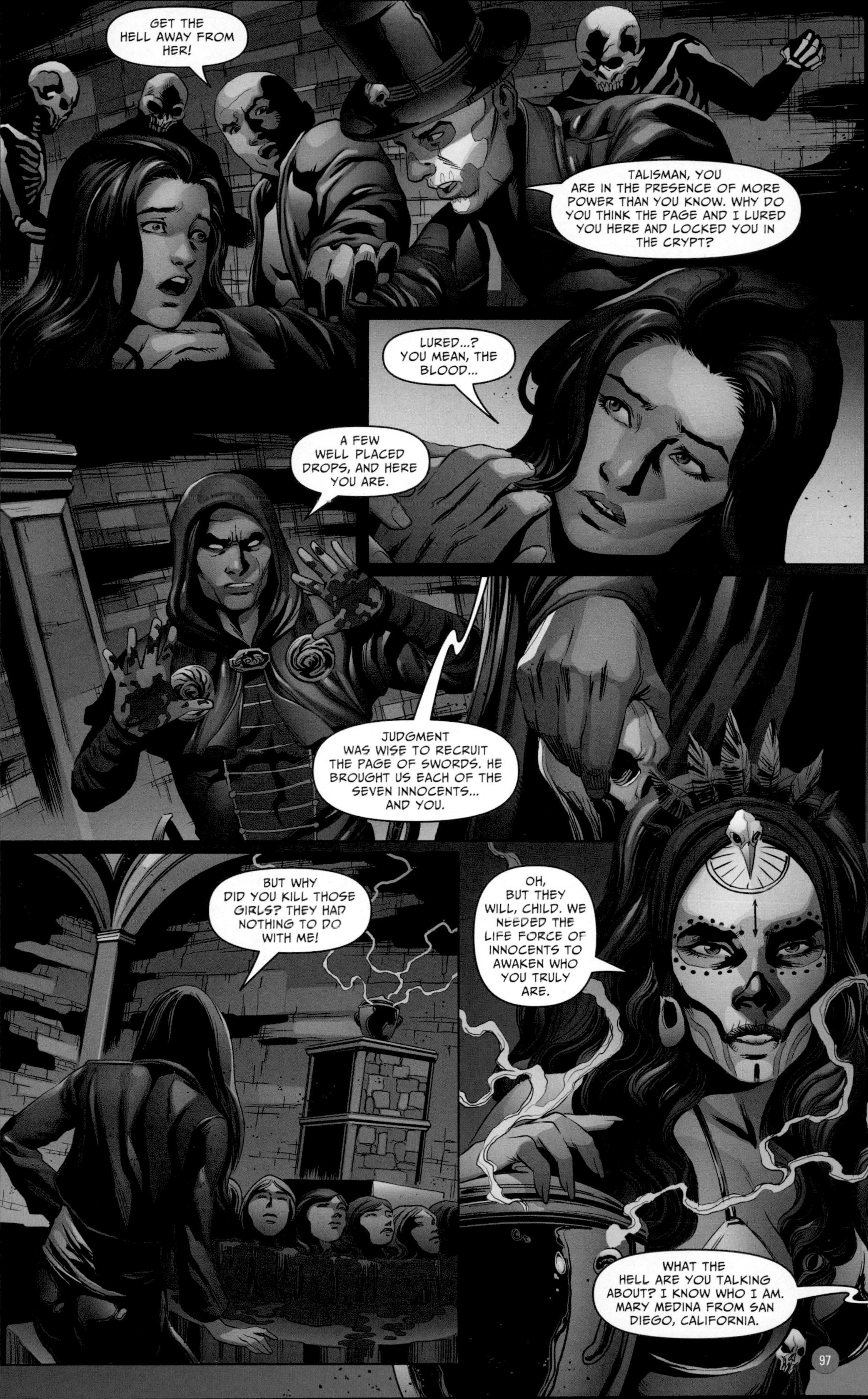
GET THE HELL AWAY FROM HER!
TALISMAN, YOU ARE IN THE PRESENCE OF MORE POWER THAN YOU KNOW. WHY DO YOU THINK THE PAGE AND I LURED YOU HERE AND LOCKED YOU IN THE CRYPT?
LURED...? YOU MEAN, THE BLOOD...
A FEW WELL PLACED DROPS, AND HERE YOU ARE.
JUDGMENT WAS WISE TO RECRUIT THE PAGE OF SWORDS. HE BROUGHT US EACH OF THE SEVEN INNOCENTS... AND YOU.
BUT WHY DID YOU KILL THOSE GIRLS? THEY HAD NOTHING TO DO WITH ME!
OH, BUT THEY WILL, CHILD. WE NEEDED THE LIFE FORCE OF INNOCENTS TO AWAKEN WHO YOU TRULY ARE.
WHAT THE HELL ARE YOU TALKING ABOUT? I KNOW WHO I AM. MARY MEDINA FROM SAN DIEGO, CALIFORNIA.

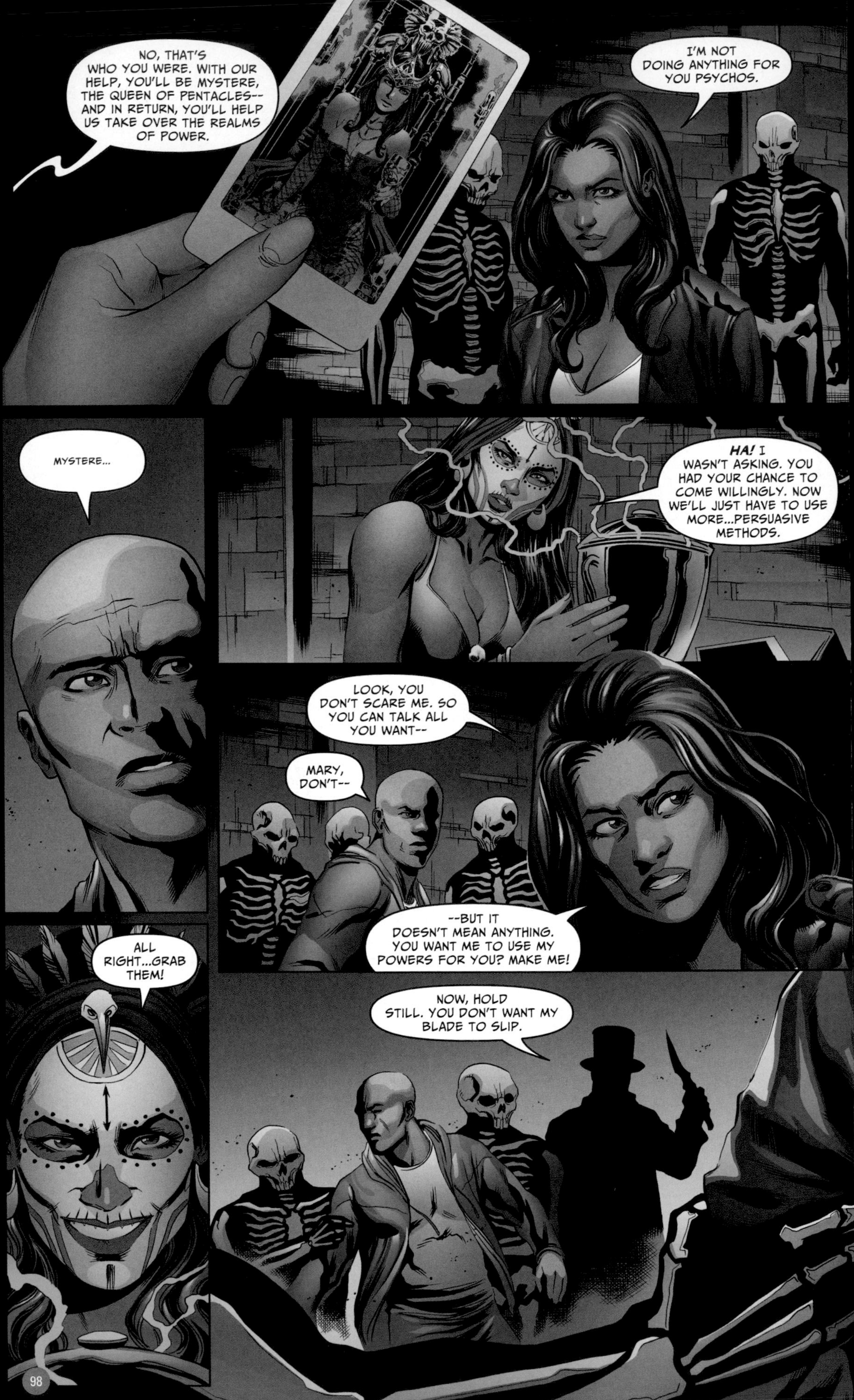
NO, THAT'S WHO YOU WERE. WITH OUR HELP, YOU'LL BE MYSTERE, THE QUEEN OF PENTACLES--AND IN RETURN, YOU'LL HELP US TAKE OVER THE REALMS OF POWER.
I'M NOT DOING ANYTHING FOR YOU PSYCHOS.
MYSTERE...
HA! I WASN'T ASKING. YOU HAD YOUR CHANCE TO COME WILLINGLY. NOW WE'LL JUST HAVE TO USE MORE...PERSUASIVE METHODS.
LOOK, YOU DON'T SCARE ME. SO YOU CAN TALK ALL YOU WANT--
MARY, DON'T--
--BUT IT DOESN'T MEAN ANYTHING. YOU WANT ME TO USE MY POWERS FOR YOU? MAKE ME!
ALL RIGHT...GRAB THEM!
NOW, HOLD STILL. YOU DON'T WANT MY BLADE TO SLIP.

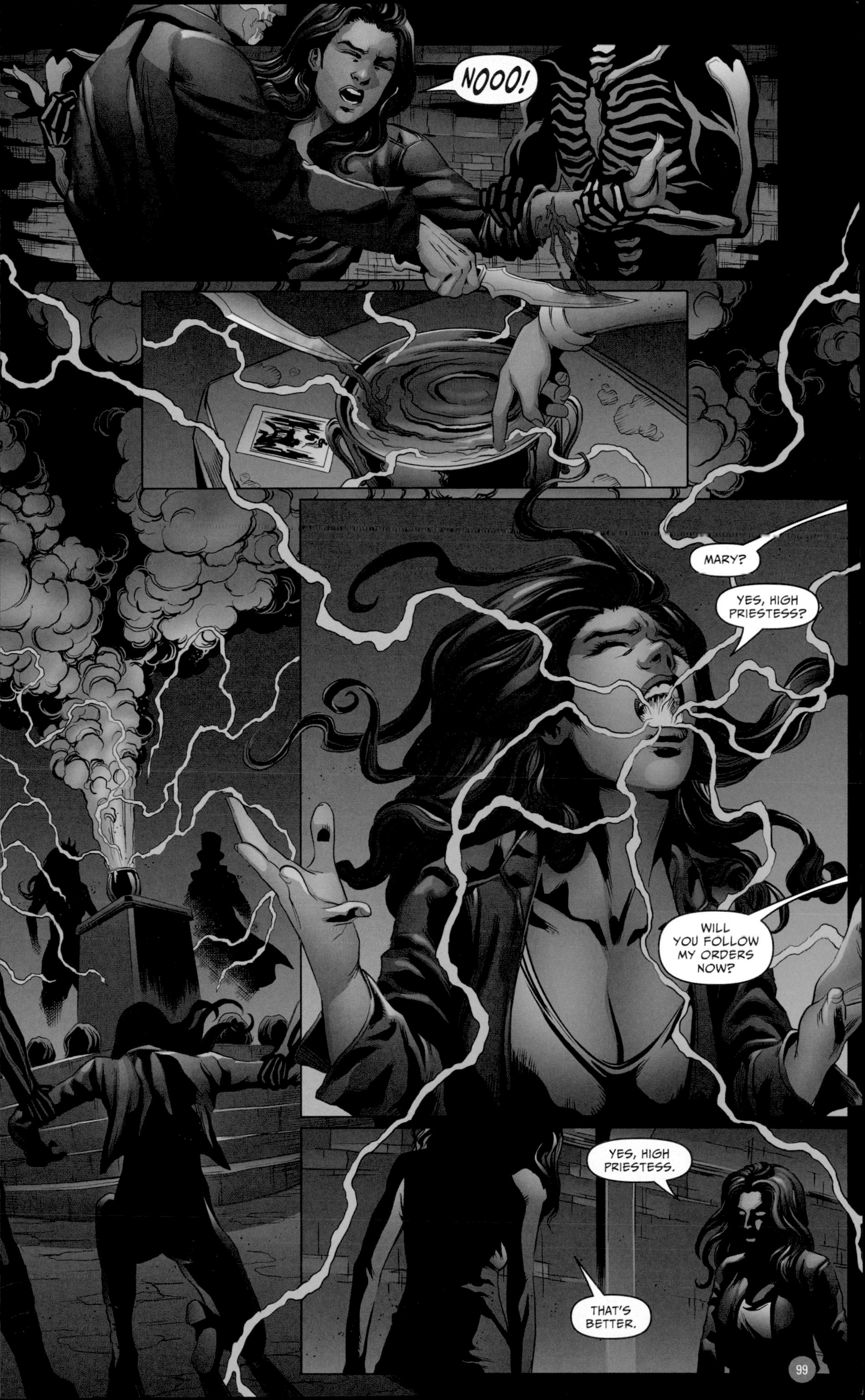

NOOO!
MARY?
YES, HIGH PRIESTESS?
WILL YOU FOLLOW MY ORDERS NOW?
YES, HIGH PRIESTESS.
THAT'S BETTER.

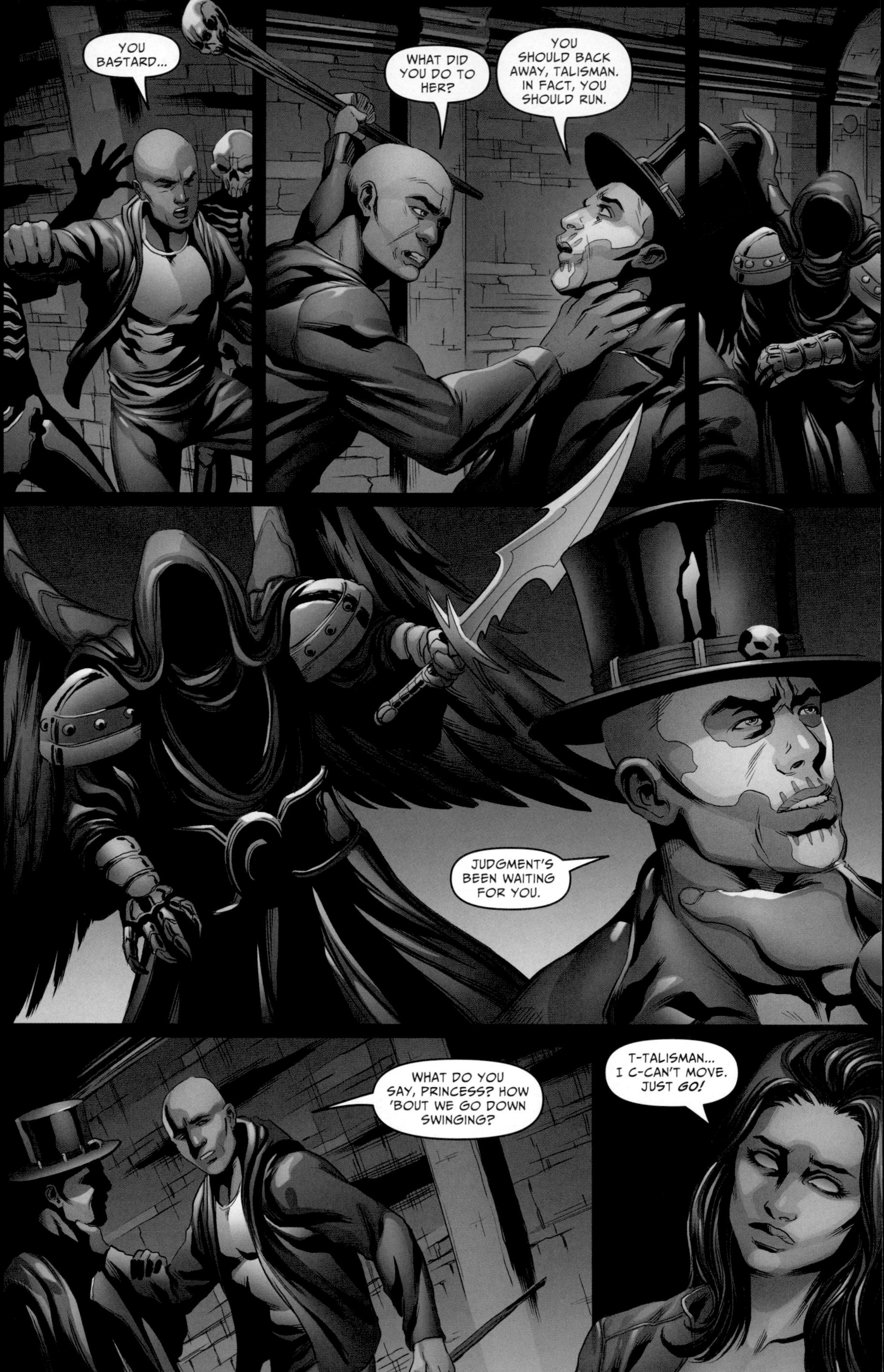
YOU BASTARD...
WHAT DID YOU DO TO HER?
YOU SHOULD BACK AWAY, TALISMAN. IN FACT, YOU SHOULD RUN.
JUDGMENT'S BEEN WAITING FOR YOU.
WHAT DO YOU SAY, PRINCESS? HOW 'BOUT WE GO DOWN SWINGING?
T-TALISMAN... I C-CAN'T MOVE. JUST *GO!*

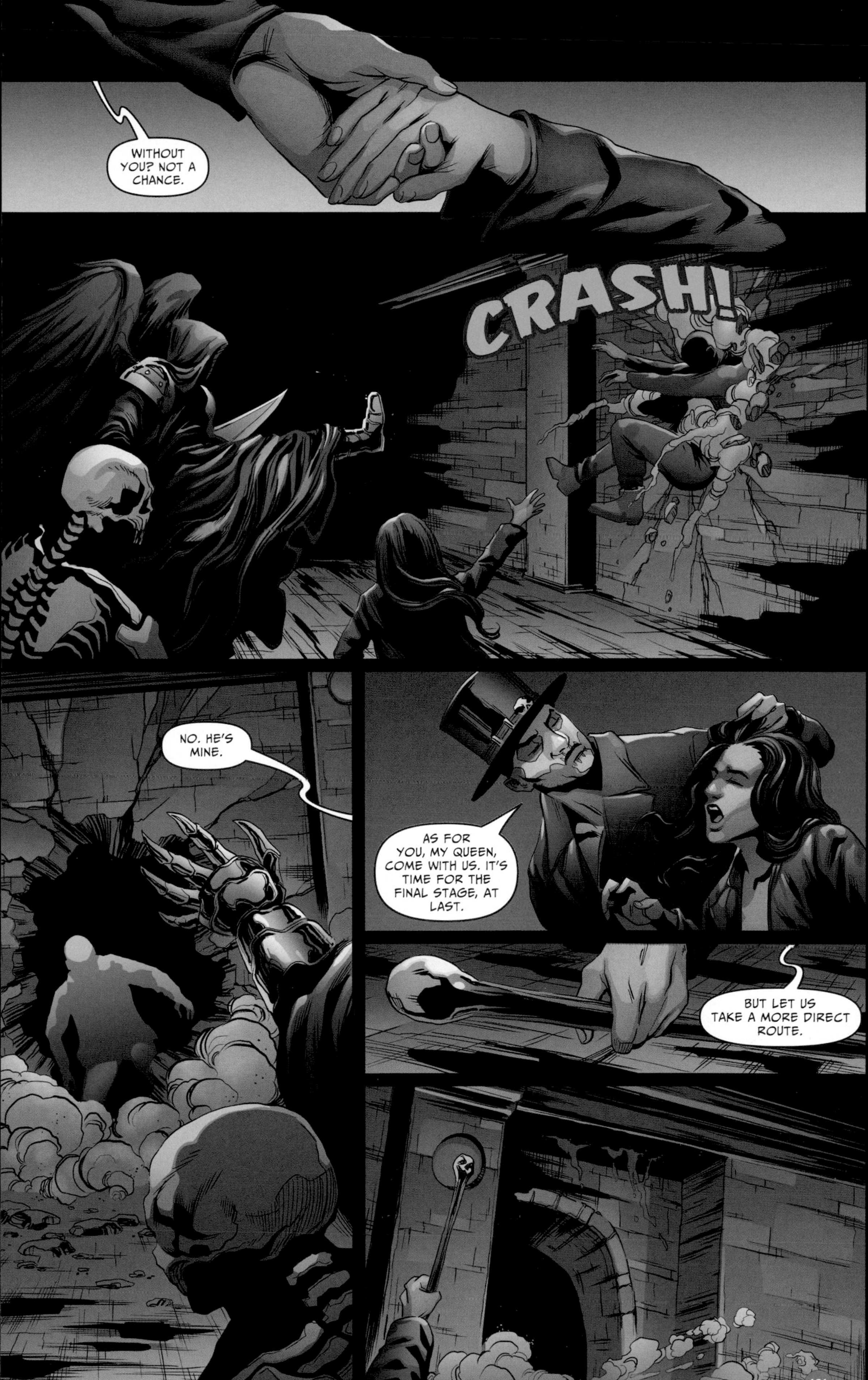
WITHOUT YOU? NOT A CHANCE.
CRASH!
NO. HE'S MINE.
AS FOR YOU, MY QUEEN, COME WITH US. IT'S TIME FOR THE FINAL STAGE, AT LAST.
BUT LET US TAKE A MORE DIRECT ROUTE.

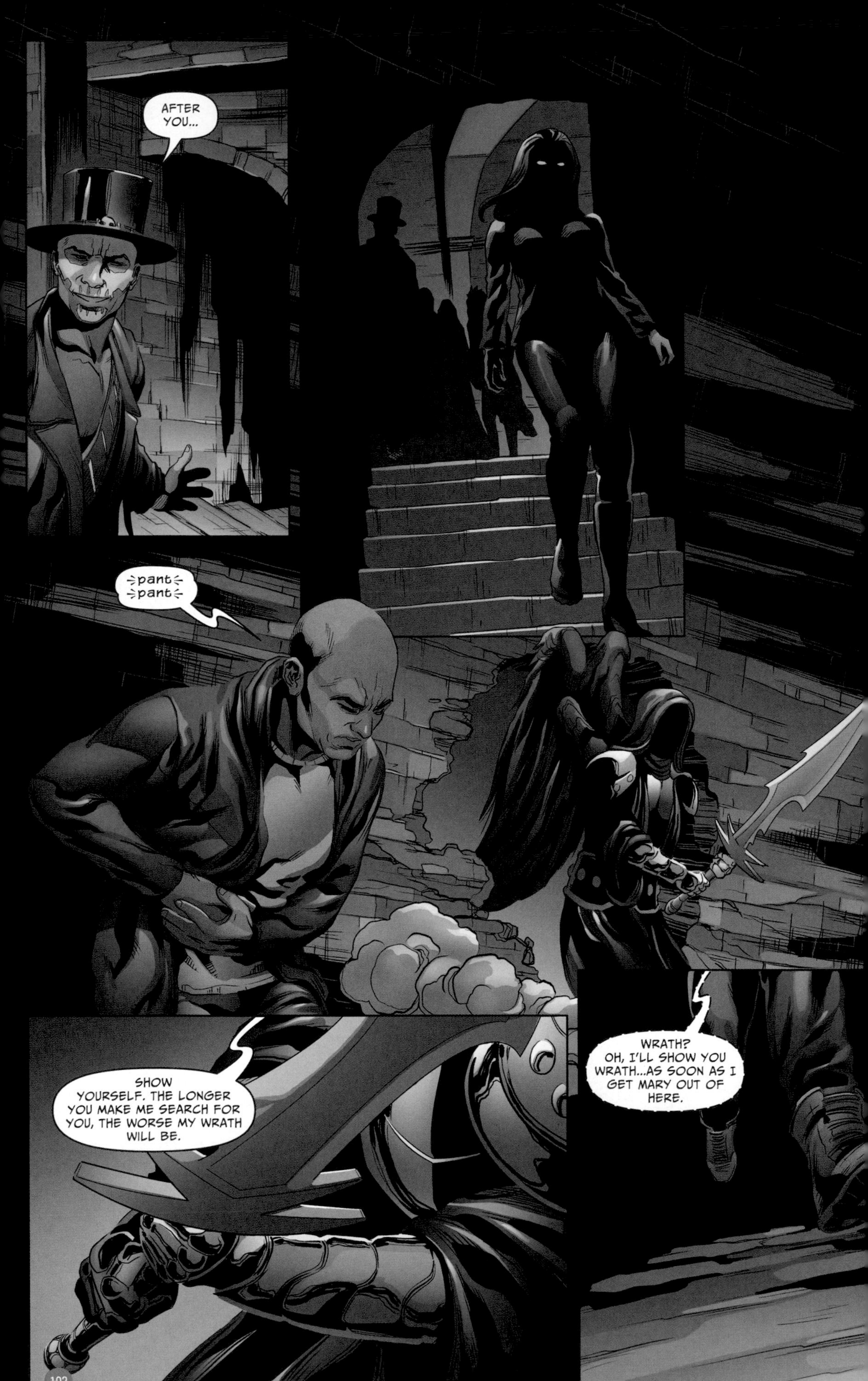
AFTER YOU...
pant pant
SHOW YOURSELF. THE LONGER YOU MAKE ME SEARCH FOR YOU, THE WORSE MY WRATH WILL BE.
WRATH? OH, I'LL SHOW YOU WRATH...AS SOON AS I GET MARY OUT OF HERE.

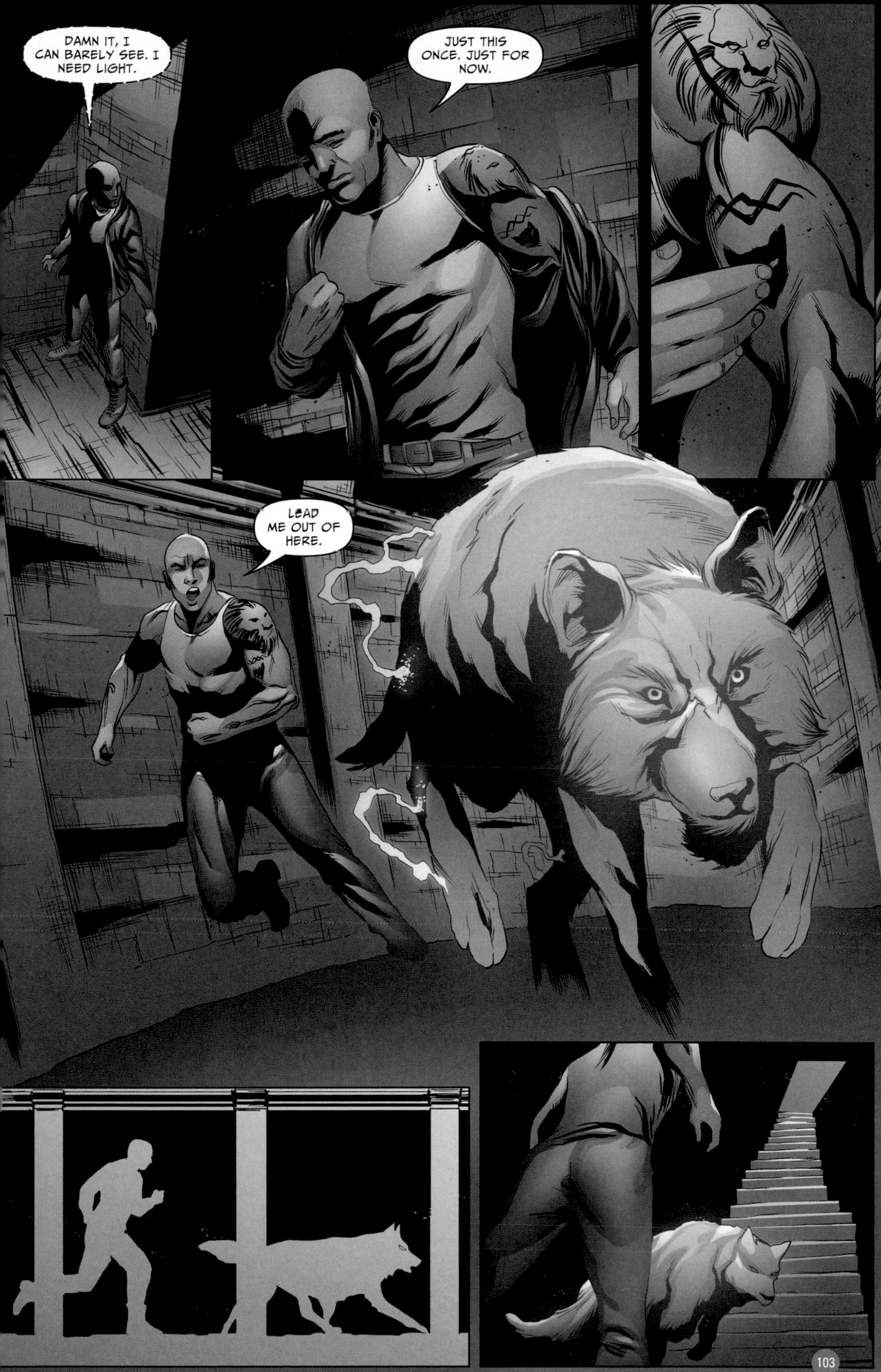
DAMN IT, I CAN BARELY SEE. I NEED LIGHT.
JUST THIS ONCE. JUST FOR NOW.
LEAD ME OUT OF HERE.

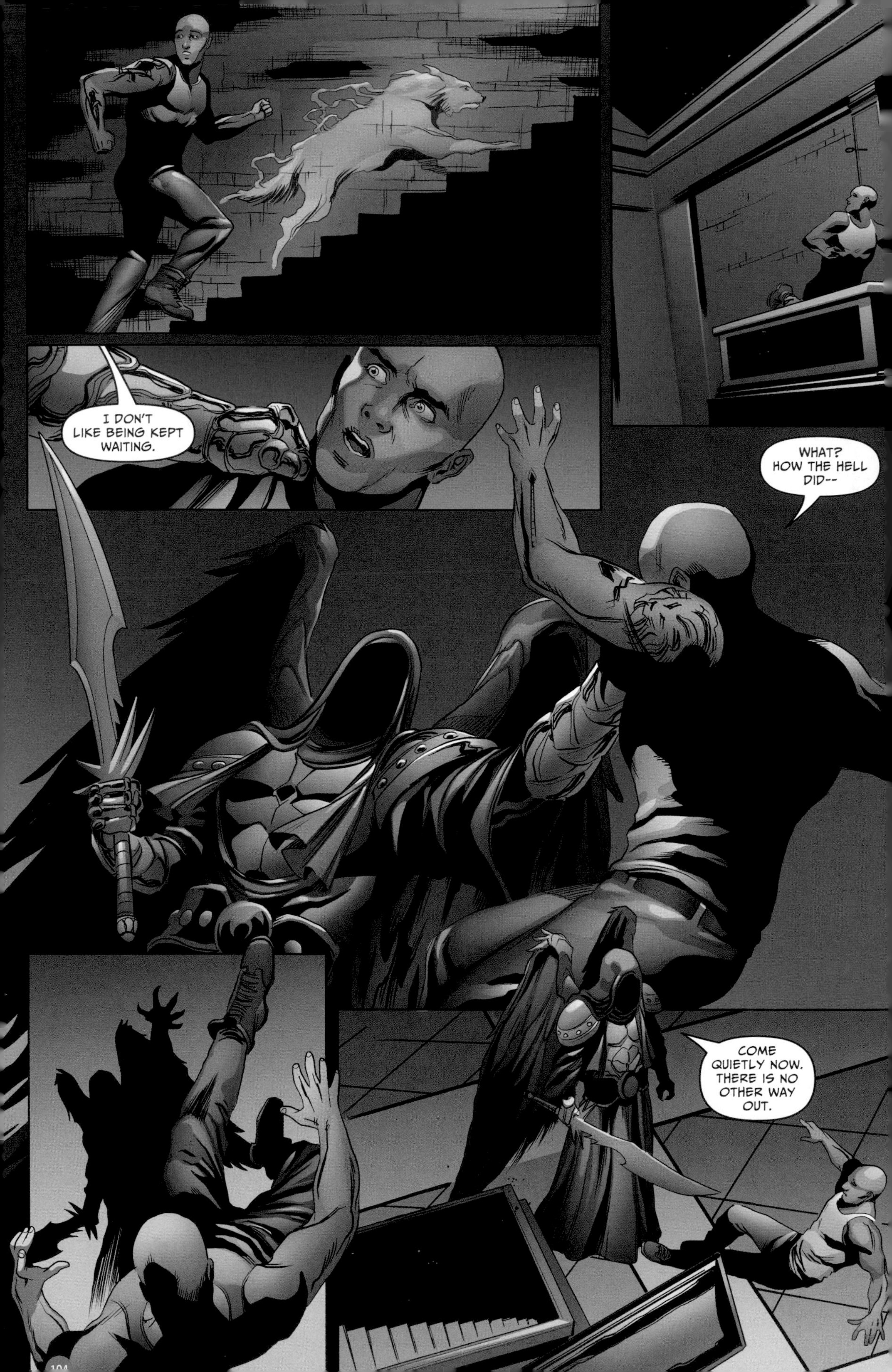
I DON'T LIKE BEING KEPT WAITING.
WHAT? HOW THE HELL DID--
COME QUIETLY NOW. THERE IS NO OTHER WAY OUT.

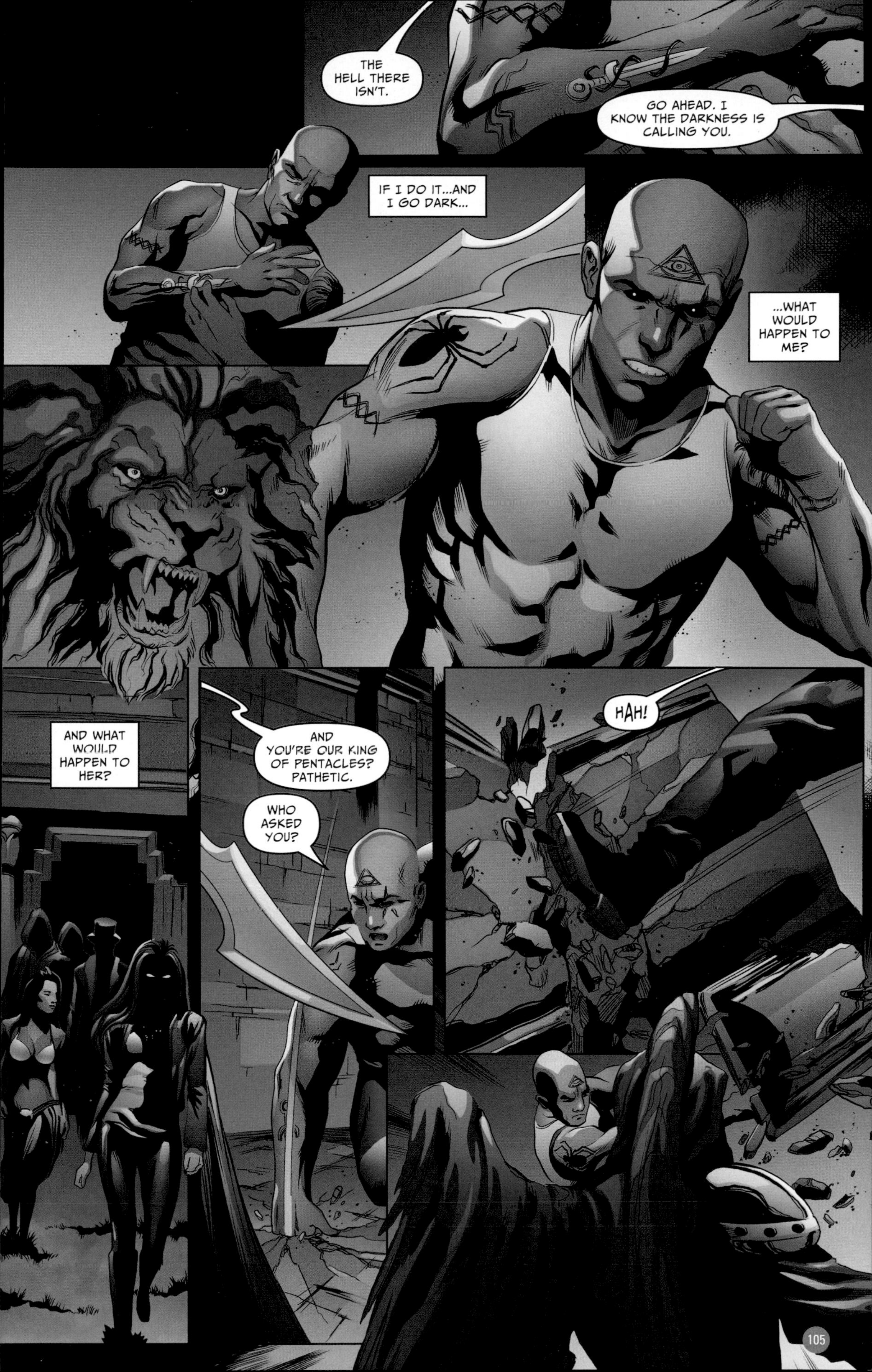
THE HELL THERE ISN'T.
GO AHEAD. I KNOW THE DARKNESS IS CALLING YOU.
IF I DO IT...AND I GO DARK...
...WHAT WOULD HAPPEN TO ME?
AND WHAT WOULD HAPPEN TO HER?
AND YOU'RE OUR KING OF PENTACLES? PATHETIC.
WHO ASKED YOU?
HAH!

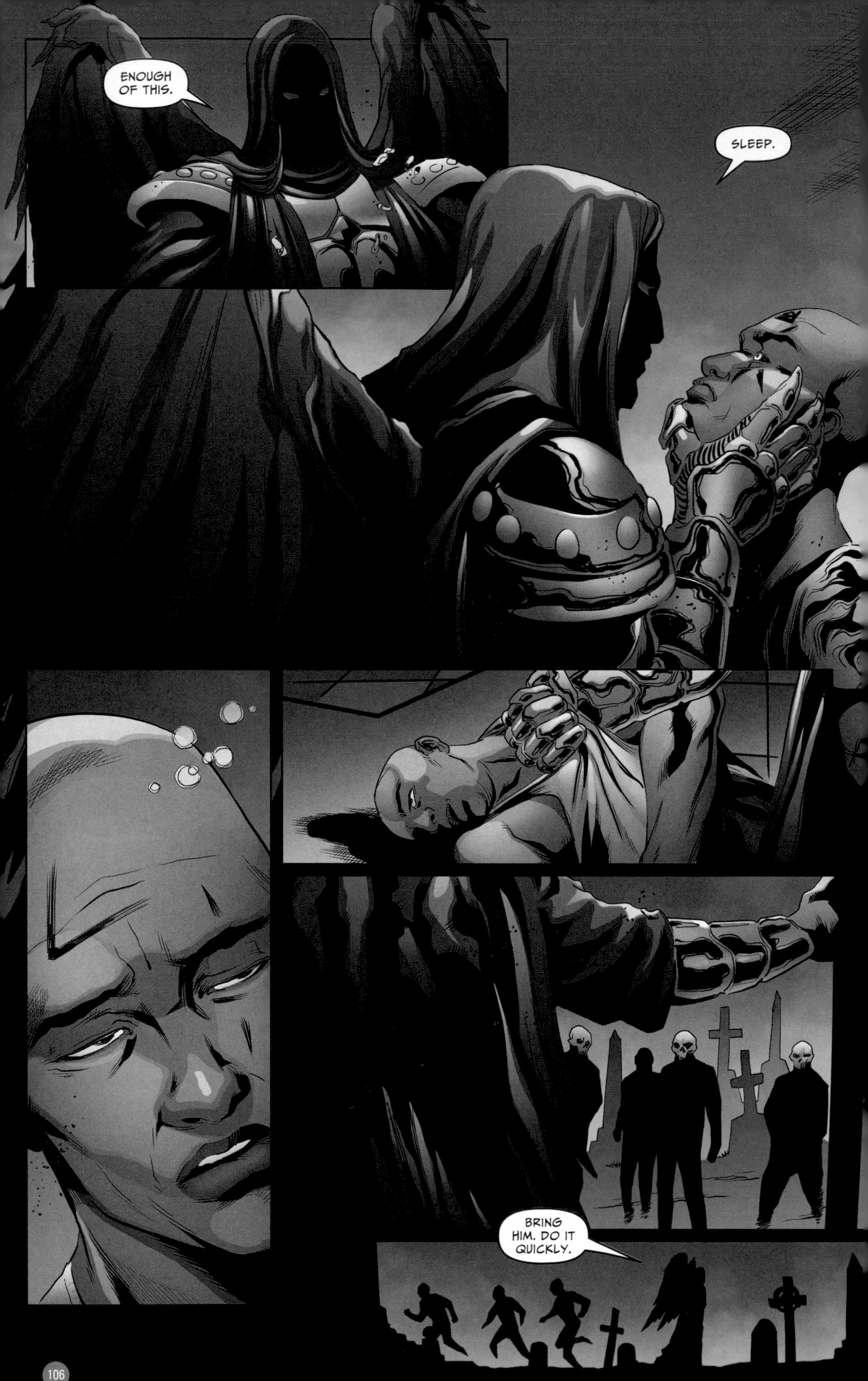
ENOUGH OF THIS.
SLEEP.
BRING HIM. DO IT QUICKLY.

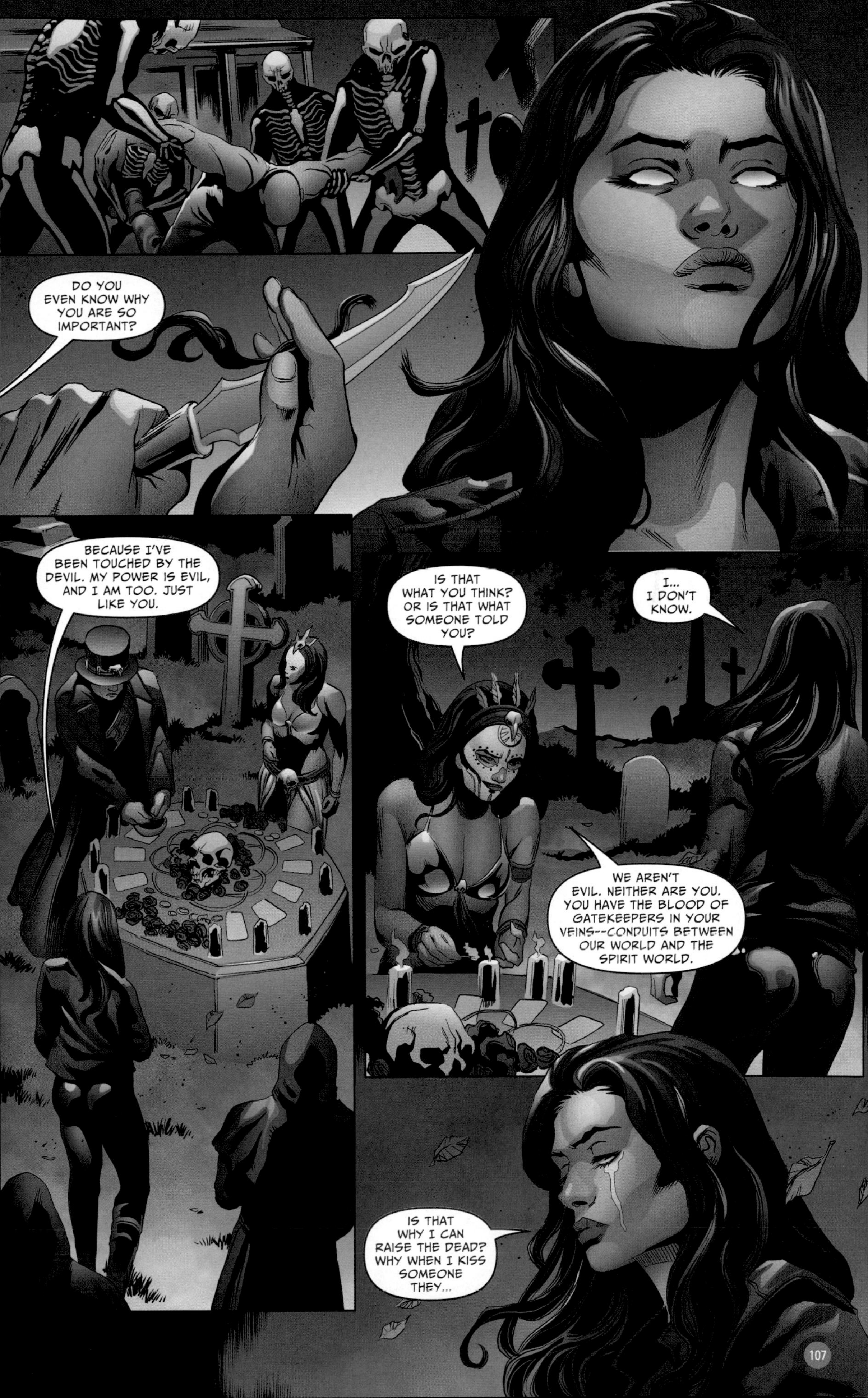
DO YOU EVEN KNOW WHY YOU ARE SO IMPORTANT?
BECAUSE I'VE BEEN TOUCHED BY THE DEVIL. MY POWER IS EVIL, AND I AM TOO. JUST LIKE YOU.
IS THAT WHAT YOU THINK? OR IS THAT WHAT SOMEONE TOLD YOU?
I... I DON'T KNOW.
WE AREN'T EVIL. NEITHER ARE YOU. YOU HAVE THE BLOOD OF GATEKEEPERS IN YOUR VEINS--CONDUITS BETWEEN OUR WORLD AND THE SPIRIT WORLD.
IS THAT WHY I CAN RAISE THE DEAD? WHY WHEN I KISS SOMEONE THEY...

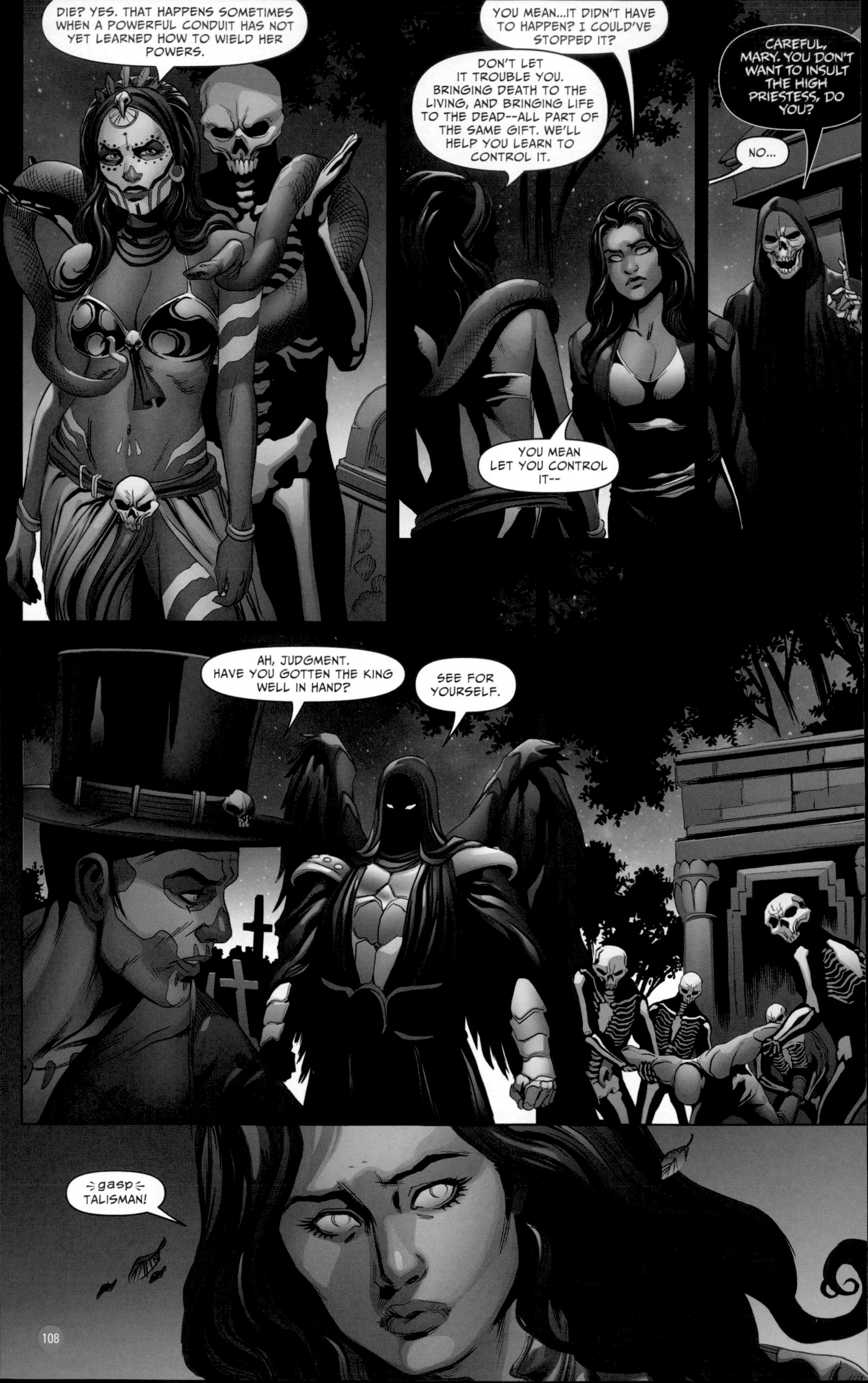
DIE? YES. THAT HAPPENS SOMETIMES WHEN A POWERFUL CONDUIT HAS NOT YET LEARNED HOW TO WIELD HER POWERS.
YOU MEAN...IT DIDN'T HAVE TO HAPPEN? I COULD'VE STOPPED IT?
DON'T LET IT TROUBLE YOU. BRINGING DEATH TO THE LIVING, AND BRINGING LIFE TO THE DEAD--ALL PART OF THE SAME GIFT. WE'LL HELP YOU LEARN TO CONTROL IT.
YOU MEAN LET YOU CONTROL IT--
CAREFUL, MARY. YOU DON'T WANT TO INSULT THE HIGH PRIESTESS, DO YOU?
NO...
AH, JUDGMENT. HAVE YOU GOTTEN THE KING WELL IN HAND?
SEE FOR YOURSELF.
gasp
TALISMAN!

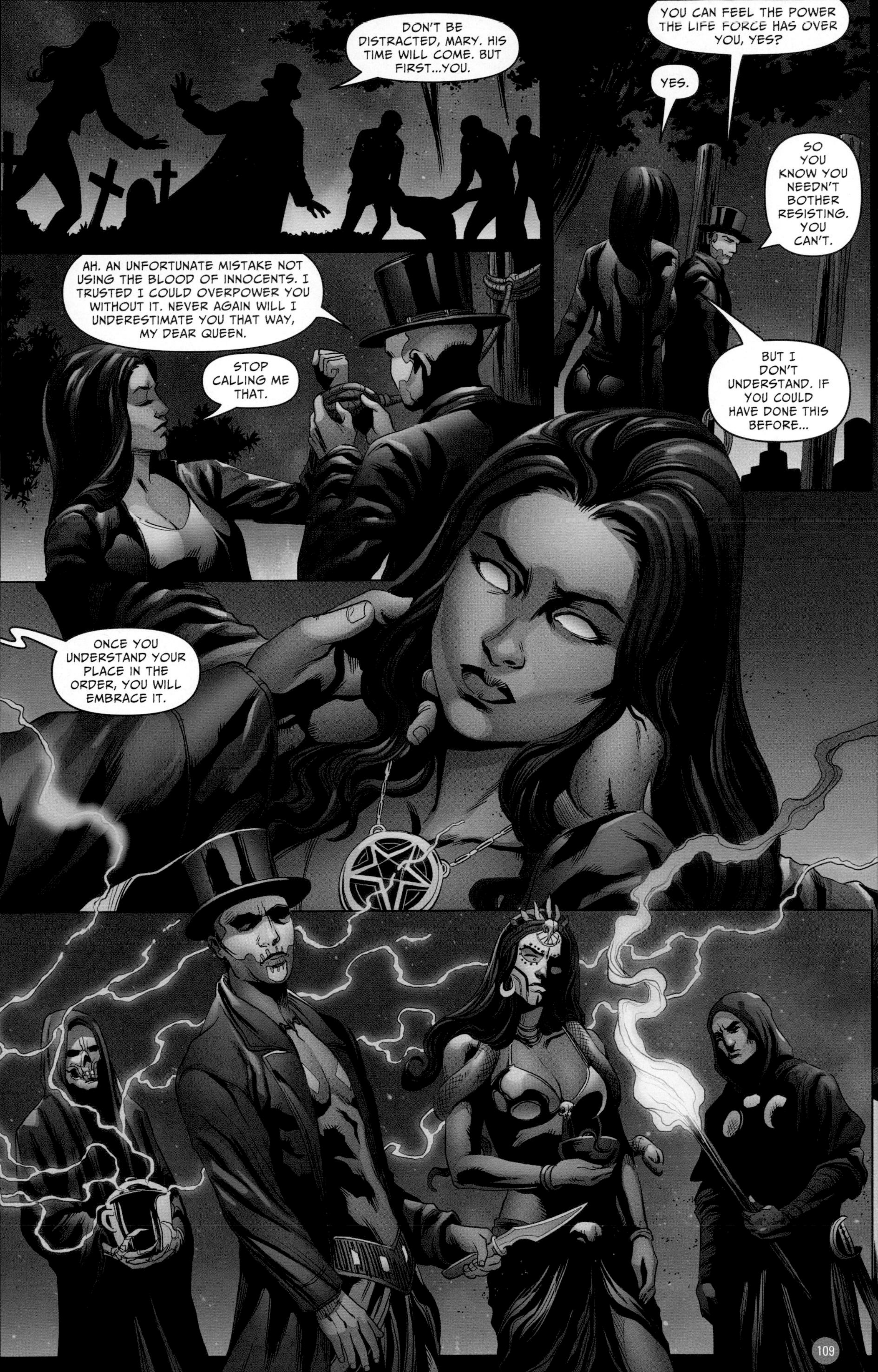
DON'T BE DISTRACTED, MARY. HIS TIME WILL COME. BUT FIRST...YOU.
YOU CAN FEEL THE POWER THE LIFE FORCE HAS OVER YOU, YES?
YES.
SO YOU KNOW YOU NEEDN'T BOTHER RESISTING. YOU CAN'T.
AH. AN UNFORTUNATE MISTAKE NOT USING THE BLOOD OF INNOCENTS. I TRUSTED I COULD OVERPOWER YOU WITHOUT IT. NEVER AGAIN WILL I UNDERESTIMATE YOU THAT WAY, MY DEAR QUEEN.
STOP CALLING ME THAT.
BUT I DON'T UNDERSTAND. IF YOU COULD HAVE DONE THIS BEFORE...
ONCE YOU UNDERSTAND YOUR PLACE IN THE ORDER, YOU WILL EMBRACE IT.

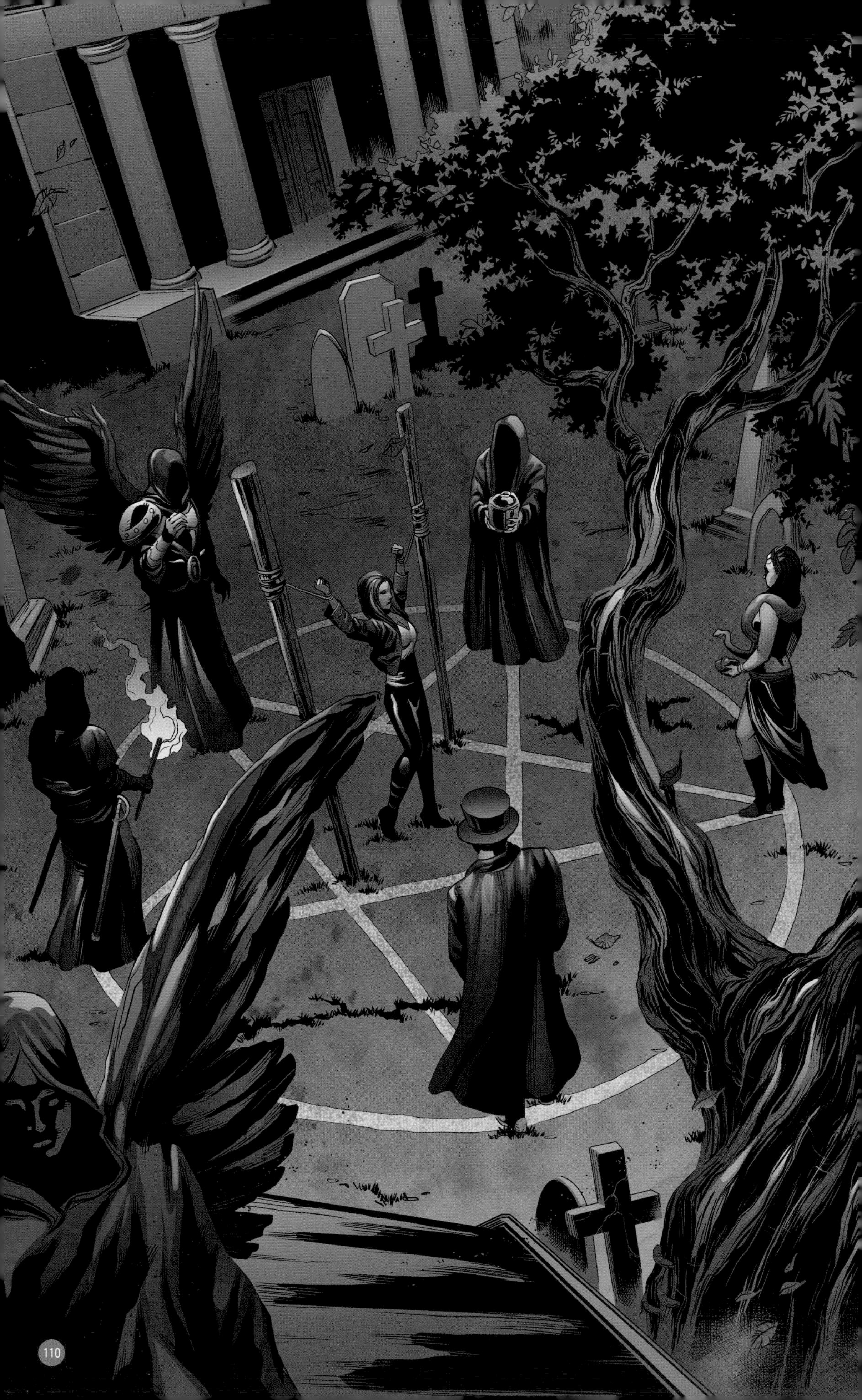

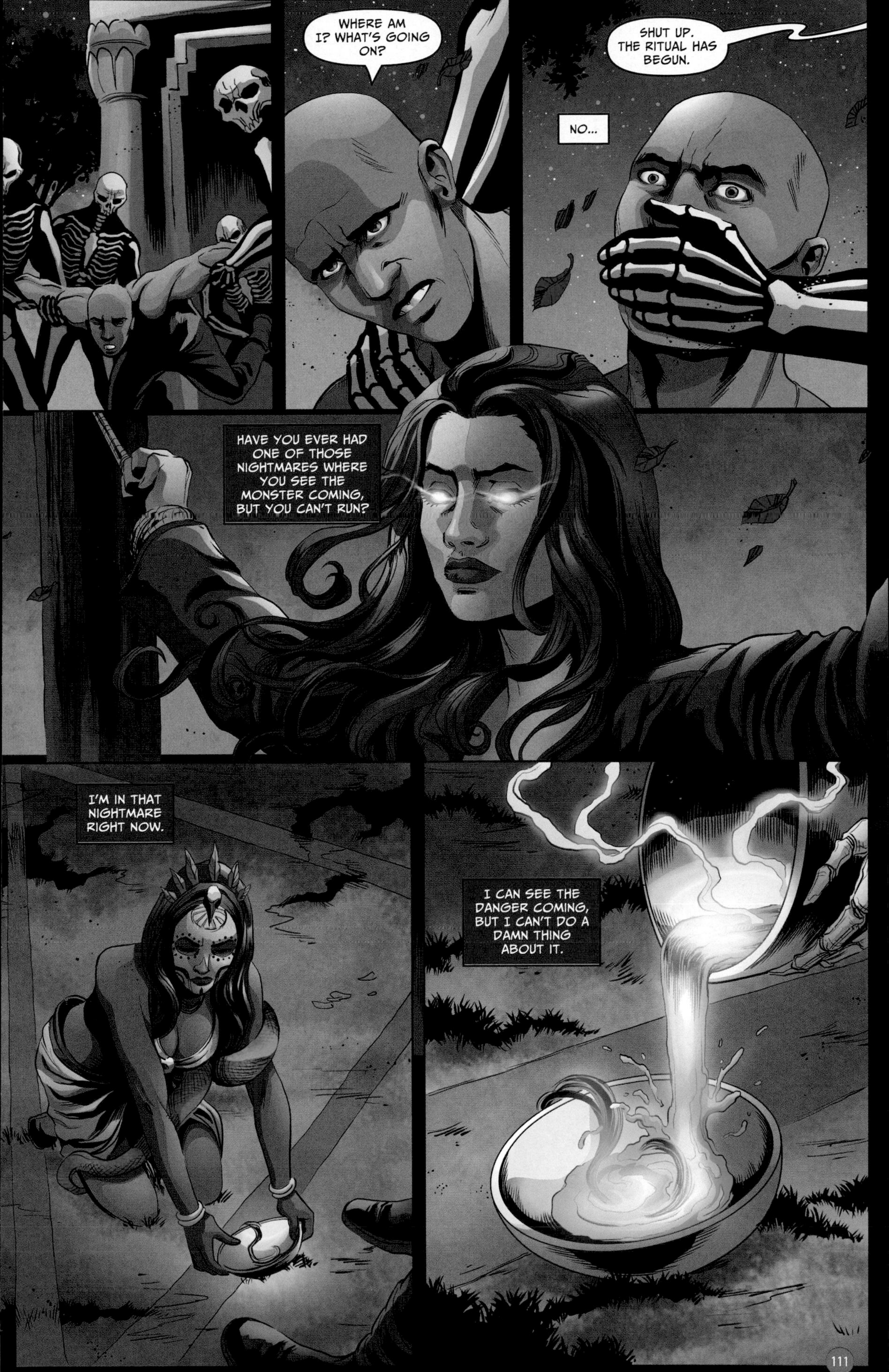
WHERE AM I? WHAT'S GOING ON?
SHUT UP. THE RITUAL HAS BEGUN.
NO...
HAVE YOU EVER HAD ONE OF THOSE NIGHTMARES WHERE YOU SEE THE MONSTER COMING, BUT YOU CAN'T RUN?
I'M IN THAT NIGHTMARE RIGHT NOW.
I CAN SEE THE DANGER COMING, BUT I CAN'T DO A DAMN THING ABOUT IT.

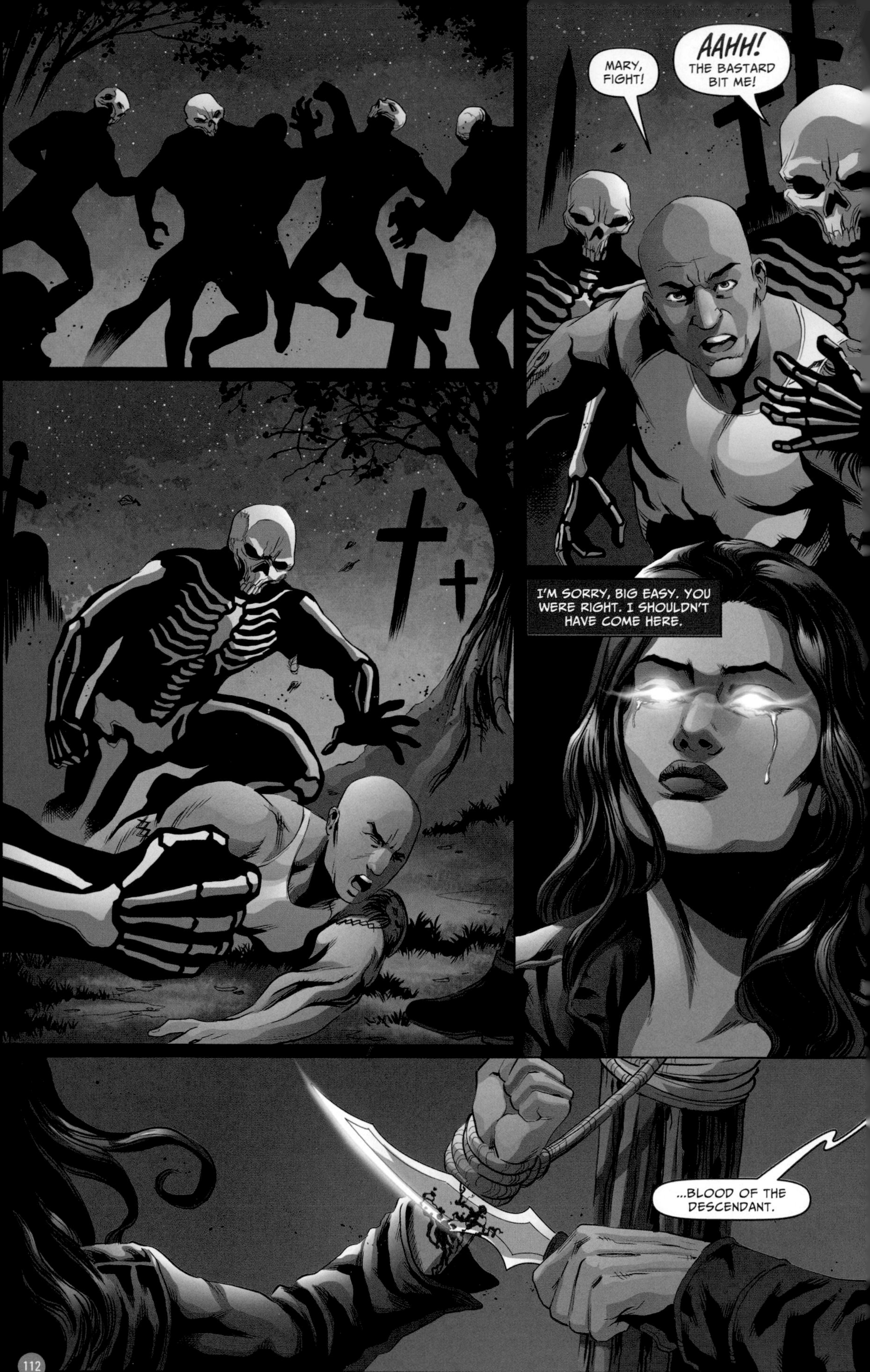
MARY, FIGHT!
AAHH! THE BASTARD BIT ME!
I'M SORRY, BIG EASY. YOU WERE RIGHT. I SHOULDN'T HAVE COME HERE.
...BLOOD OF THE DESCENDANT.

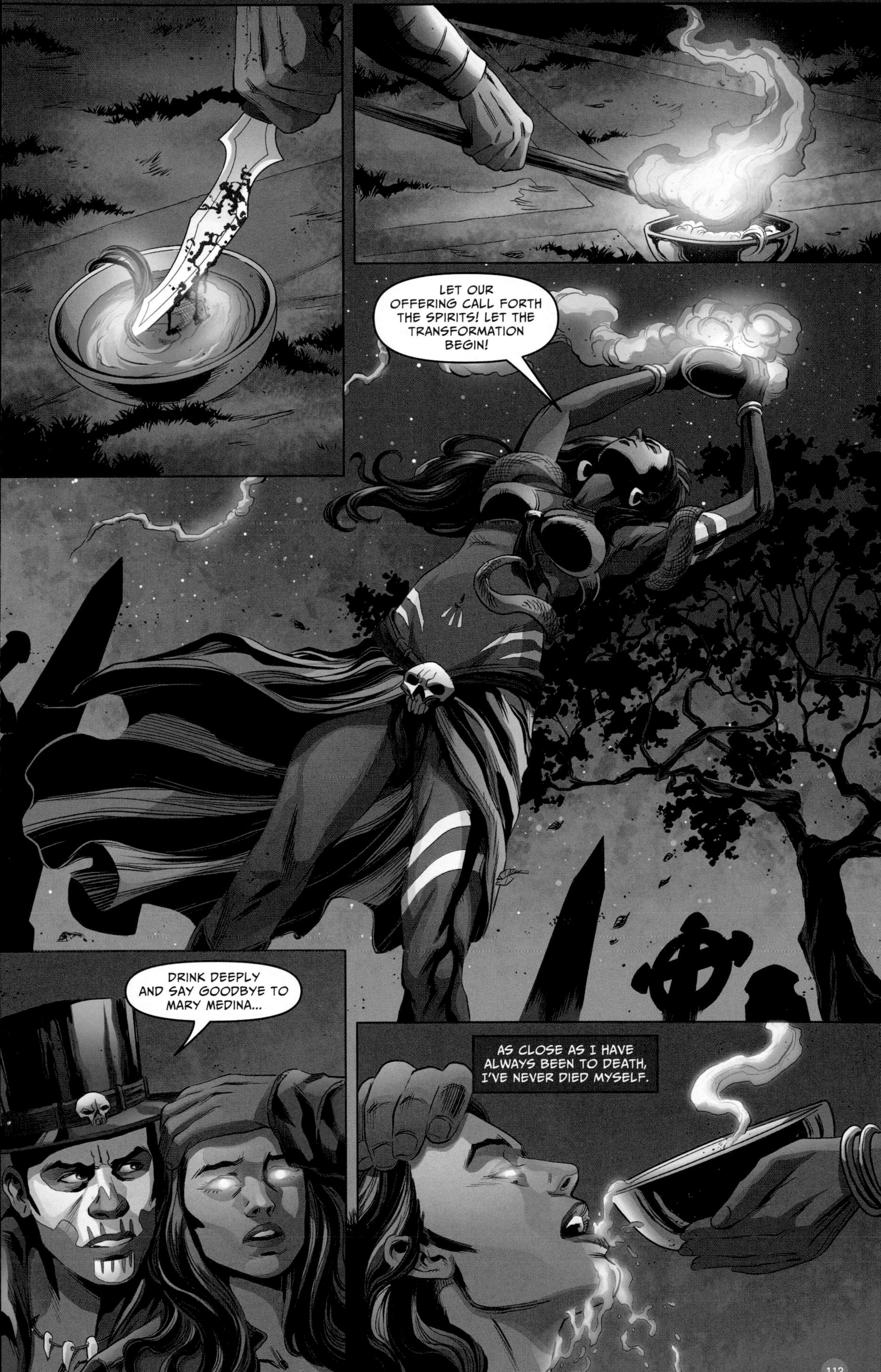
LET OUR OFFERING CALL FORTH THE SPIRITS! LET THE TRANSFORMATION BEGIN!
DRINK DEEPLY AND SAY GOODBYE TO MARY MEDINA...
AS CLOSE AS I HAVE ALWAYS BEEN TO DEATH, I'VE NEVER DIED MYSELF.

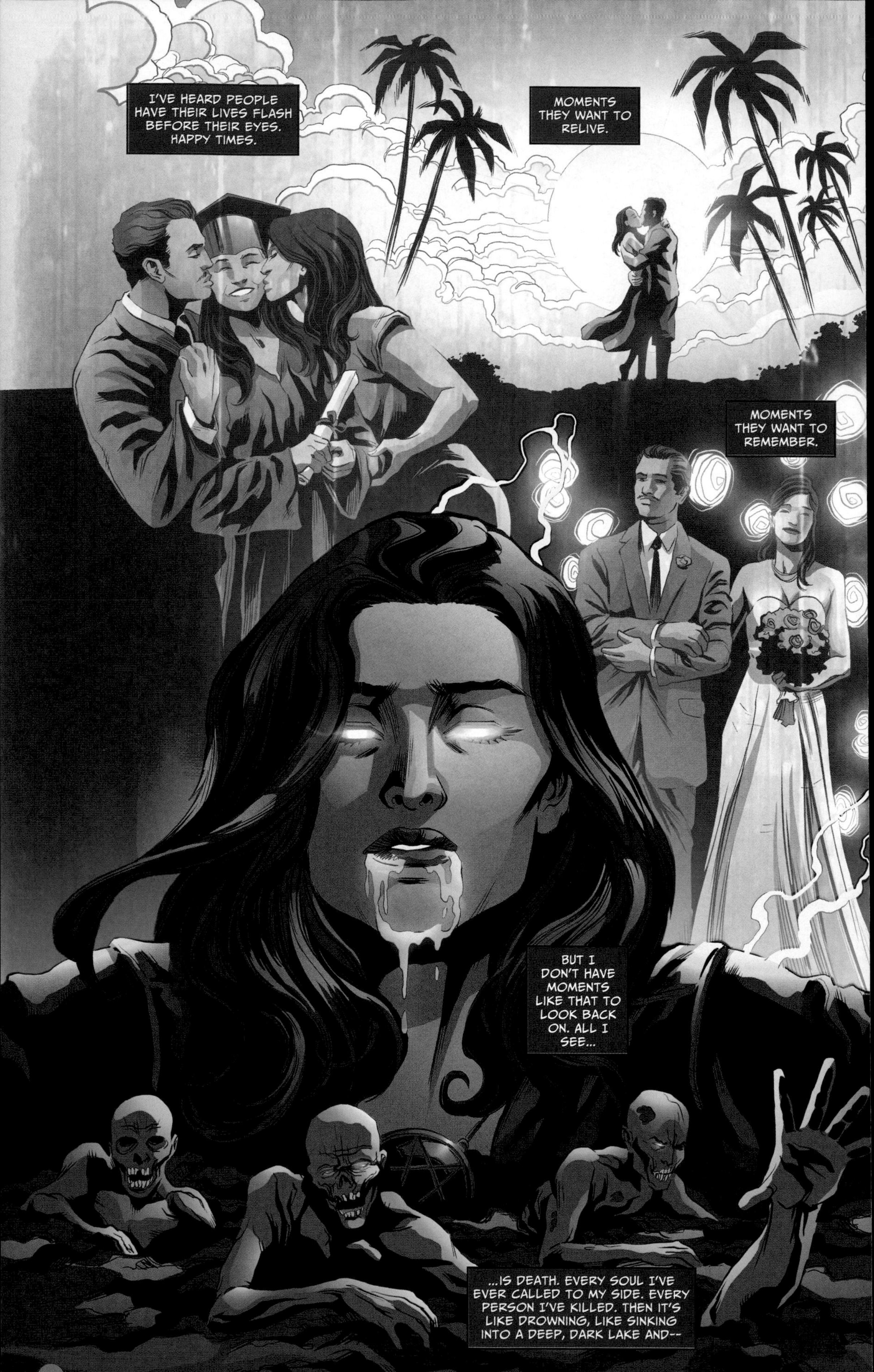
I'VE HEARD PEOPLE HAVE THEIR LIVES FLASH BEFORE THEIR EYES. HAPPY TIMES.
MOMENTS THEY WANT TO RELIVE.
MOMENTS THEY WANT TO REMEMBER.
BUT I DON'T HAVE MOMENTS LIKE THAT TO LOOK BACK ON. ALL I SEE...
...IS DEATH. EVERY SOUL I'VE EVER CALLED TO MY SIDE. EVERY PERSON I'VE KILLED. THEN IT'S LIKE DROWNING, LIKE SINKING INTO A DEEP, DARK LAKE AND--

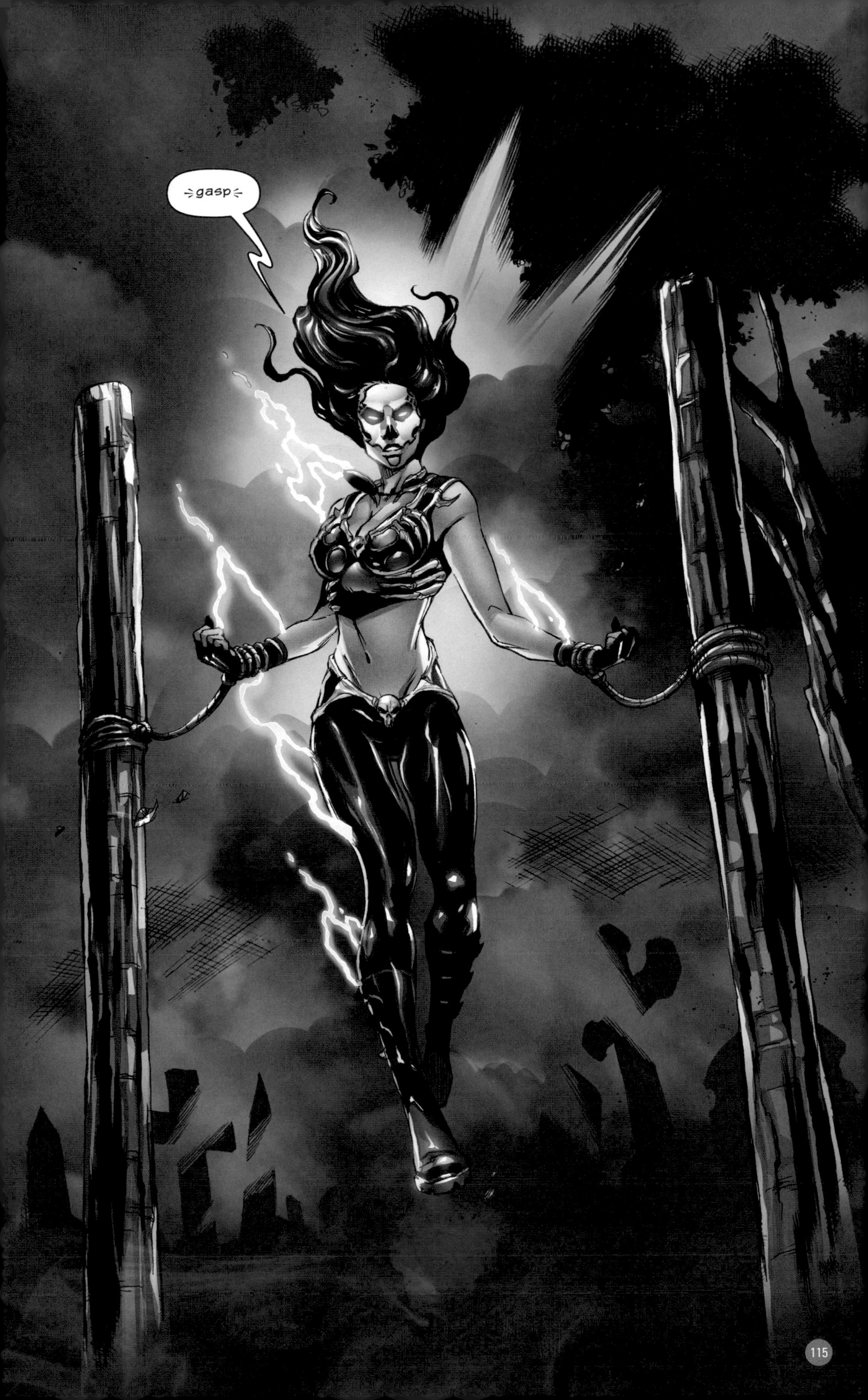
gasp

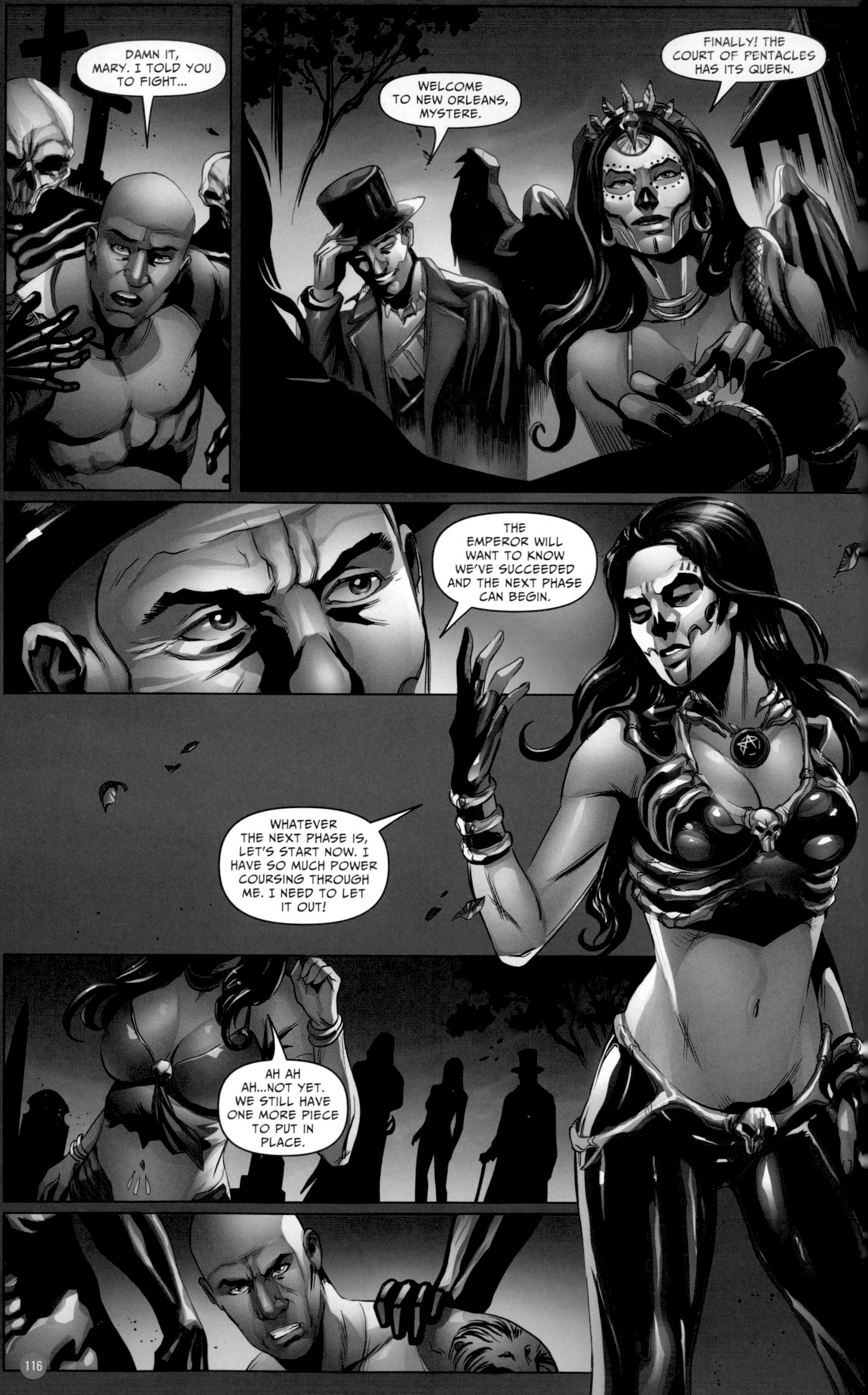
DAMN IT, MARY. I TOLD YOU TO FIGHT...
WELCOME TO NEW ORLEANS, MYSTERE.
FINALLY! THE COURT OF PENTACLES HAS ITS QUEEN.
THE EMPEROR WILL WANT TO KNOW WE'VE SUCCEEDED AND THE NEXT PHASE CAN BEGIN.
WHATEVER THE NEXT PHASE IS, LET'S START NOW. I HAVE SO MUCH POWER COURSING THROUGH ME. I NEED TO LET IT OUT!
AH AH AH...NOT YET. WE STILL HAVE ONE MORE PIECE TO PUT IN PLACE.

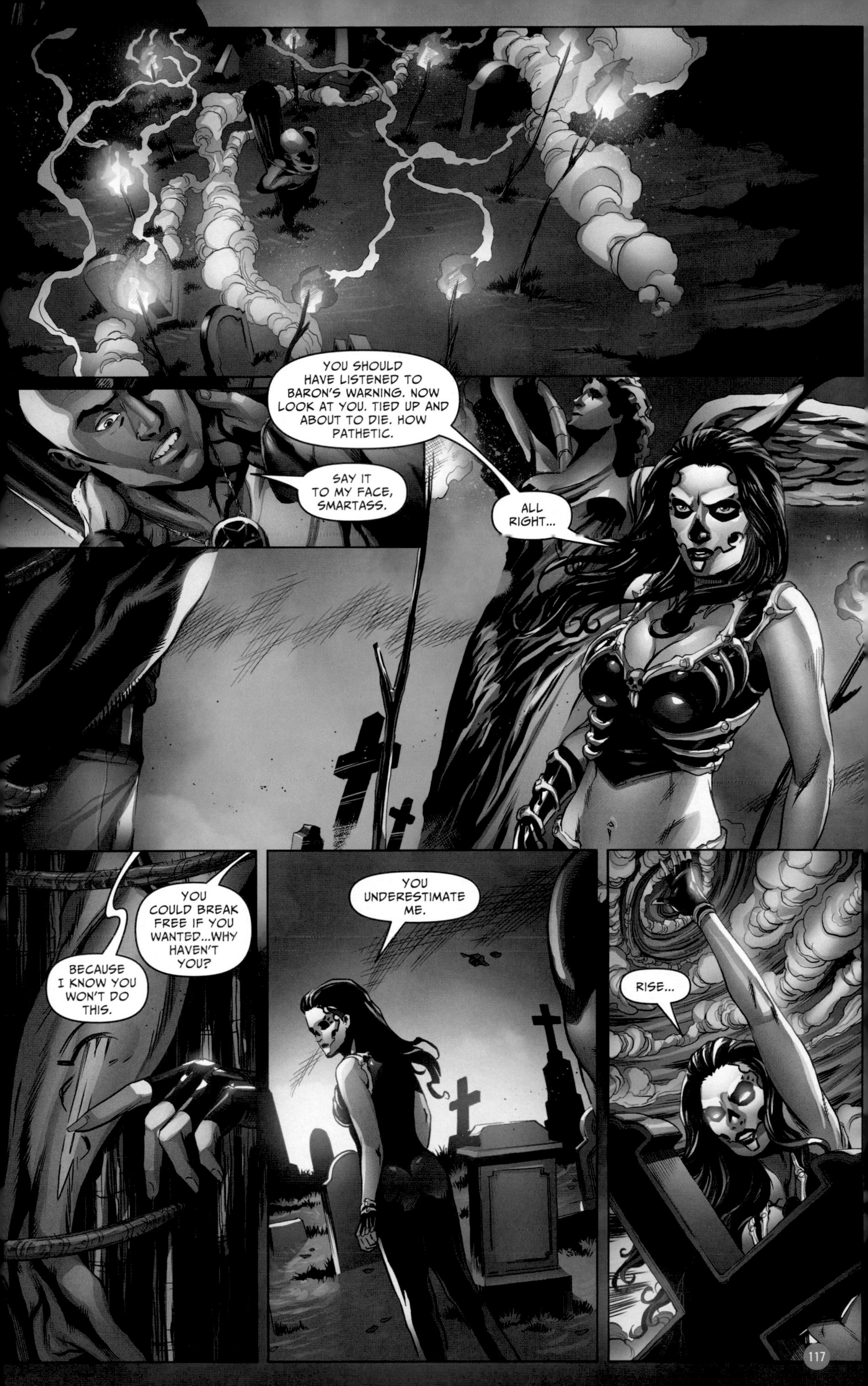
YOU SHOULD HAVE LISTENED TO BARON'S WARNING. NOW LOOK AT YOU. TIED UP AND ABOUT TO DIE. HOW PATHETIC.
SAY IT TO MY FACE, SMARTASS.
ALL RIGHT...
YOU COULD BREAK FREE IF YOU WANTED...WHY HAVEN'T YOU?
BECAUSE I KNOW YOU WON'T DO THIS.
YOU UNDERESTIMATE ME.
RISE...

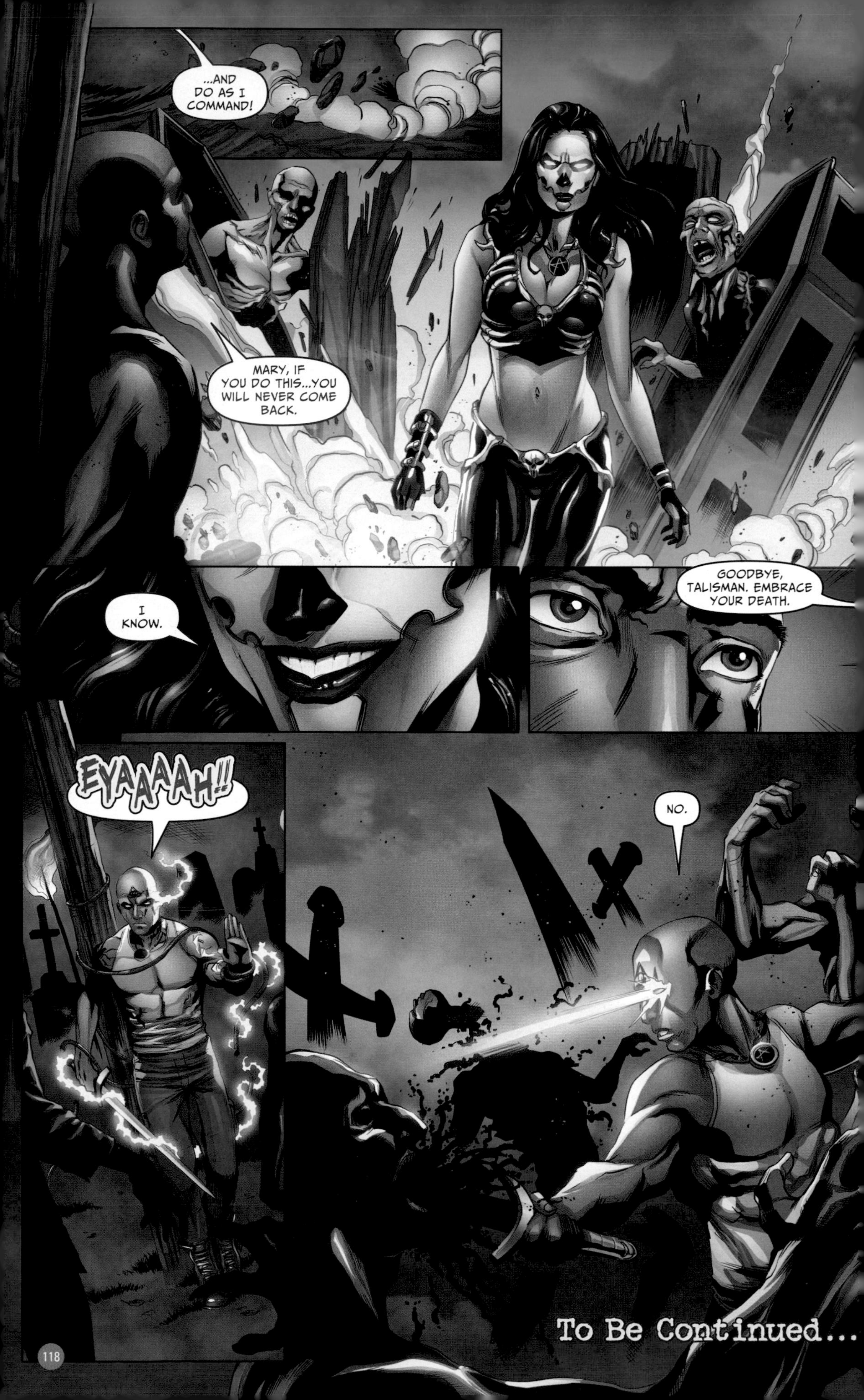
...AND DO AS I COMMAND!
MARY, IF YOU DO THIS...YOU WILL NEVER COME BACK.
I KNOW.
GOODBYE, TALISMAN. EMBRACE YOUR DEATH.
EYAAAAH!!
NO.
To Be Continued...

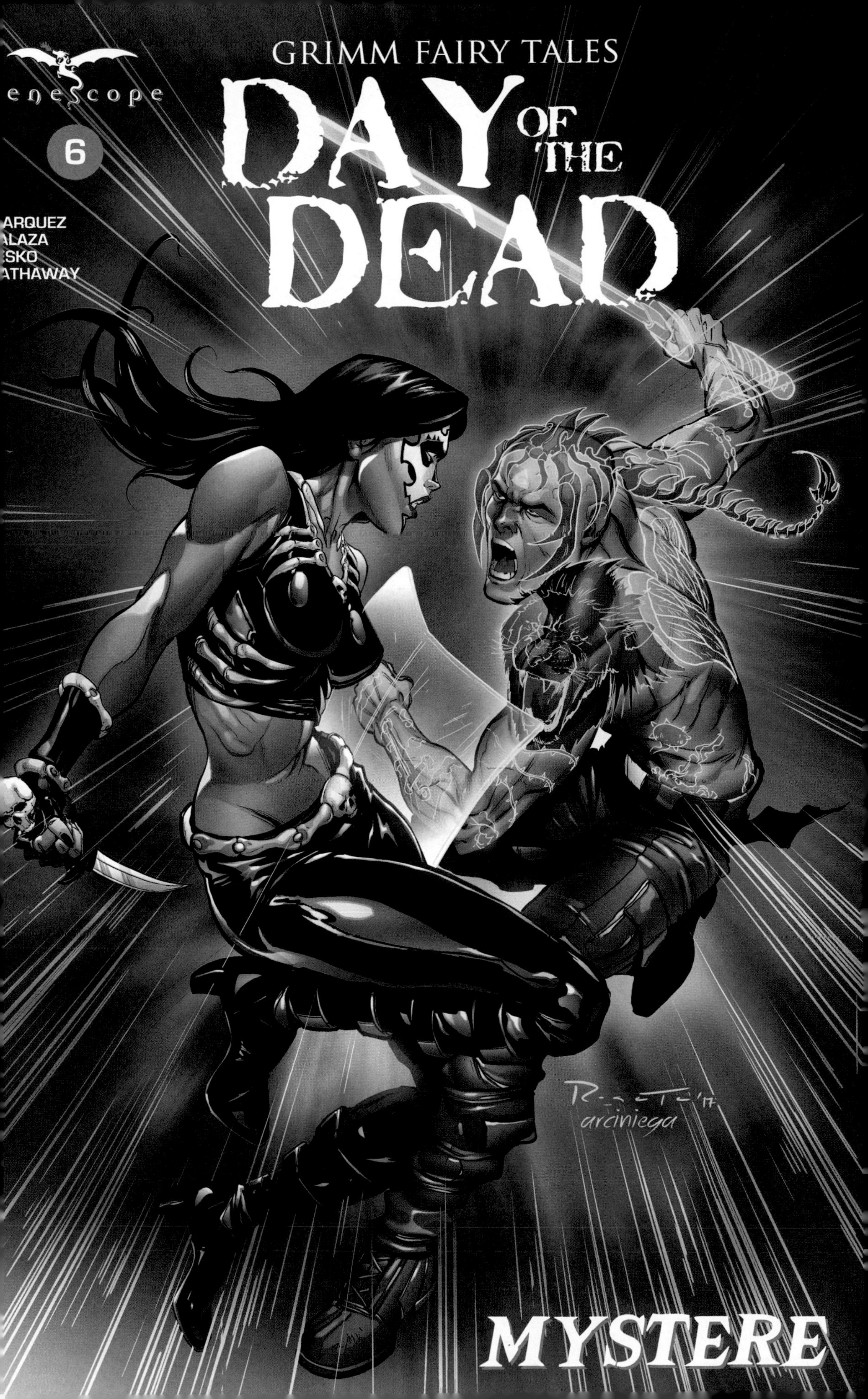
GRIMM FAIRY TALES
DAY OF THE DEAD
6
ARQUEZ
ALAZA
SKO
ATHAWAY
arciniega
MYSTERE

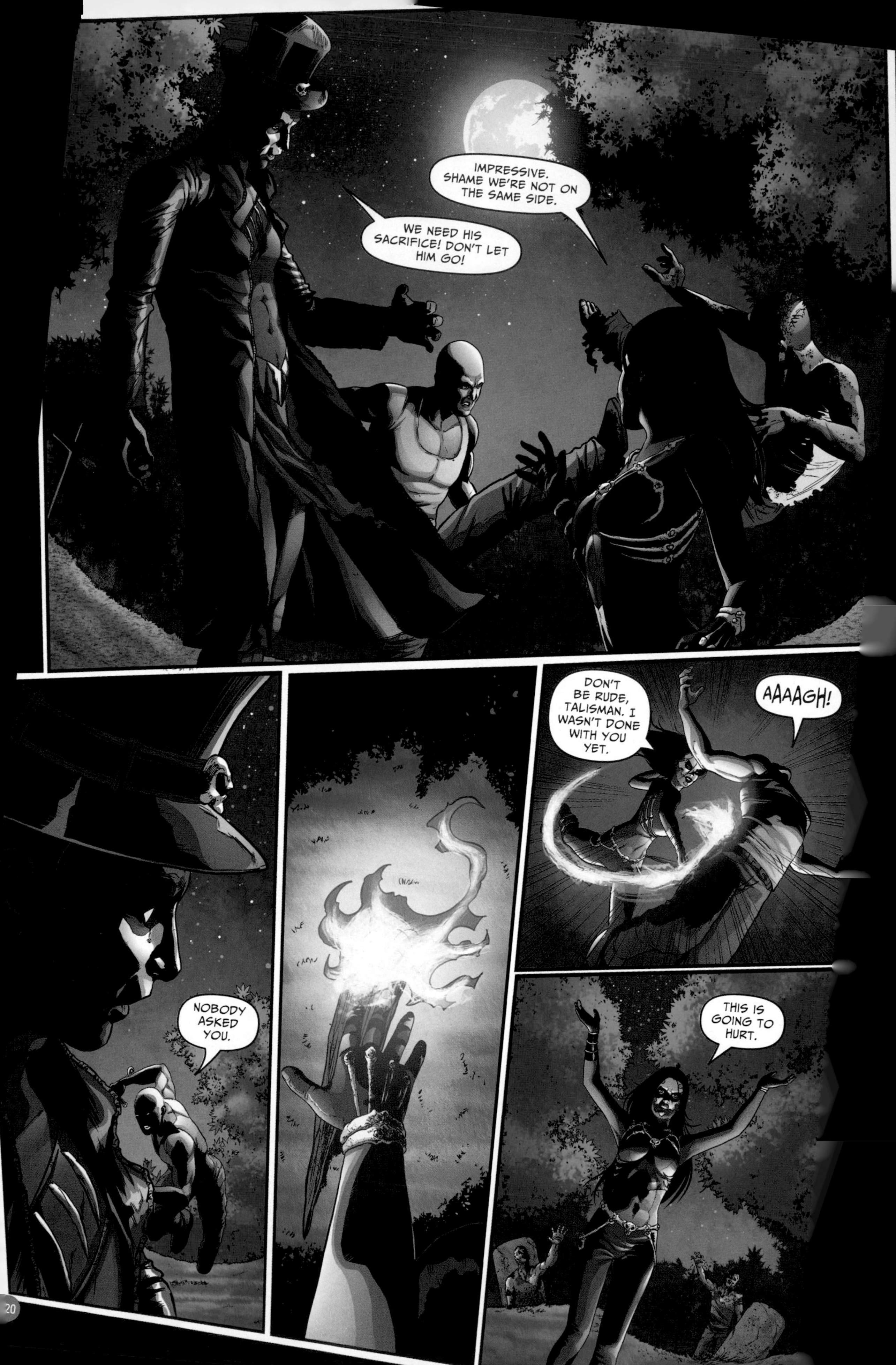

WE NEED HIS SACRIFICE! DON'T LET HIM GO!
IMPRESSIVE. SHAME WE'RE NOT ON THE SAME SIDE.
NOBODY ASKED YOU.
DON'T BE RUDE, TALISMAN. I WASN'T DONE WITH YOU YET.
AAAAGH!
THIS IS GOING TO HURT.

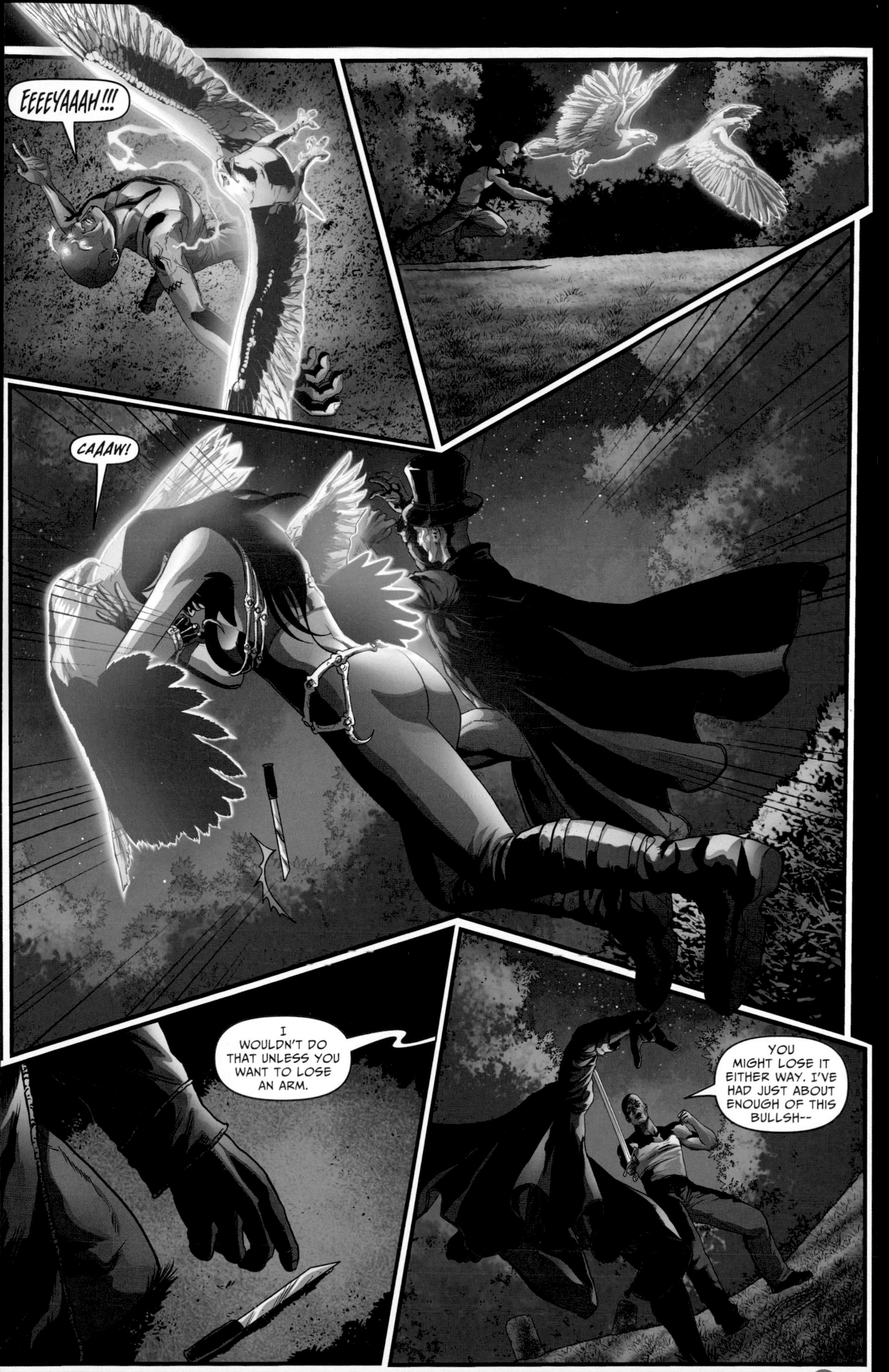
EEEEYAAAH!!!
CAAAW!
I WOULDN'T DO THAT UNLESS YOU WANT TO LOSE AN ARM.
YOU MIGHT LOSE IT EITHER WAY. I'VE HAD JUST ABOUT ENOUGH OF THIS BULLSH--

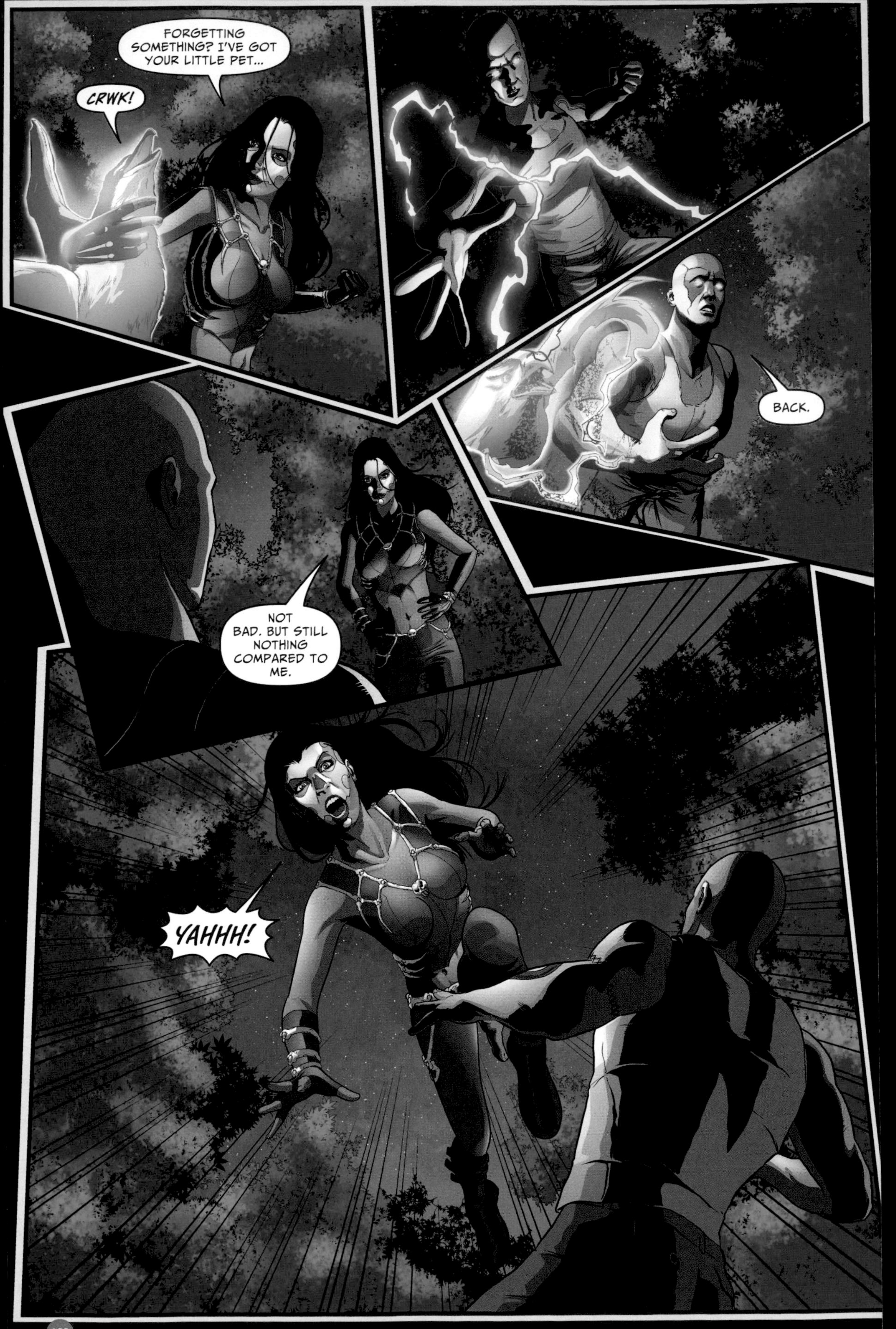
FORGETTING SOMETHING? I'VE GOT YOUR LITTLE PET...
CRWK!
BACK.
NOT BAD. BUT STILL NOTHING COMPARED TO ME.
YAHHH!

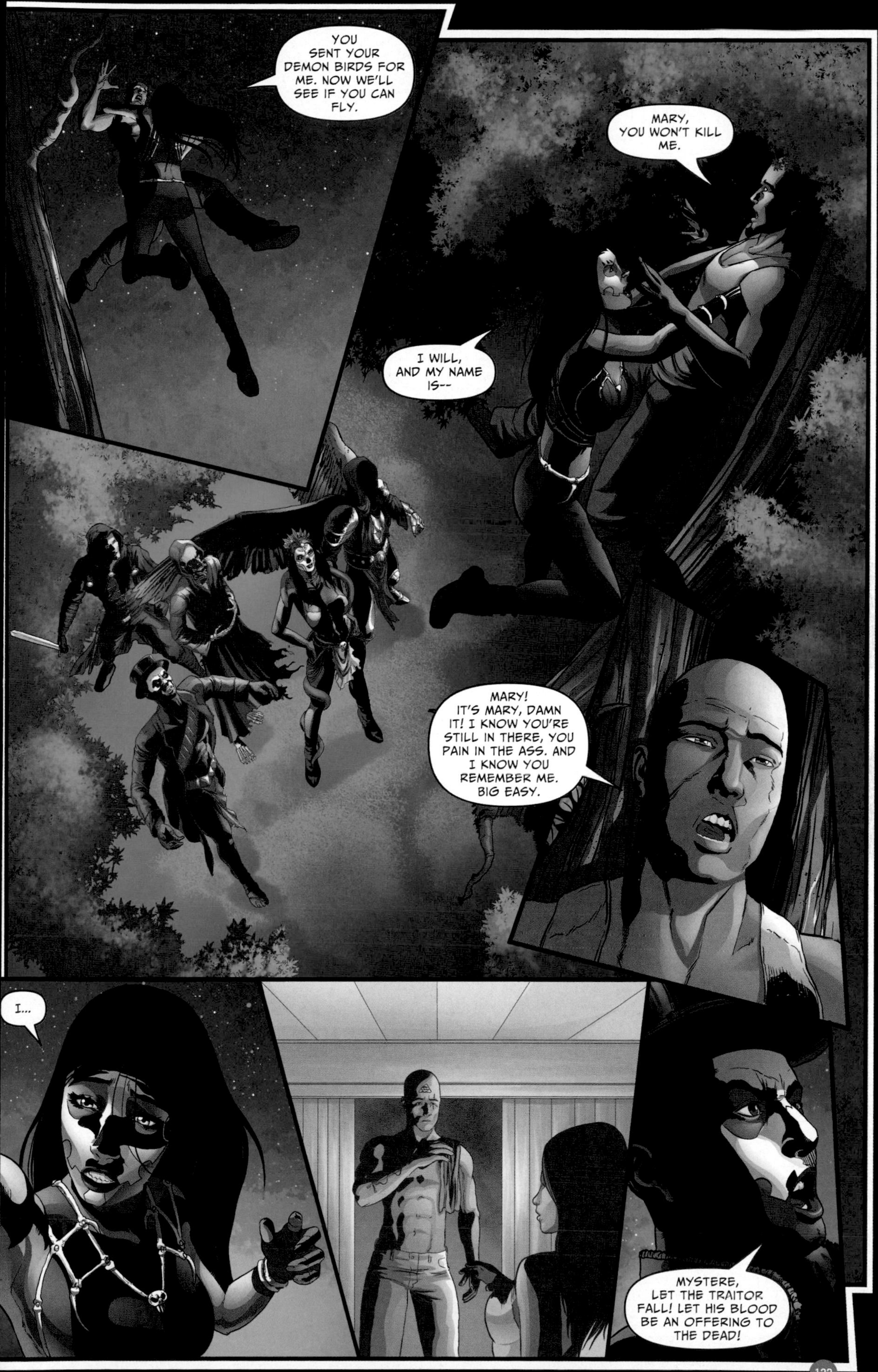
YOU SENT YOUR DEMON BIRDS FOR ME. NOW WE'LL SEE IF YOU CAN FLY.
MARY, YOU WON'T KILL ME.
I WILL, AND MY NAME IS--
MARY! IT'S MARY, DAMN IT! I KNOW YOU'RE STILL IN THERE, YOU PAIN IN THE ASS. AND I KNOW YOU REMEMBER ME. BIG EASY.
I...
MYSTERE, LET THE TRAITOR FALL! LET HIS BLOOD BE AN OFFERING TO THE DEAD!

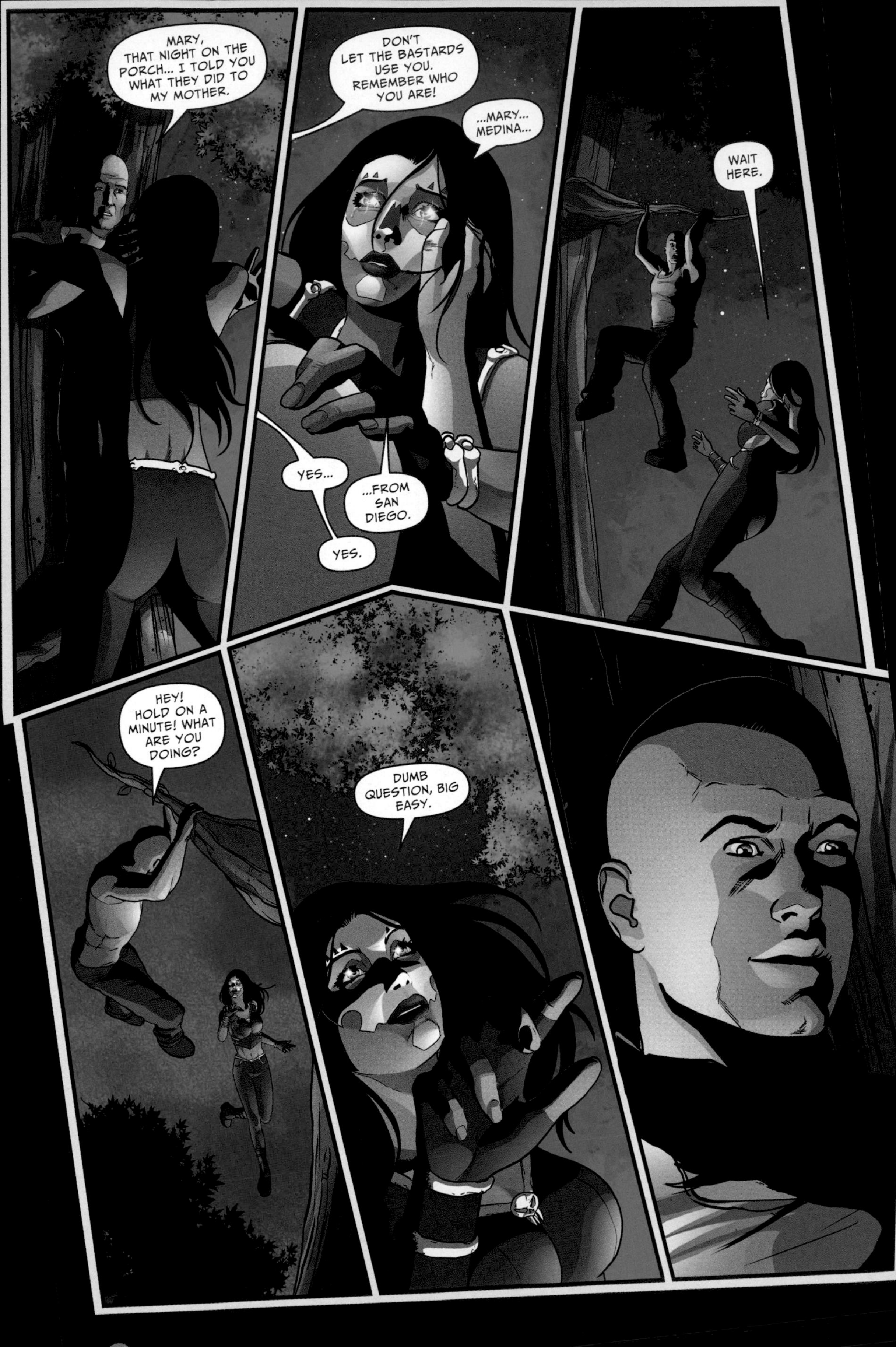
MARY, THAT NIGHT ON THE PORCH... I TOLD YOU WHAT THEY DID TO MY MOTHER.
DON'T LET THE BASTARDS USE YOU. REMEMBER WHO YOU ARE!
...MARY... MEDINA...
YES...
...FROM SAN DIEGO.
YES.
WAIT HERE.
HEY! HOLD ON A MINUTE! WHAT ARE YOU DOING?
DUMB QUESTION, BIG EASY.

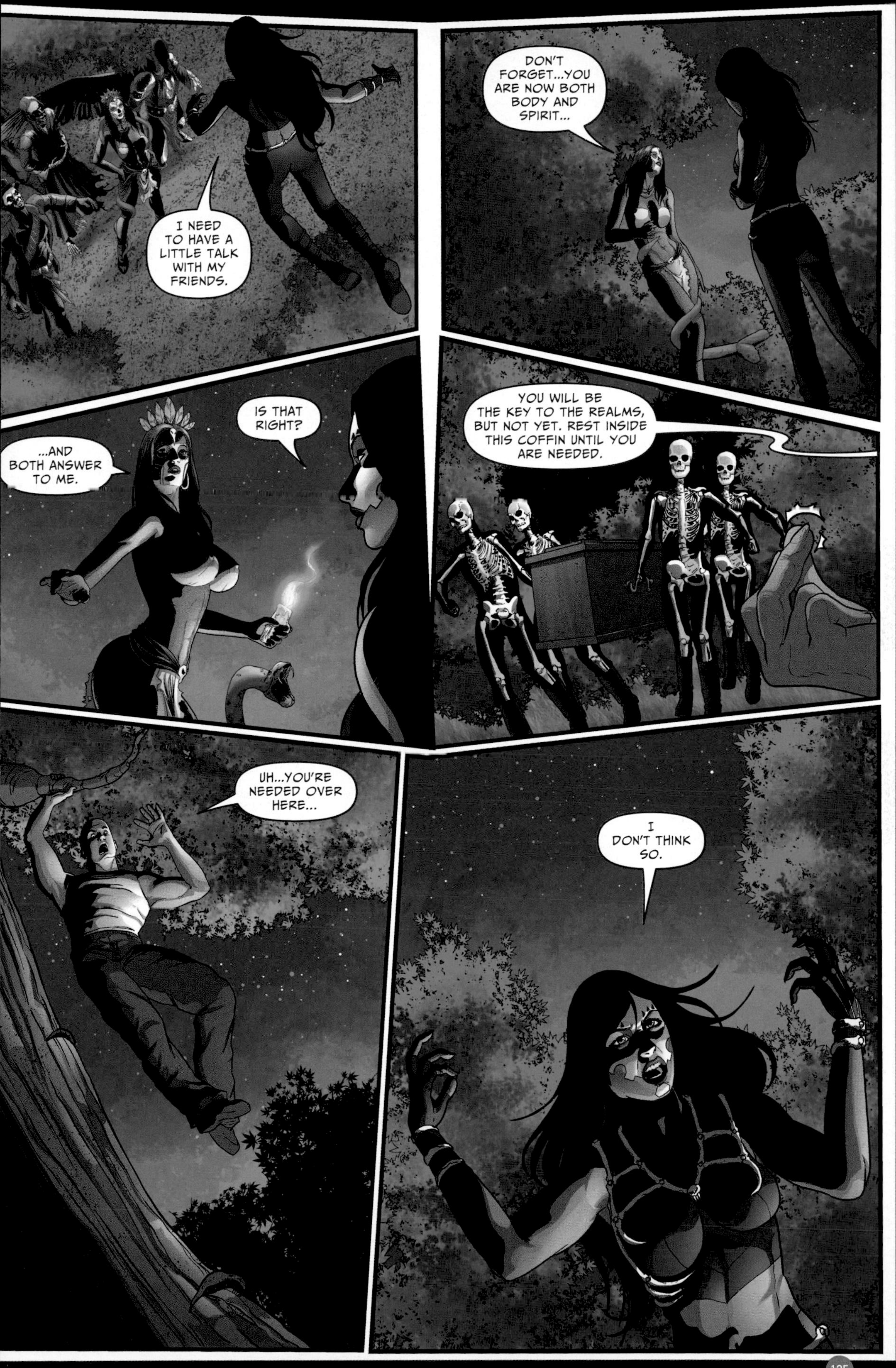
I NEED TO HAVE A LITTLE TALK WITH MY FRIENDS.
DON'T FORGET...YOU ARE NOW BOTH BODY AND SPIRIT...
...AND BOTH ANSWER TO ME.
IS THAT RIGHT?
YOU WILL BE THE KEY TO THE REALMS, BUT NOT YET. REST INSIDE THIS COFFIN UNTIL YOU ARE NEEDED.
UH...YOU'RE NEEDED OVER HERE...
I DON'T THINK SO.

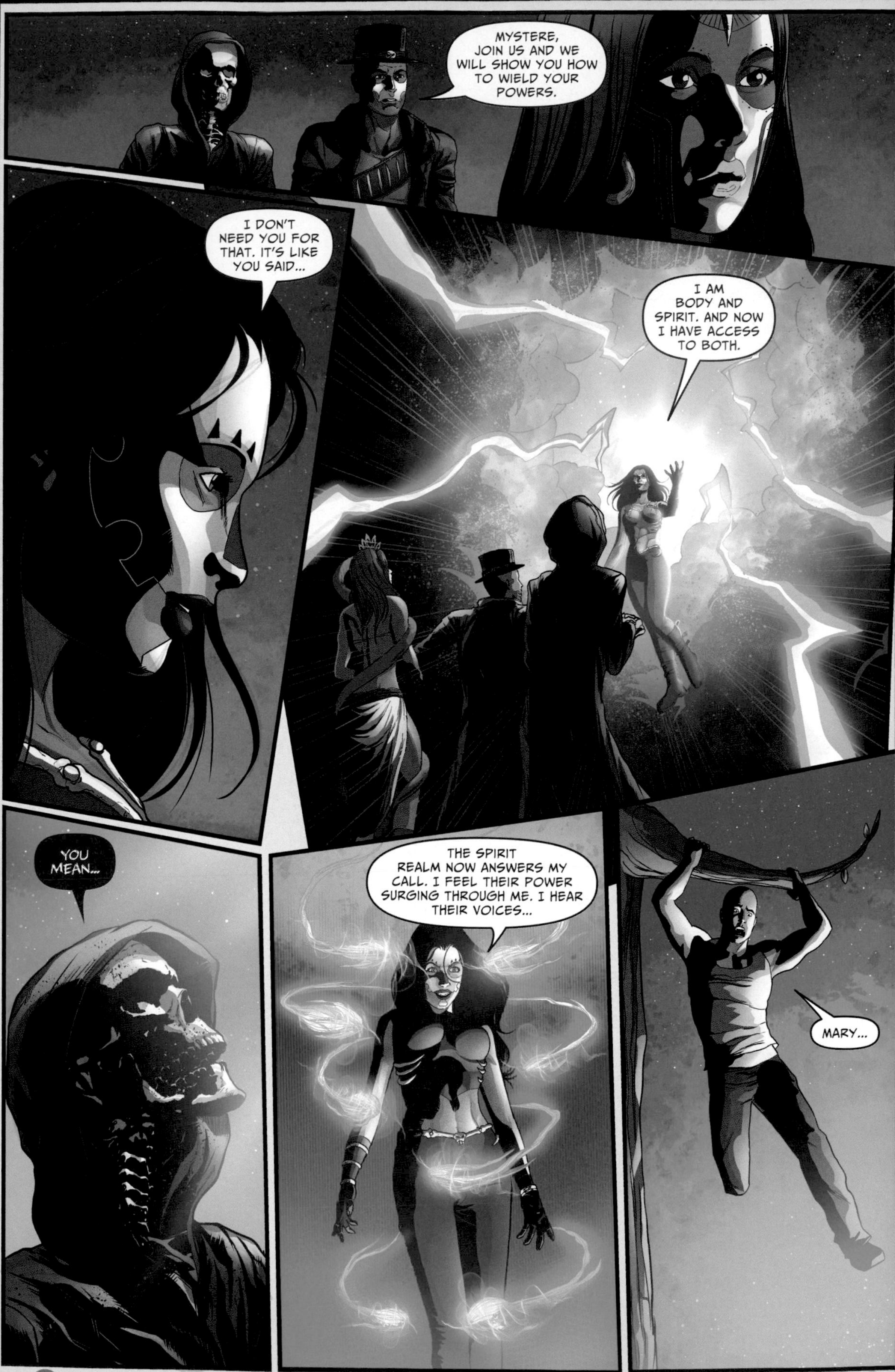
MYSTERE, JOIN US AND WE WILL SHOW YOU HOW TO WIELD YOUR POWERS.
I DON'T NEED YOU FOR THAT. IT'S LIKE YOU SAID...
I AM BODY AND SPIRIT. AND NOW I HAVE ACCESS TO BOTH.
YOU MEAN...
THE SPIRIT REALM NOW ANSWERS MY CALL. I FEEL THEIR POWER SURGING THROUGH ME. I HEAR THEIR VOICES...
MARY...

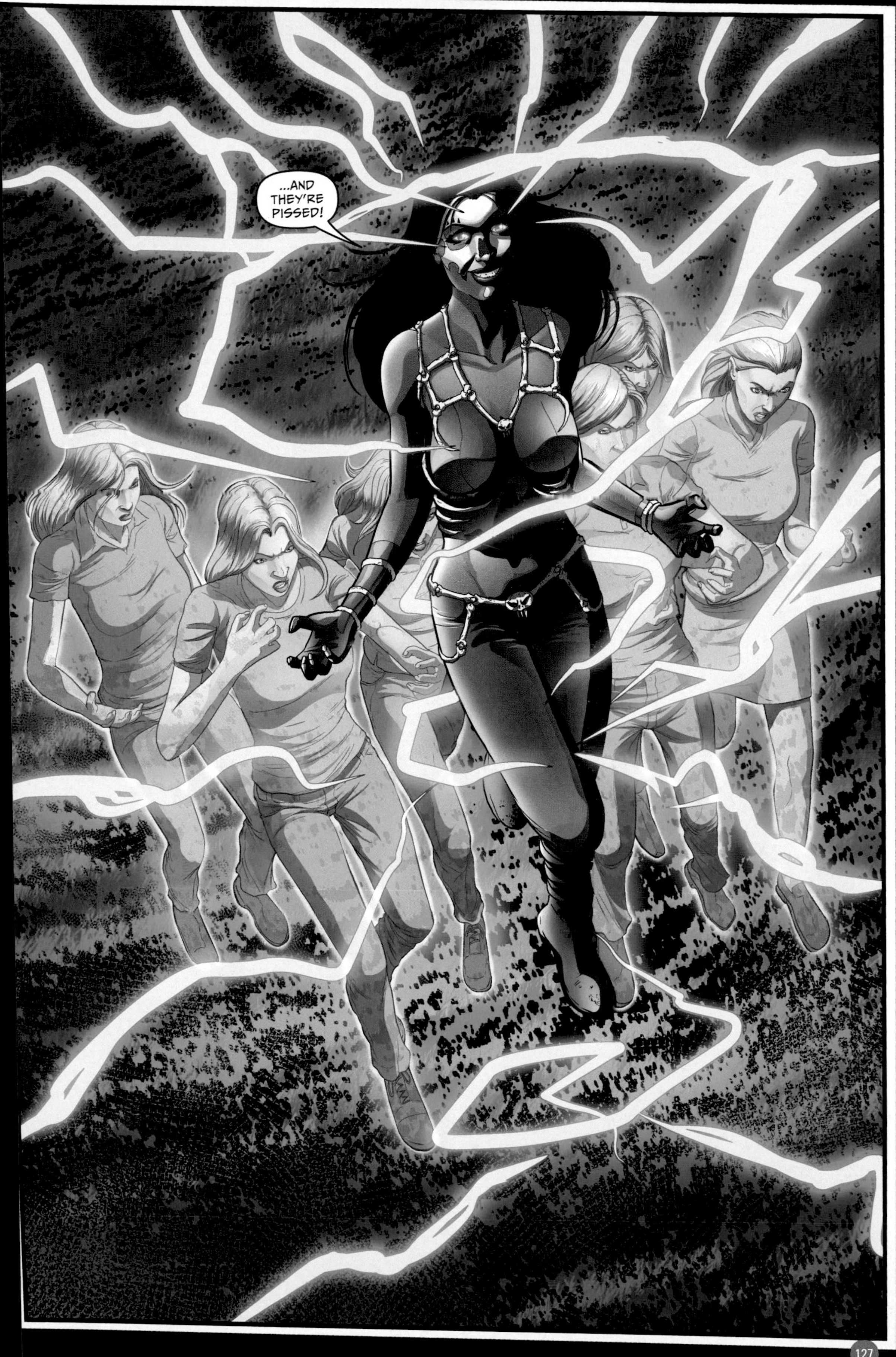
...AND THEY'RE PISSED!

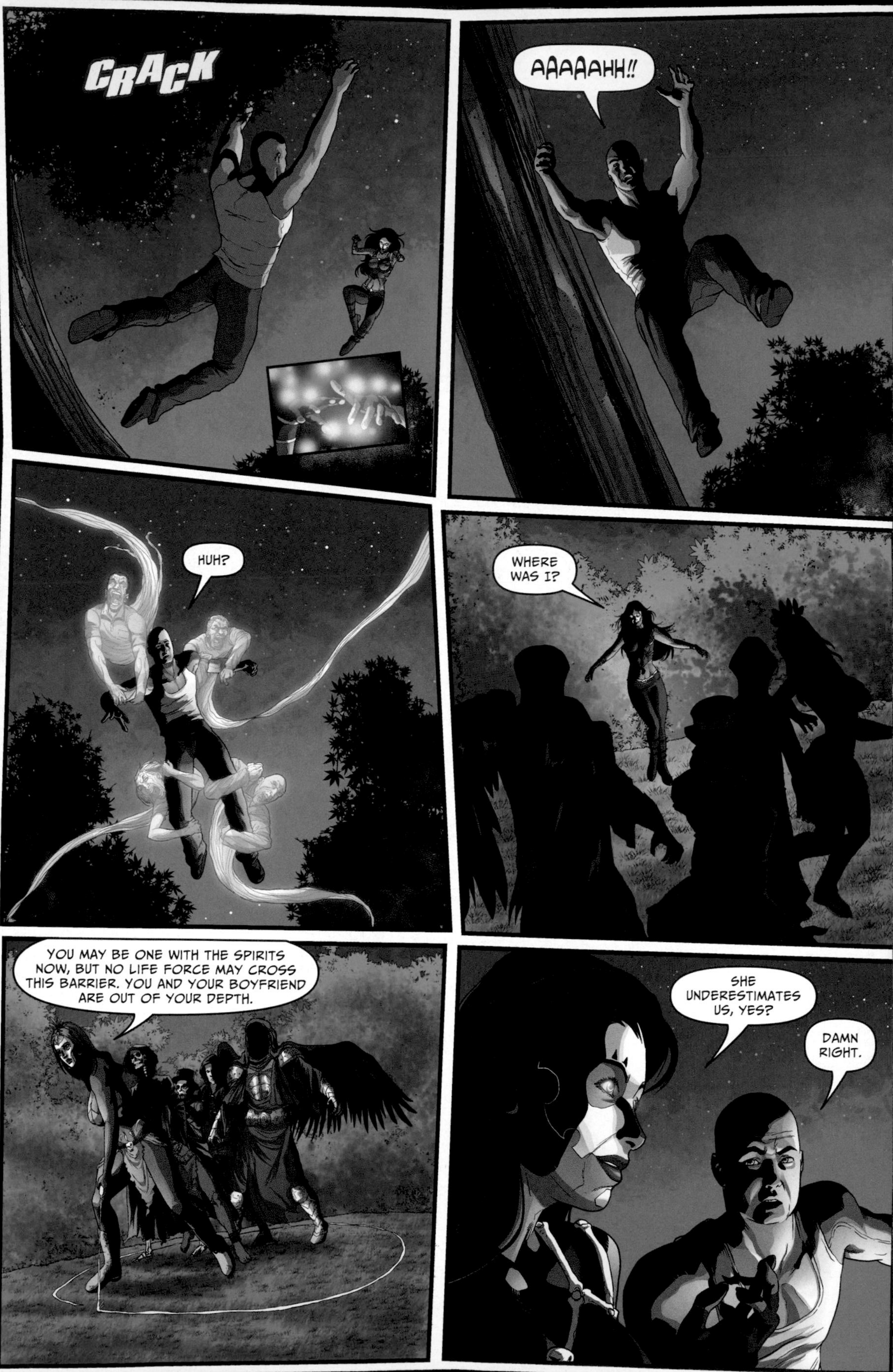
CRACK
AAAAAHH!!
HUH?
WHERE WAS I?
YOU MAY BE ONE WITH THE SPIRITS NOW, BUT NO LIFE FORCE MAY CROSS THIS BARRIER. YOU AND YOUR BOYFRIEND ARE OUT OF YOUR DEPTH.
SHE UNDERESTIMATES US, YES?
DAMN RIGHT.

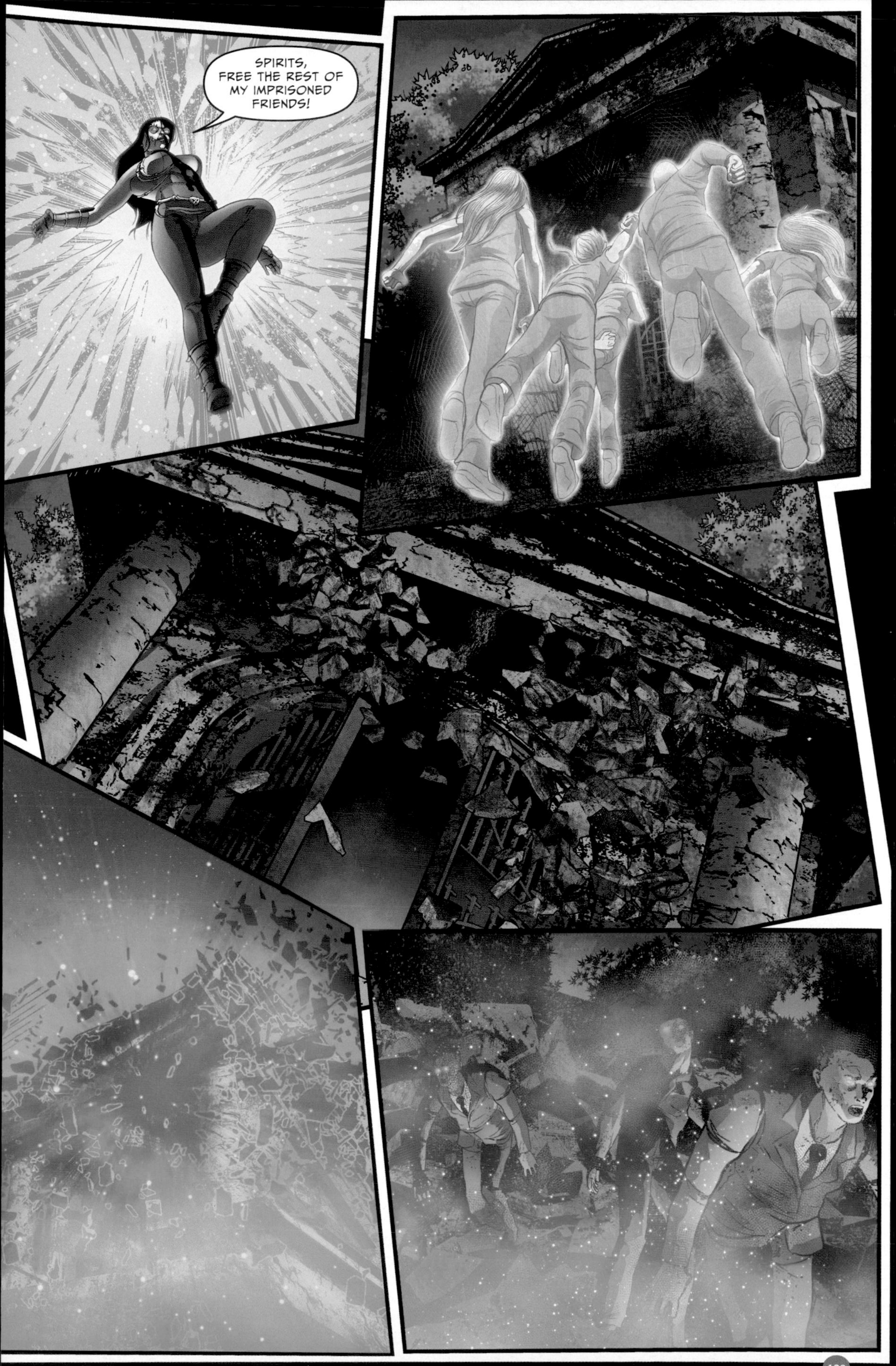
SPIRITS, FREE THE REST OF MY IMPRISONED FRIENDS!

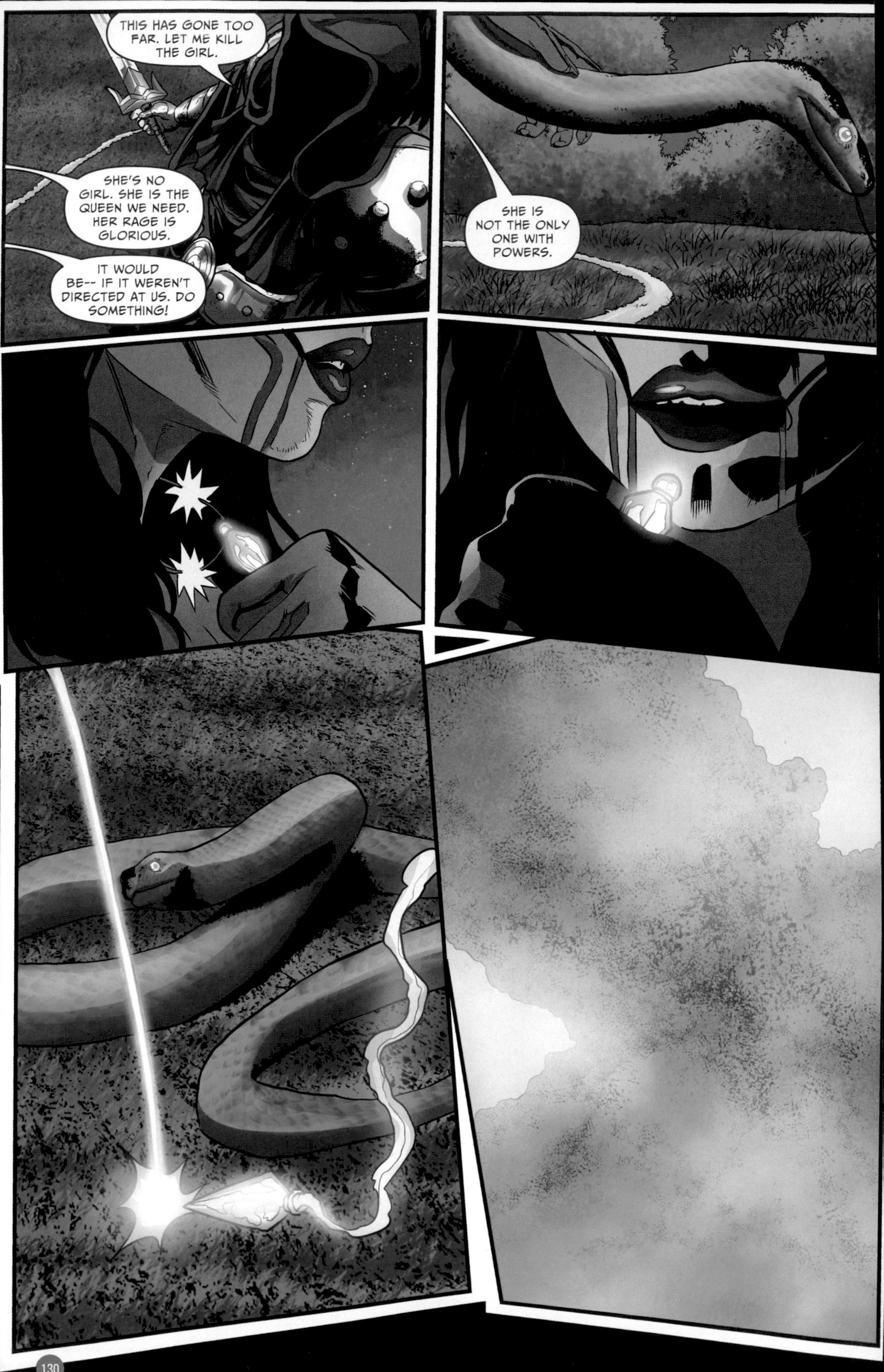
THIS HAS GONE TOO FAR. LET ME KILL THE GIRL.
SHE'S NO GIRL. SHE IS THE QUEEN WE NEED. HER RAGE IS GLORIOUS.
IT WOULD BE-- IF IT WEREN'T DIRECTED AT US. DO SOMETHING!
SHE IS NOT THE ONLY ONE WITH POWERS.

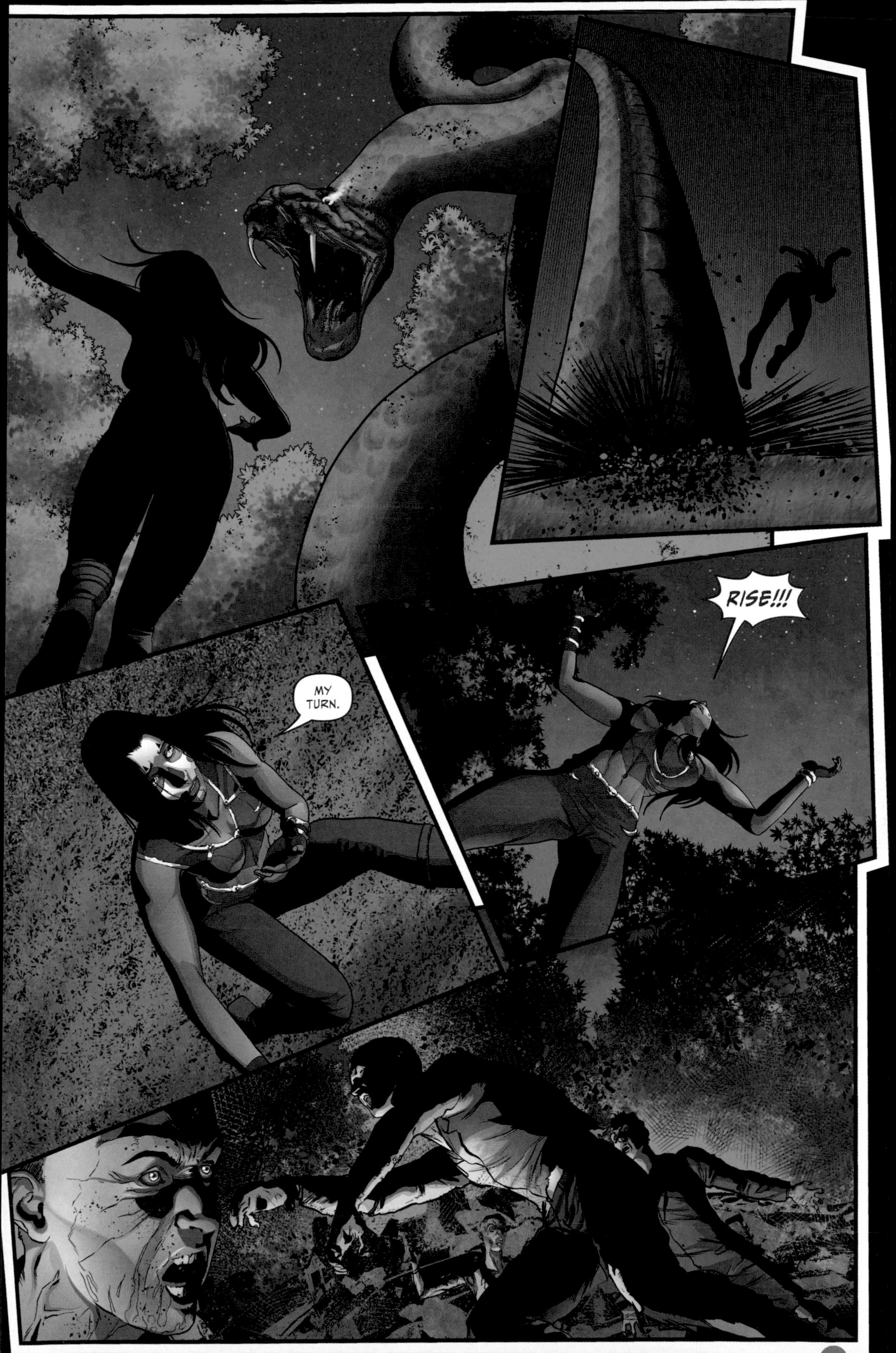
RISE!!!
MY TURN.

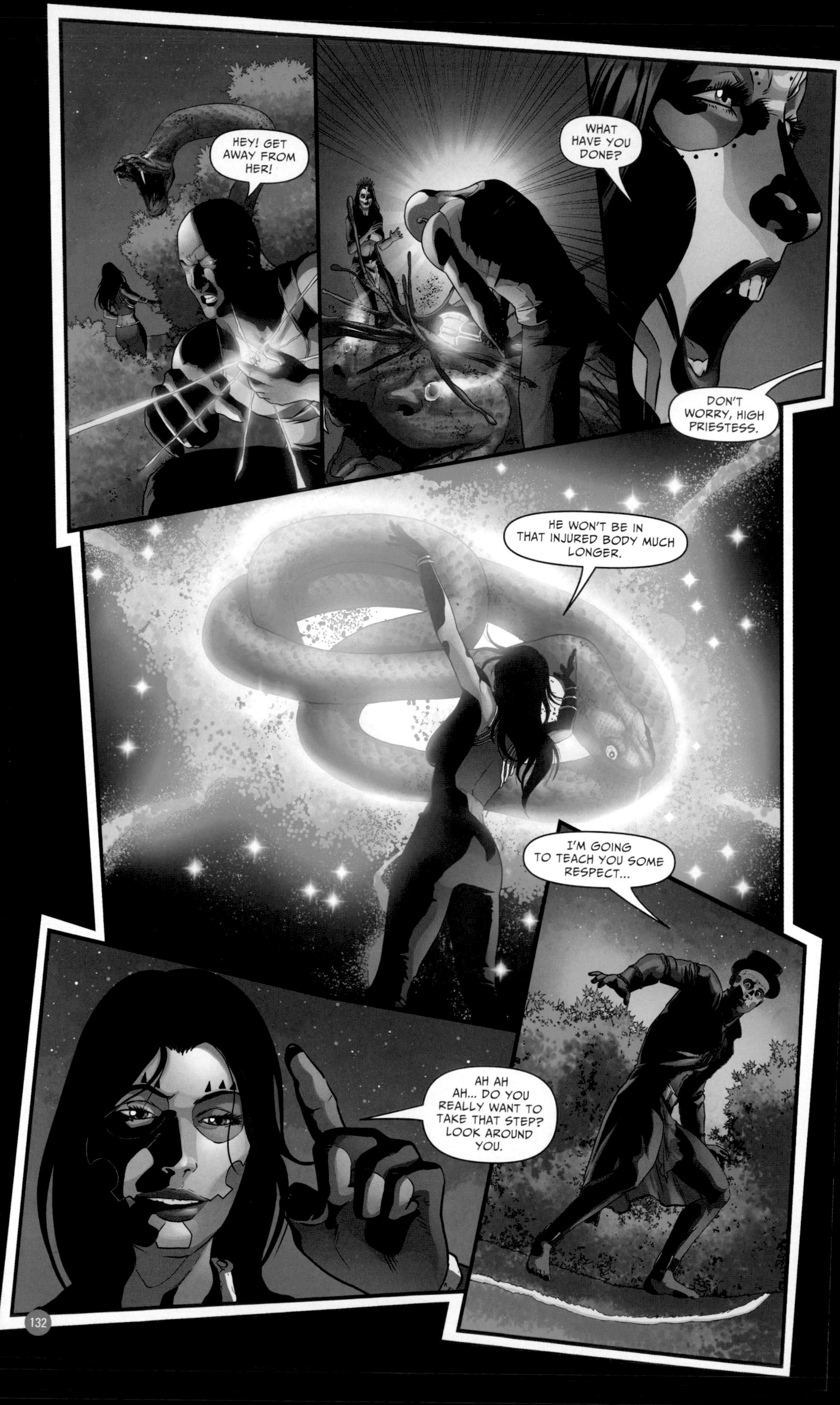
HEY! GET AWAY FROM HER!
WHAT HAVE YOU DONE?
DON'T WORRY, HIGH PRIESTESS.
HE WON'T BE IN THAT INJURED BODY MUCH LONGER.
I'M GOING TO TEACH YOU SOME RESPECT...
AH AH AH... DO YOU REALLY WANT TO TAKE THAT STEP? LOOK AROUND YOU.

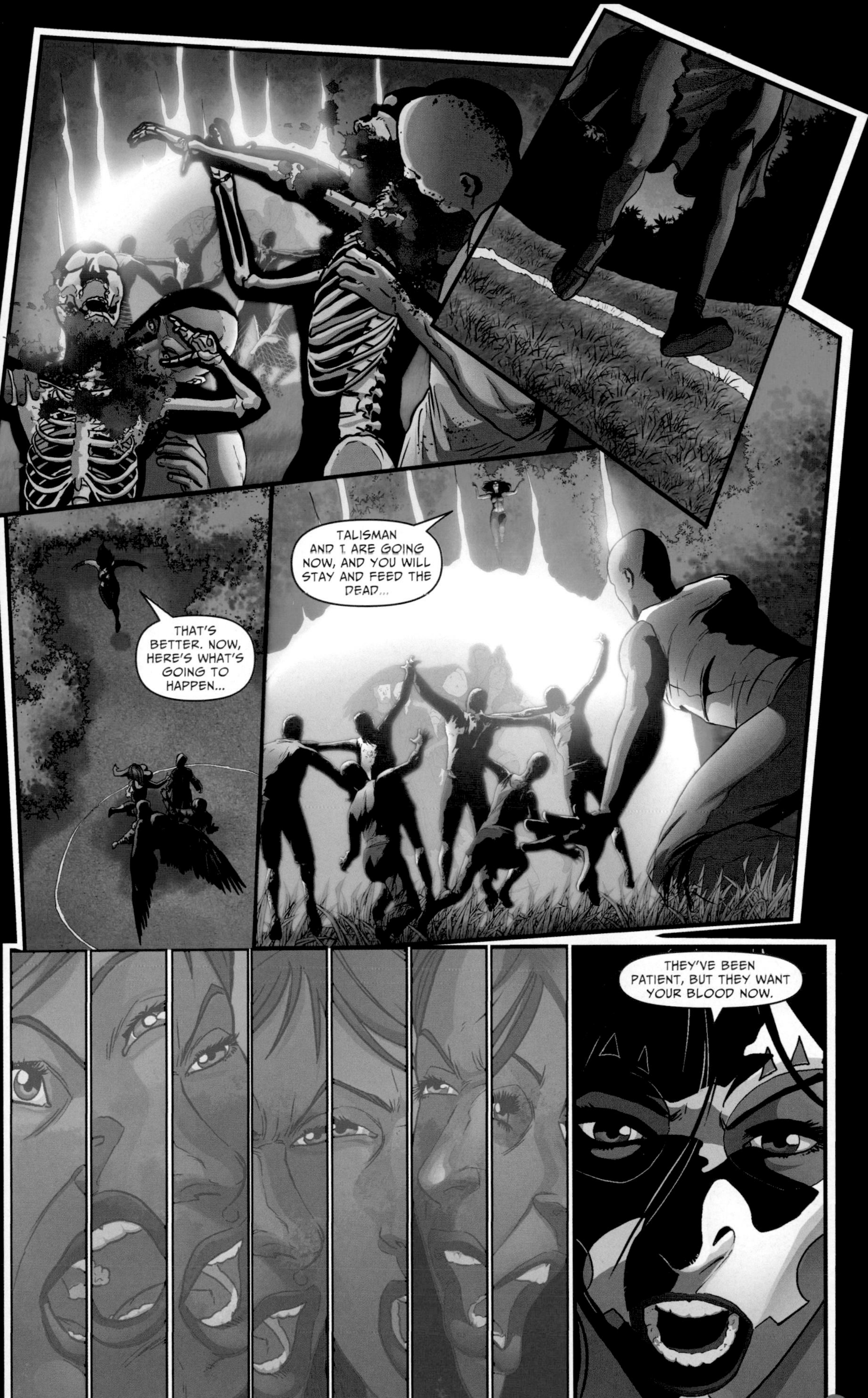

THAT'S BETTER. NOW, HERE'S WHAT'S GOING TO HAPPEN...
TALISMAN AND I ARE GOING NOW, AND YOU WILL STAY AND FEED THE DEAD...
THEY'VE BEEN PATIENT, BUT THEY WANT YOUR BLOOD NOW.

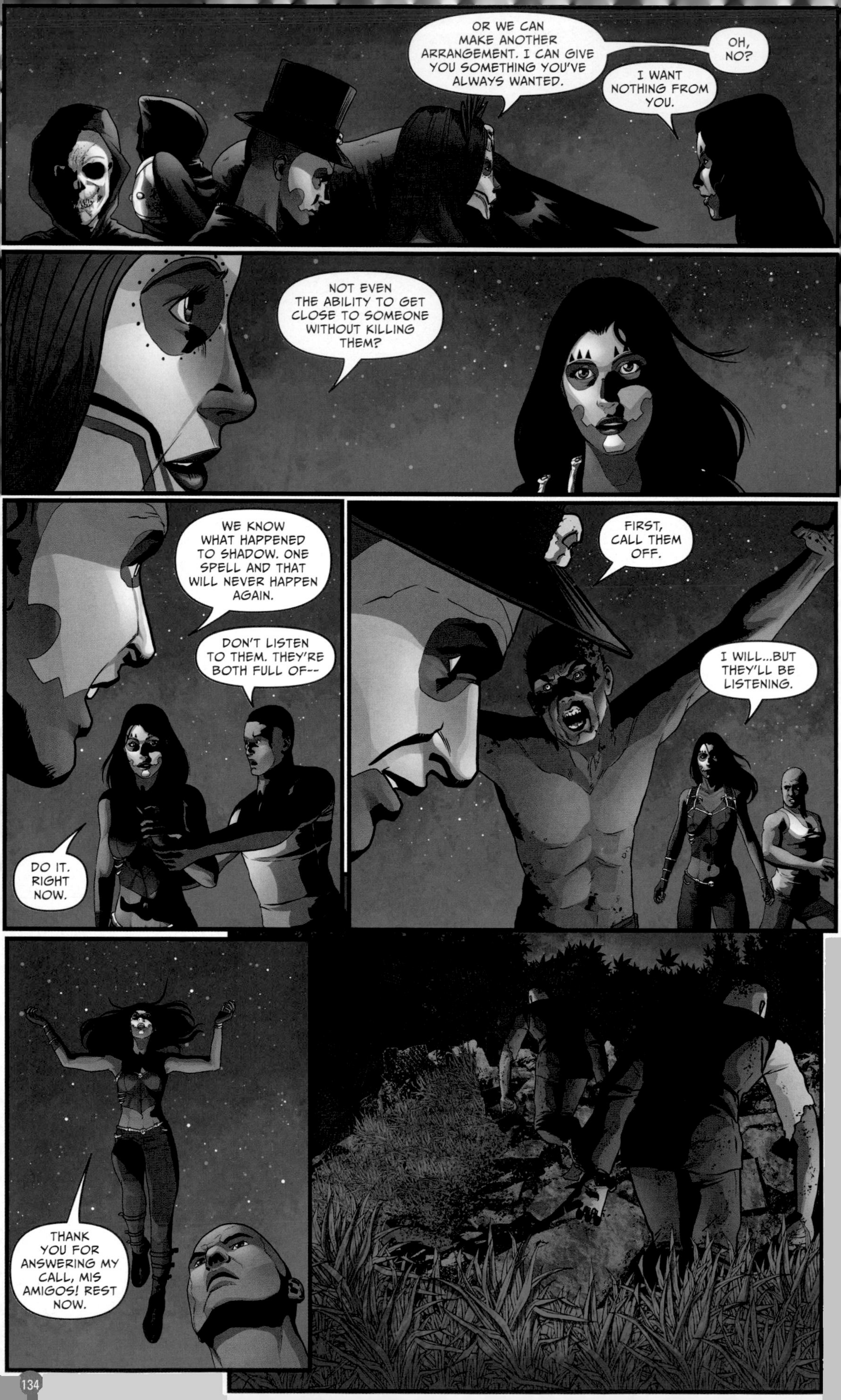
OR WE CAN MAKE ANOTHER ARRANGEMENT. I CAN GIVE YOU SOMETHING YOU'VE ALWAYS WANTED.
OH, NO?
I WANT NOTHING FROM YOU.
NOT EVEN THE ABILITY TO GET CLOSE TO SOMEONE WITHOUT KILLING THEM?
WE KNOW WHAT HAPPENED TO SHADOW. ONE SPELL AND THAT WILL NEVER HAPPEN AGAIN.
DON'T LISTEN TO THEM. THEY'RE BOTH FULL OF--
DO IT. RIGHT NOW.
FIRST, CALL THEM OFF.
I WILL...BUT THEY'LL BE LISTENING.
THANK YOU FOR ANSWERING MY CALL, MIS AMIGOS! REST NOW.

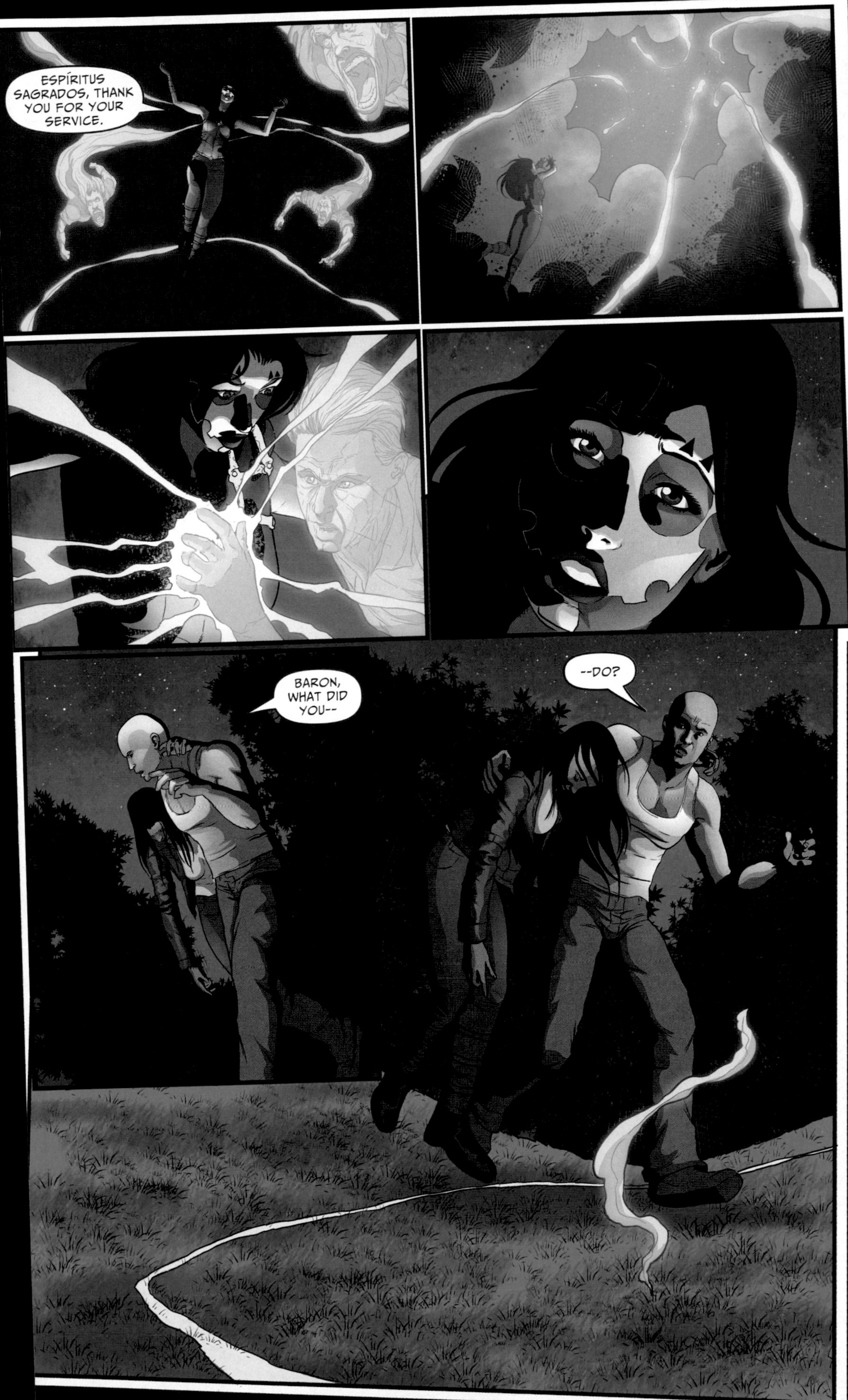
ESPÍRITUS SAGRADOS, THANK YOU FOR YOUR SERVICE.
BARON, WHAT DID YOU--
--DO?

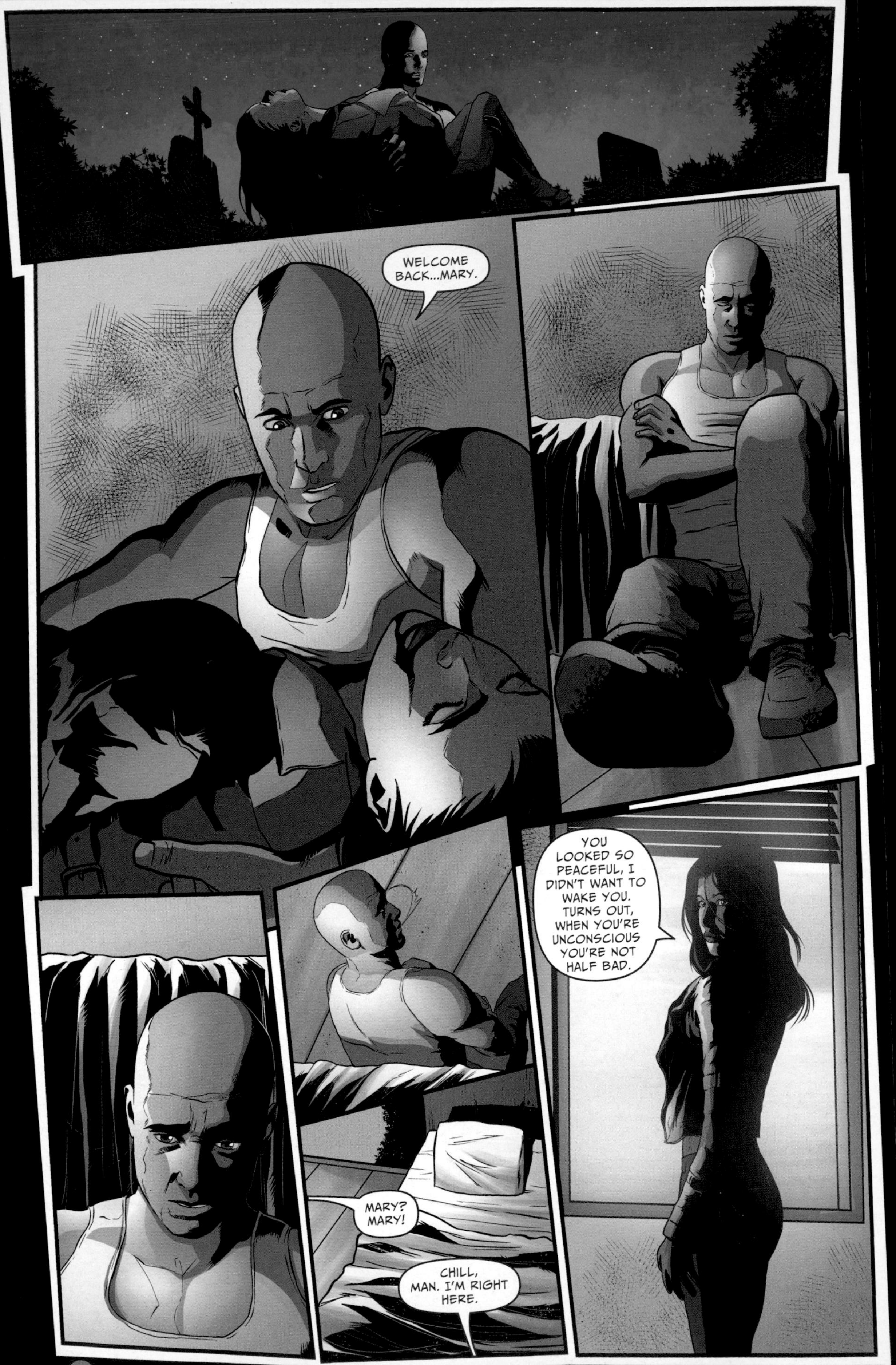
WELCOME BACK...MARY.
MARY? MARY!
CHILL, MAN. I'M RIGHT HERE.
YOU LOOKED SO PEACEFUL, I DIDN'T WANT TO WAKE YOU. TURNS OUT, WHEN YOU'RE UNCONSCIOUS YOU'RE NOT HALF BAD.

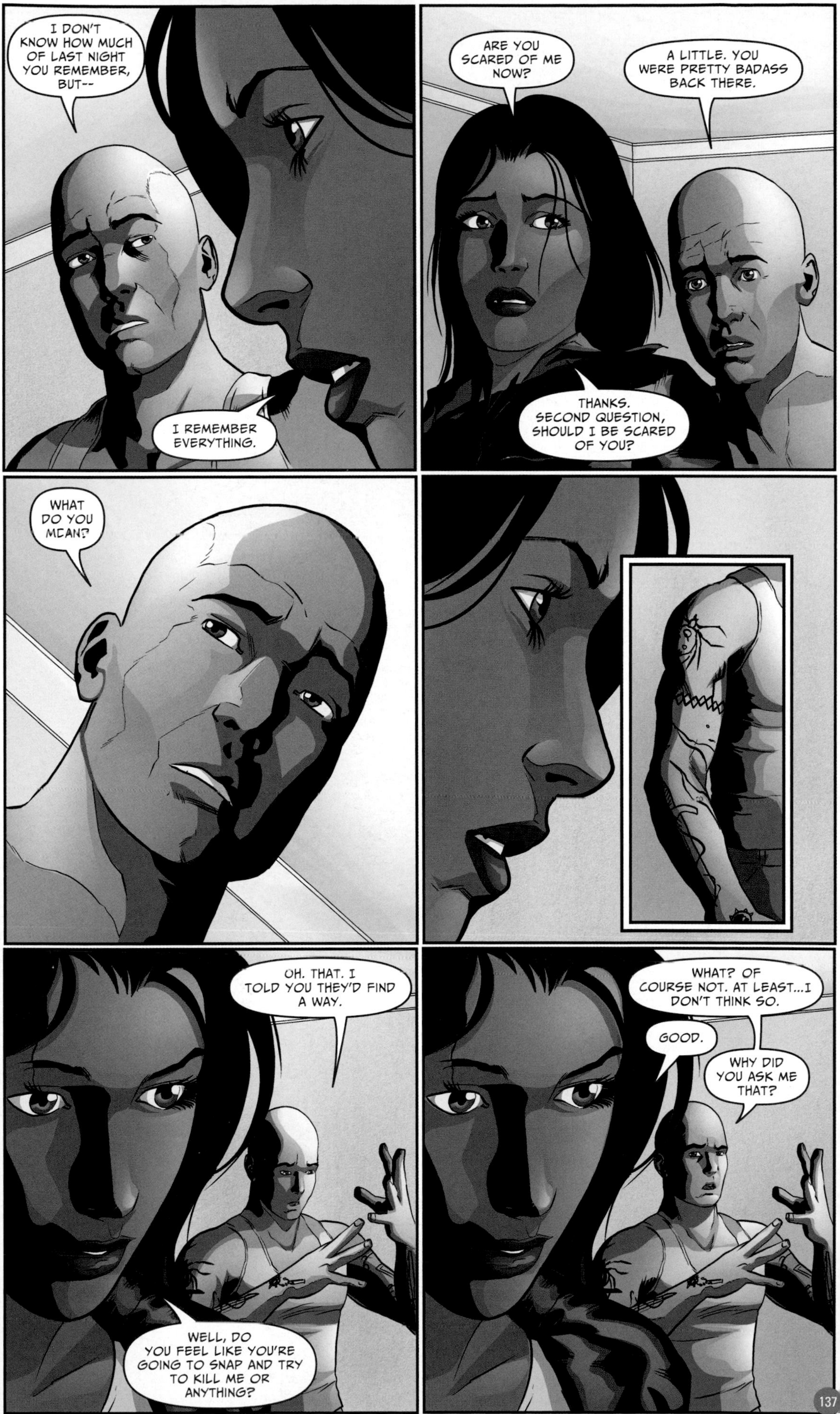
I DON'T KNOW HOW MUCH OF LAST NIGHT YOU REMEMBER, BUT--
I REMEMBER EVERYTHING.
ARE YOU SCARED OF ME NOW?
A LITTLE. YOU WERE PRETTY BADASS BACK THERE.
THANKS. SECOND QUESTION, SHOULD I BE SCARED OF YOU?
WHAT DO YOU MEAN?
OH. THAT. I TOLD YOU THEY'D FIND A WAY.
WELL, DO YOU FEEL LIKE YOU'RE GOING TO SNAP AND TRY TO KILL ME OR ANYTHING?
WHAT? OF COURSE NOT. AT LEAST...I DON'T THINK SO.
GOOD.
WHY DID YOU ASK ME THAT?

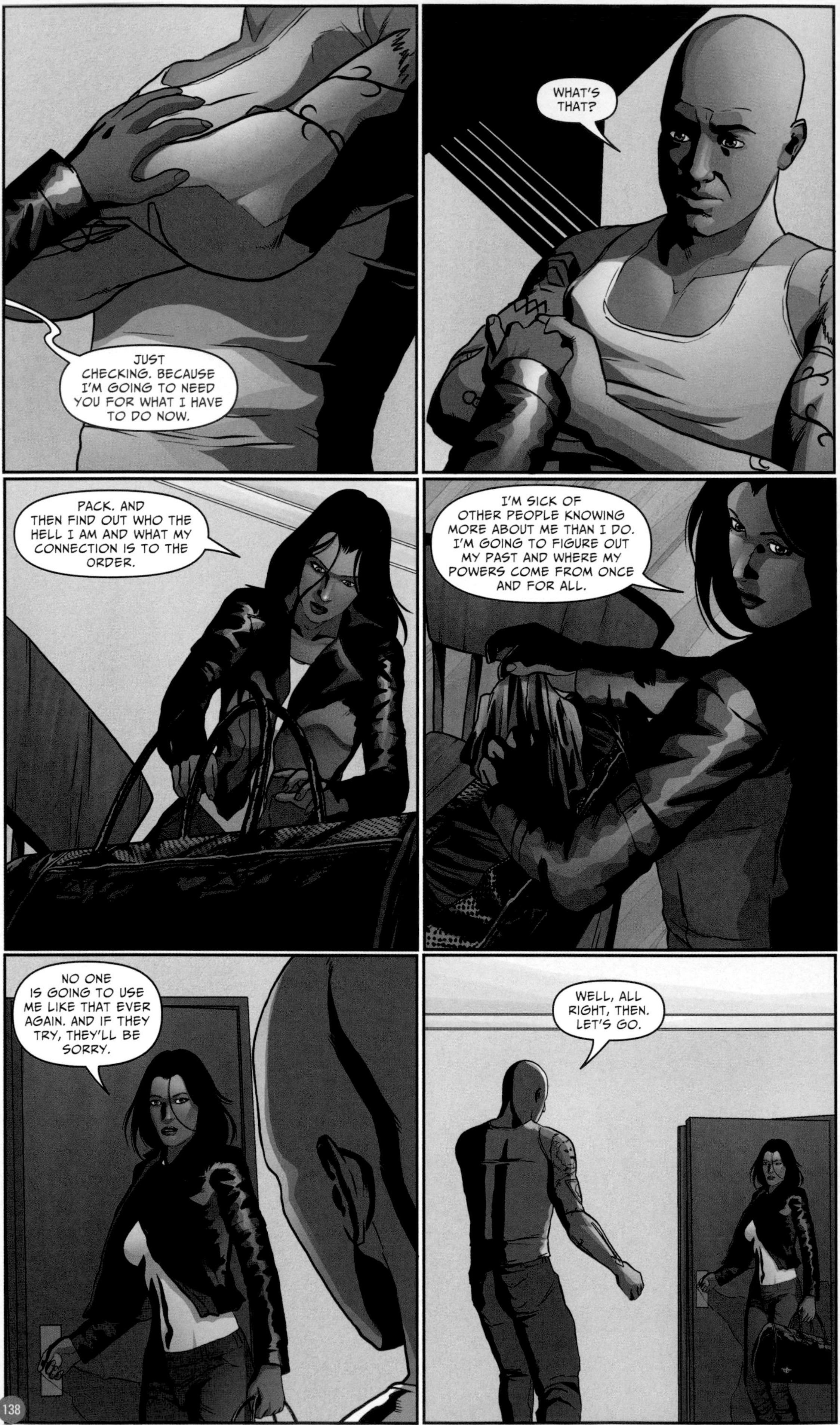
JUST CHECKING. BECAUSE I'M GOING TO NEED YOU FOR WHAT I HAVE TO DO NOW.
WHAT'S THAT?
PACK. AND THEN FIND OUT WHO THE HELL I AM AND WHAT MY CONNECTION IS TO THE ORDER.
I'M SICK OF OTHER PEOPLE KNOWING MORE ABOUT ME THAN I DO. I'M GOING TO FIGURE OUT MY PAST AND WHERE MY POWERS COME FROM ONCE AND FOR ALL.
NO ONE IS GOING TO USE ME LIKE THAT EVER AGAIN. AND IF THEY TRY, THEY'LL BE SORRY.
WELL, ALL RIGHT, THEN. LET'S GO.

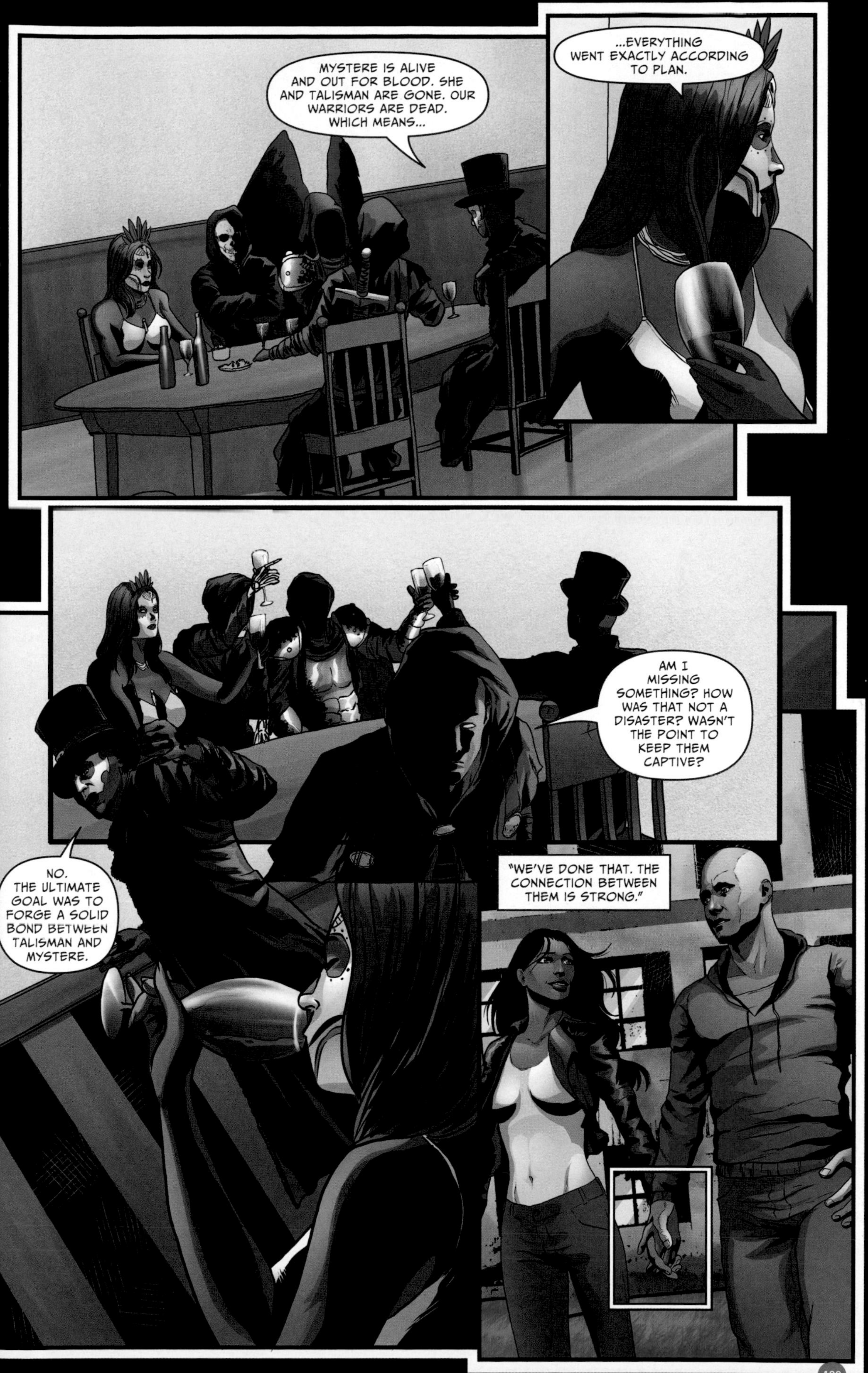

MYSTERE IS ALIVE AND OUT FOR BLOOD. SHE AND TALISMAN ARE GONE. OUR WARRIORS ARE DEAD. WHICH MEANS...
...EVERYTHING WENT EXACTLY ACCORDING TO PLAN.
AM I MISSING SOMETHING? HOW WAS THAT NOT A DISASTER? WASN'T THE POINT TO KEEP THEM CAPTIVE?
NO. THE ULTIMATE GOAL WAS TO FORGE A SOLID BOND BETWEEN TALISMAN AND MYSTERE.
"WE'VE DONE THAT. THE CONNECTION BETWEEN THEM IS STRONG."

THE WARRIORS WERE EXPECTED CASUALTIES.

ANY LOSSES WILL BE WORTH IT IN THE END.

BY THE TIME WE ARE READY TO IMPLEMENT THE NEXT PART OF OUR PLAN...

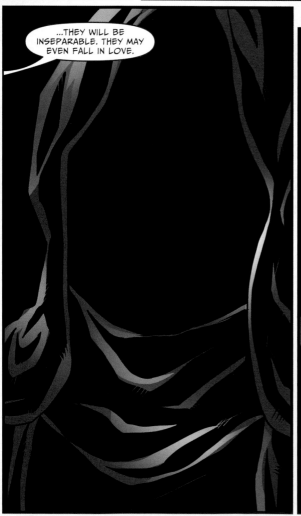

...THEY WILL BE INSEPARABLE. THEY MAY EVEN FALL IN LOVE.

IT WILL BE EASY TO MAKE THEM THE KING AND QUEEN OF PENTACLES.

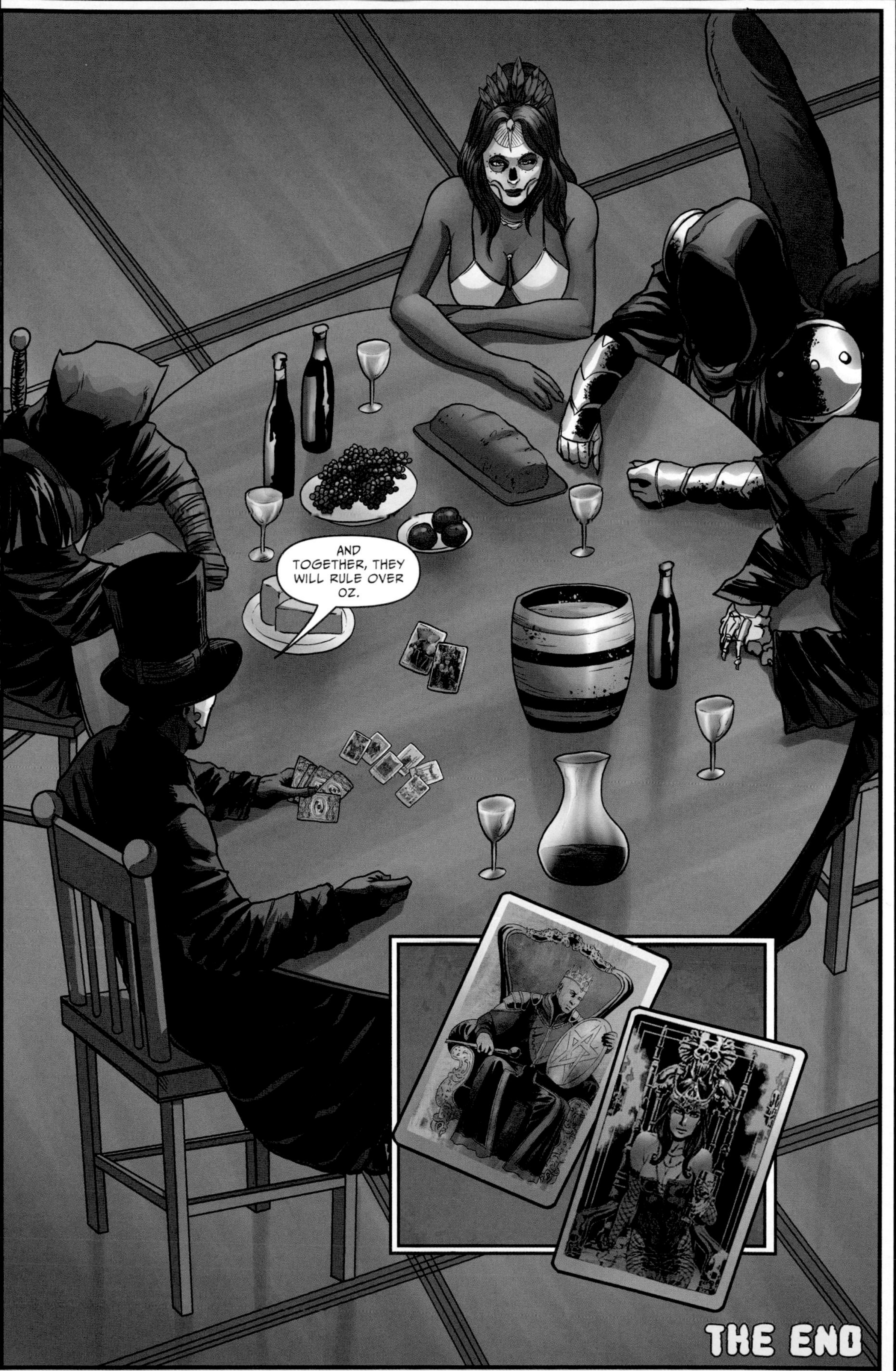
AND TOGETHER, THEY WILL RULE OVER OZ.
THE END

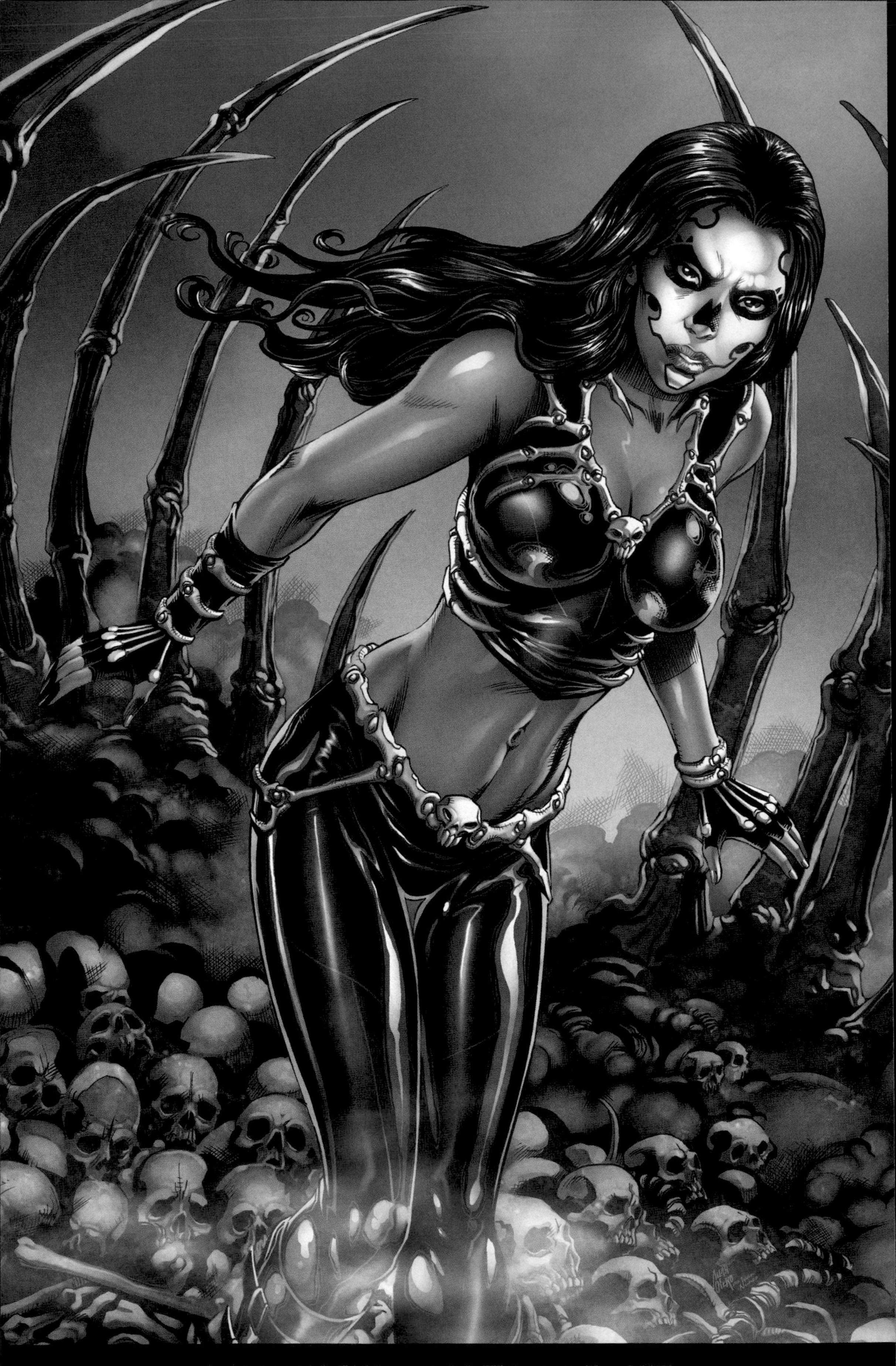

GRIMM FAIRY TALES: DAY OF THE DEAD #1 ▲ COVER A

Artwork by Allan Otero • Colors by Ivan Nunes

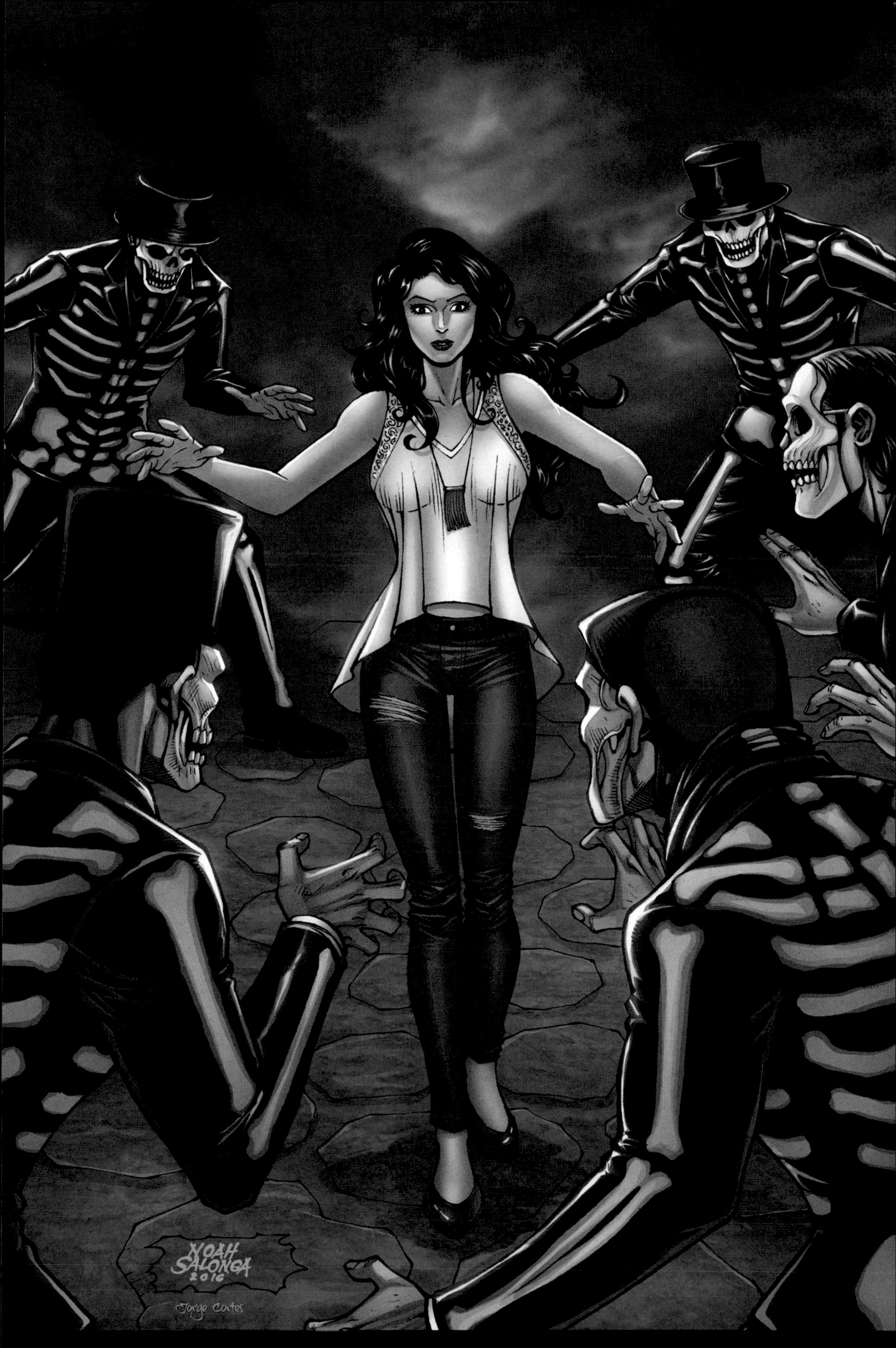
NOAH SALONGA 2016
Jorge Cortes

GRIMM FAIRY TALES: DAY OF THE DEAD #1 ▲ COVER B
Artwork by Noah Salonga • Colors by Jorge Cortes

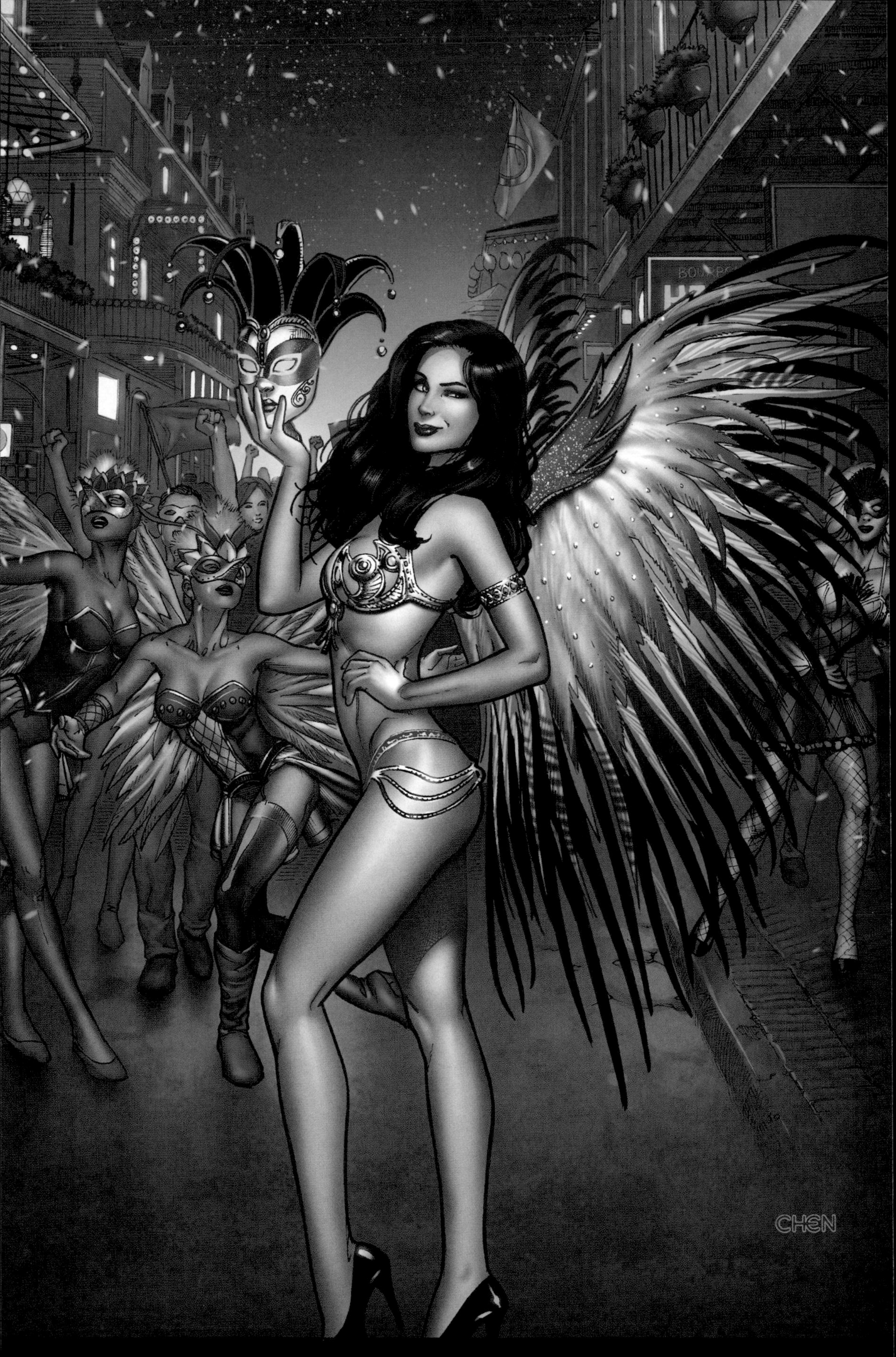
BOURBO
CHEN

GRIMM FAIRY TALES: DAY OF THE DEAD #1 ▲ COVER C
Artwork by Sean Chen • Colors by Ula Mos

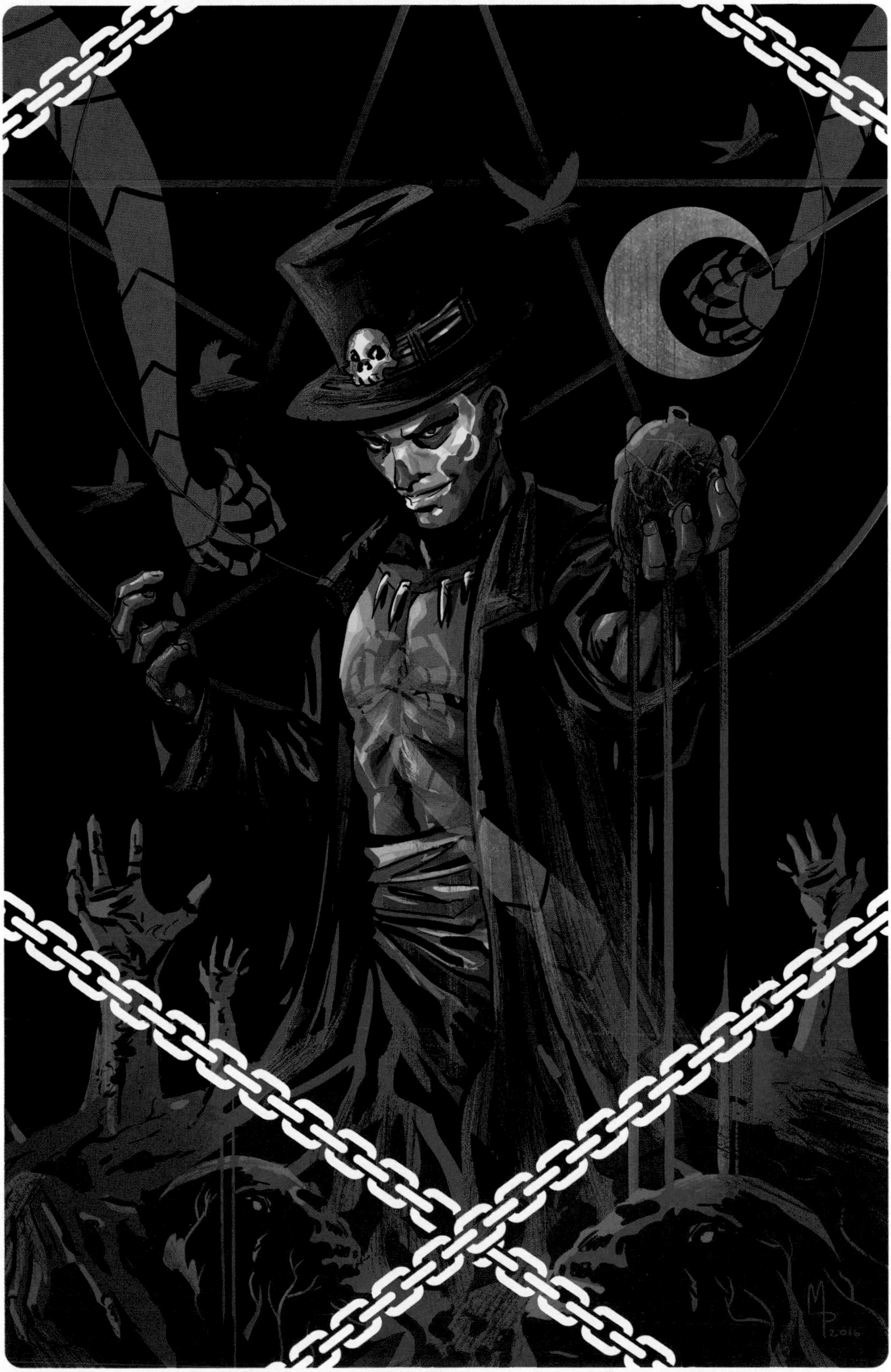

THE MAGICIAN

GRIMM FAIRY TALES: DAY OF THE DEAD #1 ▲ COVER D
Artwork by Manuel Preitano

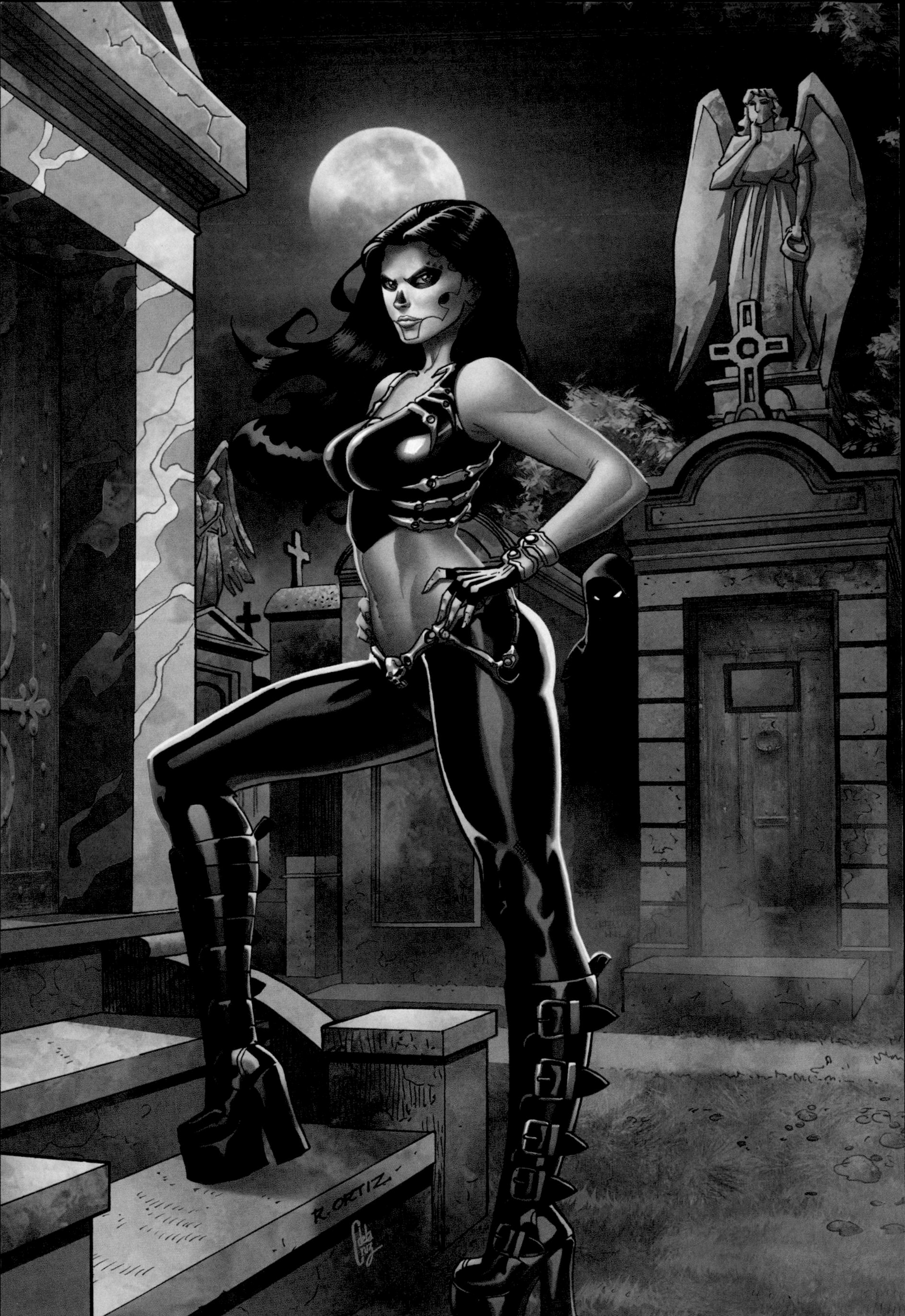
R. ORTIZ

GRIMM FAIRY TALES: DAY OF THE DEAD #2 ▲ COVER A
Artwork by Richard Ortiz • Colors by Ceci de la Cruz

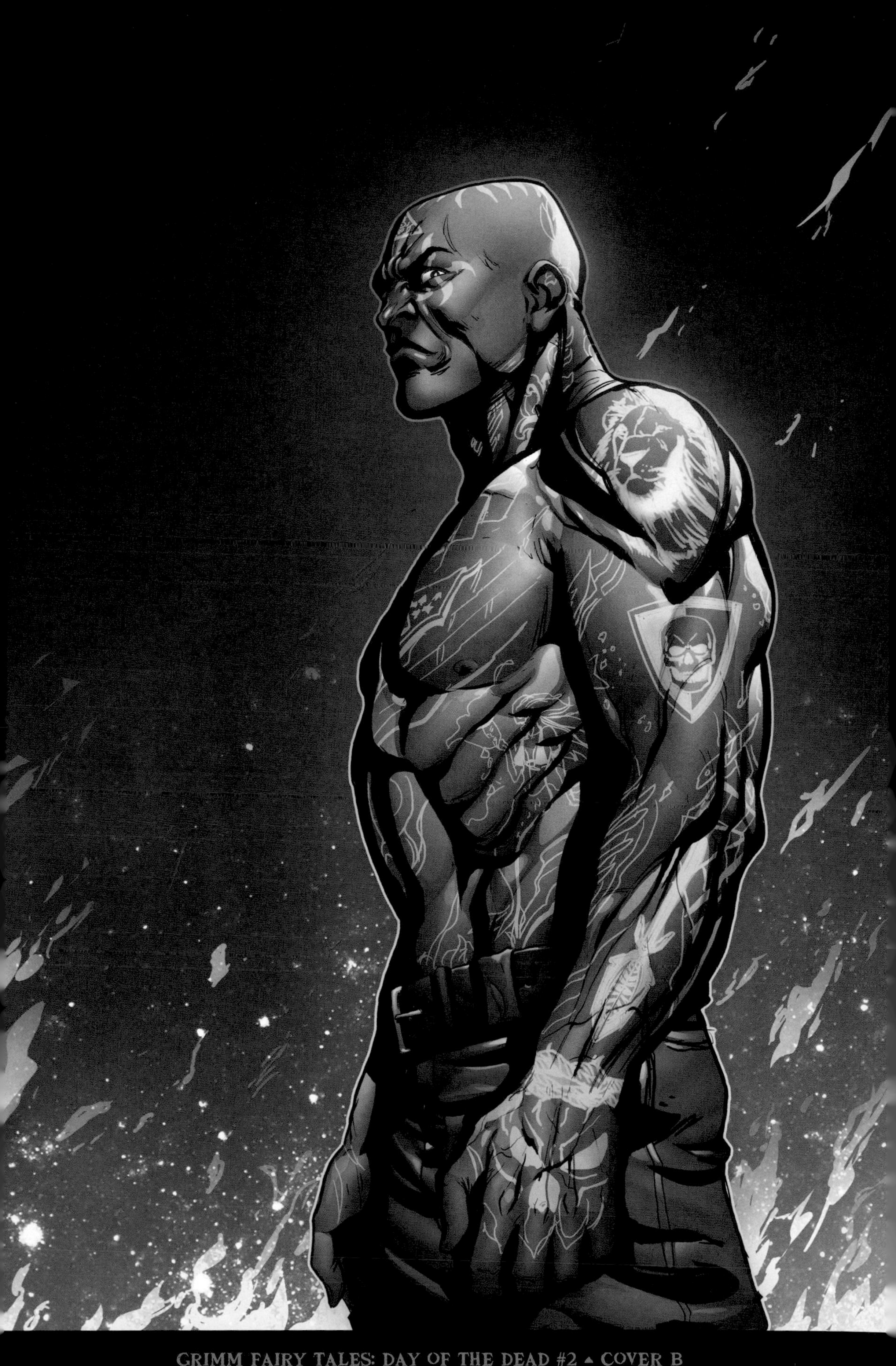

GRIMM FAIRY TALES: DAY OF THE DEAD #2 ▲ COVER B
Artwork by Marc Rosete • Colors by Erick Arciniega

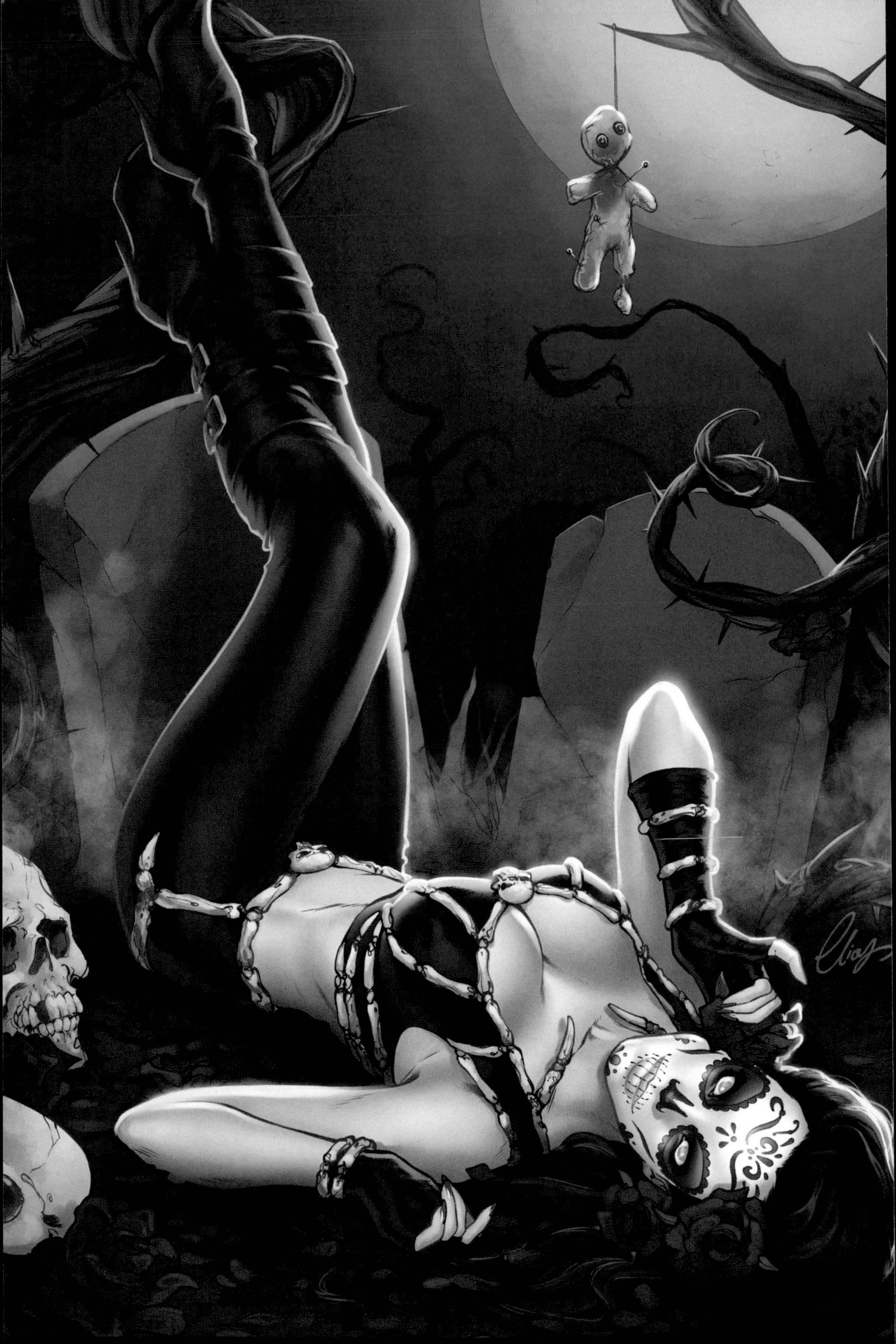

GRIMM FAIRY TALES: DAY OF THE DEAD #2 ▲ COVER C
Artwork by Elias Chatzoudis

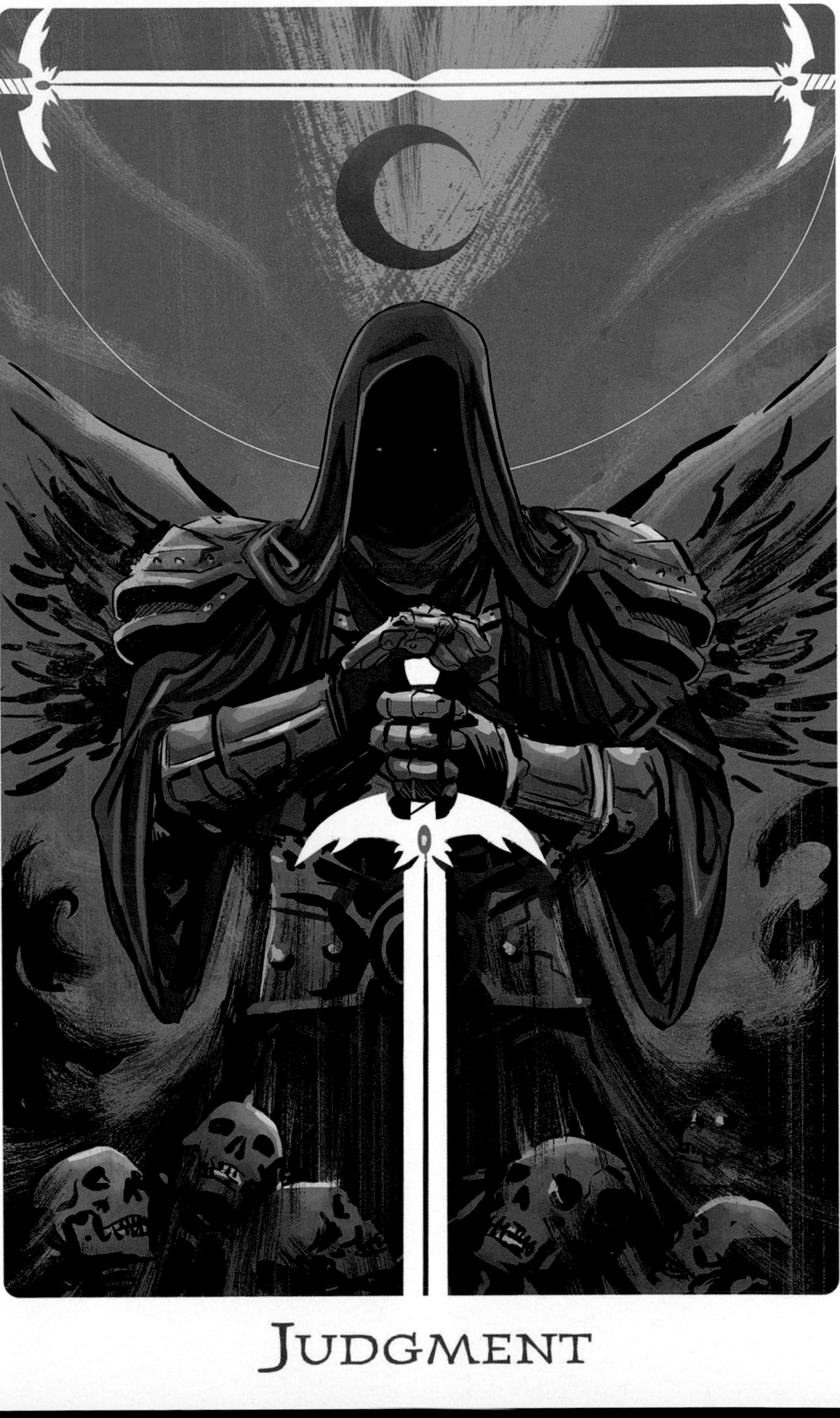
JUDGMENT

GRIMM FAIRY TALES: DAY OF THE DEAD #2 ▲ COVER D
Artwork by Manuel Preitano

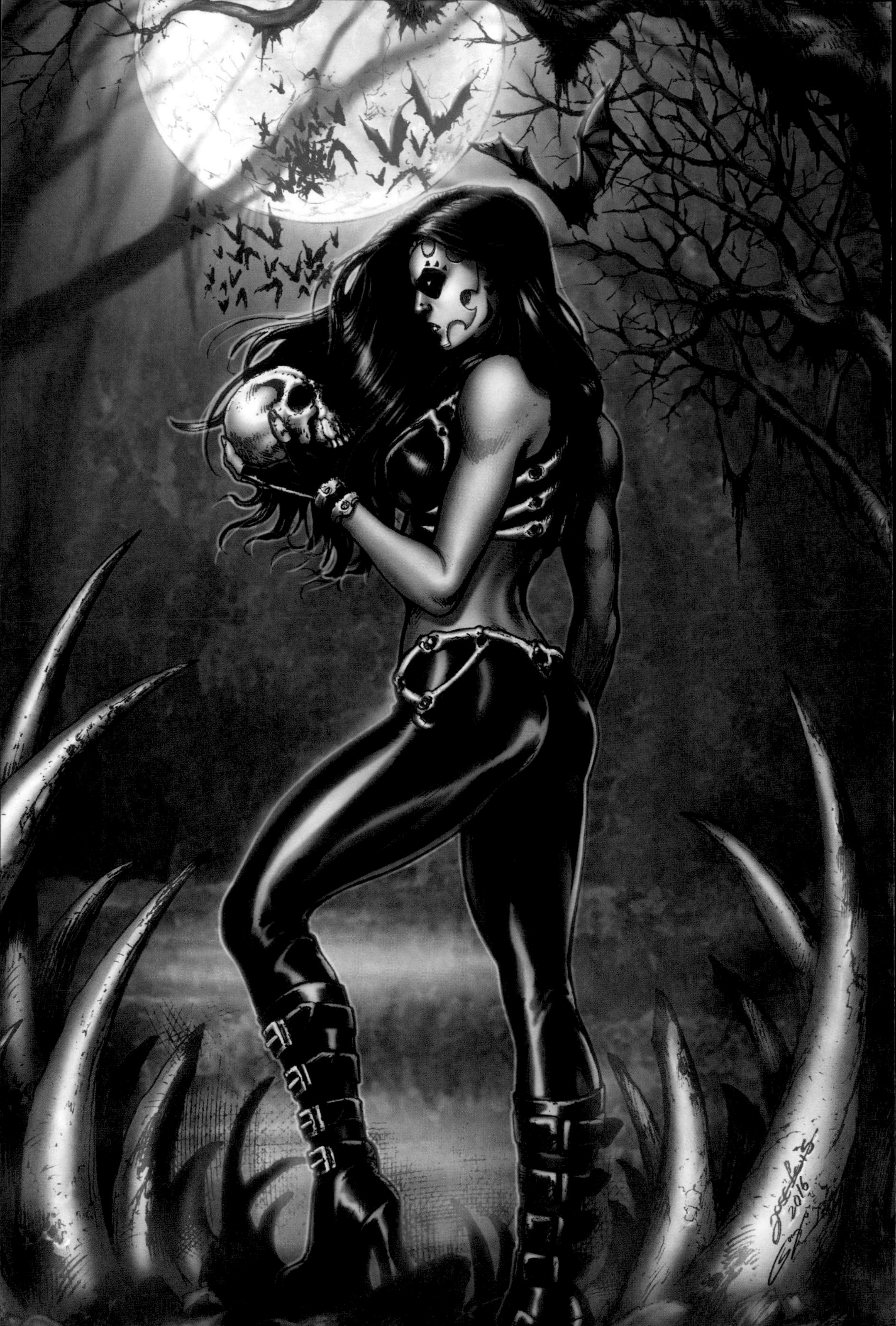

GRIMM FAIRY TALES: DAY OF THE DEAD #3 ▲ COVER A

Artwork by Jose Luis • Colors by Sanju Nivangune

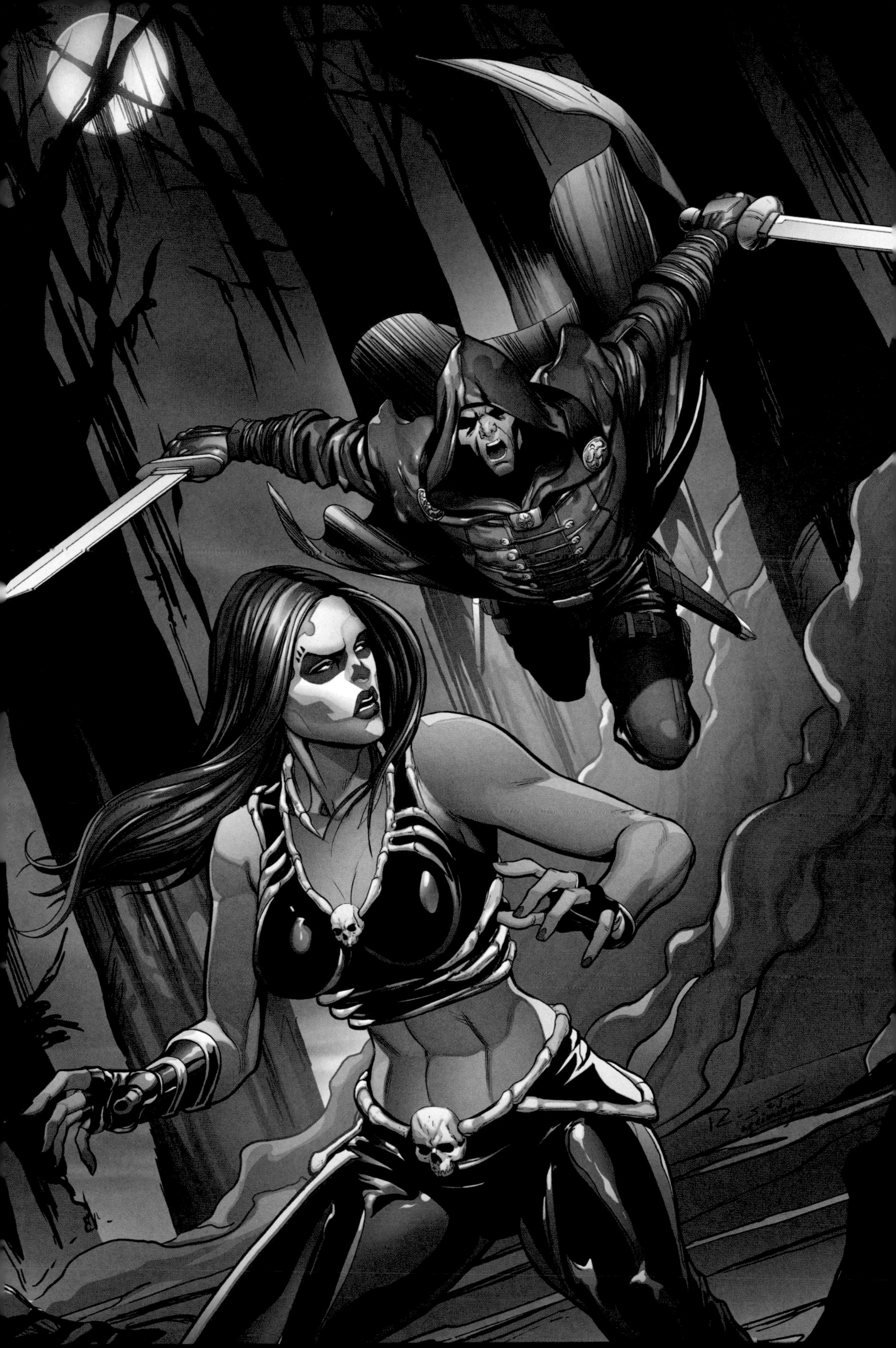

GRIMM FAIRY TALES: DAY OF THE DEAD #3 ▲ COVER B
Artwork by Marc Rosete • Colors by Erick Arciniega

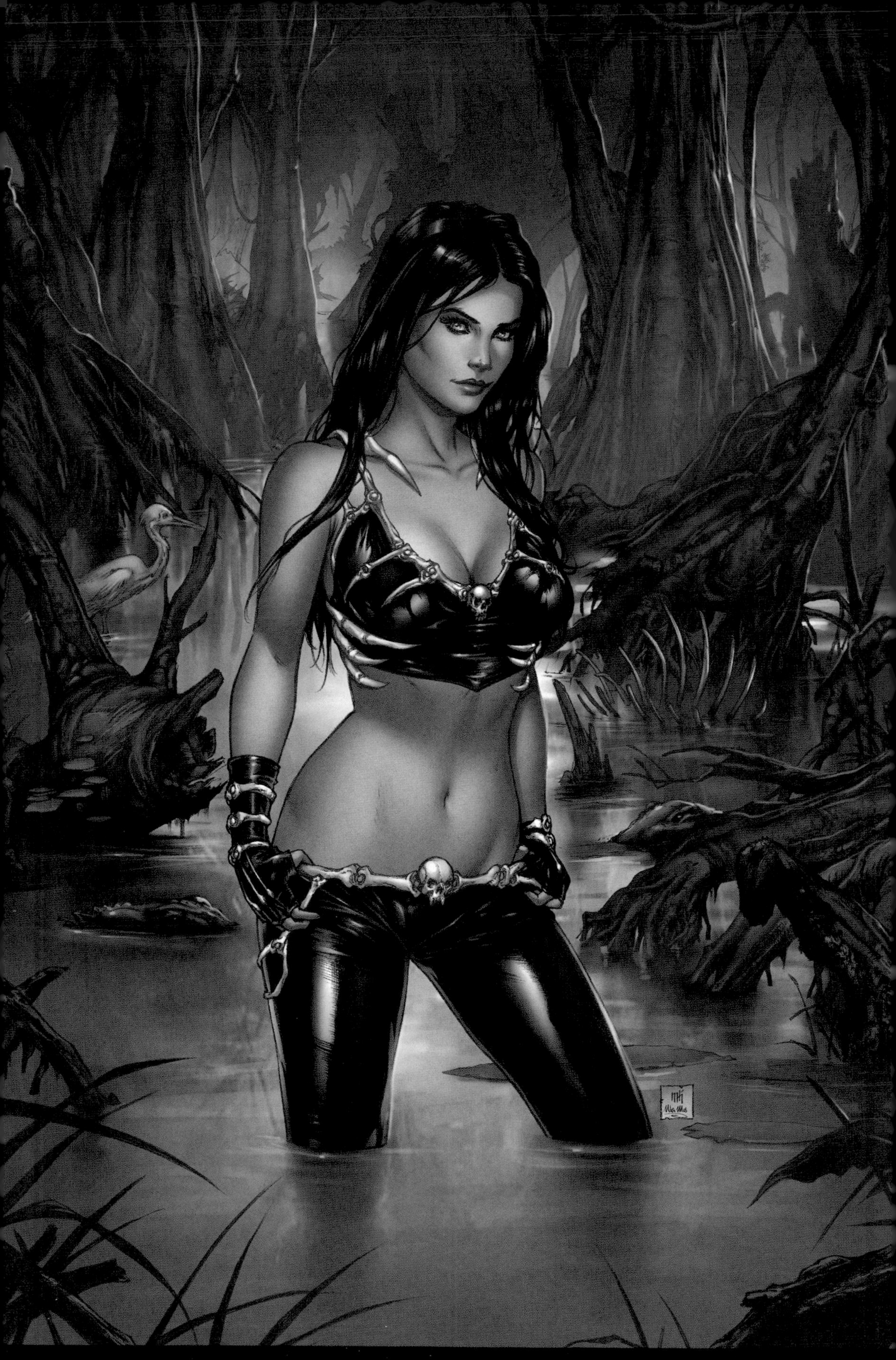

GRIMM FAIRY TALES: DAY OF THE DEAD #3 ▲ COVER C
Artwork by Mike Krome • Colors by Ula Mos

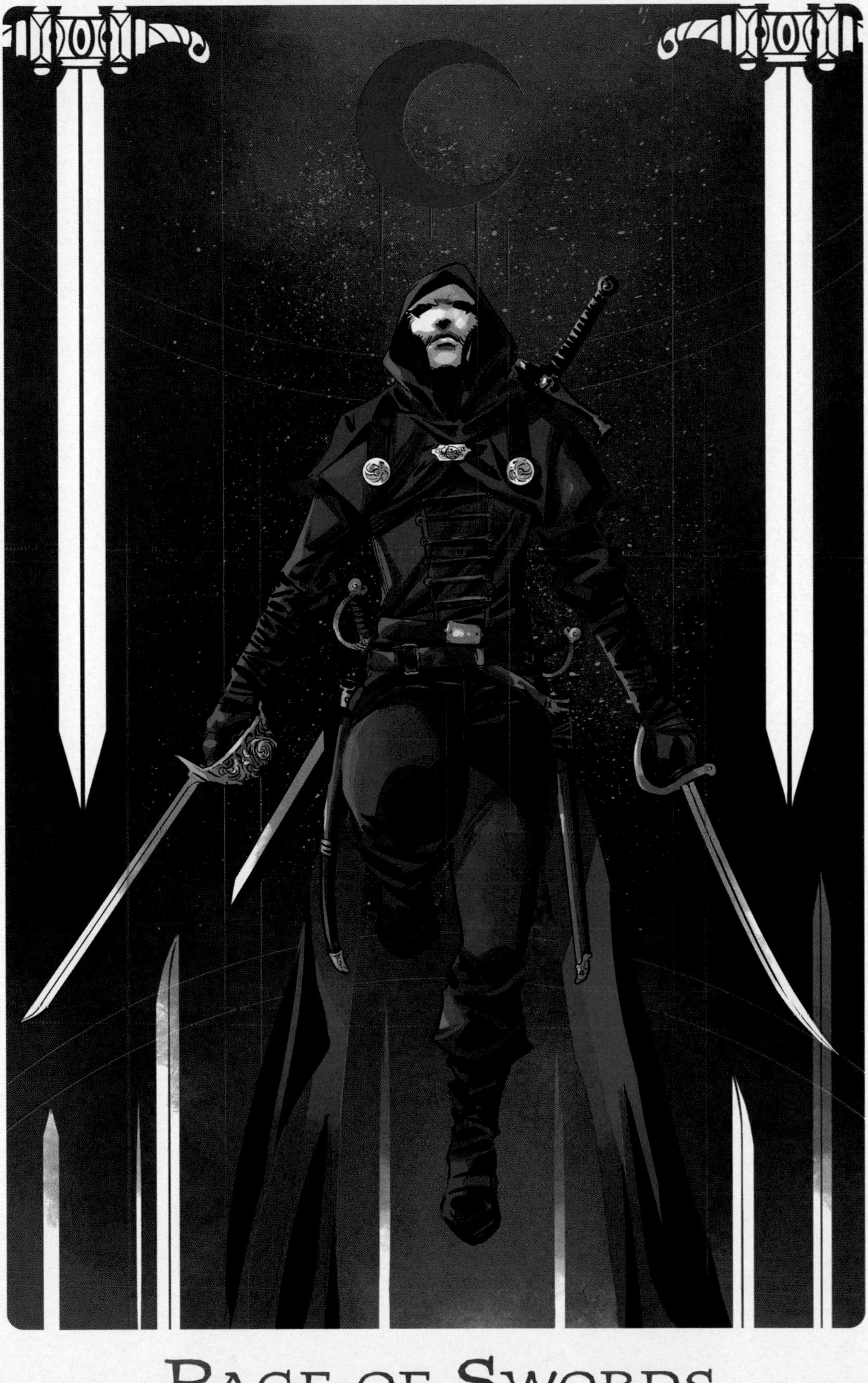
PAGE OF SWORDS

GRIMM FAIRY TALES: DAY OF THE DEAD #3 ▲ COVER D
Artwork by Manuel Preitano

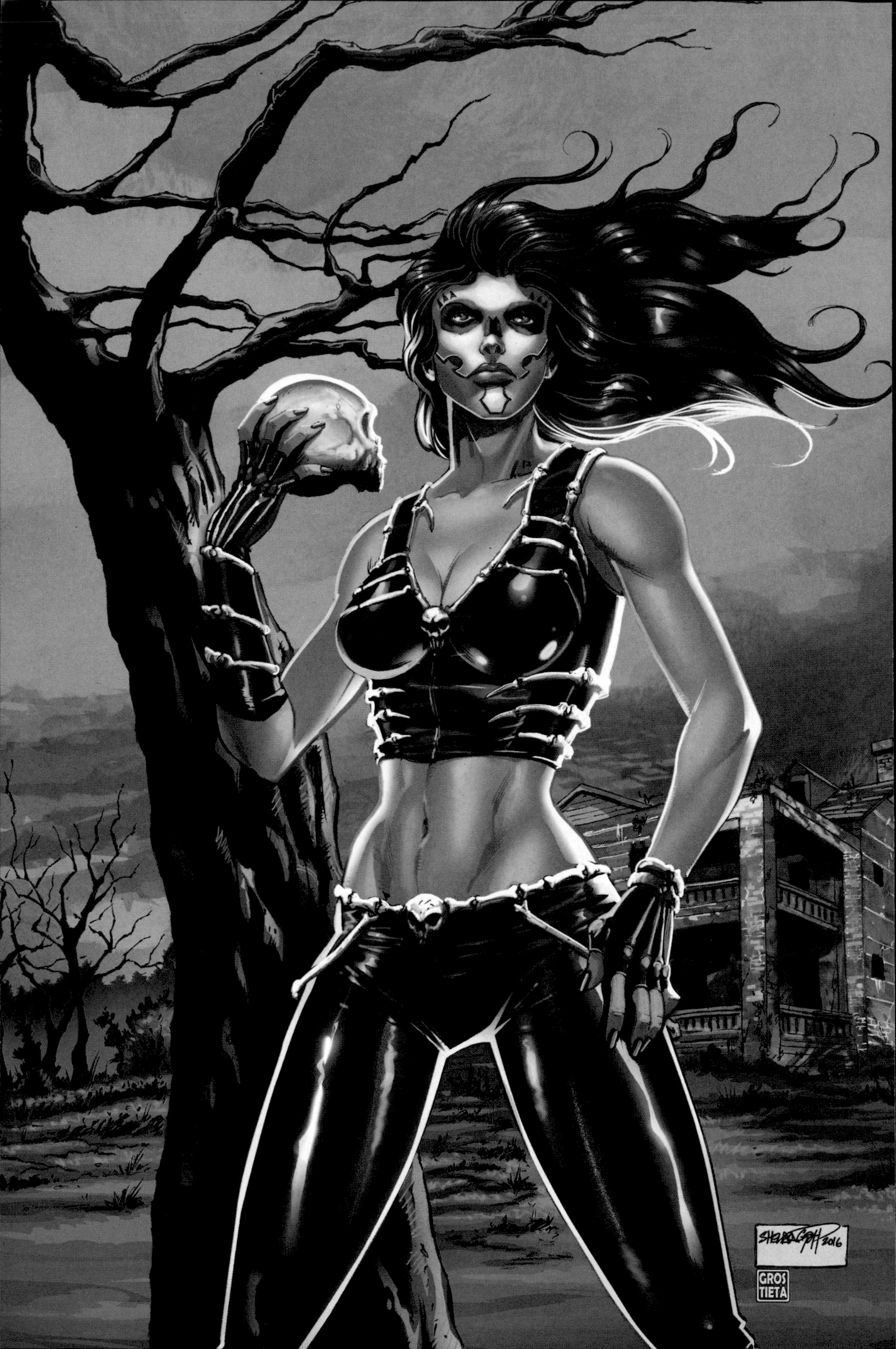
SHELDON GOH 2016
GROS TIETA

GRIMM FAIRY TALES: DAY OF THE DEAD #4 ▲ COVER A
Artwork by Sheldon Goh • Colors by Grostieta

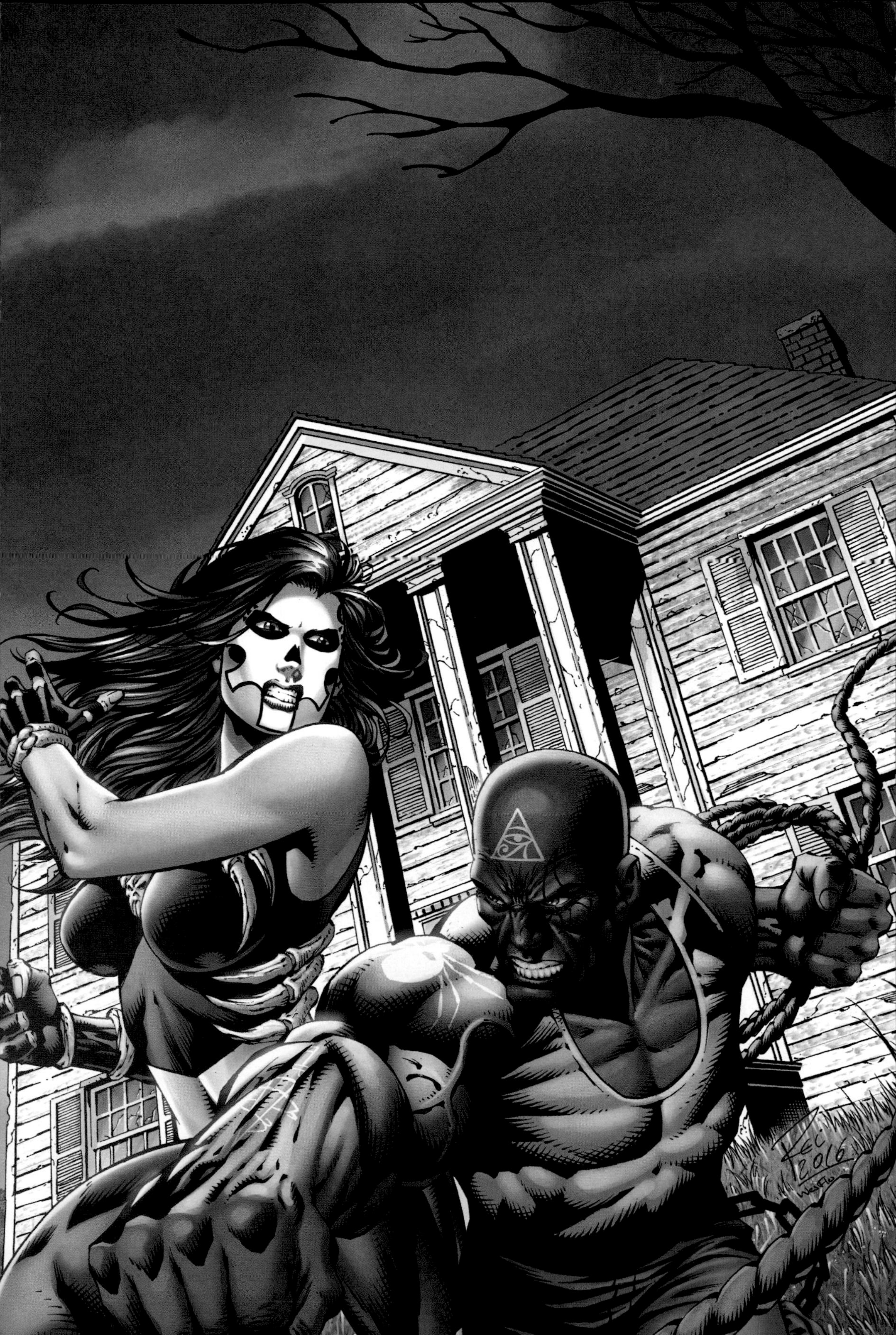

GRIMM FAIRY TALES: DAY OF THE DEAD #4 ▲ COVER B

Artwork by Renato Rei • Colors by Wes Hartman

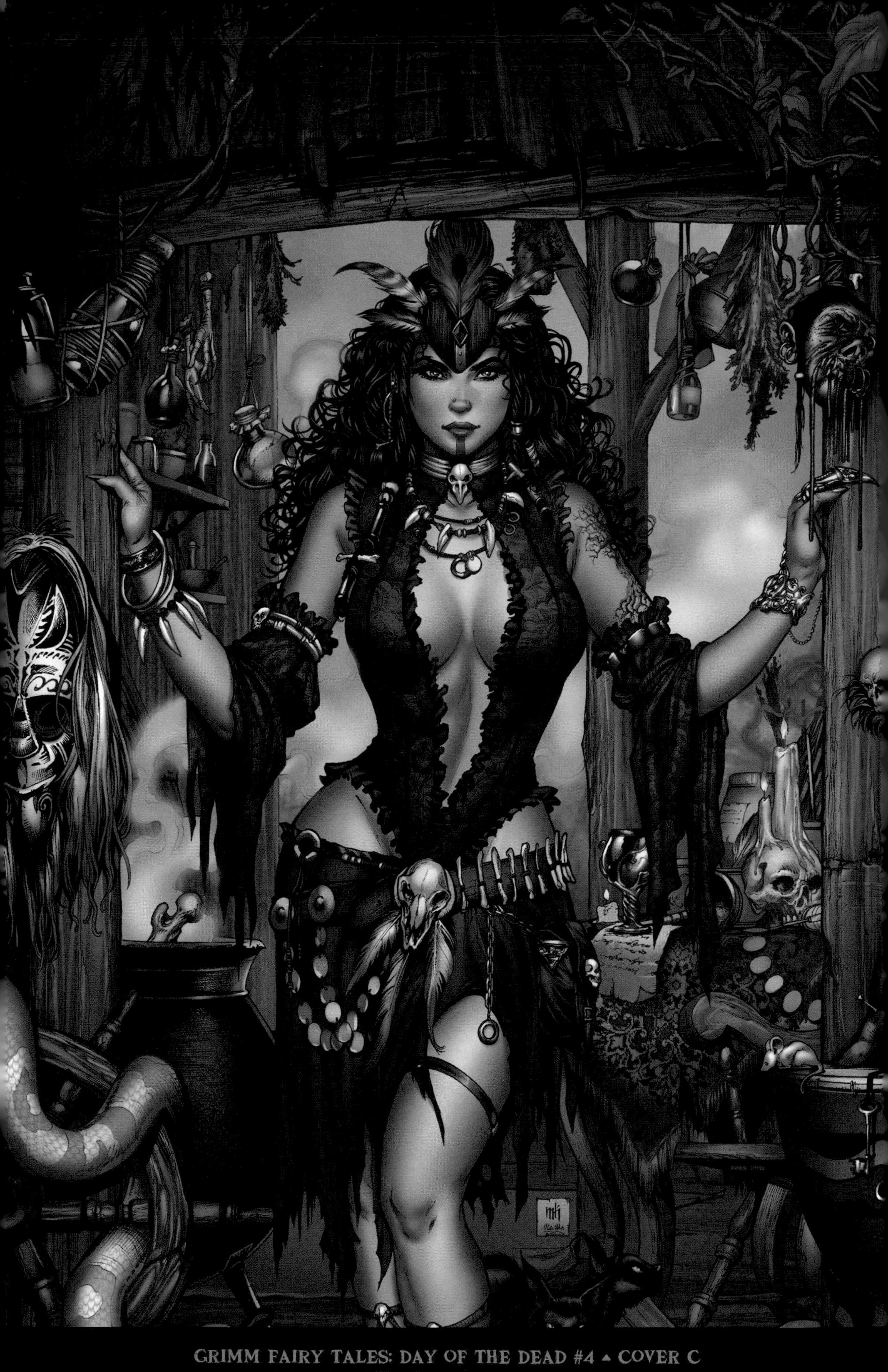

GRIMM FAIRY TALES: DAY OF THE DEAD #4 ▲ COVER C
Artwork by Mike Krome • Colors by Ula Mos

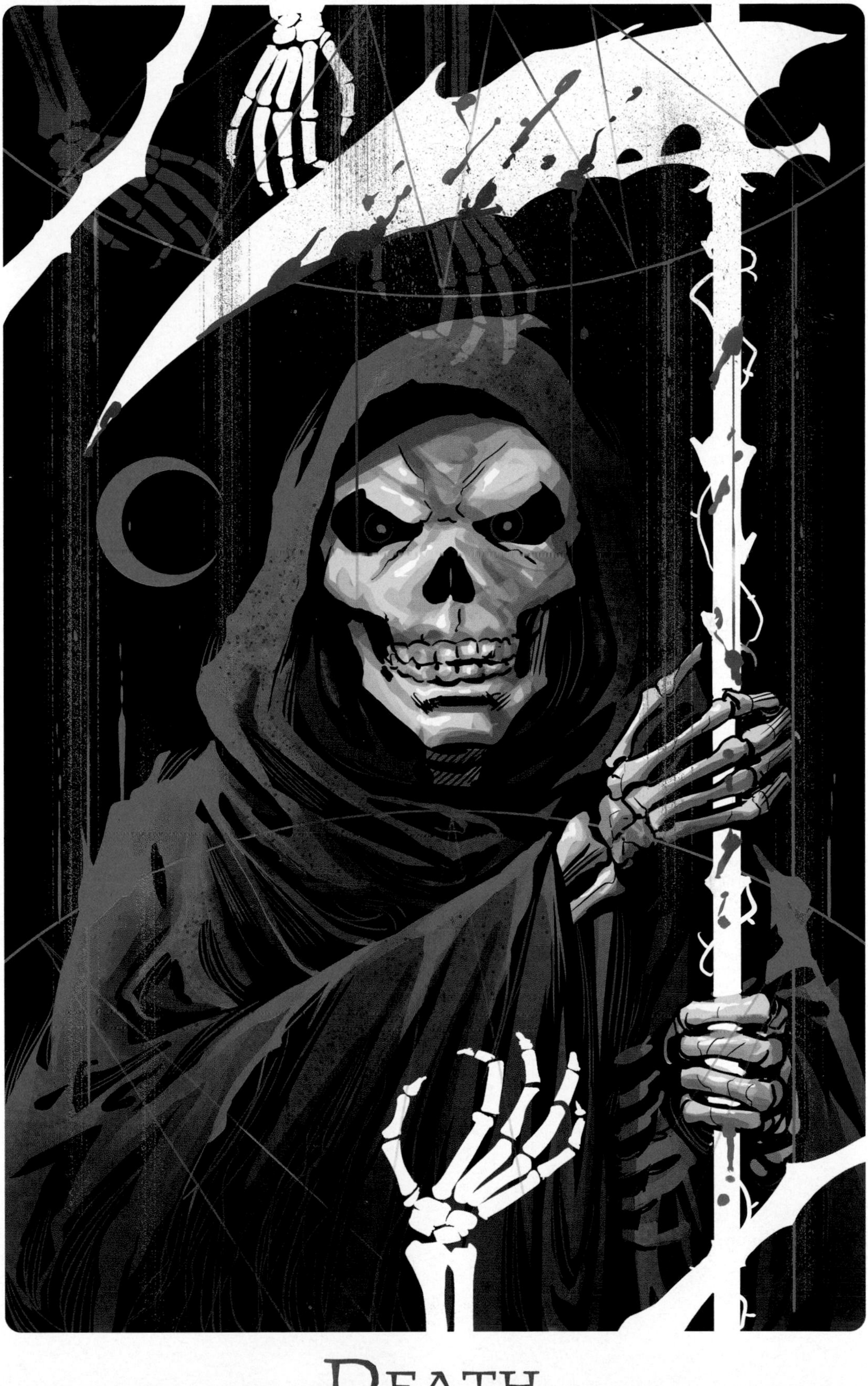

DEATH

GRIMM FAIRY TALES: DAY OF THE DEAD #4 ▲ COVER D
Artwork by Manuel Preitano

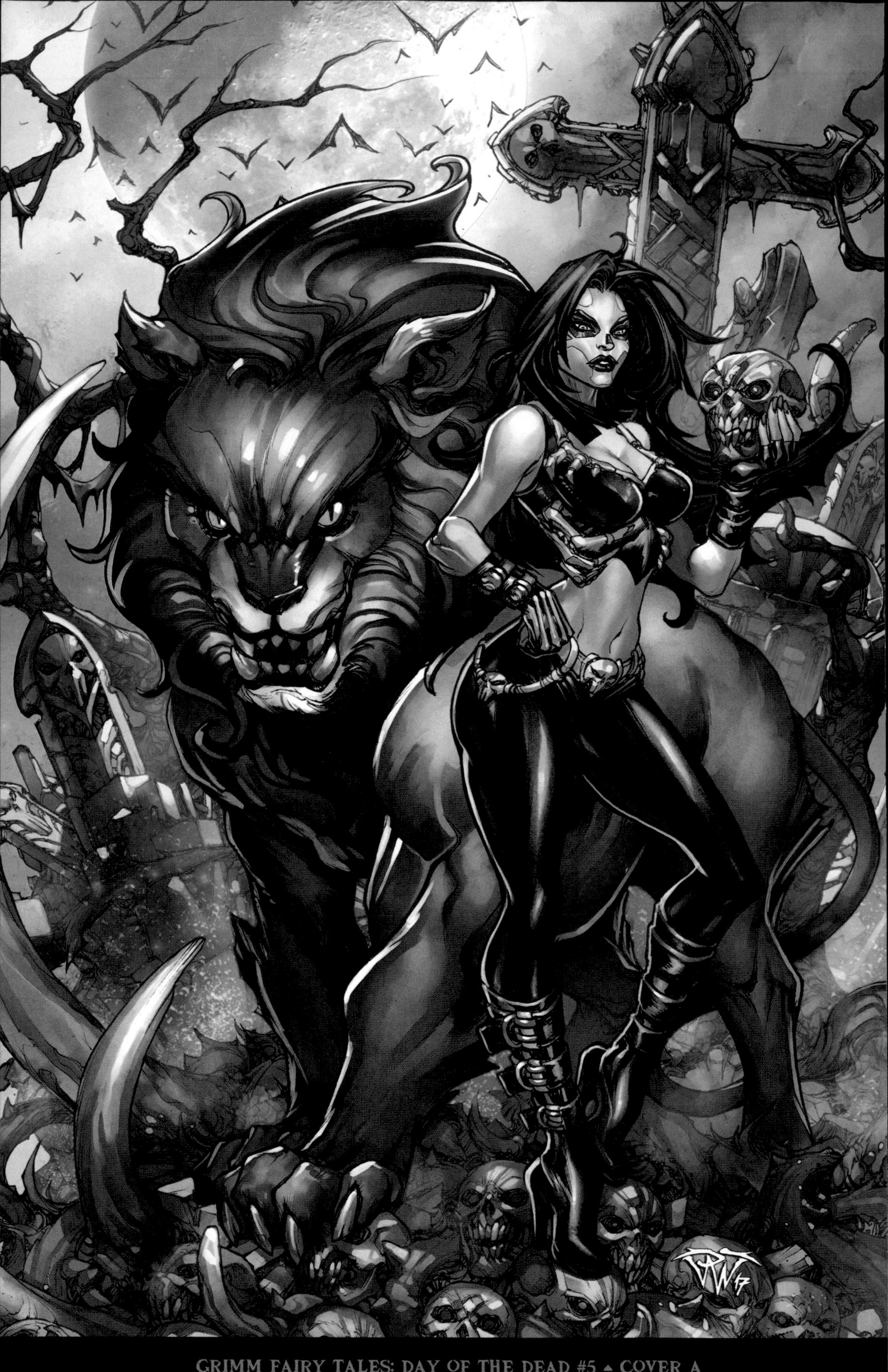

GRIMM FAIRY TALES: DAY OF THE DEAD #5 ▲ COVER A

Artwork by Paolo Pantalena • Colors by Arif Prianto

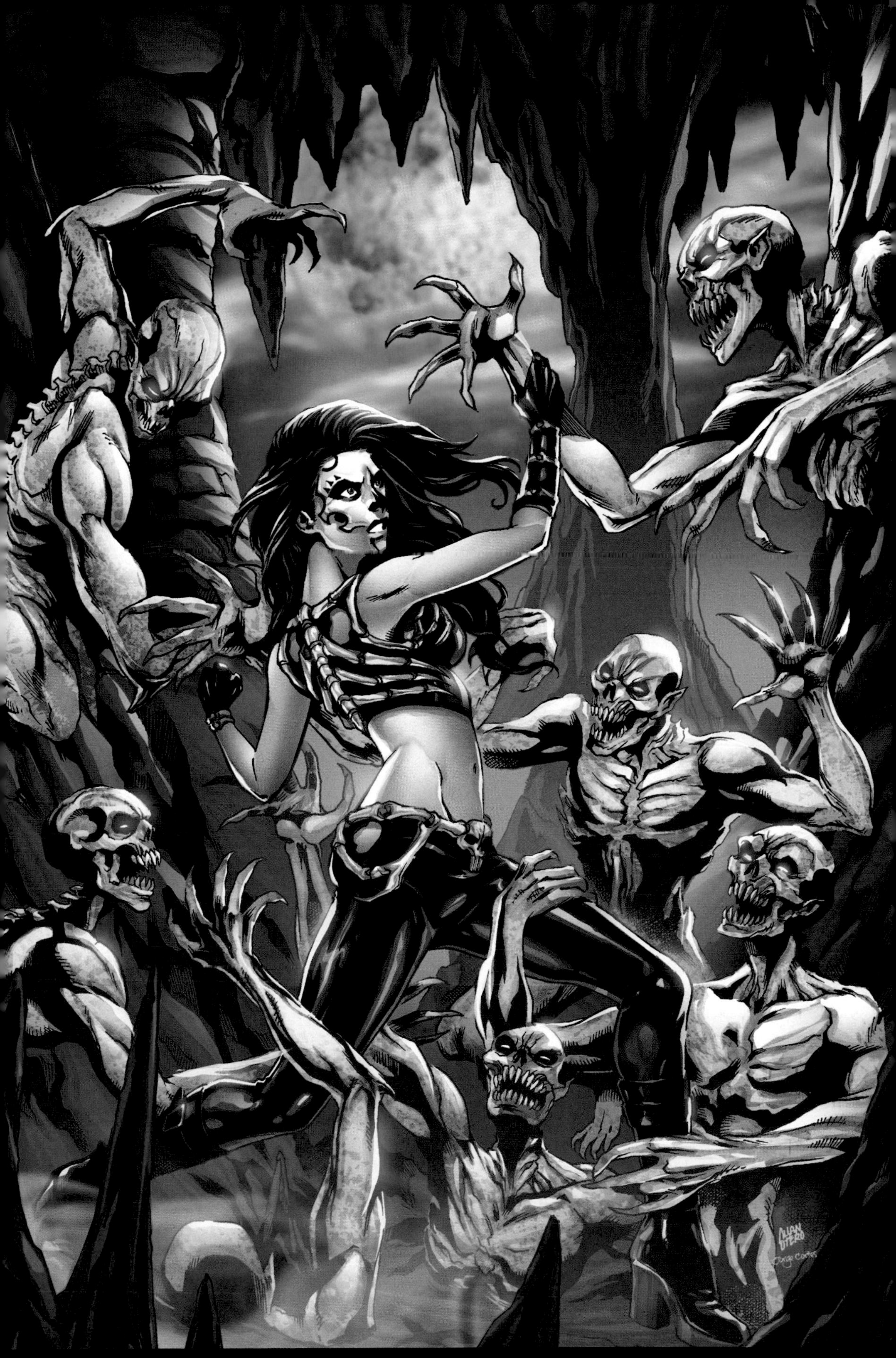

GRIMM FAIRY TALES: DAY OF THE DEAD #5 ▲ COVER B
Artwork by Allan Otero • Colors by Jorge Cortes

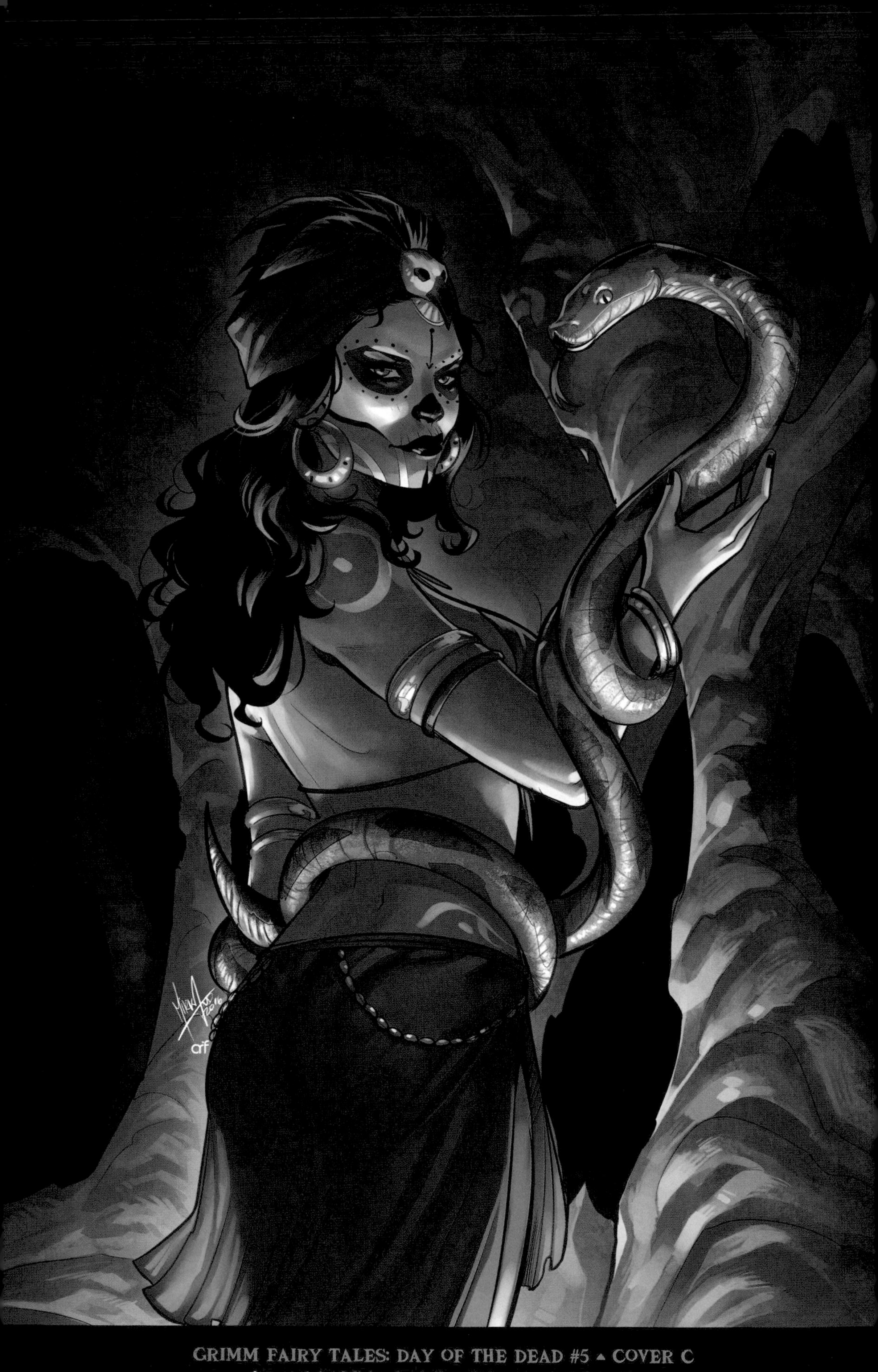

GRIMM FAIRY TALES: DAY OF THE DEAD #5 ▲ COVER C
Artwork by Mirka Andolfo • Colors by Arif Prianto

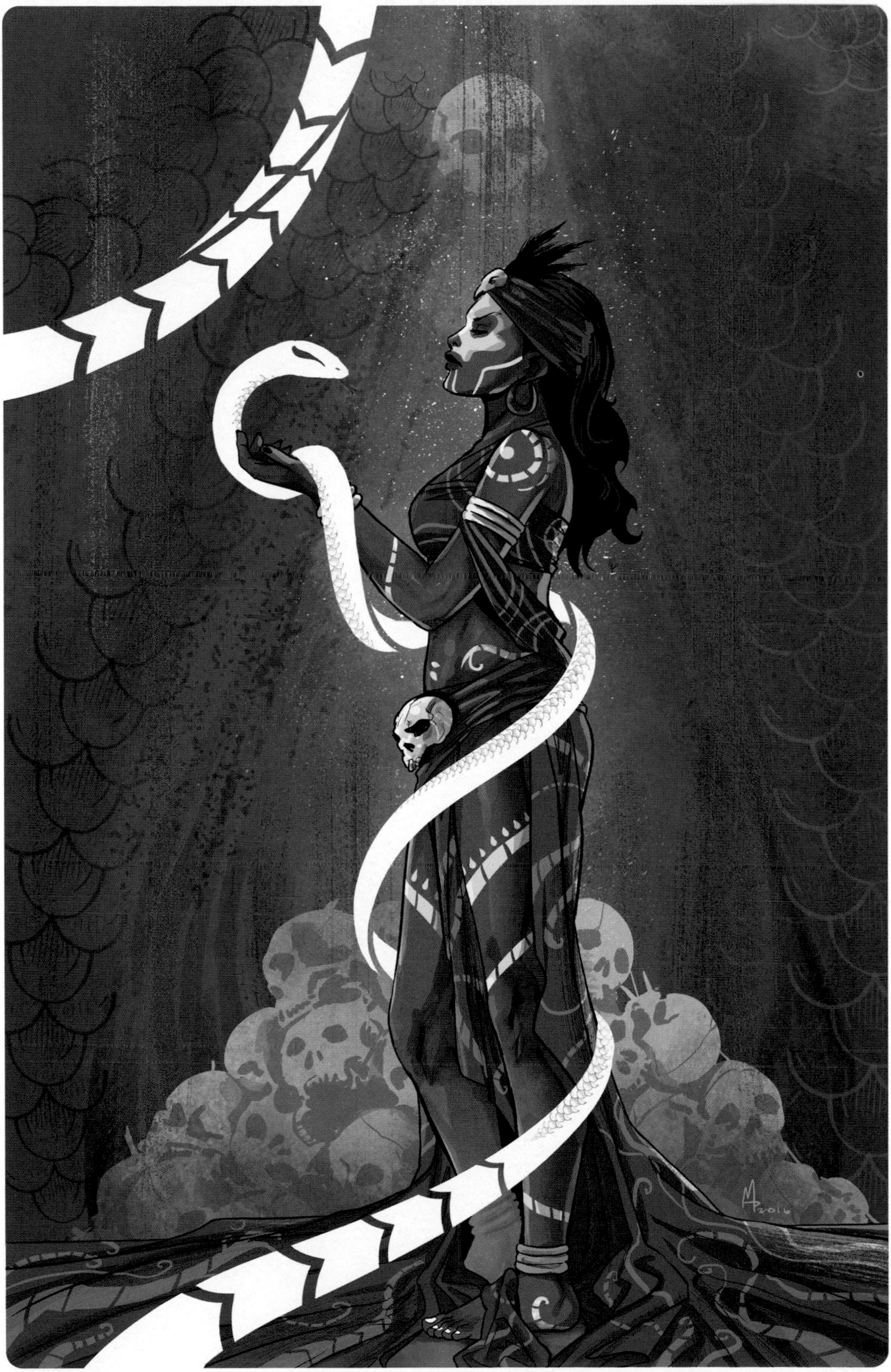
MP 2016

HIGH PRIESTESS

GRIMM FAIRY TALES: DAY OF THE DEAD #5 ▲ COVER D
Artwork by Manuel Preitano

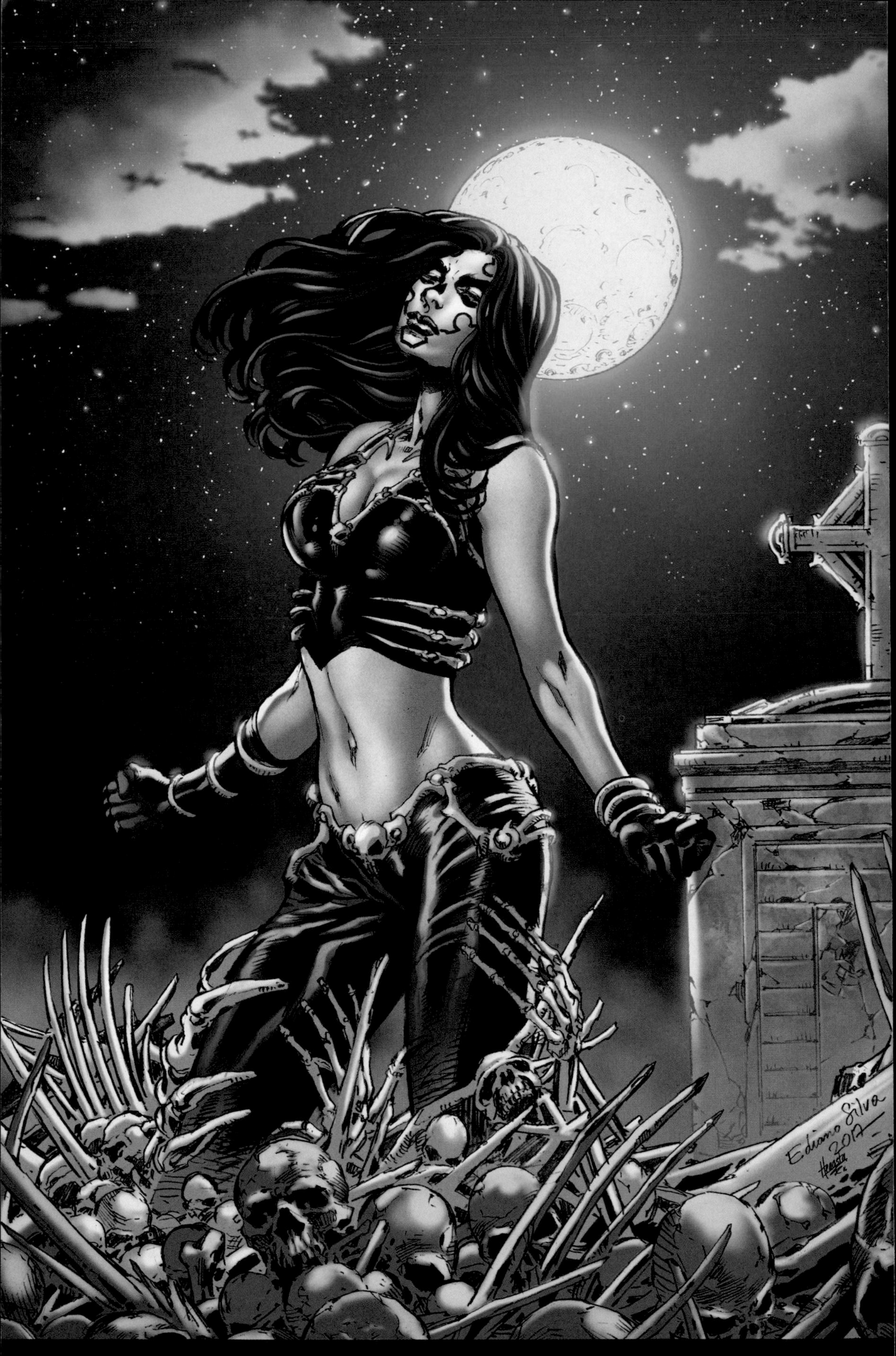

GRIMM FAIRY TALES: DAY OF THE DEAD #6 ▲ COVER A

Artwork by Ediano Silva • Colors by Jesse Heagy

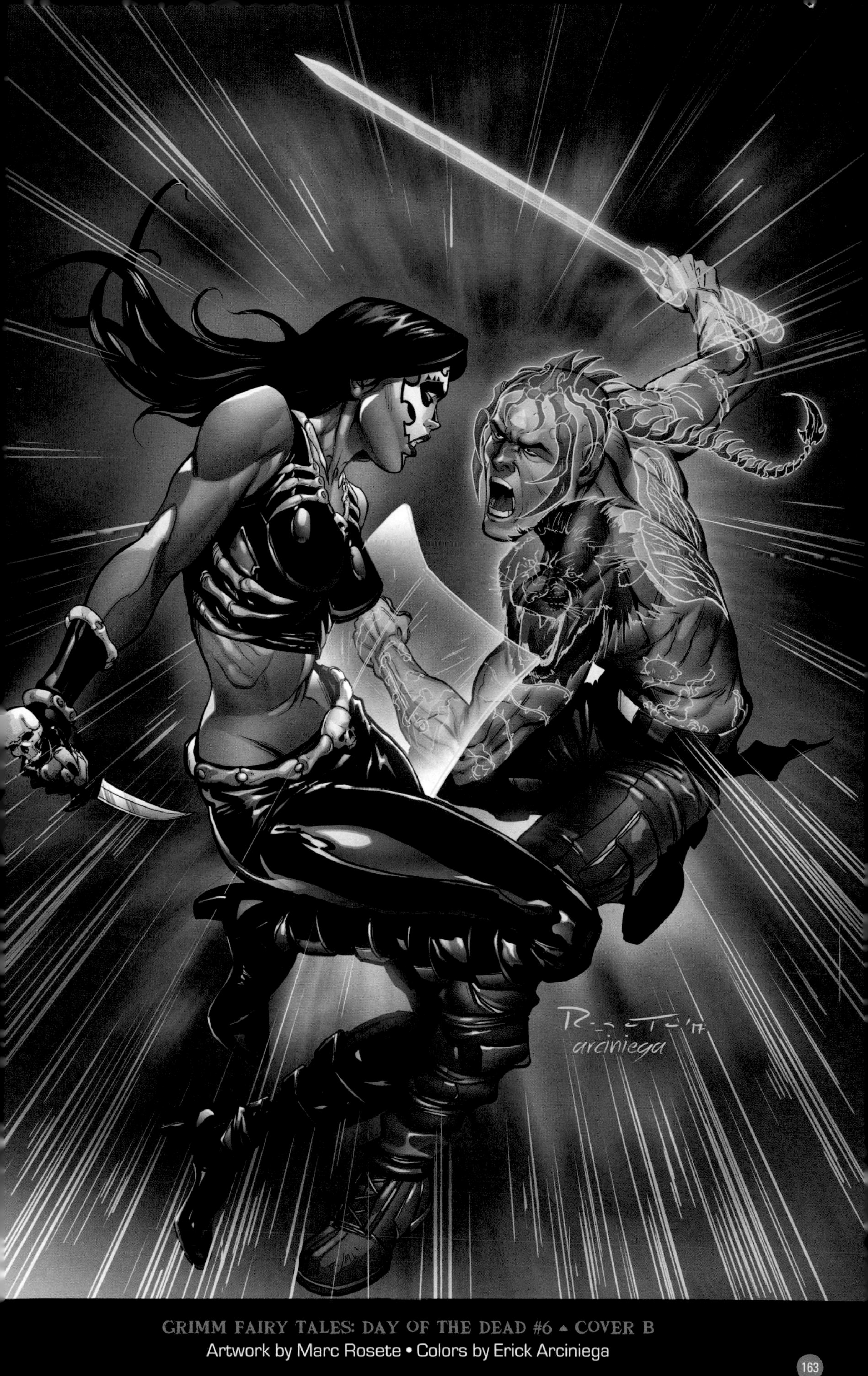
arciniega

GRIMM FAIRY TALES: DAY OF THE DEAD #6 ▲ COVER B
Artwork by Marc Rosete • Colors by Erick Arciniega

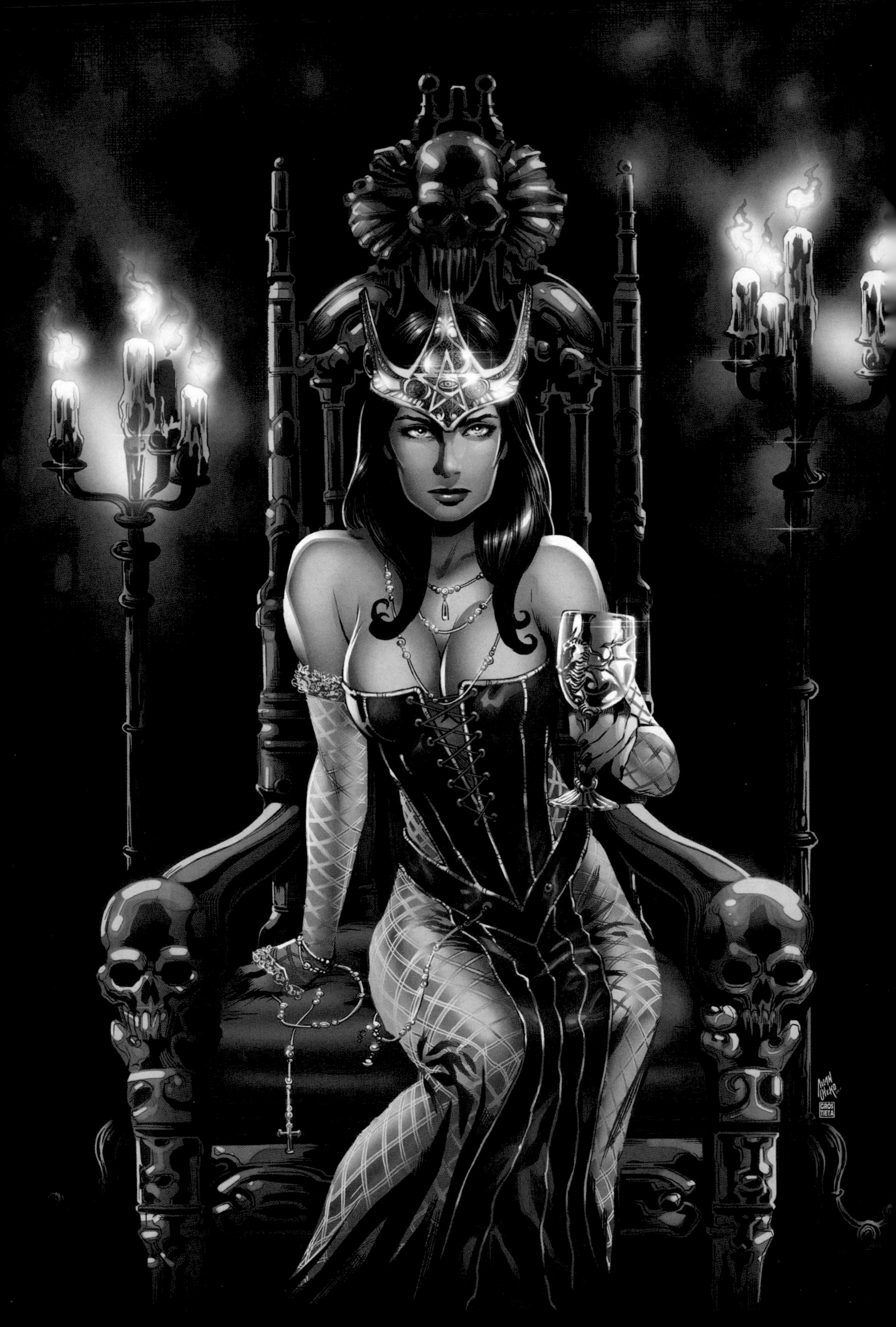

GRIMM FAIRY TALES: DAY OF THE DEAD #6 ▲ COVER C

Artwork by Allan Otero • Colors by Grostieta

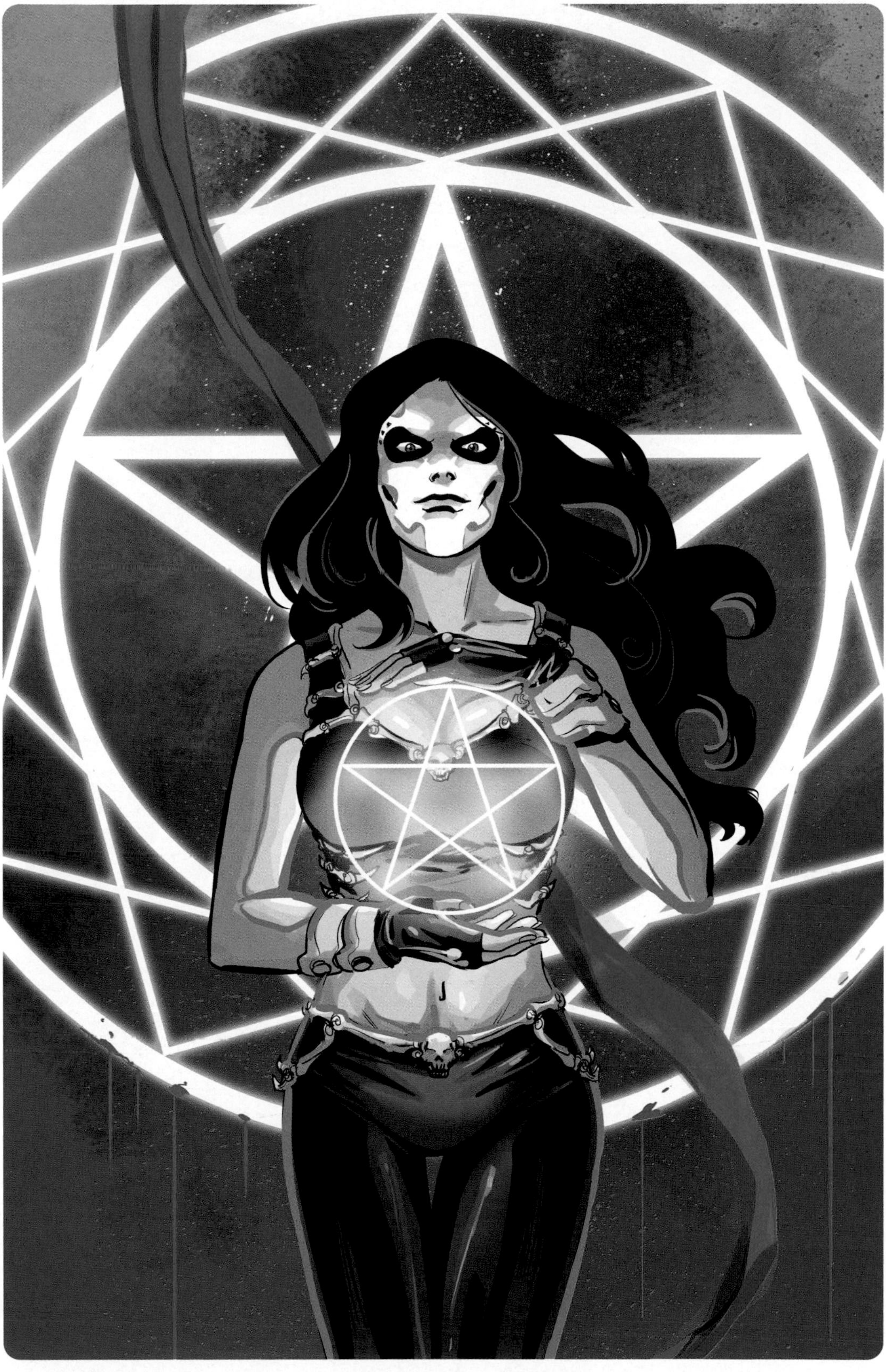

Queen of Pentacles

GRIMM FAIRY TALES: DAY OF THE DEAD #6 ▲ COVER D

Artwork by Manuel Preitano

GRIMM FAIRY TALES
THE ART OF DAY OF THE DEAD

Artwork by **ALLAN OTERO**

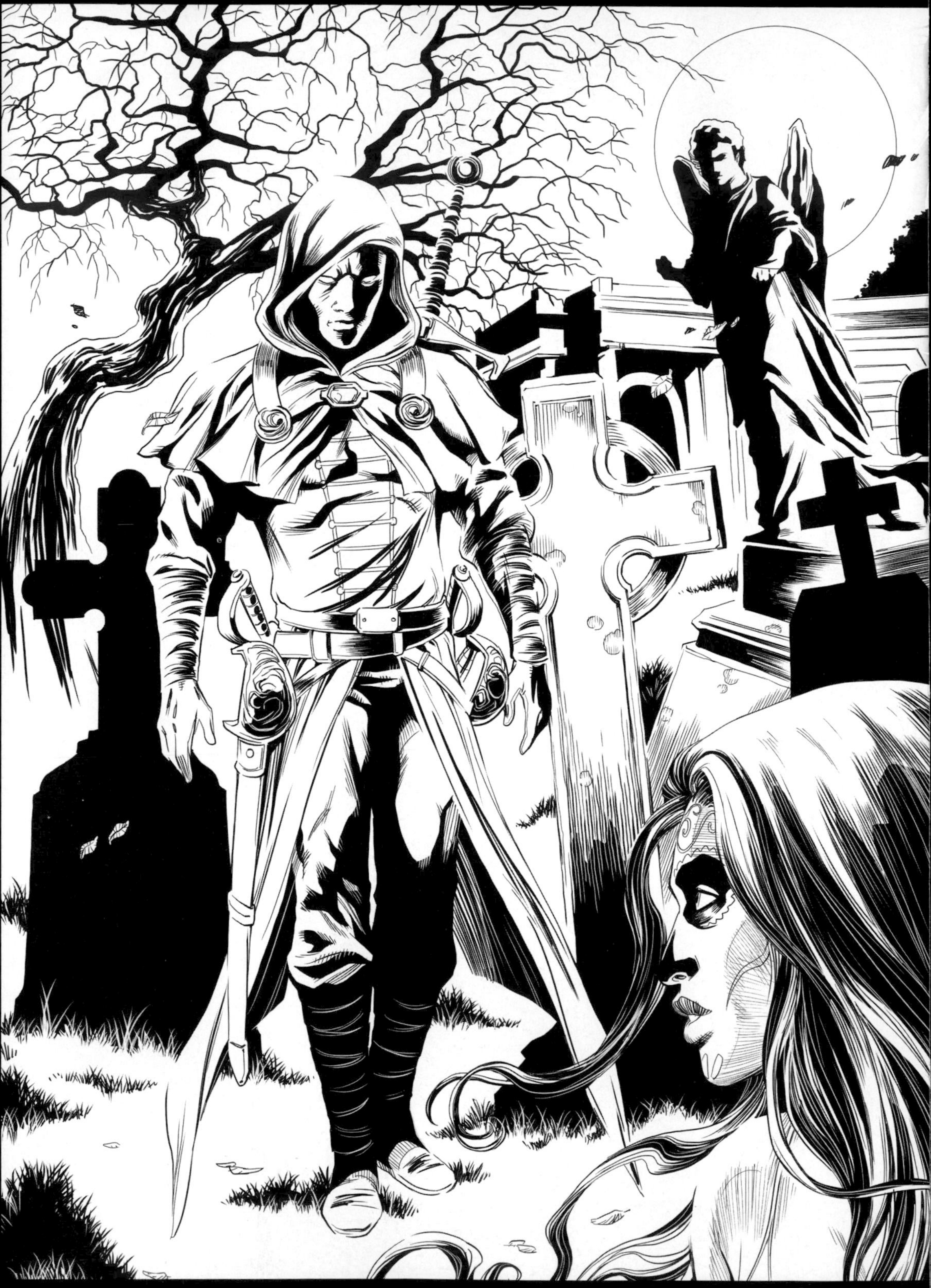